D1260261

Soldiers and States
Civil-Military Relations
in Modern Europe

STUDIES IN HISTORY AND POLITICS
Under the editorial direction of Gerald E. Stearn

RUSSIA AND THE WEST FROM PETER TO KHRUSHCHEV
Edited by L. Jay Oliva, New York University

THE DEVELOPMENT OF THE COMMUNIST BLOC
Edited by Roger Pethybridge, University College, Swansea

CHURCH AND STATE IN AMERICAN HISTORY
Edited by John F. Wilson, Princeton University

BRITISH POLITICS
PEOPLE, PARTIES AND PARLIAMENTS
Edited by Anthony King, University of Essex

SOLDIERS AND STATES
CIVIL-MILITARY RELATIONS IN MODERN EUROPE
Edited by David B. Ralston, Massachusetts Institute
of Technology

Other volumes in preparation

STUDIES IN HISTORY AND POLITICS

Soldiers and States
Civil-Military Relations
in Modern Europe

Edited with an introduction by

David B. Ralston
Massachusetts Institute of Technology

D. C. HEATH AND COMPANY: BOSTON

Englewood · Chicago · Dallas · San Francisco · Atlanta

Library of Congress Catalog Card Number 66-25073

COPYRIGHT © 1966 BY D. C. HEATH AND COMPANY

PRINTED IN THE UNITED STATES OF AMERICA.

PRINTED AUGUST 1966

Table of Contents

1. Machiavelli on the Problem of the Army and the State   1

I. THE MILITARY FORCES OF THE DYNASTIC STATE
THE ORIGINS OF THE STANDING ARMY
2. *Michael Roberts:* The Military Revolution   13
3. Cardinal Richelieu on the Need for a Permanent Army   20
4. *Louis André:* Michel Le Tellier and the Founding of the
   French Army   23
5. Louis XIV on the Military Duties of the French Monarch   28
SEVENTEENTH- AND EIGHTEENTH-CENTURY PRUSSIA: A STATE FOUNDED ON AN ARMY
6. *Ferdinand Schevill:* The Great Elector and the Founding of
   the Prussian Army   31
7. The Political Testament of Frederick William I   36
8. *Leopold von Ranke:* The Army under Frederick William I   40
9. *Robert Ergang:* The Growth of the Prussian Bureaucracy   43
10. Frederick the Great on the Military Bases of Prussian
    Statecraft   46
SEVENTEENTH-CENTURY ENGLAND: THE ORIGINS OF AN ANTI-MILITARIST TRADITION
11. The New Model Army   48
12. *C. H. Firth:* Cromwell's Army   52
13. James II and the Army   56
14. The Bill of Rights and the Mutiny Act   58
15. *J. S. Omond:* Parliament and the Army   60
ARMY AND STATE IN THE AGE OF THE FRENCH REVOLUTION
16. The Levée en Masse   66
17. The Representatives on Mission   67
18. Saint-Juste on the Army of the Revolution   70
19. *Robert R. Palmer:* The Military Achievements of the
    Committee of Public Safety   73
20. *Ramsey W. Phipps:* The Armies of the First French Republic   78
21. *Albert Sorel:* The Emergence of the Army as a Political Force . . .   80
22. The Rise of Napoleon Bonaparte   85
23. *Godefroy Cavaignac:* The French Revolution and the Reform
    of the Prussian Army   88

II. THE ARMED FORCES OF THE NATIONAL STATE
THE PRUSSIAN ARMY AND THE FOUNDING OF THE GERMAN EMPIRE
24. *Herbert Rosinski:* The Prussian Army, 1815–1870   99

25. Bismarck on the Army and Parliamentary Liberalism 103
26. *Gordon A. Craig:* The Prussian Army in the German Empire 109
27. William II on the Military Prerogatives and Duties
of the German Emperor 114
NINETEENTH-CENTURY FRANCE: THE ARMY AND THE CHANGING
REGIMES
28. *Raoul Girardet:* The Army in the State, 1815–1870 116
29. Debate on the Political Rights of the French Soldier 122
30. *David Thomson:* The Army under the Third Republic 124
31. General André on the Politics of Officer Promotion 128
WORLD WAR I: ARMY AND STATE IN TOTAL WAR
32. Walther Rathenau on the Industrial Mobilization of Germany . . . 131
33. David Lloyd George on British Democracy in Total War 135
34. Ludendorff on the Failure of the German Home Front 143
35. *Arthur Rosenberg:* The Dictatorship of Ludendorff, 1916–1918 . . . 146

III. **ARMY AND STATE IN AN AGE OF TOTALITARIANISM**
SOVIET RUSSIA: THE ARMY OF THE REVOLUTIONARY STATE
36. The Founding of the Red Army 156
37. *D. Fedotov White:* The Military Commissars 161
38. The Scheme for a Soviet Militia 163
39. *Leon Trotsky:* The Revolution Betrayed 164
40. *Leonard Schapiro:* The Great Purge 169
41. Marshal Voroshilov on the State of the Army in 1939 173
42. Khrushchev on the Military Consequences of the Purges 175
THE GERMAN ARMY UNDER THE WEIMAR REPUBLIC AND THE NAZIS
43. General von Seeckt's 1920 Order to the German Army 177
44. *Harold Gordon:* The Reichswehr and the German Republic 179
45. The Oath of the German Soldiers to Hitler 182
46. *Hans Rothfels:* The Military Resistance to Hitler 183
47. General Guderian on the July 20, 1944, Plot 187
48. *Telford Taylor:* The Guilt of the Generals 189
FRANCE: FROM MILITARY DEFEAT TO MILITARY REVOLT
49. De Gaulle on the Origins of the Free French Movement 194
50. *Paul-Marie de la Gorce:* The Collapse of the Traditional
Military Order 198
51. *Marshal Alphonse Juin:* Vichy, De Gaulle, and the French
Army 202
52. General Boyer de la Tour on the Martyrdom of the French
Army 207
53. *Raoul Girardet:* The Politicization of the French Army under
the Fourth Republic 209
54. De Gaulle on the 1960 and 1961 Uprisings in Algeria 214
Suggestions for Reading 217

Introduction

The primary task of any government is the maintenance of some measure of peace and order within a given community. This civil imperative holds for any political grouping, be it a primitive tribe or a twentieth-century superpower, and unless it is met, no organized society can exist. In addition to regulating the internal affairs of a community, the government may also be required to provide for its defense against external foes. The requirements of this military imperative are starkly evident in time of war, but they are also present to some degree in time of peace as well, since a government must generally take some precautions against possible conflict with other communities.

Although these two imperatives are complementary in that the orderly and peaceful domestic life of a community may depend on its being secure against its predatory neighbors, and vice versa, they are at the same time basically incompatible in terms of the demands they make on the individual members of the community. In responding to the civil imperative, the government encourages its people to behave in an essentially pacific way, while the military imperative obliges them to show some capacity for violence.

The civil imperative applies to every society, but there are those for whom the military imperative is all but nonexistent. A community which is geographically isolated or which is surrounded by peaceful neighbors is to all intents and purposes relieved of the necessity of taking any measures to insure its security. During most of its history, the United States, primarily because of geography, could afford practically to ignore the problem of national defense and thus to allow itself the luxury of a small peacetime military establishment. On the other hand, there have been societies which for a variety of reasons are constantly organized for war.

Among more primitive peoples living in the midst of predatory neighbors, some kind of orderly domestic social existence can be enjoyed only on condition that the community be prepared to fight at any time, either to defend itself or perhaps to appropriate the more desirable lands and goods of a nearby tribe or clan. Even in modern times, one may see something analogous in the history of the Prussian state, whose seventeenth- and eighteenth-century rulers realized that the safety of their poor and geographically defenseless lands demanded the creation of an extremely powerful military force. They thus subordinated the total energies of their realm to the building and the maintenance of a standing army, which was equal in size to the military machines of far wealthier states possessing several times the population of Prussia. Since civil society in Prussia was organized and functioned almost exclusively in terms of the needs of the army, with its inhabitants obliged to lead a spartan, harshly disciplined existence, there was little incompatibility between the civil and military imperatives.

Incompatibility becomes more likely when a community has been able for an extended period of time to maintain an independent political existence and to devote its energies to other pursuits than simply defending itself. As the rigors of civic life are alleviated and as the whole ethos and moral code of the society come to emphasize the more peaceful human qualities, the members of the community become increasingly unwilling to make the sacrifices demanded by the military imperative. The history of Rome provides a case in point. In the early days of the Republic, military service was a clearly recognized part of the civic duty of every citizen. The armies by which the small city state defended itself and advanced its frontiers were made up of farmers and towns-people who served on a temporary basis over a limited period of time. In so doing they were motivated by a high sense of civic pride and patriotism. By the end of the Republic, however, military and civic duty had ceased to complement each other. Nevertheless, in a society whose style of life and whose dominant ideals had grown to have little in common with either the military ethos or the military virtues, the military imperative still remained. The frontiers of the Empire still had to be defended against the barbarian peoples pressing in from the north and east. This led to an increasingly dangerous expedient, the maintenance on a permanent basis of a mercenary army. At first it was recruited from among the poor and dispossessed of Roman society for whom military service became a way to make their fortunes. By the second century A.D., however, the armies serving on the frontiers were being recruited more and more from among recently conquered and subdued barbarians, and there was a growing danger of the government losing control of these permanently organized armed forces. No longer simply the visible manifestation of imperial power, the armies gradually began to act as powers in their own right, ready and able to dispute the decisions of the government, and even to impose their will upon it. By the middle of the third century, the armies had become in fact the political arbiters of the Roman Empire, making and deposing emperors at will. Who was chosen as emperor and how he conducted himself in office was only occasionally determined by the needs of the body politic.

In the political order which took shape in the West following the break-up of the Roman Empire the separation between the civil and military functions within society tended to disappear. Certainly one reason for this was the sharp decline in economic activity which accompanied the collapse of the imperial system. One thousand years were to pass before European society as a whole was again wealthy enough to support permanent mercenary armies. There was thus a reversion to the conditions of more primitive times. The structure of the feudal system under which Europe was governed was primarily military. Political prerogatives, the right of one man to rule over others, depended on the ability and the willingness to render military service. Even the serf, who supposedly filled no military function in society and on whose shoulders the economic life of the system rested, might occasionally be called upon to assist his lord in battle, if only with a staff or a scythe.

It was in that area of Europe which was most advanced economically and culturally, Italy, that it first became possible again to depend on purely mercenary armies for the military needs of society. During the Middle Ages, the Italian city states had relied on citizen militias for defense, but as the wealth of these merchant republics grew, their oligarchic ruling factions became increasingly disinclined to undergo even the occasional rigors of military life. Then too, the decline of the citizen militia may also have been due to the unwillingness of these ruling factions to place weapons in the hands of the lower classes, who over the preceding few centuries had been progressively disenfranchised. As a result, the city states of Renaissance Italy came to rely on mercenary soldiers in time of war.

These armies of mercenary soldiers, under their leaders or *condottieri*, were likely to have no connection or bond of loyalty with the city state for whom they fought beyond the wages they were paid. The mercenary captain who dealt with the political authorities and who contracted for a particular military enterprise was understandably reluctant to commit his men too wholeheartedly to battle, since they represented his effective professional capital. His ideal was a long campaign, punctuated by a few bloodless battles.

Politically, the system of hired soldiers could lead to the most unfortunate consequences, the authorities of a given city being on occasion unpleasantly surprised to find that the mercenary captains had ambitions quite apart from their desire for money or their lust for military glory. There was little the ruling oligarchy of a city state could do to protect itself if the hired head of its military forces sought to overthrow it in his own interests. The advent of the Sforza in Milan was symptomatic of what might happen when the leading elements in the state ceased to concern themselves directly with the harsh but necessary tasks of military defense.

The doleful effect of these mercenary armies on the political and military development of Italy was vividly depicted by Niccolo Machiavelli. Machiavelli, who occupied an important post in the government of the Florentine state during the early years of the sixteenth century, was a penetrating observer of the contemporary Italian scene and a shrewd, dispassionate commentator on man's political behavior. It was on the basis of his insights and through his wide reading, particularly in the history of Rome, that Machiavelli sought to approach the practice of government as an autonomous study, possessing its own canons and its own rationale, and thus to treat politics as a science. In his best known treatise, *The Prince*, Machiavelli as a matter of course deals with the military imperative, which is an inherent part of the life of any political organism. He advises the ruler who wishes to maintain himself in power to pay special attention to military matters. For both the political and the military security of his state, he counsels a prince to raise his armed forces from among its citizens and to eschew the use of mercenary armies of any sort. (See selection 1.) Because the city states had ignored this fundamental principle of statecraft and had allowed the old citizen militia, the embodiment of both civic spirit and military virtue, to decay, there had been a consequent decline in the vigor of Italian political life.

For a period of some five years prior to his exile from Florence, Machiavelli was in a position to put his politico-military theories into practice. Under his inspiration and guidance, a serious effort was made to reconstitute the old

Florentine militia. Machiavelli hoped thereby to rekindle the civic pride and municipal patriotism which he believed to have been characteristics of the city state in the Middle Ages, but his aspirations came to nought when the militia collapsed before the advancing Spaniards in 1512. This defeat brought about the fall of the restored Florentine Republic and the return of the benevolent Medici despotism, which had been overthrown in 1494. It also meant exile for Machiavelli.

Aside from its deficiencies in both training and organization, there was another, more fundamental reason for the failure of the revived Florentine militia. The city state of Renaissance Italy was no longer a viable unit, either politically or militarily, compared to the new states which were emerging beyond the Alps. Political and military power in these states was vested in the person of the monarch, and they were organized on a scale which was far beyond the capacity of any Italian city state to equal. From the moment when the rulers of France and Spain looked toward Italy as an area in which to advance the interests of their respective dynasties, the existence of these city states as autonomous, sovereign entities was doomed. For the next three centuries the history of Europe would be written in terms of the needs and ambitions of these dynastic monarchies. Their needs and their ambitions would also provide the setting and the rationale for the problem of the place of the armed forces within the state.

1. MACHIAVELLI ON THE PROBLEM OF THE ARMY AND THE STATE

The study of politics as it is treated by Machiavelli in *The Prince* is simply a study in the technique of power. An interest in military matters and some skill in the art of war are necessary attributes of anyone who wishes to practice this technique. Machiavelli did not, as other political theorists before him had done, take into consideration the moral and political implications of war, when and under what condition it is justified. War and the problems of military organization which it raised were simply questions with which any ruler had to be conversant if he were to govern effectively. It is because of his dispassionate, detached attitude toward war as a political phenomenon that Machiavelli may be taken as the first to treat the problem of civil-military relations in the history of Modern Europe.

The chief foundations of all states, new as well as old or composite, are good laws and good arms; and as there cannot be good laws where the state is not well armed, it follows that where they are well armed they have good laws. I shall leave the laws out of the discussion and shall speak of the arms.

I say, therefore, that the arms with which a prince defends his state are either his own, or they are mercenaries, auxiliaries, or mixed. Mercenaries and auxiliaries are useless and dangerous; and if one holds his state based on these arms, he will stand neither firm nor safe; for they are disunited, ambitious and without discipline, unfaithful, valiant before friends, cowardly before enemies; they have neither the fear of God nor fidelity to men, and destruction is deferred only so long as the attack is; for in peace one is robbed by them, and in war by the enemy. The fact is, they have no other attraction or reason for keeping the field than a trifle of stipend, which is not sufficient to make them willing to die for you. They are ready enough to be your soldiers whilst you do not make war, but if war comes they take themselves off or run from the foe; which I should have little trouble to prove, for the ruin of Italy has been caused by nothing else than by resting all her hopes for many years on mercenaries, and although they formerly made some display and appeared valiant amongst themselves, yet when the foreigners came they showed what they were. Thus it was that Charles, King of France, was allowed to seize Italy . . . ; and he who told us that our sins were the cause of it told the truth, but they were not the sins he imagined, but those which I have related. And as they were the sins of princes, it is the princes who have also suffered the penalty.

I wish to demonstrate further the infelicity of these arms. The mercenary captains are either capable men or they are not; if they are, you cannot trust them, because they always aspire to their own greatness, either by oppressing you, who are their master, or others contrary to your intentions; but if the captain is not skilful, you are ruined in the usual way.

And if it be urged that whoever is armed will act in the same way, whether mercenary or not, I reply that when arms have to

From *The Prince* by Nicolo Machiavelli, chapters 12, 13, and 14, abridged. Translated by W. K. Marriott. Everyman's Library. Reprinted by permission of E. P. Dutton & Co., Inc., and J. M. Dent & Sons Ltd.

be resorted to, either by a prince or a republic, then the prince ought to go in person and perform the duty of captain; the republic has to send its citizens, and when one is sent who does not turn out satisfactorily, it ought to recall him, and when one is worthy, to hold him by the laws so that he does not leave the command. And experience has shown princes and republics, single-handed, making the greatest progress, and mercenaries doing nothing except damage; and it is more difficult to bring a republic, armed with its own arms, under the sway of one of its citizens than it is to bring one armed with foreign arms. Rome and Sparta stood for many ages armed and free. The Switzers are completely armed and quite free.

Of ancient mercenaries, for example, there are the Carthaginians, who were oppressed by their mercenary soldiers after the first war with the Romans, although the Carthaginians had their own citizens for captains. After the death of Epaminondas, Philip of Macedon was made captain of their soldiers by the Thebans, and after victory he took away their liberty.

And as with these examples I have reached Italy, which has been ruled for many years by mercenaries, I wish to discuss them more seriously, in order that, having seen their rise and progress, one may be better prepared to counteract them. . . .

The first who gave renown to this soldiery was Alberigo da Conio, the Romagnian. From the school of this man sprang, among others, Braccio and Sforza, who in their time were the arbiters of Italy. After these came all the other captains who till now have directed the arms of Italy; and the end of all their valour has been, that she has been overrun by Charles, robbed by Louis, ravaged by Ferdinand, and insulted by the Switzers. The principle that has guided them has been, first, to lower the credit of infantry so that they might increase their own. They did this because, subsisting on their pay and without territory, they were unable to support many soldiers, and a few

infantry did not give them any authority; so they were led to employ cavalry, with a moderate force of which they were maintained and honoured and affairs were brought to such a pass that, in an army of twenty thousand soldiers, there were not to be found two thousand foot soldiers. They had, besides this, used every art to lessen fatigue and danger to themselves and their soldiers, not killing in the fray, but taking prisoners and liberating without ransom. They did not attack towns at night, nor did the garrisons of the towns attack encampments at night; they did not surround the camp either with stockade or ditch, nor did they campaign in the winter. All these things were permitted by their military rules, and devised by them to avoid, as I have said, both fatigue and dangers; thus they have brought Italy to slavery and contempt.

Auxiliaries, which are the other useless arm, are employed when a prince is called in with his forces to aid and defend, as was done by Pope Julius in the most recent times, for he, having, in the enterprise against Ferrara, had poor proof of his mercenaries, turned to auxiliaries, and stipulated with Ferdinand, King of Spain, for his assistance with men and arms. These arms may be useful and good in themselves, but for him who calls them in they are always disadvantageous; for losing, one is undone, and winning, one is their captive. . . .

The Florentines, being entirely without arms, sent ten thousand Frenchmen to take Pisa, whereby they ran more danger than at any other time of their troubles.

The Emperor of Constantinople, to oppose his neighbours, sent ten thousand Turks into Greece, who, on the war being finished, were not willing to quit; this was the beginning of the servitude of Greece to the infidels.

Therefore, let him who has no desire to conquer make use of these arms, for they are much more hazardous than mercenaries, because with them the ruin is ready made; they are all united, all yield obedience to others; but with mercenaries, when they have conquered, more time and better opportunities are needed to injure you; they are not all of one community, they are found and paid by you, and a third party, which you have made their head, is not able all at once to assume enough authority to injure you. In conclusion, in mercenaries dastardy is most dangerous; in auxiliaries, valour. The wise prince, therefore, has always avoided these arms and turned to his own; and has been willing rather to lose with them than to conquer with others, not deeming that a real victory which is gained with the arms of others. . . . David offered himself to Saul to fight with Goliath, the Philistine champion, and, to give him courage, Saul armed him with his own weapons; which David rejected as soon as he had them on his back, saying he could make no use of them, and that he wished to meet the enemy with his sling and his knife. In conclusion, the arms of others either fall from your back, or they weigh you down, or they bind you fast.

Charles the Seventh, the father of King Louis the Eleventh, having by good fortune and valour liberated France from the English, recognized the necessity of being armed with forces of his own, and he established in his kingdom ordinances concerning men-at-arms and infantry. Afterwards his son, King Louis, abolished the infantry and began to enlist the Switzers, which mistake, followed by others, is, as is now seen, a source of peril to that kingdom; because, having raised the reputation of the Switzers, he has entirely diminished the value of his own arms, for he has destroyed the infantry altogether; and his men-at-arms he has subordinated to others, for, being as they are so accustomed to fight along with Switzers, it does not appear that they can now conquer without them. Hence it arises that the French cannot stand against the Switzers, and without the Switzers they do not come off well against others. The armies of the French have thus become mixed, partly mercenary and partly national, both of which arms together are much better than mercenaries

alone or auxiliaries alone, yet much inferior to one's own forces. And this example proves it, for the kingdom of France would be unconquerable if the ordinance of Charles had been enlarged or maintained.

But the scanty wisdom of man, on entering into an affair which looks well at first, cannot discern the poison that is hidden in it, as I have said above of hectic fevers. Therefore, if he who rules a principality cannot recognize evils until they are upon him, he is not truly wise; and this insight is given to few. And if the first disaster to the Roman Empire should be examined, it will be found to have commenced only with the enlisting of the Goths; because from that time the vigour of the Roman Empire began to decline, and all that valour which had raised it passed away to others.

I conclude, therefore, that no principality is secure without having its own forces; on the contrary, it is entirely dependent on good fortune, not having the valour which in adversity would defend it. And it has always been the opinion and judgment of wise men that nothing can be so uncertain or unstable as fame or power not founded on its own strength. And one's own forces are those which are composed either of subjects, citizens, or dependants; all others are mercenaries or auxiliaries. And the way to make ready one's own forces will be easily found if the rules suggested by me shall be reflected upon, and if one will consider how Philip, the father of Alexander the Great, and many republics and princes have armed and organized themselves, to which rules I entirely commit myself. . . .

A prince ought to have no other aim or thought, nor select anything else for his study, than war and its rules and discipline; for this is the sole art that belongs to him who rules, and it is of such force that it not only upholds those who are born princes, but it often enables men to rise from a private station to that rank. And, on the contrary, it is seen that when princes have thought more of ease than of arms they have lost their states. And the first cause of your losing it is to neglect this art; and what enables you to acquire a state is to be master of the art. Francesco Sforza, through being martial, from a private person became Duke of Milan; and the sons, through avoiding the hardships and troubles of arms, from dukes became private persons. For among other evils which being unarmed brings you, it causes you to be despised, and this is one of those ignominies against which a prince ought to guard himself, as is shown later on. Because there is nothing proportionate between the armed and the unarmed; and it is not reasonable that he who is armed should yield obedience willingly to him who is unarmed, or that the unarmed man should be secure among armed servants. Because, there being in the one disdain and in the other suspicion, it is not possible for them to work well together. And therefore a prince who does not understand the art of war, over and above the other misfortunes already mentioned, cannot be respected by his soldiers, nor can he rely on them. . . .

I. *The Military Forces of the Dynastic State*

A dynastic state, such as France by the year 1650, represented a sum of real political power greater than anything seen in Europe since the end of the Roman Empire, and this power was wielded by one man. During the Middle Ages, military, and along with it political, power had of necessity been decentralized, for with the relative stagnation of economic activity in Medieval Europe, the monarchy had lacked the means to maintain peace and order throughout the realm. The direct beneficiaries of this state of affairs were the great vassals of the King, to whom he delegated the task of administering the different parts of his kingdom. Many of them were in fact stronger than the monarch, their supposed lord. The political and military prerogatives of this great feudal nobility were based on the holding of land, for with a given quantity of land one could maintain a corresponding number of armed men. The fact that the nobles were obliged to come to the armed assistance of the king only under certain specified conditions gave them a high degree of control over him, whatever his titles and pretensions.

The drawback in this system of decentralized administration was that it was conducive to endemic petty warfare among the various members of the nobility, each one of whom could call upon his armed men to defend his particular rights and claims. To restore true peace and internal order throughout his kingdom, a monarch had thus to deprive his vassals of their capacity to make war on each other whenever it pleased them. The efforts of the monarchy in this direction were greatly facilitated by the growth of a money economy in Europe, and the emergence of a class, the bourgeoisie, whose power was based on money and whose basic interests coincided with those of the crown. Money was a flexible dynamic instrument of political power, as opposed to land, for with it a ruler could hire soldiers when and as he needed them. In this way he was able to escape one of the most effective checks which his vassals could exercise over him, their hitherto exclusive ability to provide him with armed men. Thus fortified, the monarch was slowly able to dispossess his vassals of their discretionary military power and thereby to obtain a virtual monopoly of violence within his kingdom.

Having established his dominance at home, the monarch then moved to defend and advance the claims of his dynasty in foreign lands. As a result, the dynastic states of the sixteenth, seventeenth, and eighteenth centuries were often at war with each other. Furthermore, the introduction of new and expensive weapons, demanding the tactical reorganization of the armies and consequently trained manpower in greater numbers than ever before, all added to the high cost of military endeavor. To raise the needed money, it was necessary to marshal the resources of the realm, both human and economic, more rationally and efficiently than had been done in the past. This in turn had a profound effect on the institutional development of the state. (See selection 2.)

The consolidation in the power and authority of the dynastic monarchy during the sixteenth and seventeenth centuries and the resulting decline in the effective strength of the feudal nobility was by no means a steady, uninterrupted process. This may be clearly seen in the case of France. Although by the year 1500, the prestige of the crown had been immeasurably enhanced through the defeat of the English in the Hundred Years War and through the victory of the king over his great vassal, Charles the Bold, Duke of Burgundy, nevertheless, the French nobility was on at least three occasions over the next two centuries to rebel against their monarch in an effort to regain some portion of their lost prerogatives.

The first and most serious of these rebellions coincided with and became part of the religious wars wracking France in the last half of the sixteenth century. There was another outbreak of feudal turbulence after the assassination of Henry IV in 1610. It was climaxed by a revolt of the Huguenots, the French Protestants. This last outbreak of domestic violence was quashed and order reestablished through the efforts of Cardinal Richelieu, the great minister of Louis XIII. Any group within society which disturbed the peace and stability of the realm and thereby threatened the authority of the crown was anathema to Richelieu: hence the enmity he felt toward the French nobility, who seemed unable to subordinate their particular whims and their supposed class interests to the good of the whole commonwealth. Richelieu believed that the solution to this problem lay in the creation of a permanent standing army in which the nobility would be enrolled. Not only would they thus be made to serve the interests of the state, protecting the kingdom against its foreign foes, they would also be much more easily subject to royal discipline and control. (See selection 3.) Such a standing army was never organized in Richelieu's lifetime. His death in 1642, followed by that of his royal master a year later, left a child of five as king, Louis XIV, under the regency of his mother, and provided the occasion for the last great armed rising of the French nobility, the Fronde. This disorganized and chaotic rebellion lasted from 1648 to 1652.

Louis XIV never forgot the Fronde or forgave his proud and disloyal nobility the indignities that as a child he had been obliged to suffer at their hands. He was determined that it should never again be possible for royal authority to be so disdained. The most effective guarantee against such a calamity being repeated was for the king to possess a strong, disciplined military force. Prior to the accession of Louis XIV, France could not be considered to have had a permanent army. At the beginning of a war, the crown, dealing with individual captains and colonels, raised an army. At the end of hostilities, it was disbanded. Even though the soldiers were paid by the crown, the monarch enjoyed only an uncertain and intermittent authority over his armies. The real control of the armed forces of the kingdom lay with the great military chiefs, who were generally members of the higher nobility and whose obedience to the monarch was therefore conditional.

It was the achievement of the great Ministers of War of Louis XIV, Michel Le Tellier and his son, Louvois, to bring this insubordinate and disorganized body under the absolute control of the state. In their efforts, they were vigorously seconded by the king himself, who had a passionate interest in military matters, even to the most minute details. (See selection 5.) The primary means by which they accomplished this goal was through the establishment of the armed forces on a permanent basis, maintaining at least a nucleus of every unit in time of peace as well as war. Then by assuming direct responsibility not only for the recruitment but also for both the pay and the provisioning of these units, the government was able to free itself from its former reliance on a multitude of semi-independent agencies, each of which had sought to assert its special rights against the sovereign pretensions of the crown. All of this involved great increases in the size and the complexity of the machinery of state, but it also provided the means to subject the armed forces of the country to the direct and constant control of the king. (See selection 4.) They were thus transformed from a quasi-autonomous group within the body politic, and a potential source of trouble and disorder, into a docile instrument for the carrying out of royal policy at home and abroad.

The dynastic monarchies of France, Spain, and England which took shape in the sixteenth and seventeenth centuries were the result of a long process of evolution, a process which was facilitated by the fact that their peoples tended to have a common cultural background and a shared history. Then too, the territories occupied by these kingdoms were from a geographical point of view relatively well defined. To that degree, these states might be considered as "natural" political phenomena. They provide a sharp contrast to that state which came into existence in the seventeenth century and which over the course of the next two hundred years was to become the dominant power on the European continent, for Prussia was in a very real sense an "artificial" creation, a monument to the grim determination and tenacity of purpose of its remarkable rulers.

The dynastic inheritance of the House of Hohenzollern in 1648, at the moment of the Peace of Westphalia, comprised six separate pieces of territory stretching across the sandy plains of North Germany, from the Rhineland to the Duchy of Prussia in Poland, the most important of which was the Margravate of Brandenburg. These lands were not contiguous, nor did they possess any common legal and political institutions. Their only common bond was the fact that they were all ruled by the same man, although in each case under a different title. Out of this hodgepodge of principalities a powerful unitary state was to be forged. This new state corresponded to no natural ethnic or linguistic grouping, nor did it possess any natural frontiers. Almost the sole reason for its coming into existence was the military imperative as it was first recognized by Frederick William, Margrave of Brandenburg and Elector of the Holy Roman Empire, who succeeded to the title in 1640 at the age of twenty.

Having seen his small and insignificant lands the prey to every marauding army marching across northern Germany during the Thirty Years War, the Great Elector, by which title Frederick William was to be known in history, realized that the only possible security against a similar catastrophe in some future war lay in the creation of a competent military force. Such a force would make him a worthy ally of some greater power, thereby affording his lands a measure of protection. The greatest obstacle to the plans of Frederick William was the unwillingness of the landed nobility to provide the funds necessary for an institution which could well mean the end of their power and independence within the realm. The Great Elector was obliged to display considerable ingenuity and ruthlessness in virtually extorting the money from his nobility, but he was nevertheless successful. (See selection 6.) By the time of his death in 1688 the house possessed a well trained army of some 30,000 men.

The Great Elector's son and successor, Frederick III, a mild mannered gentleman with a weakness for pomp and ceremonial, was more interested in the arts and sciences than in military matters. Even so, he did not let slip any of the rights and prerogatives which had been won by his father. He was in fact able to add some 10,000 men to the army, but probably his most significant accomplishment was to obtain the royal dignity for his dynasty from the Holy Roman Emperor. Throughout his various lands, the Margrave of Brandenburg was henceforth to be called King in Prussia.

Frederick William I, the second Prussian king, cared nothing for either ceremony or culture. His one all-consuming passion was the army. (See selection 7.) Convinced that the 40,000 man army which he found at the moment of succession in 1713 was not large enough, Frederick William had by the time of his death a quarter of a century later doubled its size and had made it the most efficient fighting force in Europe. (See selection 8.) Furthermore he paid for this army out of the resources of his own poor and economically backward kingdom, for he believed that he would never be truly independent until he could foreswear the foreign subsidies upon which his predecessors had relied. To accomplish this tour de force Frederick William was quite prepared to subordinate the whole energies of the Prussian state to the needs of the army. The bureaucracy which he created for the rational administration of his kingdom in the interests of his army had no parallel in any contemporary state with regard to its honesty, efficiency, and devotion to duty. (See selection 9.) It was in the functioning of the Prussian bureaucracy, minutely regulating the life of every subject of the king that the process begun by the Great Elector was brought to its logical conclusion. The dissimilar and disparate lands of the House of Hohenzollern had been welded into a unified state. This state existed and its subjects labored incessantly for no other reason than to support a standing army.

Frederick William I never cared to risk his cherished army in war. His son,

Frederick the Great, was not so prudent. Some six months after he had succeeded to the throne in 1740, he seized by force of arms the rich and populous neighboring province of Silesia, part of the domain of the House of Habsburg, and for the next twenty-three years he fought a series of increasingly desperate wars against a formidable coalition of enemies in a successful effort to retain it. With the annexation of Silesia, Prussia became a European power.

For all the achievements of the great Hohenzollerns, a vigorous and healthy society could not be built solely on the principles of the barracks room, with all initiative coming from above and the people expected to do nothing but obey. As long as the body politic received its impulsion from men of the caliber of Frederick the Great or his father, it functioned well enough, but their successors had neither the force of character nor the dynamism which such a system of government required. The resulting ossification in both the army and the state was to be revealed in the shattering defeat of Jena at the hands of Napoleon. For a moment it seemed as if this catastrophe had deprived the Kingdom of Prussia of its raison d'être. The military imperative alone, in the name of which both army and state had been called into existence, ultimately proved to be an inadequate basis for a viable polity.

Purely geographical factors did much to determine the military problem as it was faced by either the Prussian or the French government in modern times. By the same token, the fact that England is an island has had considerable bearing on her peculiar military requirements and her consequently unique constitutional development. With the defense of the realm assured above all by the sea, the government has never been obliged to maintain a large permanent military establishment or to create an imposing apparatus of state to finance and administer it. Nevertheless, a strong standing army was instituted in England during the course of the seventeenth century, but unlike what took place on the continent, it was not created in response to a recognized military imperative. Rather its origin was to be found in the great struggle between parliament and the crown which in 1642 led to the outbreak of civil war. Although the basic issue over which they had fallen out was ostensibly a constitutional one—which of the two organs of the government was to possess the ultimate sovereign power in the state—it was the religious question which supplied the real acrimony in their dispute. The royal party championed a church episcopal in organization and vaguely Roman in much of its doctrine and service, while the parliamentary party, which was puritan in its beliefs, advocated a presbyterian organization for the church.

The decisive element in the victory of the parliamentary party was the New Model Army, whose most noted leader was Oliver Cromwell. Organized in 1644, following the inconclusive opening battles of the war, this military force was remarkable for the religious fervor of its officers and men. This ardor was the basis for their splendid discipline and their grim efficacy on the field of battle, but it was to prove highly inconvenient once the Civil Wars were over. In their ideas regarding the organization of the church, and by implication, the state, the men of the New Model Army were far more radical than the great majority of the parliamentary party, or for that matter, most other Englishmen. Having fought and won the Civil War, the army was determined to have the decisive voice in the political and religious settlement which would follow. (See selection 11.) It was a pretension which parliament was unwilling to admit. The quarrel between the two factions and the efforts of the king to profit by it finally led the army to resort to force and to "purge" parliament of its moderate elements. Under the direction of Cromwell, the radical remnants of parliament, having been constituted as a high court of justice, then proceeded to the trial and condemnation of the king on a charge of treason. With the execution of Charles on January 30, 1649, all effective political power had come to rest in the army. For the next nine years, Cromwell ruled England as a military dictatorship.

Throughout the years he was in power, Cromwell vainly sought a permanent constitutional settlement which would be consonant with the aspirations and the desires both of the "godly" men of the army and of the English people as a whole. Each successive failure to arrive at such a settlement obliged him once again to turn to the army as the only reliable political force in the country. (See selection 12.) As a system of government, "godliness" supported by a standing army could not function without someone of Cromwell's prestige and strength of character at its head. He died in 1658 and it outlasted him by less than two years.

The whole Cromwellian experience served to give Englishmen a profound and durable distaste for the institution of standing armies. When after the restoration of the monarchy in 1660, parliament sought to provide for the defense of the realm, they thought primarily in terms of a local militia. Funds for a few regiments of regular troops were voted only grudgingly. Harboring a well founded distrust of the policies and motives of both Charles II and his brother and successor, James II, parliament feared that the army could well become an instrument of royal despotism in their hands. Even though there were perfectly sound military reasons for James to wish to increase the size of the army at the expense of the rather ineffective militia, parliament stubbornly resisted him. (See selection 13.) The Glorious Revolution of 1688 whereby parliament deposed James and presented the crown jointly to his daughter Mary and her husband William of Orange, established once and for all its prerogatives as the ultimate sovereign power within the kingdom. Parliamentary control over the army was enshrined in the Bill of Rights of 1689 and the Mutiny Act of the same year. (See selection 14.) These guarantees, along with the custom of annual or semiannual appropriations of money for the army, which over the next 200 years became embedded in constitutional practice, were sufficient to reconcile the English to the existence of an adequate military establishment, minuscule as it may have been by continental standards. (See selection 15.)

England's insular situation, which in the eighteenth century permitted her to rely on so small an army, also protected England against the full effects of the French Revolution, for it was by force of arms that the Revolution was carried beyond the borders of France. The army of Revolutionary France was in many ways a new and unique body, and yet at the same time it was a direct, lineal descendant of the royal army created by Le Tellier and Louvois. When, under the impact of the Revolution, the Old Regime began to fall apart, the military institutions of the dynastic state demonstrated more durability and resilience than almost any other part of the traditional body politic. Despite the incipient chaos caused by the collapse of royal authority and by the emigration of a large part of the officer corps in the person of the French nobility, the remnants of the old royal army were still able to provide a nucleus for the new armed forces which were in the process of formation and to embody those principles of order, discipline, and cohesion which would seem to be essential to the functioning of any military body. An amalgam of the traditional with the new and untried, the Revolutionary armies were to prove themselves a superbly effective instrument of war.

Unlike the army of the Old Regime, existing apart from the rest of society, the military forces of the Revolution were meant to be intimately bound up with the French people as a whole. They were, in a sense, the personification of the patriotic enthusiasm of a newly self-conscious nation. By the decree of August 23, 1793, calling for a *levée en masse*, the Republic sought to mobilize the total energies of the French people for war. (See selection 16.) No government as yet possessed the technical capabilities to realize such a grandiose ambition, but the very fact that men now were coming to conceive of the military imperative in these terms was a grim portent for the future. Some of the more fanatical leaders of the ruling Jacobin party, such as Saint-Juste, the implacable young colleague of Robespierre on the Committee of Public Safety, even advocated fundamental changes in the tactics and the principles of organization of the army, to make them more "revolutionary." (See selection 18.) As experience on the field of battle was to prove, however, tactical problems could not be resolved by revolutionary enthusiasm alone and nationalistic exaltation was to little avail unless channelled through conventional military forms. The revolutionary government was therefore obliged to avail itself of military talent wherever it could be found, even among the officers of the suspect royal army. To insure the obedience and the loyalty of this new, necessarily heterogenous army, as well as its military effectiveness, the Committee of Public Safety, which served as the government of France during the most desperate period of the Revolution, employed the so-called representatives on mission. For the carrying out of their assigned mission, these delegates of the government were given practically unlimited powers. (See selection 17.) Whether the great victories of the year of crisis 1793–1794 were achieved through the new nationalistic fervor of the soldiers, as aided and abetted by the representatives of the people, or whether they were won primarily through the reintroduction of the traditional qualities of discipline and military training is difficult to answer in a definitive way. (See selections 19 & 20.) In any case, the newly reinvigorated army, having beaten back a formidable coalition of enemies and thereby saved the Republic, then went on the offensive. The army thus became the instrument by which the doctrines of the French Revolution were disseminated to neighboring lands, dissolving traditional ideals and institutions.

The revolutionary enthusiasm of the years 1792–1794 could not be sustained indefinitely. There thus followed a rather abrupt reaction to the extreme Jacobin policies of the Committee of Public Safety, and consequently a reorganization of the regime. Executive power was now vested in a Directory, consisting of five men. The chief beneficiaries of this new regime were the French bourgeoisie, who believed that the moment had come to "stabilize" the gains of the Revolution and to reestablish a measure of order within the nation. Enjoying little or no personal prestige, and lacking widespread popular support, the politicians of the Directory found it to be an impossible task. Beset by the resurgent monarchists on one side and the Jacobins on the other, they were increasingly driven to rely on the army, the one solidly organized element within the persistent chaos and confusion of French national life, as the means through which they might maintain themselves in power and make a pretense of governing the country. Drawn into the political struggle at the behest of the government, the army ceased to be what it had been under the Committee of Public Safety, purely an instrument for the defense of the nation. Having already become the chief financial support of the French state through its foreign conquests, the army also became in the years 1795–1799 the essential element in its political life. It was thus only a matter of time before a victorious general, clothed with the prestige of his military exploits, would overturn the Directory and its rickety facade of constitutionalism and would begin to govern in his own name. (See selection 21.)

That political power should fall to General Napoleon Bonaparte was no doubt a question of chance and his own immense good fortune. It was even more the result of his military genius, as seen in the Italian Campaign of 1796-1797, and of his skill in publicizing his achievements to promote his political ambitions. (See selection 22.) On November 9, 1799, or by the Revolutionary calendar, 18 Brumaire of the year VIII, Bonaparte and his accomplices staged the coup d'état which overthrew the Directory. After ten years of revolutionary upheaval, France had a new master, a general who reestablished civil order and who governed not by military force but through civilian institutions of his own devising. These were to provide the essential adminstrative framework of the French state down through the nineteenth century. Nevertheless the history of his regime was one of war. Before his career was over, Napoleon would have conquered most of the European continent. To defeat him, the old dynastic states would all to some degree be obliged to remake their military institutions after the French model. (See selection 23.)

THE ORIGINS OF THE STANDING ARMY

Michael Roberts

2. THE MILITARY REVOLUTION

The great dynastic states which emerged in the two centuries between 1500 and 1700 could support armies on a scale that had been previously impossible. Certain long-term social and economic processes may well have underlain this decisive political development, but it can be argued that the essential motive force behind the dynastic state was ultimately military. Such is the contention of Professor Michael Roberts of Queen's University, Belfast. In the following selection taken from his brilliant essay, *The Military Revolution, 1560–1660*, he discusses the changing techniques of war, and in particular, the introduction of the first crude firearms, which of necessity led to the creation of new and different tactical units on the field of battle. They in turn required the reorganization of the traditional military institutions of the monarchy. These ultimately promoted far reaching changes in both state and society.

The effective combination of missile weapons with close action has always been one of the central problems of tactics; and in the sixteenth century it was posed afresh. For a thousand years the battlefields of Europe had been dominated by heavy cavalry, and on the whole arrows had not availed much against them. In the fifteenth century that domination had been overthrown. But it was not that chivalry had succumbed to the power of hand-gun or arquebus; it was not that firearms had for the moment the advantage over the tactics of the *mêlée*: it was rather that a form of close action dependent upon the impact and mass of heavy cavalry was displaced by a form of close action dependent upon the impact and mass of heavy infantry. The line of charging knights was smashed by the massed pikes of the Swiss column. Firearms did, indeed, batter down the feudal castle; and the social and constitutional significance of that achievement needs no emphasis. But on the battlefield firearms for long represented a big step backward. The effective combination of archers and men-at-arms, not uncommon in the Middle Ages, reached its climax, perhaps, at Agincourt: the following generations, turning increasingly to firearms, and abandoning the bow, groped in vain for a tactical form that should take its place. For by a curious paradox the coming of the hand-gun brought with it a steep decline in firepower: the superiority of the longbow, in speed, accuracy, and mobility, was so marked that even in the late seventeenth century military writers were pleading for its reintroduction.

The tacticians of the sixteenth century, seeking an effective form for the combination of firearms and *l'arme blanche,* had to take account of the fact that military fashion, and a well-grounded faith in the moral effect of loud detonations, had provided them with a thoroughly inefficient missile weapon. It followed that the missile arm must make up by numbers what it lacked in

From Michael Roberts, *The Military Revolution, 1560–1660* (Belfast, 1956), pp. 4–12, 16–23, abridged. Reprinted by permission of the Librarian, Queen's University Library, Belfast, Northern Ireland.

individual effectiveness. At the same time they saw no reason to abandon those huge squares of pikemen and halberdiers with which the Swiss had routed the chivalry of Burgundy. Thus massed pikemen must somehow be combined with massed musketeers. The upshot of this state of affairs was the Spanish *tercio*, 3000 strong, in which a square of pikemen was surrounded by a deep bordure of shot; while to counteract the slowness and inaccuracy of musket-fire commanders evolved the countermarch. By 1560 this formation, or something like it, was dominant all over western Europe. The pike was "queen of the battlefield"; the millennial ascendancy of cavalry was broken; the Chevalier Bayard fought on foot.

The invention of the wheel-lock pistol, about 1515, seemed for a time to offer to the mounted arm a chance of revival. The horseman equipped both with lance and pistol might seem to embody in his own person an economical combination of arms. And so no doubt he would have done, if the pistoleers could have been persuaded to use both their weapons. But after about 1560, the cavalryman, deterred by the bristling and uninviting aspect of the *tercios* which he was called upon to attack, his lance outranged by the infantryman's eighteen-foot pike, preferred to confine himself to discharging his pistol by successive ranks, in that intricate but futile manoeuvre known as the caracole. Since the effective range of the cavalry pistol was perhaps as little as five paces, this did no great harm to anybody, except possibly to the cavalry themselves, who became very generally perverted and degenerate. . . .

The effect of these developments was to hobble the conduct of operations. The huge size of infantry units forbade the practice of minor tactics. The refusal of cavalry to behave as cavalry deprived commanders of their aid in attack. . . . The steady increase in the proportion of musketeers to pikemen strengthened that element in the infantry which was least apt to the offensive. Contemporary theorists, rationalizing their own

impotence, extolled the superior science of the war of manoeuvre, and condemned battle as the last resort of the inept or unfortunate commander. Strategic thinking withered away; war eternalized itself.

Upon this military *ancien régime* there now fell a major revolution. The first of the revolutionaries was Erik XIV of Sweden, in the 'sixties; but his experiment passed unnoticed, and it was not until after 1590 that the revolution can really be said to have got under weigh. It took place in two stages: the first, from about 1590 to 1609, under the leadership of Maurice of Orange; the second, from about 1617 to 1632, under the leadership of Gustavus Adolphus. Maurice and his cousins, inspired by a study of Vegetius, Aelian, and Leo VI, . . . attempted to return to Roman models in regard to size of units, order of battle, discipline, and drill. Their new infantry unit, the battalion, was about the size of a cohort; and they ranged their battalions *quincunx*-wise, to form a *duplex* or *triplex acies*. They thus reverted, for the first time for more than a century, to a linear order of battle, with a proper reserve; by their arrangement of shot and pikes within the unit they avoided the great waste of manpower implicit in the *tercio*, and were thus able to increase the proportion of pikes to muskets (a reversal of previous trends); and by their drastic reduction in the size of the tactical unit they were able to achieve much greater elasticity and flexibility within the framework of their battle-line: a Spanish army of 12,000 men would have only 4 units, a Dutch would have 24, and the task of reinforcing a threatened sector of the line was proportionately simplified.

These were great innovations; but they did not at once gain general acceptance, nor were those who adopted them able to point to much success against the *tercios*. Maurice's reforms, indeed, were a revolution that stopped half-way, and their lack of success on the battlefield is to be attributed to that fact. They made little real advance towards solving the problem of combining firepower and shock; they left cavalry still in the hands of the pistoleers; and above all they were essentially defensive in spirit, for Maurice shared to the full the contemporary dislike of battle. It was left to Gustavus Adolphus to remedy most of the defects of Maurice's system, and in doing so to stereotype European warfare in that linear pattern which it retained, on the whole, until our own day.

The essential contribution of Gustavus Adolphus was to demonstrate the ability of linear formations to defeat mass, not only in defence, but in attack. And he did this by combining firepower and shock as nobody had been able to do since firearms replaced bows, while developing the characteristic offensive qualities of each arm. The pike was rehabilitated, for the last time, as an offensive, battlewinning, weapon; but at the same time it was linked in the closest tactical combination with musketeers. And the effectiveness of the musketeers was secured by the device of the salvo, which replaced the desultory rolling fire of the countermarch. The characteristic method of this last period, whether for attack or defence, whether for horse or foot, was an alternation of missile shock and mass impact. And this in turn implied the emancipation of cavalry from the caracole, and a return to its natural reliance upon the weight of man and horse to disrupt enemy formations. At the same time, the effectiveness of missile support was revolutionized, first by the use of a light three-pounder gun, which, since it could be manhandled, could be used in intimate collaboration with infantry; and secondly by decisive improvements in the mobility of field artillery. All these advances rested upon a thorough reform of military administration, along lines later to be familiar to Le Tellier and Louvois, and upon a discipline and drill which were superior even to the Dutch. Gustavus took over the smaller units of the Maurician system, with their minor articulations; but he stabilized, as Maurice had not been able to do, the relationship between the tactical and administrative unit, and above all he developed the initiative of subalterns and N.C.O.'s in an entirely novel manner. The importance of the platoon-commander begins with Gustavus; and all the manuals on section-leading in attack and defence may justly claim him as their progenitor.

The battles of Breitenfeld, Wittstock, Rocroi and Jankow marked the success of the revolution. They revealed the recovery of the art of war from the debility which had been the result of the invention of firearms. They laid down the pattern which warfare would follow until the close of the eighteenth century. And they entailed consequences of the most far-reaching kind.

The most obvious of these were purely military. The soldier of the middle ages had been, on the whole, an individualist; and he (and his horse) had been highly trained over a prolonged period. The coming, first of firearms, then of the Swiss column, put an end to this state of affairs. The mercenary in the middle of a pike-square needed little training and less skill: if he inclined his pike in correct alignment and leaned heavily on the man in front of him, he had done almost all that could be required of him. So too with the musketeer: a certain dexterity in loading, a certain steadiness in the ranks, sufficed to execute the countermarch, since no one could reasonably demand of a musket that it should be aimed with accuracy. The training of a bowman, schooled to be a dead shot at a distance, would be wasted on so imperfect an instrument as an arquebus or a wheel-lock pistol; and the pike, unlike the lance, was not an individual weapon at all. One reason why firearms drove out the bow and the lance was precisely this, that they economized on training. Moreover, deep formations, whether of horse or foot, dispensed with the need for a large trained corps of officers, and required a less high morale, since it is difficult to run away with fifteen ranks behind you.

The reforms of Maurice inaugurated a real, and a lasting, revolution in these matters. Maurice's small units had to be highly trained in manoeuvre; they needed many more officers and N.C.O.'s to lead them. The tactics of Gustavus postulated a vastly improved fire-discipline, and long practice in the combination of arms. . . . And so officers became not merely leaders, but trainers, of men; diligent practice in peacetime, and in winter, became essential; and drill, for the first time in modern history, became the precondition for military success. And since individual initiative was expected at a far lower level of command than ever before; and since the slowly-increasing technical complexity of firearms was already beginning the process of forcing the soldier to be (on however primitive a level) a technician; the revolution in drill, while it implied a new subordination of a soldier's will to the command of a superior, implied also intelligent subordination. Henceforth it might not be the soldier's business to think, but he would at least be expected to possess a certain minimal capacity for thinking. The army was no longer to be a brute mass, in the Swiss style, nor a collection of bellicose individuals, in the feudal style; it was to be an articulated organism of which each part responded to impulses from above. The demand for unanimity and precision of movement led naturally to the innovation of marching in step, which appears at some date impossible to establish about the middle of the seventeenth century. And the principle of mass-subordination, of the solution of the individual will in the will of the commander, received a last reinforcement with the slow adoption of uniforms: "without uniforms," said Frederick the Great, "there can be no discipline.". . . The way was clear for the armies of the nineteenth century: it remained only for the twentieth to complete the process by replacing dolmans, busbies, eagles' wings, and all the flaunting *panache* of Cossack and Hussar, by the flat uniformity of field-grey and khaki. . . .

The armies which carried through the military revolution — or upon which that revolution impinged — were nearly all mercenary armies. It has indeed been argued, and with some force, that the great military innovations throughout history have generally coincided with the predominance of mercenaries; and it has been urged, more specifically, that the Maurician reforms were possible only in a mercenary force, since the prolonged drilling and high degree of professional skill which they demanded would have been impossible to obtain from a citizen militia. But though this last contention (as we shall see in a moment) cannot be sustained, there is no doubt that the use of mercenaries was attended with certain obvious advantages. A mercenary army cared not at all if the war were prolonged, or fought far from home; it economized the state's own manpower, and hence its wealth; the system of recruiting through captains relieved the government of a good deal of administrative work. There were, of course, many countervailing disadvantages: the mercenary was undisciplined, unreliable, and averse to battle; his arms and equipment were unstandardized and often bad; the employer was invariably swindled by the captains; and the whole system was ruinously expensive. So expensive, indeed, that the smaller and poorer states were forced to look for alternatives. Around the turn of the century, many of the lesser German states — and even some quite big ones such as Saxony, Brandenburg and Bavaria — began to experiment with local militias. Military writers such as Machiavelli and Lazarus von Schwendi had urged the superiority of the citizen army, with many a backward glance at the military virtues of republican Rome. But it was forgotten that the classical authors whose military teachings formed the basis of the Maurician reforms all dated from times when the Roman forces were citizen-armies no longer. The event proved that the half-trained militias were incapable of mastering the modern art of war. Their failure in Germany was universal, ignominious and complete; and it seemed that those were right who contended that in the new conditions only mercenary armies could be effective. The

Swedish victories, however, were a warning against too hasty a conclusion; for the Swedish army was a conscript national militia—the first truly national European army—and it proved capable of mastering military techniques much more complex than had been seen before. The second and more important stage of the military revolution, in fact, was launched, not by highly-skilled professionals, but by conscript peasants; and experienced mercenary soldiers such as Robert Monro had to go to school again to learn the new Swedish methods. And not only were the Swedish armies better than any mercenaries; they were also incomparably cheaper. There was no peculation by captains; and payment could be made in land-grants, revenue-assignments, tax-remissions, or in kind.

But conditions in Sweden were exceptional, and other European countries felt unable to follow the Swedish example. The Spanish army under Philip II did indeed contain some conscripts, as well as international mercenaries and Spanish "gentlemen-rankers," and the Prussian army of Frederick William I was a mixed army too; but on the whole the rulers found no feasible alternative to a mercenary force: some of them, like Christian IV of Denmark and John George of Saxony, were not willing to put arms into the hands of their peasantry. But if mercenaries thus appeared inevitable, something at least could be done to make them less burdensome to the state. Already before the end of the sixteenth century it was realized that the practice of disbanding and paying-off regiments at the end of each campaigning season, and re-enlisting them the following spring, was an expensive way of doing business. Large sums were payable on enlistment and mustering, and (in theory at least) all arrears were paid up on disbandment. But between mustering and disbandment pay was irregular and never full, despite the so-called "full-pays" which occurred from time to time. If then a mercenary force were not disbanded in the autumn, but continued from year to year, the calls upon the exchequer were likely to be considerably lessened, and the general nuisance of mutinous soldiery would be abated. Moreover, if the army remained embodied throughout the winter, the close season could be used for drilling and exercising, of which since the tactical revolution there was much more need than ever before. . . . From this practice arose the modern standing army; and it is worthwhile emphasizing the fact that it was the result of considerations of a military and financial, and not of a political or constitutional nature. . . . There is little basis for the suggestion that standing armies were called into being by artful princes in order to provide employment for their turbulent nobility; or that they were a sign of the inherent *Drang nach Machtentfaltung* of the monarchs; or that they were designed to support the rulers in their struggles against constitutional limitations—though they did, no doubt, prove very serviceable instruments of despotism. Where absolutism triumphed in this century, it did so because it provided the response to a genuine need; and though an army might be useful for curbing aristocratic licence, it was but an accessory factor in the general political situation which produced the eclipse of the Estates. Essentially the standing armies were the product of military logic rather than of political design. . . .

Nevertheless, it is obvious that the military changes of the seventeenth century had important consequences in the political and constitutional fields. The stricter discipline, the elaborately mechanical drilling, required by the new linear tactics, matched the tendency of the age towards absolute government, and may well have reinforced it: if discipline proved so successful in obtaining results in the military sphere, it might well be worthwhile trying the experiment of applying it to civilian life. The ruler was increasingly identified with the commander-in-chief; and from the new discipline and drill would be born not merely the autocrat, but that particular type of autocrat which delighted in the name of

17

Kriegsherr. It was perhaps not the least of England's good luck, that for the whole of the critical century from 1547 to 1649 she was ruled by monarchs with neither interest nor capacity for military matters. It was certainly no accident that Louis XIII should have been "passionately fond" of drill; nor was it a mere personal quirk that led Louis XIV to cause a medal to be struck, of which the reverse displays him in the act of taking a parade, and correcting, with a sharp poke of his cane, the imperfect dressing of a feckless private in the rear rank. The newly-acquired symmetry and order of the parade-ground provided, for Louis XIV and his contemporaries, the model to which life and art must alike conform; and the *pas cadencé* of Martinet's regiments echoed again in the majestic monotony of interminable alexandrines.

The military character of monarchy was further emphasized by the adoption of uniforms: the soldier became the king's man, for he wore the king's coat. And it was the king's coat indeed; for by the close of the century there was already a tendency in monarchs of an absolutist cast to consider military uniform as their normal attire—as Charles XII did, for instance, and Frederick William I. It was not a fashion that would have commended itself to Henry VIII, or Gustav Vasa, or Philip II.

Moreover, the new style of warfare made demands upon the adminstration which could be met only by new methods, new standards, and new officers; and it soon became clear that this implied an increasing measure of centralization, and hence of royal control. Secretaries of State for War are born; War Offices proliferate; Gustavus Adolphus creates something like the first General Staff. Military needs were forcing the monarchs into ever-increasing interference in the lives of their subjects: even in peaceful England, under the unwarlike Stuarts, the activities of the saltpetreman were no less a matter of popular complaint than in contemporary Sweden. New fortresses for the *pré carré* meant heavier *corvées*, the subversion of municipal liber-

ties, and the increased power of the sovereign: "fortresses," says Montecuccoli, "are the buttresses of the crown," and the fact that "licentious" nations such as the English disliked them merely proved their utility. The urgent need for the standardization of weapons, calibres, and powder drove the rulers to armaments-monopolies or state supervision of supply. It was a policy dictated by obvious military necessity; but it had constitutional repercussions too, for "self-equipment is conducive to the relaxation of discipline—that is, to the flattening of the pyramid of subordination." Above all, the ever-increasing cost of war—the result of larger armies and navies, in an age when prices were still rising —embarrassed the finances of every monarchy in Europe. Everywhere kings found that though they might still—with care —live of their own in peacetime, they plunged into debt in wartime. And in this period it was almost always wartime. The monarchs fell back on *ad hoc* financial devices—on currency debasement, sale of monopolies, sale of crown lands, sale of offices (which first becomes a general European phenomenon in this century)—but sooner or later they found themselves forced to parley with their Estates, or to violate the ancient constitutional liberties. Behind all the great insurrectionary movements of the age—the Thirty Years' War, the English rebellion, the Fronde, the revolts in the Spanish realms—there lay, as one major element in the situation (though of course not the only one) the crown's need for money; and that need was usually produced by military commitments whose dimensions were in part the result of the military revolution. On the whole, the monarchs prevailed; the income for maintaining standing armies was taken out of control of the Estates; sometimes military finance—as in Brandenburg—was wholly separated from the ordinary revenues. And in Germany this issue of the conflict resulted, in part, from the fact that in the last resort the Estates had rather sacrifice a constitutional principle, and retain the security afforded by a standing army, than risk the appalling sufferings and crushing financial exactions which, as the experience of the Thirty Years' War had shown, awaited the militarily impotent or old-fashioned. Sweden, with her relatively inexpensive conscript army, escaped this constitutional crux, and her Estates were in consequence able to weather a period of semi-absolutist rule: the contrast with the constitutional history of Brandenburg is a reflection of the differences in the military organization of the two countries. Nevertheless, though the standing army thus came to be accepted as the lesser of two evils, it was a grievous burden to the smaller and financially weaker states. They had discarded the alternative of a militia; a standing army seemed inescapable; but many of them could scarcely finance it from their own resources. It was this situation which presented such opportunities to that subsidy-diplomacy upon which the aggressive policies of Louis XIV were to thrive.

If liberty, then, were thus to be sacrificed to the army, it ought at least to be an army that was really the property of the king, and not a mere agglomeration of recruiting speculators. The free bargaining between recruiting captain and employing prince, the Articles of War which partook more of the nature of an industrial agreement than of a code of military discipline,—these things were repugnant to the orderliness and efficiency of the new military ideal. The larger the army, the greater the need for disciplining it from above. The monarch must take over the business of recruiting and paying men, as he was already beginning to take over the business of supplying material and supervising war-industries. And the monarchs, in fact, did so. The Articles of War of Gustavus Adolphus set a new standard of royal control, and were imitated even in countries which employed a predominantly mercenary army. In curbing the independence of the recruiting colonels a start was made by Wallenstein; and a generation later Louvois and the Great Elector were to profit from his example. By the end of the century the monarchs had mostly gained effective control of their armies. It was a significant development; for once the armies became royal (as the navies already were) the way was open for their eventually becoming national. . . .

3. CARDINAL RICHELIEU ON THE NEED FOR A PERMANENT ARMY

The absolute monarchies of the seventeenth and eighteenth centuries sought to monopolize the military potential of their peoples for two reasons. First, a government which had gained complete control over its armed forces was obviously in a far better position to utilize them for the protection of the kingdom against its foreign enemies and for advancing the international interests of the state than one which did not. Secondly, the maintenance of internal peace and order would be facilitated if the traditionally factious elements within the country, in particular the great feudal nobility, were deprived of their discretionary military power. Nowhere was this more true than in France, the wealthiest and most populous state in Europe. Because she was at the center of all continental affairs, her foreign interests and foreign enemies were correspondingly numerous. At the same time, the French nobility, not yet reconciled to their loss of power within the kingdom, represented a constant potential danger to the crown. The greatest exponent of the power of the monarchy in the seventeenth century, as well as its most skilled practitioner, was Cardinal Richelieu, the minister of Louis XIII. In his *Political Testament,* which was written for the instruction and edification of the king, and from which the following passages are taken, Richelieu discusses why the French monarchy must maintain a large military establishment.

The most powerful state in the world cannot be certain that it will be able to enjoy an assured peace if it is not in a condition to protect itself at all times from a sudden invasion or a surprise attack.

Thus, a great realm such as this one must always maintain a sufficient body of men at arms, who will serve to ward off the designs that are formulated through hatred and envy against its prosperity and grandeur. . . .

In matters of state, whoever is strong is often in the right, while he who is weak may find, according to the opinion of most people, that he is in the wrong.

Just as the soldier who does not wear his sword at all times may suffer all sorts of difficulties, so too a realm which is not always on its guard and prepared to protect itself against surprise attack, has much to fear.

The public interest demands that those to whom is entrusted the leadership of a state govern it in such a way that it is sheltered not only from all avoidable misfortunes but even from the fear to which they give rise.

Since reason dictates that the thing which supports be geometrically proportionate to the thing supported, it is evident that so great a realm as this cannot be defended by an inconsiderable force. . . .

For the garrisoning of the frontier towns and the maintenance of a permanent force strong enough to thwart any unexpected schemes, at least 4000 horses and 40,000 infantrymen must be kept in a constant state of readiness, and if it can be done without placing too much of a burden on the state, a reserve of 1000 gentlemen for the cavalry and 5000 for the infantry, who can be called upon any time the occasion should demand it.

From Cardinal Richelieu, *Testament politique,* Part 1, Chapter III, section 1 and Part 2, Chapter IV, section 4. Translated by the editor.

Some may say that the defense of a state does not require such elaborate preparations. But aside from the fact that this establishment is far from being a burden to France, for the nobility gain many advantages from it, while it provides relief for the common people, I declare that it is necessary to be capable of waging a long war, when the good of the state requires it. . . .

In order to wage war well, it is not enough for one to have carefully chosen the occasion, or to have on hand enough men, money, supplies, and munitions. The most important thing is that, the men be well trained; one must know how to maintain discipline and keep them in order, so that the money, the supplies, and the munitions are expended to the best effect.

To lay down general precepts is easy, but putting them into practice is difficult. And yet, if this is not done, a war will have a fortunate outcome only by chance or through a miracle and a miracle is something upon which wise men should never count. . . .

Frenchmen are capable of anything provided that those who command them are capable of teaching them the things that they must practice.

Their courage, which leads them to the four corners of the world in search of war, bears out the truth of this proposition, since they behave just as do the natives in whichever army they are serving, be it Spanish, Swedish, Croatian, or Dutch.

They observe the discipline to be found in each army, which clearly demonstrates that if they retain their natural defects in this country, it is because people put up with them and do not know how to correct them.

That they live without discipline in this realm is not so much their fault as that of their chiefs who command them and who are generally capable of drawing up fine regulations, but who do not trouble themselves to see that they are observed.

There is nothing easier than to make rules for good conduct and although it is difficult to put them into practice, it is nevertheless not impossible.

One must endeavor through reason to make people understand what is just, but then one must punish inexorably and without pity those who violate this concept.

If two or three exemplary punishments do not have some effect on this disobedience, repeated punishments will triumph over it. Here I take the liberty to state to your majesty that if he finds chiefs who are worthy of commanding, he will not lack subjects who are willing to obey, and that this idea which has spread throughout the world that the French cannot stomach discipline or regulations has no basis except in the incapacity of the chiefs who do not know how to set about accomplishing their chosen goals. . . .

He who commands must make no exception for special persons and he must have a reputation for this, for he should realize that if people see that he does not have the strength of character to be bound by his own regulations, they will not consider themselves bound by them either, or at least many will take the chance of violating them, thinking that they can do so with impunity. But if a chief tires of meting out punishment less easily than the offenders of trespassing, then his firmness will cause a halt to our excessive frivolity. Without such a remedy, there is little hope that a nation which is as hot-headed and impetuous as ours can be kept within the bounds of reason.

Thus, perseverance in the punishment of all those who fail in their duties and their obligations will have the result that few are actually punished, for there are not many to be found who would be willing with a light heart to run the risk of wrongdoing when they know retribution to be inevitable. Through the sacrifice of a few, the lives of many will be preserved, while order in all things will be maintained. . . .

It causes me no little pain in this respect to dwell upon the defects that your majesty has several times noted in his nobility, but they are so manifest that it is impossible to avoid them. And the affection that I bear your majesty makes it necessary to examine them in order to find the reason and thus to seek a remedy.

The esteem in which the nobility has been held in the past almost does not permit one to believe that it could conduct itself so badly on certain occasions during your reign. . . .

There is not a community where there are not to be found many more bad subjects than good and so. . .it is not to be wondered that when a group of nobles is assembled, the majority corrupts the lesser though better part, that it is easy for the poor in courage and those who are but little moved by the public interest. . . to spoil the good by contagion. It is almost inevitable on such occasions, and as the best wine is worth nothing when it is mixed with the dregs, so the services rendered by the best of the nobility are not only useless, but even harmful when joined to the dregs which adulterate them. . . .

Although your majesty is better aware of these verities than I, for he has seen such things take place in his presence, my conscience demands that I state frankly, without exaggeration, the faults of an order whose virtues I would willingly depict, in order that no one should turn to them for help, such assistance being harmful rather than beneficial to the state.

But this realm should not always be deprived of the services of the nobility, which has traditionally been one of its principal supports, and which is still required to render service in time of war because of the fiefs which are held in return for this service, and also because of the advantages which are enjoyed over the common people in time of peace. Therefor, all the fiefs in each bailliwick should be taxed according to their income and with the money thus raised, regular companies should be formed, which may be joined by those among the nobility who would prefer to serve in person rather than paying taxes out of the revenues from their fiefs, pro-

vided that they agree to abide by the regulations of the company in question. . . .

The nobility, having shown in the recent successfully concluded war that they are the heirs to the virtues of their ancestors . . . they should be so treated that they regain their former reputation and that they usefully serve the state.

Since those who do not contribute to the public good are actually harmful to it, it is evident that a nobility which does not serve the state in war is not only useless but in fact a burden upon it. The state may in this case be compared to a body the arms of which are paralyzed and which act as a dead weight rather than serving any useful function.

Just as a gentleman deserves to be well treated when he does well, so one must be strict with him when he fails in that duty to which his birth obliges him. I do not hesitate to declare that those who, having degenerated from the virtues of their forefathers, refuse to serve the crown with their swords and their lives, with devotion and steadfastness, deserve to be deprived of the advantages they have by their birth and reduced to shouldering part of the burden borne by the common people. Since honor should be more dear to them than life itself it would be more effective to punish them by stripping them of the former than the latter. . . .

If we should neglect nothing in order to preserve among the nobility the true virtue of the ancestors, we should also not overlook anything that can be done to help them to hold onto such wealth as has been left to them and even to procure more. . . .

If your Majesty were . . . to establish fifty companies of men at arms and a like number of light cavalry, which would be in accordance with certain specified conditions in the provinces, it would do a great deal toward supporting the poorer nobility. . . .

Louis André

4. MICHEL LE TELLIER AND THE FOUNDING OF THE FRENCH ARMY

When in 1643, Louis XIV succeeded to the throne as a child of five under the regency of his mother, the French army, despite the efforts of Richelieu, was an unruly, semi-autonomous body within the state. It was not above rebelling against the crown if the occasion presented itself. By 1660, when Louis came of age and the period of his personal rule began, it had become a stable, orderly, and disciplined arm of the state. The man to whom more than anyone else this transformation was due was Michel Le Tellier, Secretary of State for War under Louis's great minister Cardinal Mazarin. Le Tellier and his son and successor, Louvois, gave to the French military establishment the basic constitution which it has maintained for the past three centuries. The more significant aspects of this achievement are treated in the following selection by the late Louis André, a noted French student of the period.

Up until the moment when, upon the death of his father, Louis XIV became king, the efforts that had been made to organize the military forces of the realm had been neither numerous nor noteworthy. They had not been conceived or carried out according to any overall plan carefully prepared in advance. As a result, in 1643 an army cannot really be said to have existed. Over a long period of time, indeed since the Treaty of Vervins in 1598, the French had not had to sustain a serious foreign war. It was only in 1635 that they began to intervene against the House of Habsburg which was threatening the European balance of power. During these forty years they had made no progress from a military point of view. . . .

On the contrary, when the War of Devolution broke out in 1667, this army had for a long time been engaged in combat. Within the space of a quarter of a century, it had known only six or seven years of relative peace. It had had to sustain the shock of the Spanish and German troops, which until then had been reputed to be the best in Europe, and it had defeated them. It had been inured to the hardships of war. By the general discharge of 1659 the worst elements had been extirpated, and if a few indisciplined troops remained, the monarchy, following an old custom, had sent them off to perish in expeditions to Hungary, North Africa, or Chios.

The troops who made up the army were an elite. They had been involved and taken an active part in the disturbances of the Fronde. Its lamentable failure had been very instructive for them. Ever since then they had understood that in France a single will represented the law. . . . The army was monarchical. . . .

Where formerly everything within the army had been regulated according to the arbitrary whim of different individuals, logic and method had penetrated into its most remote parts and in the process had effected a profound change. This army now

From Louis André, *Michel Le Tellier et l'organisation de l'armée monarchique* (Montpellier, 1906), pp. 115–126, 199–205, 657–659, abridged. Translated by the editor.

possessed cadres of officers, who if not numerous, were adequate. The military chiefs who were either too powerful or who were filling some useless post had been banished. Those who remained were bound one to another in accordance with a hierarchy the stages of which were clearly defined. Although compulsory military service could not as yet be introduced, there were enough voluntary enlistments to fill the vacancies and bring the units up to their full strength. A hurried levying of men was no longer necessary, nor was there even need to have recourse to foreign troops, who were particularly greedy and difficult to get along with. A sufficient number of Frenchmen were ready to enlist. The king had only to make a sign and he had more men than he required, and these men were certain not to be *passevolants* — men who served only to beef up the muster roles, thus permitting the chiefs to draw a larger allowance from the government – or deserters, but real soldiers.

These men recognized that where formerly they had been paid only infrequently, now they would receive their money every month. Thanks to the surveillance exercised by civilian agents of the king, they were no longer robbed by their commanding officers; they received their pay. If they compared this pay to what their predecessors had received, they would have doubtless found that even if it had not increased, now at least it was real and not imaginary. In general, the troops clothed and outfitted themselves according to the whims of each individual; nevertheless, in certain units the clothing . . . was already alike. Uniformity was appearing and replacing the former diversity. Their weapons, the pike and the musket had not changed, but with regard to the latter, the government had prescribed certain regulation models. . . .

The administration of the army was entrusted to special war commissioners and to the military intendants, whose functions were innumerable, who counted, checked, inspected, curbed abuses, and kept a register of everything they did. They sent regular reports to the Secretary of State. He, being precisely informed, oversaw matters from his office . . . taking the requisite measures, dictating orders, and, in a word, directing things. All thus was referred back to the king, the sole uncontested master, who with good reason could now count on the fact that the army had become absolutely obedient and impregnated with a monarchical spirit.

Behind this transformation, there were a number of possible causes. Perhaps a comparison between the German bands and the Swedish troops during the Thirty Years War had had something to do with inducing the French government to draw its inspiration from Gustavus Adolphus. More probably, the absolutist ideas which in the middle of the seventeenth century were being implanted in the various groups within the nation, inevitably came to penetrate the army, that last refuge of insubordination and independence. But the essential cause in all likelihood was the fact that at the right moment there appeared the necessary man.

Michel Le Tellier possessed in effect the desired qualities for the carrying out of this task – patience, moderation, and at the same time, firmness. It was necessary that he not offend the point of view of the warriors who if treated too roughly would have balked. Consequently, he had to let himself be guided by circumstances in a troubled period of transition, in which the theory of absolute power although accepted in principle, was not yet the general practice. . . . Rather than imposing himself and his theories, he caused them to be accepted. But behind his amiable appearance he hid a strong, steady mind, essentially that of an organizer, and an unbreakable determination to make everything subject to the will of his sovereign. He was a conciliatory authoritarian.

In this work of organization, the most dangerous adversaries for a civilian Secretary of State were . . . the officers themselves. Out of a spirit of caste, they were determined to hold onto their privileges. . . .

Michel Le Tellier saw things in a completely different way from them. In his view, the army was to be the army of the king, while the idea of duty was to take precedence over more selfish preoccupations. He therefor intended to restrict the individual prerogatives of the military chiefs and to indicate to each in a precise manner their duties and their rights, to establish, in a word, a logical, clearly defined hierarchy. But the task was arduous, for it was necessary to break with traditions that until that time had been considered as sacred. . . .

For the nobles, in effect, the profession of arms was one of the few lucrative careers upon which they could embark without losing caste. The sole obligation which they felt they had vis-à-vis the state was to fight well. In return, they considered that they had the right to as much as they could get from it, not only in order to acquire the necessities of life but also its luxuries. They doubtless gave some thought to the interests of their soverign and even of the country, but the advancement of their own personal, immediate interests came before anything else. The usual way to speed up their promotion and to acquire a fortune was to hold several posts at the same time. All the chiefs as a consequence sought a plurality of offices. They were at one and the same time majors and captains, or they served simultaneously in different regiments. . . . Since they were willing to augment their personal fortunes by all manner of means, the nobles were determined to preserve within the army the traditional hierarchy which was until that time confused and incomplete. The plurality and venality of offices, which were a consequence of this state of affairs, were very much to their advantage. Thus, the practice became universal. What was at first thought of as a special favor by the nobles had by the middle of the seventeenth century come to be looked upon as a right. The government which paid a great deal of money to a single warrior holding several posts was not any better served by that token. However, the government had not

yet been able, despite its efforts, . . . to break this coalition of interests.

Then too, the absence of clarity and stability in the hierarchy promoted a weakening of discipline. Each man acted as he pleased, in an independent fashion. Each, from the general down to the most subaltern officer, thought of himself as master in his own little domain. This was the reason behind those leaves of absence and furloughs which were taken freely by all who needed them, despite repeated ordinances against this practice. It was the reason behind troublesome rivalries, especially those that arose when in a single army there were several men in command who had at one and the same time equal rights and unyielding pretensions. It was the reason for those conflicts between individuals and those refusals to obey, examples of which were too frequently given by the generals themselves. . . .

Finally from a special point of view, there were serious gaps in the hierarchy. While certain functions that were practically the same were occupied by a great number of officers of different ranks, . . . on the other hand there were vitally important, even essential, functions that were non-existent. The tactical units of today, the battalion, . . . the brigade, and the division were only imperfectly organized in the army at the end of the reign of Louis XIII. . . .

By the force of circumstances, Le Tellier could not have a single system of command. In the beginning he did no more than continue Richelieu's policies. Often he divided the command of an army between two, and sometimes three chiefs. This mode of operation can be very easily explained. The periods when the king was a minor were always critical. In this case, affairs were complicated by the effects of the Fronde. The royal government had to take precautions against all kinds of plots and intrigues. In particular, it had to be careful vis-à-vis the great nobles, who, once Richelieu was gone, expected to regain their special advantages and particularly the independence that they had enjoyed in former times. The Secretary of State for War appeared to be afraid of placing a single general at the head of a large army and thus making him into too important a figure. Who was to say whether this chief, elated by a few victories and able to take advantage of the weakness of the royal authority, might not try to impose his own conditions on the monarch. . . . A few years later, after the king had seen his authority firmly established and incontestably recognized by all, that is to say, after the proclamation of his majority and his coronation at Reims, there was no longer any danger of this nature to fear. It was only then that Le Tellier believed that he could, without creating any serious difficulties, bestow upon a single man the command of an army. . . . He had only adopted the policy of dual command in self defense, and it had been the frequent cause of terrible difficulties. He returned as soon as he could to the principle of unity in command, the advantages of which he had a most exact appreciation. . . .

The number of Marshals of France, already numerous during the reign of Louis XIII, increased in a regular fashion during the first part of Le Tellier's administration. There were sixteen by 1651. Why there were so many of them is explained by the date, for it was the most confused and disturbed period of the Fronde. Exploiting the awkward situation of the monarchy for their own benefit, certain military chiefs such as Daugnon had as the price of their adhesion and assistance extracted some truly princely concessions, in particular, the baton of a Marshal of France. A few received this dignity from Mazarin on condition that they not exercise it or that they not make their nomination public until they were specifically permitted to do so. . . . The government, by fostering this particular expectation, had thereby a means by which it could maintain a hold on the loyalties of those whose spirits were wavering, or even restore it in those malcontents who might be dangerous. Le Tellier, however, was not the author of this prolif-

eration in the number of marshals and the consequent depreciation in the value of the title. Rather, it was Mazarin who distributed these favors, either openly or in clandestine fashion. He did not take into consideration the military services that had been rendered, but was directed solely by political necessity. As for the Secretary of State, Le Tellier did no more than record these nominations.

There was certainly no lack of candidates, and with good reason. . . . The Marshal, in effect, commanded over all; he had no one above him but the king. In addition, there were numerous and important material advantages attached to this dignity. . . .

In spite of all this, they were never happy. Not only did they refuse to accept positions of command, when they did accept them, they could not get along with each other. They quarrelled, going as far as to draw their swords. A more serious matter was that they would not coordinate their movements or would remain in unpardonable inactivity. Interventions were constantly having to be made to reconcile them. Mazarin, the Duke of Orleans, and still others had to go and reside with the army in an effort to keep them on good terms with each other, or at least to prevent an explosion. . . .

A rule could almost be established in this regard. If there were two marshals in the same army, disunion was inevitable. If by any chance an exception occurred, people spoke of it as a miracle. . . .

Yet it was possible for a humble Secretary of State to put a stop to these disputes between the marshals . . . which were so contrary to the interests of the monarch. For a long time, Michel Le Tellier could not without great risk mount a frontal assault on the inborn pride, the pretensions, as well as the insolence of these warriors who often belonged to the highest nobility. He had to employ great discretion with them and to rely on mere palliatives, such as sending the young Louis XIV on frequent visits to the army. His presence prevented all quarrels. Then when both the foreign and domestic troubles had subsided, Le Tellier quickly brought these turbulent and undisciplined marshals to their senses. His reforms were neither numerous nor harshly imposed. Two measures sufficed. . . . Le Tellier assigned to each army a single chief, thereby concentrating the power of command instead of dispersing it. Further, he subordinated all the marshals to the most glorious of them, Turenne. In all of this there was no hint of high-handed, brutal measures such as were to be seen under Louvois. These were simply administrative acts against which no one could protest. Unity in the high command, along with the elevation of Turenne, were enough in themselves to bring about a diminution in the power of the marshals. . . .

In sum, Michel Le Tellier, continuing the work of his predecessors, completed and organized methodically the military hierarchy. It was his intention to bind together the officers of the army, or rather to subordinate them, one to another in a rational fashion, and further to suppress useless posts wherever they were to be found, and to create and fill them wherever there was the need. . . .

In the regiments the succession of ranks was constituted such as it still exists today. The colonel became the commanding officer of the unit, while the lieutenant-colonel . . . was now named by the king and served as second in command. The prerogatives of the majors were also determined. The captains and lieutenants had their respective ranking regulated in accordance with their length of service. . . .

The establishment of this hierarchy should have led, it would seem, to the suppression of venality, but nothing of the kind happened. If the posts of the general officers were no longer to be bought, venality of office persisted and indeed was rampant throughout the rest of the army. Doubtless, the monarchy recognized the disadvantages in this state of affairs and therefor promulgated on April 2, 1654 an "ordinance to prevent the sale of the posts of infantry officers." . . . Nevertheless, the

traffic continued and the government itself fostered it through the issuing of "bestowal warrants" which permitted certain persons to dispose of military posts as they saw fit.

On the other hand, precise fixing of each rank and of its prerogatives had significant and beneficial consequences. First and foremost, it put a stop to . . . the holding of a plurality of offices. . . . Le Tellier proceeded to take direct action against this abuse as soon as he had become Secretary of State. Either through peremptory ordinances or through severe letters, he never wearied of declaring that the king forbade "any officer to hold two posts." Up until about 1655, that is to say, until the moment when royal authority was only just regaining its former strength, he was content to provide a solution to each special case as it arose. Then, to the degree that his reforms were put into effect and the military hierarchy became more complete and more explicit, there was no longer any need for ordinances. Each person knew what rank he was to hold and what specific duties would thereby devolve upon him. The confusion and waste, which resulted from the persistence of the plurality of offices in the army, disappeared to make way for order and economy.

Then too, and more important, the establishment of the hierarchy resulted in a total transformation in the character of the French army. Before 1643, it had still resembled in no small way the German bands of the Thirty Years War. All the officers great or small had had a large measure of independence, disregarding the regulations and orders of the monarch, or rather of his Secretary of State for War. Such were the two principal distinguishing features of the army of that era. Imperceptibly, however, this army became accustomed to think of itself as having one sole master, the king. He, for his part, no longer wished to be merely its nominal commander, but rather its real chief. By 1666 it was he who distributed all the ranks, from the least important to the most elevated. As a consequence, it was he who accorded all favors and who was the sole and principal author of an officer's fortune. Those officers who obstinately tried to maintain the old traditions could only end by compromising their own careers. By being obedient to the king, on the other hand, by following the hierarchical path which the monarchy had created, they could be certain of their livelihood and could even hope for a brilliant future. Thus, they came to place all their expectations in the sovereign. Where they had once been irreverent and contentious, always ready to dispute the royal will, they had now been transformed into men who respectfully conformed to that same will. Thus it was, thanks to the constant and patient efforts of Le Tellier, that the authority of the sovereign and of his Secretary of State for War were no longer disregarded. The army which in 1643 consisted of a series of little republics, boisterous and undisciplined, had little by little become an army that was clearly hierarchized and submissive to a single chief, a monarchical army. . . .

5. LOUIS XIV ON THE MILITARY DUTIES OF THE FRENCH MONARCH

Louis XIV, in whose reign the French monarchy became unquestionably the paramount power on the European continent, was passionately interested in military matters. Even if he himself was not a great soldier in the sense of being a leader of men in battle, he recognized how vitally important it was for the welfare of the kingdom that the army be maintained in a constant high state of discipline and readiness, even in time of peace. Drills and parades were the aspect of military life which appealed most naturally to his orderly and authoritarian spirit, as can be seen from the following extract from the memoir he wrote for his successor, the Dauphin.

This is a maxim that the most experienced captains of this era hold to be true: that many more battles are won by well ordered ranks and by a fine appearance than by gun shot or blows from a sword. Such well ordered ranks make one appear confident, and it seems that it is sufficient merely to give the appearance of being brave, since most often our enemies will not await us long enough to let us show if we are in actual fact. . . .

Marching well and keeping ranks are skills which can only be acquired through long drill. The most valiant men in the world would fight very badly if they were not trained, and it is clear that men of the most moderate courage can become warlike by working hard at this profession. . . . Veteran troops who are permitted to vegetate in idleness will never do so well as new troops who have been well drilled. . . . That is why diligence in the drill of your troops is one of the things in which I advise you to imitate me as closely as possible. . . . In truth, you will be able to make brave through practice those who are not so by nature and to show that with care one can make good soldiers out of all sorts of men. . . .

Whoever has men in abundance will always have soldiers when he wants them, that is to say, whenever he is willing to take the trouble to train them and to encourage them to do well, so that one may

From *Mémoires de Louis XIV pour l'instruction du Dauphin*, ed. Ch. Dreyss (Paris, 1860), pp. 112–114, 119–124, 130–134, abridged. Translation by the editor.

say that a prince who has many subjects and few soldiers has only his lack of industry or his excessive laziness to blame. . . .

I . . . took the trouble to attend to the most minor questions pertaining to the infantry, which is something which my forebears never did, since they always relied on the great officers for whom these functions were an attribute of their dignity. I even took care of the quartering of the troops. I settled disputes between the different units and even between individual officers. I believed that I could never count on anything except through the assiduity of my own labors. . . .

For my part, I do not understand how princes who neglect their own affairs can imagine that those on whose good faith they rely will be more concerned about them than they themselves. . . .

I neglected none of the means which I believed appropriate for putting my troops in good order, and, not being satisfied to make this matter the most important part of my official duties, I even wished to have my usual amusements serve this end. The conversations which gave me the most pleasure were those in which I could praise officers who took good care of the units under their command, or in which I was told of all that went on in the different barracks. . . .

I thenceforth cut down on what I had been accustomed to spend each year on furniture, on precious stones, on paintings, and on other things of a similar nature, no longer finding that any expenditures were pleasurable except those which I made for armaments or for the comfort of my warriors. And instead of amusing myself as formerly in hunting or in promenades, I often used my leisure hours by having this or that body of troops drill before me, and sometimes several together. . . .

It is generally agreed that of all situations in which the uncontested authority of one man may be necessary to the public good, it is most evidently so in war. Here everyone knows that resolutions must be prompt, discipline exact, orders unquestioned, and obedience absolute, that the least instant that is lost in discussion may cause a golden opportunity to escape forever and that the slightest mistakes that one commits are often paid for in blood. . . .

Indeed what may one expect but tumult and confusion in a body where those who must obey cannot be sure who has the right to give them commands, where those who aspire to authority think more of settling their own private disputes than of looking out for the welfare and the security of the troops that have been entrusted to them.

There is nothing which arouses men's feelings so much as envy of superior rank or position. The pretensions of the chiefs naturally commit the feelings of the men who are under their command and each soldier thus comes to believe that it is a matter vitally affecting his own particular interests. All are aroused by emulation and in a single camp there are soon two enemy armies drawn up, both of which, forgetting in an instant the duties they owe their prince, and the security of their country, no longer think of anything except to satisfy, even at the cost of their own blood, the brutal passion which has seized them. These calamities may only be avoided for sure if one does as I did, settling all such disputes so that whatever troops might henceforth be brought together, there was no longer any question about the rank or the authority of the one who commanded them. . . .

There was nothing new in such disputes over rank and precedence, but those who had governed before me seeing them everywhere asserted with such excessive fervor, had not dared to try to settle them, possibly because they doubted if their decisions would be carried out by the parties in question, or if the benefits that would be achieved for the public would not be offset by the hatred of the individuals affected.

In this case, I was certain enough of the respect of my subjects not to be stayed by such considerations, but I must admit that the resolution that I had taken to make this settlement did cause me to suffer in that, cherishing equally all of my troops, I foresaw that I could not reduce the ranking of any of them without bringing upon myself a portion of the chagrin that they would feel. However, I did not believe that such sentiments should move me in what was a matter of the highest importance.

It is evident that a taste for plunder has up until now been one of the principal attractions that has caused many to choose the soldier's trade and that in the present time debauchery and plunder have on occasion taken the place of pay for very many of the troops. A wise prince may tolerate it, although for the apparent good that it seems to accomplish, it causes an infinite number of great evils. All writers on political subjects are agreed that if there is one area where severity is absolutely necessary for a sovereign, it is with regard to his soldiers. The oppression that people suffer from them is so evident that there is no need to embark on a long discourse to convince you of it, or to show how the sovereign suffers indirect losses from it through a reduction in his revenues. . . . Being by honor bound to secure their states from the violence of foreigners, they should be even more eager to protect them from pillage by their own troops. And you must not delude yourself, in weighing the interests of the peasant and the soldier, as many others do, that those men who have enlisted in your troops should mean that much more to you than the rest of your subjects, or that it is to your interests to favor them more than the others.

All that is to be found within the borders of our kingdom of whatever nature it may be has been equally committed to our care and should be equally dear to us. One must not think that . . . the troops who serve in our name are more dependent on us than other people and that those who bear arms are under a greater obligation to serve us than all other men who live under our dominion. All men owe us the same respect and we owe to all the same justice. We are never bound to take the side of one against the other; rather, we must always be disinterested judges and the common fathers of all.

Each profession contributes according to its ability to the support and the grandeur of the monarchy. Farm laborers are perhaps more necessary than soldiers since without them the soldiers could not live. . . . None of these professions should be held in contempt. All have their place and if most of them seem to be less dangerous, they are not for that reason useful or less difficult. If a prince, moved by the realization of the constant dangers to which his soldiers are exposed or by the admiration that any noble spirit has for men who follow this trade, should want to favor them in some way, it should be by taking pains to establish their fortune and not in letting their morals be corrupted.

Ferdinand Schevill

6. THE GREAT ELECTOR AND THE FOUNDING OF THE PRUSSIAN ARMY

In the Thirty Years' War, the various territories of the Elector of Brandenburg which lay scattered and defenseless across Northern Germany were ravaged on numerous occasions by invading armies. To avert the reoccurrence of such a catastrophe, Frederick William, who succeeded to his inheritance in 1640 at the age of twenty and who was to be known to posterity as the "Great Elector," resolved to build a permanent standing army. In undertaking this revolutionary innovation, he quickly found himself at odds with the essentially feudal institutions through which his lands were governed. Undaunted, he set about breaking these institutions to his will and abolishing those which would not give way. In so doing, he laid the foundations of what over the following century was to become a modern bureaucratic state. The manner in which Frederick William set about this great work is described by Professor Ferdinand Schevill in the following selection from his book *The Great Elector*.

Because he [Frederick William] began his rule as the impotent victim of a war that had been raging through the German lands ever since two years before his birth, . . . he was obliged to inaugurate his government by concentrating all but exclusively on the bare issue of self-preservation. When, eight years after his accession, the Treaty of Westphalia brought peace to Germany, he was indeed relieved of the immediate pressure of war by this happy event but found himself in a hardly less perilous situation than before. Immediately to the north, in the lost western section of Pomerania, towered the solidly founded might of Sweden, casting its long shadow southward all the way to his very seat and capital. To his east spread the vast, chaotic mass of Poland, perpetually giving off ominous, deep-toned rumbles like a volcano on the point of eruption. To his west lay his Westphalian territory of Cleve-Mark, of which, in spite of unremitting efforts, he had up to the peace settlement been unable to obtain clear and unchallenged possession. And chiefly to his south, but clockwise all around him, stirred futilely but feverishly the innumerable Lilliputian states into which the Holy Roman Empire had been broken as by a shattering interior explosion.

Confronted by these uncertainties threatening from every side, the young prince, apart from a momentary indecision on first assuming office, had proceeded on a plan which he never afterward abandoned. He provided himself with an army, at first a very small army, since that was all that the exhausted mark could support. This force he then proceeded, in measure as his several territories regained their strength, to swell to a larger figure. His centrally motivating thought was that, in view of the permanent perils by which he was encircled, he would see to it that his army, too, his necessary sword and buckler,

Reprinted from *The Great Elector*, by Ferdinand Schevill, pp. 186–196, 219–220, 237–238, abridged, by permission of the University of Chicago Press. Copyright 1947 by The University of Chicago. All rights reserved.

should be permanent, that is, that it should be not a temporary or emergency army dependent on the capricious favor of his diets but a standing army dependent solely on himself.

To make his plan effective, it would have to be supported by taxes, and taxes could not be had constitutionally except with the consent of the Landtag which in each of his provinces shared the rule with him. Whenever they were approached on this head, these bodies, without exception, manifested a stubborn disinclination to vote the desired supplies, in part no doubt because they were unwilling to load themselves with the proposed new burdens, but overwhelmingly because of their distaste for the very institution the tax money was intended to create and which in the discussions that raged unchecked in these assemblies was held up to infamy in the shape of that bogeyman of seventeenth-century parliaments throughout Europe, the *miles perpetuus*. The result was a hotly contested and long-drawn-out constitutional struggle between the prince and his various diets. . . .

In the later Middle Ages there had everywhere in Europe come into existence a representative political body which constituted a variously effective check on the authority of the ruler. It was called parliament in England, estates-general in France, Reichstag in Germany, and Landtag or Landstände (estates) in the all but independent principalities into which Germany had gradually dissolved. When, in 1640, Frederick William succeeded his father, he came into possession of three of these principalities . . . : the electorate and mark of Brandenburg, the duchy of Prussia, and the duchy of Cleve-Mark. In each of them . . . existed a Landtag endowed with a varying body of rights but embracing in each instance control of taxation as the undisputed minimum of its extensive prerogative. . . .

When on reaching the Westphalian milestone the elector made no move to reduce the army, the Brandenburg Landtag grew more and more vigorous in its re-

monstrances against his headstrong conduct. In a last effort to solve the crisis amicably Frederick William in 1652 summoned an extraordinary, that is, a full, Landtag to Berlin. A full Landtag had been but rarely called in Brandenburg history, in all probability because it was too large and unwieldy a body for the orderly transaction of business. In a Landtag of this kind every knight had the right to attend in person and might cause the assembly to swell to a multitude of fifteen hundred heads. The usual Landtag, officially called a *Deputationstag*, was a representative body made up of two knights from each of the fifteen districts (*Kreise*), into which the electorate was for administrative purposes divided, and of one or two delegates from each of the towns. It would seem that the elector was moved to call together the unusual or full Landtag by the hope that the whole body of knights would show a better understanding of his military necessities than their chosen delegates.

What therefore, when the Landtag met, he was encouraged to demand was the startling innovation of a perpetual tax sufficient to support an army, small indeed but as perpetual as the tax for its support. True, it was not quite a perpetual tax which he requested, since he knew that the word alone would suffice to set the jaws of the estates like flint against him. His actual proposal was for a contribution of five hundred thousand talers distributed over the next six years. As ever since 1643 he had been collecting one hundred and fifty thousand talers per annum, he was in fact making a not inconsiderable concession to the estates on the material side, and he counted heavily on its effect. But against the easement in money stood the stretch of years, and not even the dullest cabbage-patch Junker failed to seize the implication: An army sanctioned for six years would be an army sanctioned for eternity! At the very least it would signify the surrender by the Landstände of their most cherished right, their dearly treasured "liberty," coupled with the triumph of that abomination of an encroaching absolutism, the perpetual soldier.

Since the full Landtag turned out to be as opposed to Frederick William's army plans as the usual representative Landtag had been, he made no headway with it. It was presently prorogued by him in the forlorn hope that reflection would make the members more amenable to his proposal. In the course of the next fifteen months he prorogued it seven times and then, persuaded that he would, after all, fare better with a restricted Landtag, in the summer of 1653 returned to the smaller and more business-like Deputationstag. From this he succeeded in wringing the substance of what he was after. The representatives at last submitted to the masterful prince, in part because he had worn them down by his stubborn dilatory tactics, but overwhelmingly because the knights, the dominant element of the assembly, gained the conviction that they could secure highly important class concessions in exchange for their vote. On August, 5, 1653, the elector, in return for the inexorably demanded subsidy, gave his assent to an ordinance (more properly a sweeping constitutional enactment) which, although not containing anything startlingly new, so fortified the existing politicosocial structure of the mark that it endured substantially unchanged until its convulsive overthrow by Napoleon one hundred and fifty years later. Let us have a closer look at this ordinance officially called the *Landtagsabschied* of 1653.

Every European state with a parliament inherited from the Middle Ages was a hierarchized society of the privileged few and the unprivileged many. While in Brandenburg the ruling classes were, in a strictly constitutional sense, the knights and the burghers, owing to the settled stagnation and resulting poverty of the towns, there was in reality only one ruling class, the knights. It was this fact that the enactment of 1653 heavily underscored, for its main significance may be declared to lie in its setting the knights apart as a distinct and dominant caste. And let it be said in respect to the knights, as already said in respect to the general constitution of the electorate, that the Abschied did not so much introduce novelties as that it gave a more precise formulation to privileges already in possession of the knights and repeatedly confirmed to them by Frederick William's predecessors.

To substantiate this statement it will suffice to refer to the developments recounted in connection with the financial difficulties of Joachim II. By this elector's time, which was also the time of the Reformation, the knights had changed their character and been transformed from medieval warriors into profit-seeking agricultural producers. To employ the expressive German terms indicative of this transformation, they had given up being medieval *Grundherrn*, content to live frugally on ground rents, and become *Gutsherrn*, that is, agricultural entrepreneurs less interested in ground rents than in large-scale production on a capitalist basis. In measure as this transformation proceeded they had been prompted to increase their own land, the demesne, by appropriating the land of the peasants, and to provide themselves with the necessary labor force by increasing the obligatory workdays owed them by the peasants and by making this service permanently available by attaching the peasants to the soil. By these encroachments the formerly free peasants had been reduced to a grinding serfdom and what, under pressure from the knights, Joachim, supposed fountain of justice, had done was to forgive them their heaped illegalities by stamping these illegalities with the seal of the law.

In the circumstances one questions why it was that, a century after the decisive concessions they had wrung from Joachim II, the knights should have felt moved to secure their renewal from Frederick William. The answer is not only that renewal is in the nature of insurance but also that it may be utilized for the introduction of additions and clarifications. Conceding such alterations to be present in the Abschied of 1653, we may nonetheless assert that the privileges secured to the knights by Joachim II were not in any substantial way enlarged by it. The document made clearer than before that peasants who had lost their freedom could never again regain it; that in addition to service in the field they owed domestic service as well; and that they were amenable to the lord in his capacity of judge (*Gerichtsherr*), for he presided over the manorial court. While the peasants retained the right to appeal from the court of the Gerichtsherr to that of the elector, the right was nullified in practice by the power of the Gerichtsherr to punish with imprisonment a peasant guilty of preferring a baseless complaint (*mutwillige klage*), the baselessness being left to the judgment of the Gerichtsherr. A final matter worthy of attention was the acceptance by the Abschied of the pretention of the knights to the status of a privileged hereditary nobility, for the document declared that not only were *Lehngüter*, that is, knights' fiefs, immune from every form of taxation but also that they might not pass by sale or testament into other than noble hands. Lands designated as "noble" in 1653 must remain noble and could not come into the possession of commoners.

In the light of this legislation the knights figured as the feudal subjects of the elector, but the peasant serfs, all but completely cut off from contact with the head of the state, figured as the subjects of their lords and were juridically, economically, and financially at their mercy.

That Frederick William had pretty much broken the back of the diet with the settlement of 1653 was made evident with little delay. Two years later the Swedes undertook the drive into Poland which at once threw the whole Baltic area into turmoil. The elector's unhesitating response to the danger in which he found himself was to recruit an army large enough to enable him to become a factor in the situation of sufficient importance not to be contemptuously ignored by the two combatants. By the year 1656 his army had swollen to almost twenty thousand men maintained by supplies wrung from his several dominions by whatever measures served his purpose. Inevitably, on these capricious terms the largest part of the army as well as of the money required for its support had to come from Brandenburg, and as the subsidy granted by the Landtag in 1653 served to satisfy no more than a fraction of the costs incurred, the elector possessed himself of the revenue needed to meet the remaining expenses by the use of force. . . .

Held fast in the east by the exigencies of the constantly expanding war, he sent orders to his agents in Brandenburg to collect forty and fifty thousand talers a month over and above the contribution to which he was legally entitled. These backbreaking burdens laid on the impoverished inhabitants so soon after the Thirty Years' War were an all but unbearable load, but the elector, while regretting their necessity, saw no escape from their infliction save by sacrificing the advantages he had gained through joining the struggle. And that sacrifice he was unwilling to make.

Before the Baltic war came to an end in 1660 by the Treaty of Oliva the elector must by the rude method of military execution have sluiced some millions of Brandenburg talers into his military coffers; and against this lawlessness the diet never ceased to protest. But that was as far as it got. Not until peace had been rung in and Frederick William had returned to Berlin with an enormously increased reputation did he, simultaneously with the reduction of the army to a skeleton formation, terminate his financial irregularities. His independent conduct of the war through five eventful campaigns left no doubt that he had ceased being a constitutional, and was by now quite visibly on the way to becoming an absolute, ruler. The statement should not be understood to mean that with this increase of the sovereign's prestige the Landtag abdicated its authority and disappeared from the scene. More than once, . . . it played a not unimportant part in Brandenburg developments. Undeniably, however, the relations between Landtag and elector had come to a turning. In control of a standing army, he had become the master and could give his attention not only to forging that army into a steadily improved instrument but also to the closely related task of a comprehensive reorganization of the state. . . .

. . . When the ruler of Brandenburg determined not to be overlooked in the settlement of the Thirty Years' War, he imparted by this decision an overshadowing importance to the problem of the army. The army thereupon became the first link in a long chain of causation. It led to taxes, and these in their turn to the necessity of bending the diets to his tax proposals. Army, taxes, diets, were the closely interlocked elements of the domestic revolution we have just passed in review.

This revolution in its further unfolding gave birth to a whole complex of fresh problems. It was like the rebuilding of an ancient house. Whoever undertakes to make over a wing or section will presently discover that he must make over the interrelated parts of the total structure. Applied to Frederick William's reshuffling of his inheritance, this meant that the revolution he started when he undertook to provide himself with an army imposed a reconstruction of all the services of the state which would, in general terms, take some such course as follows: With a permanent army in hand he would be occupied for the remainder of his days with shaping it into an increasingly effective instrument; the army thus strengthened would call for an ampler flow of revenue; and an ampler revenue return would require a greatly intensified economy together with the setting-up of the appropriate administrative controls. With one reform leading in this way to another the whole public life would experience a gradual and, in the long run, sweeping reconstruction. . . .

A later development in both the administrative and military reorganization treated in the foregoing pages must at least be briefly noted at this point because, as the feature which more than any other charac-

terized the Brandenburg-Prussian state in the period after Frederick William, it has become associated in every reader's thought with the aspect assumed by this state in the eighteenth, nineteenth, and twentieth centuries down to its total breakdown under the impact of World Wars I and II. This outstanding development has to do with the taking over by the Junkers of the elector's two centralizing and unifying departments, the army and the civil service. Doubtless the country squires began to enter them immediately on their creation, but since the two services did not, as we have been at pains to show, achieve their full development during the reign of their founder, the story of their appropriation by the Junkers belongs to a later period and is glanced at here merely to satisfy a legitimate curiosity arising from their later history.

The fact clamoring to be noticed is that it did not take the Junkers long to become aware that new avenues of employment and power had been opened to them by the creation of a standing army and a widened public service. Consequently they, or at least their younger sons, began to offer themselves at Berlin as candidates for the new posts. At first no more than a trickle, by the eighteenth century a steady stream of ambitious youth poured from the landed estates, on the one hand, into the openings created by the expanding central administration and, on the other hand, into the officer positions made available by the gradual transformation of the original mercenary into a standing national army. We have . . . made acquaintance with the Junkers as the passionate opponents of these two monarchical innovations; but, faced by them as the irreducible minimum demand of their indomitable chief, they began to examine them in a more sober spirit and discovered that they offered originally unsuspected opportunities of a profitable livelihood and a heightened social status. In short, the Junkers stayed to worship where they had formerly cursed and by this opportune conversion regained the political ascendancy that they had apparently lost when the elector struck the formidable weapon of the diet from their hands.

We have repeatedly referred to Frederick William's novelties of a unified army and a unified administration as the companion pillars of his new state. But when, in consequence of an attraction that neither he nor anyone else could have foreseen, the originally hostile Junkers adopted these pillars as their own, they became, as it were, their living counterparts and thereby the chief sustainers of the monarchy in process of formation. Thus absorbed into the leading institutions of the new state, they experienced a revival of their traditional devotion to the head of these institutions. It was the consequent intimate co-operation between the sovereign and his feudal dependents, the Junkers, that accounted for much of the vigor shown by the Hohenzollern monarchy in the era after Frederick William; but it is no less true (and the truth became increasingly manifest with each succeeding generation) that the close union, feudal in its origin and spirit, constituted a towering, and, ultimately perilous anachronism in a world rolling on to a bourgeois and industrial expression of its energies that neither would nor could be stopped.

7. THE POLITICAL TESTAMENT OF FREDERICK WILLIAM I

More than any other dynastic monarchy of the seventeenth and eighteenth centuries, Prussia provides an almost perfect example of a state created in response to the requirements of a standing army. This achievement was primarily the work of three extraordinary representatives of the Hohenzollern dynasty: Frederick William, Elector of Brandenburg (1640–1688), Frederick William I, King of Prussia (1713–1740), and the most famous of the line, Frederick the Great, (1740–1786). Of the three, the one who contributed the most to building the Prussian army and in the process to creating a modern Sparta on the sandy plains of Northern Germany, was Frederick William I. Few monarchs have ever so indelibly stamped the whole fabric of state and society with their own peculiar outlook as did this dour, hard working Calvinist. In the following selection from his *Political Testament of 1722* are set forth his stern and simple ideas concerning the preeminent place of the army in the state and the manner in which his realm should be governed. As is to be seen in this document, Frederick William was fanatical in his attention to detail. This was typical of the almost military control exercised by the state over the lives of every one of its citizens, including the nobility, in the interests of the army.

I have set down . . . instructions concerning how my successor to the Crown of Prussia might be guided after my death and wherein he may find information about the whole state of the army and of the land.

Since I gather that my health is getting worse all the time and that I will not have long to remain in life, I have set down these instructions so that my dear successor can be guided accordingly. I stand well with the all highest and have since my twentieth year placed my whole trust firm-

From the *Acta Borussica: Denkmäler der Preussischen Staatsverwaltung im 18. Jahrhundert,* Vol. III (Berlin, 1901) pp. 441–467, abridged. Translation by the editor.

ly in God, upon whom I have always called for a gracious hearing and who has always granted my prayers, and I am assured through the grace of Jesus Christ that I will be blessed on account of his bitter agony and death. All the base and inward sins that I have committed are a pain to my heart and I ask God that I be forgiven them for Jesus Christ's sake. . . .

In order to draw up the new overall statements for war and finance, my successor should demand from the general accounting office the special provincial statements, both military and civil. You must go through these yourself and be economical where the expenditure concerned is more than 100,000 thalers. You will find many useless pensions and civil servants, a part of whom you may sack completely, leaving some. . . . With the other budgets you must start with the ministers. For example, take one who gets fifty thalers per month and cut him to thirty or thirty-five. One who gets 200 per year may be cut to between 120 and 150 in the new budgets and everything else proportionately. Through this you will benefit greatly with regard to expenditures. Next after this: all those whom you take on as civil servants in Berlin and in the provinces must depend directly on your good favor and not on your ministers or favorites. To erase things from the budget and to set salaries must be your job alone, and you must give no one else the task of arranging this, so that the whole world may know that it all comes from you and from no one else. When a year is over and you find that some of your ministers and lower ranking civil servants have carried out their tasks for you with true devotion and have distinguished themselves, so at the end of the year you must add to the salary of a few people of this kind, in order that people will have a sense of personal obligation to you. Thus you will make true servants, who are obliged to you alone and not to your ministers. But you must always work as I always have. For a prince who wishes to rule with honor in this world must manage all his affairs himself, since

princes are selected in order to work and not to lead an empty, lazy woman's life, and since my successor has all in order, it will go as easily as does a sheet of music. . . .

You yourself must manage your finances and by yourself, and you alone must hold command over the army. In that way, through the command of the army, you will have authority . . . and will be admired and respected by the whole world as a wise and capable prince. So help you the almighty God,

Amen.

I request most urgently that my dear successor deprive the senior regimental officers, subordinate officers, and the common soldiers of none of their salary . . . and that he leave the provisioning of the army as he will find it after my death. . . . [*With regard to the creation of five new regiments.*]

Your ministers will say that your budget is insufficient for the maintenance of so large an army. Calculate what the increases will cost you per year and then you will see that there will be no lack of money and other requisites. You will see that for a king in Prussia who manages everything himself and does not let his ministers lead him by the nose it is a very feasible action. The ministers will say that there are no quarters for the five new regiments. In that case, you can command that the new regiments obtain quarters in the following way, by stating that anyone who argues to the contrary is your enemy, while anyone who seconds and facilitates the task will be considered by you as your friend. Then you will see that they will all agree. . . .

What will the world say, my dear successor, about the increase in the size of the army as you succeed to the throne? That you are a formidable power vis-à-vis your enemies of which our house has many. Your friends will consider you a wise prince. God help you in that direction. I wish it from the heart. Amen. . . .

Concerning the nobility, formerly it

had great privileges, which the Elector Frederick William destroyed by means of his sovereign power. I brought them completely into a state of obedience. . . . In Prussia there is a great nobility. The counts form a group of the utmost importance. Looking on it as a political matter, my successor must try to work towards this goal: that the counts and other noblemen from all his provinces and especially from Prussia be employed in the army and that their children be taken on as cadets. It is of great value for the civil service and for the army and will be conducive to peace in his lands. My successor must also permit very few of them to travel in foreign lands, for they must first spend time in your service. Provided that they really are in your service and you are not at war, then you may allow some of them to travel in foreign lands. It will be a great advantage for you to have the whole nobility reared in your service from youth onwards and knowing no other lord but God and the King of Prussia. If, however, my successor does not do this and takes lots of foreigners into service as high ranking officers, he will find that he will not be served so well by the foreign officers, while at the same time his vassals are in service outside of the country. For those who serve outside of their country are always assured that they can constantly refuse to respect their lord. . . . If you have reliable officers who come from the families of your land, you may be sure that it is a sound army, steadfastly and capably led and that no potentate has one that is any better. You must deal with the nobility from the provinces in an obliging and gracious manner, separating the good from the bad, and distinguishing the faithful ones. Then will you deserve their love and their fear. . . .

It is a good idea to have a vault containing a considerable sum of money, since it is necessary for a prince to have ready money. For although God protects against the plague of war, it takes money when whole provinces fall casualty to the horrors of war. If you have a well lined treasury, you will be able to sustain this misfortune. There-

fore, every year you must add at least 500,000 thalers to the same vault. A formidable army and a treasury to mobilize the army in time of need can earn you great respect in the world and you can hold your own along with the other powers. . . .

The interests of your house are extensive to describe, and you can inform yourself thoroughly about them from the archives and about how I handled state affairs, since in this matter it always went well with me. . . .

Your task, my dear successor, is to protect what your forebears began and to hold onto the lands thus created and the succession that belongs to our house by right of law and through God. Pray to God and begin no unrighteous wars, but do not let go of that to which you have a right. For God will bless you in righteous matters, but will desert you in unrighteous ones, you may be sure of that. Therefore my dear successor I ask you for God's sake to preserve the army, to strengthen it more and more, to make it more formidable, and not to divide it, as my father Frederick, King in Prussia did in the last French war, but always to keep its separate components together. Then you will see how you will be sought after by all the powers of the world and will be able to hold the balance, since it depends on you. For whoever holds the balance of power in the world is always able to profit thereby for his lands and is respectable in the eyes of his friends and formidable to his enemies.

My successor must not ever divide his beautiful army or give troops for money or subsidies to England or Holland, but must reply to the powers as I have done: If you want troops, then I will march myself with my whole army, but not for a subsidy. Give me lands and peoples, for I will not march until you do. "No lands, no Prussians," is the best motto for the well-being and glory of you and your country. If they need you, they must give you what you want. If they do not need you, sit still with your army and wait for a good occasion, for your affairs are in good shape. Why should you sacrifice yourself and your army for a trifle for the sake of the miserable English, the Dutch, or the Emperor? That would be the greatest foolishness in the world, but you have too much sense to take such a step. The contingent that you owe to the Imperial army consists of 14,000 men and you must give these, but not from your own army. Rather, you must recruit foreign troops by means of subsidies from the various small German princes such as Gotha, Darmstadt, Bayreuth, Ansbach, and Eisenach. Ten squadrons and ten battalions should represent the 14,000. You must send one of your generals along as the commander. Your ministers will make every effort to divide your army, but take my advice, for it is sound and I have all this from my own experience. Why should you sacrifice your army? You will always be at war, and when your land is depopulated, then it becomes difficult to go to war again. The well-being of a prince is to have a well populated land. When your army is marching beyond your borders, the excises will not yield a third so much as when the army is at home. The price of things will fall so that the officials will not be able to pay their rents correctly and there will be total ruin. . . .

My very dear successor will wonder and ask: "Why did not my blessed father do everything as it is written here?" The reason is this. When in 1713 my blessed father died, I found that the land of Prussia had been almost depopulated by plagues that affected men and animals. All or most of the royal domains throughout the land were mortgaged. . . . I have redeemed them all. All the finances were in such poor condition as to be near bankruptcy, while the army was in so bad a state and with so small a number of men that I cannot really describe all the things that were wrong. It is surely a masterpiece that in the nine years prior to 1722 I was able to so order and arrange these affairs that there are now no debts on your domains, while your army and your artillery are in such a condition as to be on the same level as any in Europe. I assure you that I had little help from my servants, but indeed was directly and indirectly hindered by them. So I was able to do nothing more in the past nine years. But everything that is here in these instructions, my dear successor, can come to pass after my death. . . .

May God almighty help you thus through Jesus Christ. Amen.

Your faithful father unto death,

F. William

Potsdam, on February 17, 1722

Leopold Von Ranke

8. THE ARMY UNDER FREDERICK WILLIAM I

Frederick William I made the Prussian army the best trained military force in the Europe of his day. This achievement is described by possibly the greatest of German historians, Leopold von Ranke, in the following passage taken from the first volume of his *Memoirs of the House of Brandenburg*.

A union of German provinces, which altogether did not number more than two millions and a half of inhabitants, and had not even any bond of connexion among themselves, seemed, when compared with the kingdom of France, extending from the Pyrenees to the Upper Rhine, and from the Mediterranean to the Ocean, or with the neighbouring boundless empire of Russia, with the inexhaustible Austria, or with England, mistress of the seas, a very insignificant state. The only thing which gave to Prussia a certain rank among the powers of Europe, and a certain consideration in the world, was, her military force. It was reckoned that France had at that time 160,000, and Russia 130,000 regular troops; but a great part of the former were employed in the garrisons of the numerous fortresses, while in the latter the men actually under arms were very far from corresponding with the army lists. The Austrian army was computed at 80,000 to 100,000 men; but of doubtful efficiency, and dispersed through the various provinces. What Frederick William I did for Prussia in this rivalry of forces may be instantly measured, when we recollect that he increased the army from 38,000 men, — which placed her on a military level with Sardinia or Saxon-Poland, to more than 80,000, *i.e.* nearly equal to that of Austria. We possess the accurate calculation of a minister of war at the beginning of the following reign, from which it appears that Frederick William found at his accession an army of 38,459 men; which, in the very first year of his reign, he raised to 44,792. In the year 1719 the army consisted of 53,999; in the year 1729, of 69,892; and in the year 1739 of 82,352, or, including the staff, 83,486. The King's care was equally bestowed on the several arms; he increased the cavalry by more than a half, and the artillery in still greater proportion. He suffered no discrepancies between the lists and the actual corps; and the fortresses occupied but a proportionally small number of men; taking the very lowest calculation, he had 72,000 men ready at a moment's warning, or with the smallest possible delay, to take the field.

It is evident from the relative numbers, that it was impossible to raise a standing army of this strength from the populations of Brandenburg and Prussia, except by withdrawing the necessary hands from every other kind of labour. Extraordinary efforts were required to bring together the half of that number of native subjects. For a time, the King wavered between compulsory and voluntary service, between enlistment and impressment: the arbitrary power of the officers, the rivalry and mutual aggressions of the regiments, occasioned numberless disorders and complaints. To prevent these evils, Frederick William

From Leopold von Ranke, *Memoirs of the House of Brandenburg and History of Prussia during the Seventeenth and Eighteenth Centuries*, Vol. I, translated by Sir Alexander and Lady Duff Gordon (London, 1849), pp. 420–427, abridged.

gave a systematic organization to an old usage, assigning to each regiment a particular circle, out of which it should regularly keep up its numbers. All the homesteads of the country were distributed in cantons, according to their numbers, among the several regiments and companies, which were to be forcibly recruited from those members of the families who did not enjoy some peculiar exemption, or were absolutely indispensable for trade or agriculture. Neither householders nor their eldest sons or next heirs were taken; councillors of the provincial colleges were present at the levy, in order to prevent any infringement of the legal exemptions. The greater part of the additional troops thus raised, and immediately placed under the commandants, consisted of the younger sons of peasants. In the geographical descriptions of Brandenburg, it is specially remarked how healthy, robust, and laborious the people of that country are; how well they bear changes of temperature, and what excellent soldiers they become. Cato's saying—that a peasantry furnishes the bravest troops, was verified here. . . .

It were beyond our bounds to attempt to go into the details of this [the Prussian] discipline, or to describe how Prince Leopold of Anhalt laid down the first principles of it on the little meadow at Halle, and the King himself perfected the system at his own Spartan Potsdam. . . . The main thing was a regular step and rapid firing; or as the King once expressed it, "Load quickly, advance in close column, present well; take aim well;—all in profound silence." The Spanish armies had been wont to advance in deep columns, whereas the Prussian troops now presented a wide front, less exposed to the fire of artillery, and more efficient from the force of its musketry. The bayonet attached to the musket was in effect a combination of pike and firelock. The iron ramrod was a great improvement—it accomplished at one stroke what had always required several; one reason for preferring large men was that they were better fitted by nature for these manoeuvres. The

whole infantry of the Prussian army could march in four lines, of which the first and the last were composed of the tallest and strongest, and the two central of somewhat smaller, but yet full-sized men. Their flags bore an eagle gazing at the sun. Their whole aspect was martial and formidable. "Friend and foe," says Prince Leopold in one of his letters, "admire your Majesty's infantry—your friends regard it as one of the wonders of the world; your foes admire with trembling."

The leaders of these bands, whose daily business it was to go through the exercise and to drill the new recruits, were for the most part country nobles. In a census taken of the Pomeranian nobility in 1724, it is remarked that, with few exceptions, it consisted of officers of the army on service, or who had served.

One of the main objects of Frederick William was to form a thoroughly energetic and efficient corps of officers.

Great complaints were made at that time, in the Austrian service, that the post of officer was not only acquired by purchase, but that it could be sold again; it was not regarded as an honour, but as a kind of alienable property; and even where this was not the case, the deserving veteran was thrown into the background by the inexperienced young man of rank.

In the Prussian army too the universal practice still prevailed that the subordinate appointments should be made by the superior officers; ensigns were promoted to be lieutenants, and these to be captains, at their pleasure; the nomination of staff-officers alone was reserved to the King; but even these were proposed by the officers.

Frederick William now took all the nominations into his own hands; not only because he chose to be master everywhere, but because he deemed it important not to leave the appointments to the first step, on which all the succeeding ones depended, to chance, or to the influence of personal considerations; but to bestow them according to his own judgment.

The young nobles who entered the regiments as volunteer corporals formed the nursery of his army; they were trained to the greatest care both in essential and in trifling things, and subjected to the severest admonitions, nay, even punishments for the slightest neglect. Whenever the King inspected a regiment, he made minute inquiries as to their qualities and conduct, and caused them to be presented to him; and this course of discipline went on till the happy day when the young man was admitted as ensign, and received the badge which he was to guard inviolate, and which communicated somewhat of its own inviolability to his own person.

The King appointed only those who knew the exercise well, were guilty of no excesses, managed their own affairs with prudence, and had a good personal appearance. Their subsequent promotion was determined by the same motives. Lists of conduct were kept, which showed year by year how each had behaved with reference to duties of religion, to his private life, and to the service; and what degree of intelligence he possessed. The merits of the commanding officers were attested by the state of their regiments at the yearly inspection by the King in person.

It may be thought ludicrous, that every detail of the uniform, down to the most minute, was the subject of an inflexible rule; for example, the width of the ruffles and the stock, the number of buttons on the half-boots, the length of the ends of ribbon hanging from the pigtail. But the motive for this was something more than the uniformity which it is desirable for a regiment to present to the eye; it signified, that in the army all differences were to be obliterated except those dependent on rank in the service. There was little familiar intercourse except between men of the same rank, and any perceptible inequality between rich and poor would have been intolerable. Frederick William would not suffer any one to appear in civil dress when off duty; from the year 1725 he himself never wore anything but the uniform.

His reverence for the garb of a soldier is well known. Nothing displeased him so much at Dresden and Hanover as the practice of measuring rank by station at court: a general or colonel was little thought of if he had not also a place about the court; an equerry of the royal hunt was a more important man than a brigadier. He, on the contrary, rated the military service above everything. He excited in the officers a feeling for their profession — emanating from himself — which made them regard valour and efficiency in the service as the highest excellence of man, subordination as a law of nature, and duty as an honour.

Robert Ergang

9. THE GROWTH OF THE PRUSSIAN BUREAUCRACY

Relative to the population of the country, the army of Frederick William I was by far the largest in Europe. To raise the funds necessary for its maintenance from his backward and impoverished realm was a remarkable accomplishment, requiring the most careful management of the available resources. This was done through the highly efficient and honest Prussian bureaucracy. The functioning of this bureaucracy and its effect on the life of the country are described in the following passage by Robert Ergang taken from his book *The Potsdam Fuehrer*.

Soon after he became king Frederick William took up the task of reorganizing the administration of his territories. Basically the task was one of joining the scattered provinces in a closely-knit administrative system centering in the king. The immediate object of this reorganization was to insure to the crown a maximum income so that it could meet the increasing financial needs of the army. According to a German historian: "All the endeavors of the king with regard to administration and political economy had the ultimate purpose of procuring the necessary means for the support and augmentation of the army." At Frederick William's accession the administration of the Hohenzollern territories was still organized largely on a provincial basis, each province having its own laws and institutions. This aggregation of provinces was a unit only for purposes of a war and foreign policy. Nor was there any desire on the part of the inhabitants or the Estates to fuse the provincial organizations into one unified administration. Much of the administration was still in the hands of the old feudal and territorial officials, who sought in every way known to them to perpetuate

the particularism they represented. The Great Elector had taken an important step toward the creation of a unified central administration by putting the management of the military revenues under the direction of a minister of war in Berlin. But this was only a beginning. Frederick William I was to do the major part of the work of centralizing the administration, and his successors were to complete the task. . . .

This reorganization completely delocalized the entire administration. Whereas the Great Elector had been forced to promise that he would appoint as officials of a province only those who were native to that province, Frederick William ordered the chambers "not to recommend people who were born in the provinces in which there is a vacant office to be filled." In this way he succeeded in breaking the power of local families and family cliques. At the death of Frederick William, it has been said, the Prussian administration functioned like the works of a clock, with the king himself as the main spring. But the simile must not be taken too literally. Frederick William had indeed established a certain administrative unity, yet the unifica-

From Robert Ergang, *The Potsdam Fuehrer* (New York, 1941) pp. 103–104, 107–111, 119–123, abridged. Reprinted by permission of Columbia University Press.

tion was not complete. There were still many cogs missing, and others were slipping.

In an autocracy such as Frederick William had established it was but natural that the appointment of all important civil officials should be in the hands of the sovereign. The Great Elector had, by and large, gained the right to appoint most of the higher officials in his various provinces. But his choice, as already stated, had still been somewhat restricted in that he was required in Prussia, for example, to appoint only local noblemen of the Lutheran persuasion to the higher offices. During the reign of Frederick I the right of appointing subordinate officials was largely assumed by the leading ministers. Frederick William, however, claimed the sole right of appointment. "No one," he stated soon after his accession, "shall be appointed to any office unless I do it myself." This right he asserted throughout his reign.

Having gained the right to appoint all officials, Frederick William adopted measures calculated to raise the general standard of efficiency. The Great Elector had already introduced considerable improvement in this respect by trying to choose only able officials. But it was merely a beginning, and much that he accomplished was undone during the succeeding reign. Upon taking up the reins of government Frederick William decreed that officials must have the proper training for the office to which they are appointed. At various times during his reign he issued decrees regarding certain officials. He decreed, for instance, that those aspiring to become judges, lawyers, and procurators must take a specified course in a Prussian university. For other offices a prescribed course of study was not a primary requisite, but the king did demand a certain type of practical training. To demonstrate his fitness a candidate had to undergo a thorough examination. As the number of officials was large and vacancies were frequent, Frederick William had his boards draw up lists of eligibles for the various offices. Only "the most able, faith-

ful, and upright" young men, he told the boards repeatedly, were to be placed on these lists. . . .

Once in the Prussian civil service, an official became subject to a discipline no less stern than that of the Prussian army. Such a discipline Frederick William regarded as the highest form of order, as the apex of efficiency. He stated the requirements of office in no uncertain terms. To two officials who resisted transfer to Tilsit he wrote: "You must serve your master with body and soul, with goods and chattels, with honor and conscience, and stake upon this service everything but your salvation." What he specially demanded of his officials was untiring diligence, the utmost efficiency, incorruptible fidelity to duty, and above all prompt and absolute obedience. . . .

Though the requirements were high, the remuneration was so low as to make the expression *travailler pour le roi de Prusse* (to work for the king of Prussia) almost synonymous with poor stipend. Some of the higher officials, it is true, could live well, but the majority of the civil officials were paid so poorly that they found it difficult, and at times impossible, to subsist on their salaries. Only very rarely did the king grant an official a raise; when he did, it was a special mark of distinction. He would often ignore requests for salary increases. If he did answer them he would either advise the petitioners to resign if they were dissatisfied, or he would write upon the petition statements like the following: "The times are growing worse from day to day, and the country or my treasuries are to be burdened with an increase of salaries. That won't do!" To one official who complained that his salary was insufficient to meet the ordinary living expenses the king retorted: "You must follow my maxims and limit your expenses to your income." Officials, he declared, must serve rather for the honor of participating in the government than for the salaries they receive. But if the salaries the Prussian monarch paid his officials were small, he did see to it that they were paid promptly, which had not always been done in the reign of his predecessor. Frederick William knew that certain payment of the salaries, even though they were small, was a means of sustaining honesty and zeal among his officials. He also impressed upon his son that he should pay the salaries of his officials promptly, "so that they need not wait." . . .

In summary, Frederick William coördinated the various branches of the civil administration into one supreme board, the General Directory. This board supervised and controlled, with but few exceptions, the comprehensive activities of the Prussian state. All the local authorities, including the provincial chambers, the rural and local commissaries, and the municipal magistrates, were responsible to it. But even the General Directory had no independent competence. So all-embracing was the royal autocracy that the decisions of this "supreme board" were invalid without the king's approval. The higher officials of this centralized bureaucracy were chosen from both the nobility and the middle class. "In a profounder sense than was true of the army, the Prussian bureaucracy served as a loadstone which attracted and absorbed into the service of the monarchy the most industrious and intelligent section of the population, thus binding their interests closely to those of the state." By means of a severe discipline Frederick William succeeded in raising his officials to a standard of industry and honesty unrivaled in his day. . . .

Frederick William's achievement becomes striking in the light of a comparison of his officials with those of the preceding reign. The Great Elector had appointed many able officials, but after the accession of Frederick I "most of the honorable persons were forced out of the higher offices." The holding of a high civil office became, by and large, a means of enriching oneself by graft of various kinds. When Frederick William took the reins of government in hand he kept most of the old officials, but established a new discipline. Shortly after the opening of his reign he said that faithful civil servants were "so rare that one must seek them with a light during the day." There are, however, no such recorded statements for the latter part of his reign. Though he did not achieve his ideal, his desire for able, diligent, and faithful officials was in the main fulfilled. His officials complained and grumbled under the yoke of the stern military discipline, giving vent to their feelings in statements such as: "He is worse than the tsar and Charles XII"; but, and this was of primary importance to Frederick William, they did produce the revenues necessary to support his standing army. It was no small achievement, for the army was that of a first-rate power, while the resources from which the officials gathered the revenues were those of a third-rate state. Moreover, they collected enough so that the king, after paying the expenses of his army, was able to accumulate a large fund for war purposes. There were many complaints from the taxpayers about high taxes. Actually, however, the taxes were no higher than those of Austria, and they were less than those of France.

10. FREDERICK THE GREAT ON THE MILITARY BASES OF PRUSSIAN STATECRAFT

Frederick the Great, unlike his father, who never put his magnificent military machine to the test of battle, spent the first quarter century of his long reign more or less constantly at war with his neighbors. It was in this great conflict for the possession of the wealthy province of Silesia, seized by Frederick from Austria a few months after his accession and held against overwhelming odds, that the Prussian army actually proved itself to be the best in Europe. Through her army Prussia had become a great European power. It is thus understandable that in the following passage taken from his *Political Testament of 1752*, Frederick should expound at length on the place of the military as the first estate in the Prussian realm.

All branches of government are intimately related each with the others. Financial, political, and military affairs are inseparable. It is not enough that only one of these sectors be well administered, they all must be. They all must be driven in a single tandem, as were the horses that were hitched to the chariots in the Olympic games, which by making a united effort and pulling together, rapidly ran the prescribed course and brought the chariot home with its driver the winner. A prince who governs himself, who has worked out for himself his own political system, will not be embarassed on those occasions when he must promptly act, for he knows how to direct everything towards a goal which he has set for himself. It is in the details of military affairs above all that he should have acquired the widest possible knowledge. Lawyers do not draw up good campaign plans. In any case, of what use are the best plans, if the ignorance of the man who is undertaking them brings about their failure while carrying them out? He who does not know the needs of an army, who has never penetrated into the infinite details of the military commissariat, who knows nothing of how to make an army move, who is ignorant of the rules of the military art, who knows neither how to discipline troops when they are in garrison, nor how to lead them in the field, who in short is not his own general, will never accomplish great things, even if he be the wittiest of men, the best economist and the most subtle politician. I do not intend to go into details here concerning this science. . . . I only wish to encourage the ardor of those who would embrace the noble and dangerous profession of arms and to prove that it is necessary for a prince to make it his chief study.

Prussia is surrounded by powerful neighbors and in particular by an irreconcilable enemy, the House of Austria. This must condition you to the expectation of many wars. For this same reason, the military estate must be the first in the realm, just as it was among the Romans when these conquerors of the world were in their period of expansion, just as it was when Gustavus Adolphus, Charles X, and Charles XII filled the universe with their fame and made the name of Sweden known in the farthest climates. Responsibilities, honors, and rewards in turn stimulate and encourage the abilities, while praises justly bestowed on merit bring forth that generous emulation within the breast of the nobility

From *Die Politischen Testamente Friedrichs des Grossen* (Berlin, 1920), pp. 77–80. Translation by the editor.

which leads it to take up the profession of arms and to acquire the knowledge which leads it to fame and fortune. . . .To encourage a profession upon which is built the power of a realm, to value highly these columns of the state (if I may so express myself) which support it, to prefer them to that breed of soft and faint-hearted men who only serve to decorate an anti-chamber, is not to favor them too much or to act capriciously. Rather it is to render to merit its just due and to burn a feeble incense at the altar of those officers all of whom are at a moment's notice ready to shed their blood for their country.

I have made war myself and I have seen colonels who have on occasion decided the fate of a state. One cannot make war without coming upon those individual acts which determine the destiny of an empire. . . . The Battle of Ramillies led to the loss of all of Flanders by France. The Battle of Höchstadt caused the Elector of Bavaria the loss of his electorate and all of Swabia. . . . That is why Henry IV said that a battle has a long tail. It is during such important and decisive days that one gains a sense of the worth of a good officer. . . .But it is not enough to cherish them at the moment when you have need of them and when their actions wring cheers from you. It is necessary that in time of peace they enjoy the reputation that they have so justly earned and that they be signally esteemed as men who have shed their blood solely for the honor and the well-being of the state.

The sovereign in a monarchical state is the cynosure of all eyes. The people observe his actions and seem to be highly receptive to the impression that he gives. Thus it was that catholic prelates were voluptuous and magnificent under Leo X, but sly and shrewd under Sixtus V, that England, cruel under Cromwell, became gallant under Charles II. . . .and that the Roman Empire, pagan under the Antonines and the Tituses, became Christian under Constantine, who was the first to take up the new cult. In this realm, the sovereign must be that which is most useful to the good of the state and consequently he must place himself at its head as a soldier. That is the way to accentuate the importance of that profession and to maintain the excellence of our discipline and of the order which has been established in our troops. . . .

I am certain that only the sovereign can establish this admirable discipline in an army and maintain it there, because one often has to use authority, to reprimand persons regardless of their title or their rank, to reward others liberally, to pass the troops in review as often as possible, and not to permit the least negligence. Of necessity the King of Prussia must be a soldier and must be the real chief of the army, a position . . . that is somewhat scorned by most kings in Europe, who believe that they are lowering themselves if they assume command of their armies. It is shameful for a throne that these princes, soft and lazy, by relinquishing command over their troops to their generals, make a tacit admission of their faint-heartedness or their incapacity.

In this state it is certainly an honor to collaborate with the flower of the nobility and the elite of the nation in the consolidation of that discipline which underlies the glory of the fatherland, rendering it respected in peace and victorious in war. One would have to be of wretched birth, given over to sloth and enervated by voluptuousness, to complain about the trouble and the pains that the maintenance of this discipline demands. Its only recompense lies in the conquests of the army and its reputation, which is of more benefit to a prince than the greatest splendor. . . .

11. THE NEW MODEL ARMY

Because she could rely primarily on her geographical situation for her security, England was able to maintain a military establishment which was by seventeenth century continental standards ludicrously small. Only in the course of the Civil Wars beginning in 1642 did a true standing army come into existence. The New Model Army, as it was called, was raised by the parliamentary party in its struggle with the crown. Under the leadership of Oliver Cromwell, this army was inspired by a high degree of religious fervor, described in the following account by a contemporary witness. It was this fervor which more than anything else may account for its remarkable discipline and its steadiness in battle.

THE SPIRIT OF THE NEW MODEL ARMY

The English Army, being . . . new modelled, was really in the hand of . Oliver Cromwell, though seemingly under the command of Sir Thomas Fairfax. . . .

We that lived quietly in Coventry did keep to our old principles, and thought all others had done so too except a very few inconsiderable persons. . . . And when the Court News-book told the world of the swarms of Anabaptists in our armies, we thought it had been a mere lie, because it was not so with us nor in any of the garrison or county forces about us. But when I came to the Army, among Cromwell's soldiers, I found a new face of things, which I never dreamed of. . . . Abundance of the common troopers, and many of the officers, I found to be honest, sober, orthodox men, and others tractable, ready to hear the truth, and of upright intentions. But a few proud, self-conceited, hot-headed sectaries had got into the highest places, and were Cromwell's chief favourites, and by their very heat and activity bore down the rest, or

carried them along with them, and were the soul of the Army though much fewer in number than the rest. . . .

I perceived that they took the King for a tyrant and an enemy, and really intended absolutely to master him or ruin him; and that they thought, if they might fight against him, they might kill or conquer him; and if they might conquer, they were never more to trust him further than he was in their power. . . . They said, What were the Lords of England but William the Conqueror's colonels, or the Barons but his majors, or the knights but his captains? They plainly showed me that they thought God's providence would cast the trust of religion and the kingdom upon them as conquerors. They made nothing of all the most wise and godly in the armies and garrisons that were not of their way. *Per fas aut nefas,* by law or without it, they were resolved to take down not only bishops and liturgy and ceremonies, but all that did withstand their way. . . .

From *Reliquiae Baxterianae* (1696), Part I.

I found that many honest men of weak judgments and little acquaintance with such matters had been seduced into a disputing vein, and made it too much of their religion to talk for this opinion and for that. Sometimes for state-democracy, and sometimes for church-democracy; sometimes against forms of prayer, and sometimes against infant baptism (which yet some of them did maintain); sometimes against set times of prayer, and against the tying of ourselves to any duty before the Spirit move us; and sometimes about free grace and free will, . . . But their most frequent and vehement disputes were for liberty of conscience, as they called it; that is, that the civil magistrate had nothing to do to determine of anything in matters of religion by constraint or restraint, but every man might not only hold, but preach and do, in matters of religion what he pleased; that the civil magistrate hath nothing to do but with civil things, to keep the peace, and protect the churches' liberties, &c.

THE ARMY MANIFESTO

As relations between them degenerated, the extremists in the army found themselves obliged to take a stand against the moderate majority in parliament. All the while claiming their unwillingness to interfere in the government of the kingdom, the soldiers showed an increasing propensity to threaten the use of force if their views on the final settlement of the conflict with the crown were not heeded. In the following selection the leaders of the army, on their way to London at the head of their troops, the more forcibly to make their case, state their position in this matter. It is drawn from *The Letters and Speeches of Oliver Cromwell*, edited by Thomas Carlyle.

To the Right Honourable the Lord Mayor, Aldermen, and Common Council of the City of London:

Royston, 10th June 1647

RIGHT HONOURABLE AND WORTHY FRIENDS,
Having, by our letters and other addresses presented by our General to the Honourable House of Commons, endeavoured to give satisfaction of the clearness of our just demands; and "having" also, in papers published by us, remonstrated the grounds of our proceedings in prosecution thereof; — all which having been exposed to public view, we are confident have come to your hands, and at least received a charitable construction from you; — the sum of all these our Desires as Soldiers is no other than a desire of satisfaction to our demands as soldiers; and reparation upon those who have, to the utmost, improved all opportunities and advantages, by false suggestions, misrepresentations and otherwise, for the destruction of this Army with a perpetual blot of ignominy upon it. . . .

As for the thing we insist upon as Englishmen, — and surely our being soldiers hath not stript us of that interest, although our malicious enemies would have it so, — we desire a settlement of the peace of the Kingdom and of the liberties of the subject, according to the votes and declarations of Parliament, which, before we took up

From *The Letters and Speeches of Oliver Cromwell*, ed. Thos. Carlyle, Vol. I. (New York, 1904), pp. 266–269, abridged.

arms, were, by the Parliament, used as arguments and inducements to invite us and divers of our dear friends out; some of which have lost their lives in this war, which being, by God's blessing, finished, we think we have as much right to demand, and desire to see, a happy settlement, as we have to our money and the other common interest of soldiers which we have insisted upon. We find also the ingenious and honest people, in almost all the parts of the Kingdom where we come, full of the sense of ruin and misery if the Army should be disbanded before the peace of the Kingdom, and those other things before mentioned, have a full and perfect settlement.

We have said before, and profess it now, We desire no alteration of the Civil Government. We desire not to intermeddle with, or in the least to interrupt, the settling of the Presbyterial Government. Nor did we seek to open a way to licentious liberty, under pretence of obtaining ease for tender consciences.

We profess, as ever in these things, when the State have once made a settlement, we have nothing to say but to submit or suffer. Only we could wish that every good citizen, and every man that walks peaceably in a blameless conversation, and is beneficial to the Commonwealth, may have liberty and encouragement; it being according to the just policy of all States, even to justice itself.

These things are our desires, and the things for which we stand; beyond which we shall not go. And for the obtaining of these things, we are drawing near your city; — professing sincerely from our hearts, "that" we intend not evil towards you; declaring, with all confidence and assurance, that if you appear not against us in these our just desires, to assist that wicked Party that would embroil us and the Kingdom, nor we nor our Soldiers shall give you the least offence. We come not to do any act to prejudice the being of Parliaments, or to the hurt of this "Parliament" in order to the present settlement of the Kingdom. We seek the good of all. And we shall here wait, or remove to a farther distance there to abide, if once we be assured that a speedy settlement of things be in hand, — until they be accomplished. . . .

If after all this, you, or a considerable number of you, be seduced to take up arms in opposition to, or hindrance of, these our just undertakings, we hope by this brotherly premonition, to the sincerity whereof we call God to witness, we have freed ourselves from all that ruin which may befall that great and populous City; having hereby washed our hands thereof.

We rest,
Your affectionate Friends to serve you,

THOMAS FAIRFAX.   HENRY IRETON.
OLIVER CROMWELL.   ROBERT LILBURN.
ROBERT HAMMOND.   JOHN DESBOROW.
THOMAS HAMMOND.   THOMAS RAINSBOROW.
HARDRESS WALLER.   JOHN LAMBERT.
NATHANIEL RICH.   THOMAS HARRISON.
THOMAS PRIDE.

FROM THE DECLARATION OF THE ARMY, ON THE MARCH TO LONDON, 30TH NOVEMBER, 1648

Aware of the growing gulf between the army and parliament, the king sought to profit by the situation. He thus entered into negotiations with parliament against the army in the hopes of restoring his own shattered fortunes. This helped to precipitate the so-called Second Civil War in early 1648, in which Cromwell's forces were victorious. The exasperated army now resolved to settle matters in its own way. The following selection is taken from the "Declaration of the Army" of November 30, 1648, as it marched to London. Having arrived there, the army proceeded to "purge" parliament of all its moderate members. The "rump" which remained was then constituted as a high court for the trial and the condemnation of the king.

And as the incompetency of this Parliament, in its present constitution, to give an absolute and conclusive judgment for the whole (especially to be the sole judges of their own performance or breach of trust) doth make the juster way for such an appeal, so indeed we see no other way left for remedy, in regard the present unlimited continuance of this Parliament doth exclude the orderly succession of any other more equal formal judicature of men, to which we might hope in due time other ways to appeal. Thus then we apprehend ourselves in the present case, both necessitated to, and justified in, an appeal from this Parliament, in the present constitution as it stands, unto the extraordinary judgment of God and good people. . . .

. . . It should be our great rejoicing (if God saw it good), that the majority of the present House of Commons were become sensible of the evil and destructiveness of their late way, and would resolvedly and vigorously apply themselves to the speedy execution of justice, with the righting and easing of the oppressed people, and to a just and safe settlement of the kingdom upon such foundations as have been propounded by us and others for that purpose. . . .

But however, if God shall not see it good to vouchsafe that mercy to them and the kingdom, we shall, secondly, desire that so many of them as God hath kept upright, and shall touch with a just sense of those things, would by protestation or otherwise acquit themselves from such breach of trust, and approve their faithfulness by withdrawing from those that persist in the guilt thereof, and would apply themselves to such a posture whereby they may speedily and effectually prosecute those necessary and public ends. . . .

Now yet further to take away all jealousies in relation to ourselves, which might withhold or discourage any honest members from this course: as we have the witness of God in our hearts that in these proceedings we do not seek, but even resolve we will not take, advantages to ourselves either in point of profit or power, and that if God did open unto us a way wherein with honesty and faithfulness to the public interest and good people engaged for us, we might presently be discharged, so as we might not in our present employments look on, and be accessory to, yea, supporters of, the Parliament, in the present corrupt, oppressive, and destructive proceedings, we should with rejoicing, and without more ado, embrace such a discharge rather than interpose in these things to our own vast trouble and hazard. So, if we could but obtain a rational assurance for the effectual prosecution of these things, we shall give any proportionable assurance on our parts concerning our laying down of arms, when, and as, we should be required. But for the present, as the case stands, we apprehend ourselves obliged in duty to God, this kingdom, and good men therein, to improve our utmost abilities in all honest ways for the avoiding of these great evils we have remonstrated, and for prosecution of the good things we have propounded; and also that such persons who . . . the instigators and encouragers of the late insurrections within this kingdom, and (those forcible ways failing) have still pursued the same wicked designs by treacherous and corrupt counsels, may be brought to public justice, according to their several demerits. For all these ends we are now drawing up with the Army to London, there to follow Providence as God shall clear our way.

C. H. Firth

12. CROMWELL'S ARMY

The emergence of the New Model Army as the dominant political power in the country represented a decisive turning point in the course of the Civil War and indeed in the whole subsequent history of England. The stages by which this took place and the manner in which the army exercised power in England following the conclusion of the Civil Wars and the execution of the king are described below in excerpts from the classic study by C. H. Firth, *Cromwell's Army*.

In describing most armies it would hardly be necessary to devote special chapters to their religion and their politics. The Cromwellian army, however, was not an ordinary army. It was a national army in so far as it represented England in its dealings with foreign States and dependent communities. In another sense it was not a national army, for it was not drawn indifferently from every party and every sect in the nation, but represented the particular sect and the particular party which had gained the upper hand in the Civil Wars. It possessed in consequence a very definite set of opinions both in religion and politics, and exerted a distinct and a continuous influence upon the life of England from 1647 to 1660. The result of its intervention in domestic politics is part of the general history of the country during that period. . . .

The political history of the army begins in 1647. Before that date it made no attempt to influence the policy of the Parliament.

The views of officers and men were those of the authority whom they served, and if they petitioned it was only to ask that their wants might be supplied and the war more vigorously prosecuted.`. . . .

Whilst the King was unconquered his opponents could not afford to turn their arms against each other, whatever their mutual provocations might be. For the same reason the New Model army during the first two years or eighteen months of its life abstained from any direct intervention in political questions. Besides this, at the beginning it was not the homogeneous army which it subsequently became. Time and companionship in arms worked for unity and unanimity. As the adherents of independency[1] were numerous, powerful, and zealous, the whole army became per-

[1]Believers in the theory that each separate, self-governing religious congregation was responsible only to God for both its doctrine and the management of its own affairs, as opposed to a presbyterian or episcopal organization of the church. [Editor's note.]

From C. H. Firth, *Cromwell's Army* (London, 1902) pp. 346–365, abridged.

meated with their ideas, and the majority of officers and men adopted their way of thinking. The progress of independency meant the spread of democratic principles, for "Church-democracy" led by a natural sequence to "State-democracy." Thus agreement in politics accompanied agreement in religion, and by 1647 sufficient community of ideas existed to form a basis for joint action in public affairs. Moreover, in the minds of many members of the army, victory had fostered the belief that they had a mission to fulfil in the settlement which must follow the war. "They plainly showed me," says Baxter, "that they thought God's providence would cast the trust of religion and the kingdom upon them as conquerors."

The desire to intervene might never have ripened into action, the soldiers might have laid down their arms first and turned politicians afterwards, but for the unwisdom of the Parliamentary leaders. As it was, the unfairness of their scheme of disbanding the army roused an opposition which their persistence converted into a revolt. They supplied a grievance which touched every man in the ranks, and created unanimity; an opportunity which fired the hopes of the dreamer and woke the ambition of the self-seeker. . . .

The refusal of the army to disband, . . . and the decision of Fairfax and Cromwell to throw in their lot with the army against the Parliament, and to secure the redress of their grievances and the settlement of the nation by force, if force was needed, necessitated the establishment of some body qualified to direct the public action of the army. The result was the erection of the "General Council of the Army." This was defined in the "Engagement" of 5th June as "a Council to consist of those general officers of the army (who have concurred with the army in the premises) with two commission officers and two soldiers to be chosen for each regiment, who have concurred and shall concur with us in the premises and in this agreement." They were to meet in council "when they shall be thereunto called by the general." The

army at the same time took a solemn pledge that it would not "willingly disband or divide, or suffer itself to be disbanded or divided," until it obtained satisfaction for the future. The Council was to determine on behalf of the army when these conditions were fulfilled.

The demand for security for the future necessarily led to direct interference in the political settlement of the kingdom. For the soldiers held that they could not be secure if the King was restored to his authority without proper restrictions, or the Parliament left in possession of the unlimited powers it had abused. "All wise men may see," declared the army, "that Parliament privileges as well as royal prerogative may be perverted or abused to the destruction of those greater ends for whose protection and preservation they were intended, to wit, the rights and privileges of the people and the safety of the whole." This distrust of an unlimited Parliament, which is easily explained by the circumstances of the moment, is the key to the political history of the army.

To justify the claim to be heard in the settlement of the kingdom the army argued that it was not like other armies. "We were not a mere mercenary army, hired to serve any arbitrary power of state, but called forth and conjured by the several declarations of Parliament, to the defence of our own and the people's just rights and liberties." "As Englishmen," added another of their manifestoes, "and surely our being soldiers hath not stript us of that interest, though our malicious enemies would have it so, we desire a settlement of the peace of the kingdom and the liberties of the subject, according to the votes and declarations of Parliament; . . . "

The best justification of the conduct of the army, however, did not lie in these arguments and distinctions, but in the danger of a new Civil War in case the Presbyterian leaders in Parliament were allowed to carry out their plans.[2] As it was,

²They were at the time negotiating with the Scots for a military force to protect themselves against the army. The army would not accept a Presbyterian Church, but rather sought a settlement based on "Independency." [Editor's note]

after nearly two months spent in abortive negotiations between the army and the Parliament, the army occupied London and drove the Presbyterian leaders into exile. Just before it occupied London (1st August 1647) the army published its scheme for the settlement of the kingdom. The "Heads of the Proposals of the Army," as the scheme was termed, was in the main the work of Commissary-General Ireton, but it had been revised by a committee of the Council of the Army, and accepted by the Council itself. As its title showed, it was not the draught of a new constitution to be imposed by the army upon the nation, but a series of propositions meant to serve as the basis of negotiations and to show the nation what kind of settlement the army desired. Its chief characteristic was that it aimed at permanently limiting not only the power of the King but also the power of the Parliament, and therefore it naturally failed to commend itself to either. . . .

In October 1648, after the conclusion of the second Civil War, while the Commissioners of Parliament were treating with Charles the First at Newport, political excitement again rose high in the army. Regiment after regiment presented its petition to the General, demanding justice against all responsible for the war without respect of persons. In November a General Council of Officers met at St Albans and drew up a Remonstrance which was presented to the House of Commons on 20th November. It demanded that the King should be brought to justice, and his sons declared incapable of succeeding to the government. It embodied also the old proposals for biennial Parliaments, equal constituencies, and the speedy dissolution of the existing House of Commons. As the House delayed its answer . . . , the army seized the King at Newport and marched on London. The intention of the military leaders originally was to dissolve by force the existing Parliament and to call a new one as soon as possible. They were persuaded, however, by their friends in the House, to content themselves with the exclusion of all Royalist members,

or rather of all those who had voted that the King's concessions during the treaty were a satisfactory basis for a peace. The result was "Pride's Purge," by which about 140 members were either arrested or prevented from sitting. The independent minority who remained behind at the instigation of the army proceeded to establish a High Court of Justice for the trial of the King, and prepared to turn England into a republic. . . .

[*Following the execution of Charles I, the monarchy was abolished and England was proclaimed a Commonwealth. This radical step went far beyond what most Englishmen desired or considered proper, but such was the strength of the army that there were over the next few years only scattered and uncoordinated uprisings against the new government. In Ireland, however, there was an immediate and general rebellion, soon suppressed by Cromwell's forces, while in Scotland even staunch Presbyterians refused to accept the abolition of the monarchy and proclaimed Charles II king upon the news of the death of his father. Returning to Scotland in 1650 from his exile in Holland, Charles put himself at the head of the uprising there, but all his efforts were to no avail. During an abortive invasion of England at the head of a Scottish army, Charles was defeated at the Battle of Worcester and forced to flee back into exile.*]

From the beginning of the Scottish war in the summer of 1650 to its conclusion in September 1651 the army was too busily engaged in its proper business of fighting to have much time to think of politics. When peace was restored they once more began to intervene in the settlement of the nation. A Royalist writing early in 1653 says: "In regard that the whole army at present have nothing to do . . . all the chief officers are at London who meet in a grand council, called the Council of the Army, every Tuesday and Thursday.

As usual the movement commenced with a petition. On 13th August 1652 Commissary-General Whalley and five other officers appeared before Parliament with "The humble Petition of the Officers of the

Army," setting forth some dozen reforms which they desired the House to carry into effect with all possible speed. But for Cromwell's restraining influence they would probably have included in their list a demand for an immediate dissolution of Parliament. The House, as usual, thanked the officers, but did little, and during the winter of 1652 and the spring of 1653 the impatience of the army increased and the movement for intervention grew stronger. There were all the usual signs which presaged a storm. There were frequent meetings of the Council, and long prayer-meetings in which, as the phrase ran, the officers "waited upon God" and "confessed their sins." A news-letter in January 1653 significantly says: "The officers have been seeking God two days: the Grandees fear a design in hand." Then came the despatch of a series of circular letters to the regiments stationed in Scotland, Ireland and remote parts of England, which were a necessary preliminary to concerted action. Cromwell endeavoured to check the movement, and sought to effect a compromise with Parliament. When the compromise failed, owing to what he considered the bad faith of some of the Parliamentary leaders, he too lost his patience, and putting himself at the head of the movement, called in a few files of musketeers and put a stop to the sittings of the House.

The revolution of 20th April 1653 made the army the government of England. Hitherto it had contented itself with influencing and at times dictating the votes of the House; now it exercised the supreme power directly instead of indirectly. But it had no intention of retaining this power, and claimed to be merely a provisional government. Before the Parliament was expelled the army had urged it to devolve the supreme authority upon some select number of "men fearing God and of approved integrity," and to commit the government of the Commonwealth to them for a time. Since Parliament had refused to do this the army announced that it would carry out the scheme itself, and "call to the government

persons of approved fidelity and honesty." Until such persons could be got together, "for preventing the mischiefs and inconveniences which may arise in the meanwhile to the public affairs," a Council of State was appointed "to take care of and intend the peace, safety, and present management of the affairs of this Commonwealth." The councillors so appointed were thirteen in number, and nine of them were officers. While these thirteen men, with the General at their head, carried on the daily business of administration, the Council of Officers debated the nature and the composition of the body to which their tempory authority was to be transferred. Some were for a small council of ten or twelve; some for a council of seventy persons, something like the Jewish Sanhedrim. In the end it was resolved to select about 140 Puritan notables to represent the people of the three nations. Letters were sent to the Independent Churches in each county asking them to suggest the names of suitable men, and the names proposed were debated and voted upon. "In the choice of which persons such indifference was used, and so equal liberty allowed to all then present with the General, that every officer enjoyed the same freedom of nomination and the majority of suffrages carried it for the election of each single member." They were then summoned by writs, which stated that they, being "persons fearing God and of approved fidelity and honesty," had been nominated by Cromwell as commander-in-chief, with the advice and consent of his Council of Officers, to take upon themselves the trust of governing the State. With their meeting on 4th July, and the transference of authority to them by a signed indenture, the rule of the army ended. It had lasted rather more than ten weeks.

This assembly of nominees which assumed the style and claimed the rights of a Parliament failed to give satisfaction to the men who had called it into being. On 12th December 1653 a majority of their number were induced to abdicate their power. In the next three days the Council of Officers drew up the constitution known as the "Instrument of Government," and on 16th December the commander-in-chief, having accepted the limitations it imposed on his power, was installed as Protector. Thus within the short space of eight months the army had imposed upon England first a Council of State, next a Parliament, and lastly a new constitution.

While it retained power in its own hands it had ruled well, but the vice was in the origin of its power, not in the manner of its exercise. Recognizing the objections to military rule, and anxious to show what its general termed "the integrity of divesting the sword of all power in the civil administration," it had sought to establish a civil government. But it was all one to the nation whether the army governed directly or indirectly, whether the Council of Officers ruled England itself through a nominee or through an assembly of nominees. However it might be disguised by the forms and ceremonies of constitutionalism, the Protectorate rested almost entirely on the support of the army and represented military rule. Hence it was never heartily accepted by more than a section of the nation, though there was an increasing tendency to acquiesce in its authority on the part of the rest.

13. JAMES II AND THE ARMY

Possibly the most immediately significant legacy of the period of Puritan rule was a profound distaste on the part of the English people for anything savoring of military rule. Soon after the restoration of the monarchy in 1660, parliament took steps to provide against the danger to constitutional government inherent in any standing army, while at the same time taking care of the defense of the realm, by enacting two statutes on the militia. The militia being an inadequate force to assure all the military needs of the country, the crown for perfectly sound reasons constantly sought to enlarge the small standing army. Command of the armed forces was one of the accepted constitutional prerogatives of the monarch. The problem was that James II who ascended the throne in 1685 was a Catholic, opposed to the religious sentiments of the majority of his subjects. With good reason, they feared that the king might use the army, into which he had already insinuated a number of Catholic officers in defiance of the law, as an instrument to promote the Catholic cause in England. Thus parliament felt obliged to refuse the king's request for more funds for the army as well as his demands that the Catholic officers retain their posts. Both the speech of the king and the reply of parliament are reprinted below.

9 November 1685
MY LORDS AND GENTLEMEN,

After the storm that seemed to be coming upon us when we parted last, I am glad to meet you all again in so great peace and quietness. God Almighty be praised, by whose blessing that rebellion[1] was suppressed. But when we reflect what an inconsiderable number of men began it, and how long they carried it on without any opposition, I hope everybody will be convinced that the militia, which hath hitherto

[1]Rebellion led by the Protestant Duke of Monmouth, illegitimate son of Charles II [Ed. note].

been so much depended on, is not sufficient for such occasions, and that there is nothing but a good force of well-disciplined troops in constant pay that can defend us from such as, either at home or abroad, are disposed to disturb us. And in truth, my concern for the peace and quiet of my subjects, as well as for the safety of the government, made me think it necessary to increase the number to the proportion I have done. This I owed as well to the honour as the security of the nation, whose reputation was so infinitely exposed to all our neighbours, by having so evidently lain open to this late wretched attempt, that it is not to be repaired without keeping such a body of men on foot that none may ever have the thought again of finding us so miserably unprovided.

It is for the support of this great charge, which is now more than double to what it was, that I ask your assistance in giving me a supply answerable to the expense it brings along with it. And I cannot doubt but what I have begun, so much for the honour and defence of the government, will be continued by you with all the cheerfulness that is requisite for a work of so great importance.

Let no man take exception that there are some officers in the army not qualified, according to the late Tests, for their employments. The gentlemen, I must tell you, are most of them well known to me, and having formerly served with me in several occasions, and always approved the loyalty of their principles by their practice, I think fit now to be employed under me. And I will deal plainly with you, that after having had the benefit of their service in such time of need and danger, I will neither expose them to disgrace, nor myself to want of them, if there should be another rebellion to make them necessary for me.

I am afraid some men may be so wicked to hope and expect that a difference may happen between you and me upon this occasion. But when you consider what advantages have arisen to us in a few months by the good understanding we have hitherto had; what wonderful effects it hath

already produced in the change of the whole scene of affairs abroad, so much more to the honour of this nation and the figure it ought to make in the world; and that nothing can hinder a further progress in this way, to all our satisfactions, but fears and jealousies amongst ourselves, I will not apprehend that such a misfortune can befall us as a division, or but a coldness, between me and you, nor that anything can shake you in your steadiness and loyalty to me who, by God's blessing, will ever make you returns of all kindness and protection, with a resolution to venture even my own life in the defence of the true interest of this kingdom.

16 November 1685

MOST GRACIOUS SOVEREIGN,

We, your Majesty's most loyal and faithful subjects, the Commons in Parliament assembled, do in the first place, as in duty bound, return your Majesty our most humble and hearty thanks for your great care and conduct in the suppression of the late rebellion, which threatened the overthrow of this government both in Church and State and the utter extirpation of our religion by law established, which is most dear unto us, and which your Majesty has been graciously pleased to give us repeated assurances you will always defend and support, which with all grateful hearts we shall ever acknowledge.

We further crave leave to acquaint your Majesty that we have with all duty and readiness taken into our consideration your Majesty's gracious speech to us. And as to that part of it relating to the officers in the army not qualified for their employments according to an Act of Parliament made in the twenty-fifth year of the reign of your Majesty's royal brother of blessed memory, entitled, *An Act for preventing dangers which may happen from popish recusants*[2] we do out of our bounden duty humbly represent unto your Majesty that those officers cannot by law be capable of their employ-

[2]An act requiring every office holder, civil or military, to take the Sacraments of the Church of England, thus excluding Catholics from the army. [Editor;s note]

ments, and that the incapacities they bring upon themselves thereby can no ways be taken off but by an Act of Parliament.

Therefore out of that great deference and duty we owe unto your Majesty, who has been graciously pleased to take notice of their services to you, we are preparing a bill to pass both Houses for your royal assent, to indemnify them from the penalties they have now incurred. And because the continuance of them in their employments may be taken to be a dispensing with that law without Act of Parliament (the consequence of which is of the greatest concern to the rights of all your Majesty's dutiful and loyal subjects, and to all the laws made for security of their religion), we therefore, the knights, citizens and burgesses of your Majesty's House of Commons, do most humbly beseech your Majesty that you would be graciously pleased to give such directions therein that no apprehensions or jealousies may remain in the hearts of your Majesty's good and faithful subjects.

14. THE BILL OF RIGHTS AND THE MUTINY ACT

The Glorious Revolution of 1688 brought about the downfall of James II and affirmed the supremacy of parliament in the affairs of the realm. With regard to military matters that supremacy was asserted in the Bill of Rights of 1689, wherein it was declared illegal for the crown to raise and to maintain a standing army without the consent of parliament, and by the Mutiny Act of the same year. The latter act provided the legal grounds for the maintenance of discipline in the armed forces. It was originally meant to be in force for a period of six months, after which it had to be enacted again for a limited period of time. Without the provisions of the act discipline could not legally be enforced and the army would thus disintegrate.

AN ACT DECLARING THE RIGHTS AND LIBERTIES OF THE SUBJECT AND SETTLING THE SUCCESSION OF THE CROWN

Whereas the Lords Spiritual and Temporal and Commons assembled at Westminster lawfully, fully and freely representing all the estates of the people of this realm, did upon the thirteenth day of February in the year of our Lord one thousand six hundred eight-eight present unto their Majesties, then called and known by the names and style of William and Mary, prince and princess of Orange being present in their proper persons, a certain declaration in writing made by the said Lords and Commons in the words following, viz.:

Whereas the late King James the Second, by the assistance of divers evil counsellors, judges and ministers employed by him, did endeavour to subvert and extirpate the Protestant religion and the laws and liberties of this kingdom;

By assuming and exercising a power of dispensing with and suspending of laws and the execution of laws without consent of Parliament; . . .

By levying money for and to the use of the Crown by pretence of prerogative for other time and in other manner than the same was granted by Parliament;

By raising and keeping a standing army within this kingdom in time of peace without consent of Parliament, and quartering soldiers contrary to law;

By causing several good subjects being Protestants to be disarmed at the same time when papists were both armed and em-

From *Statutes of the Realm*, vol. VI, pp. 55–56, 142–145, abridged.

ployed contrary to law; . . .

All which are utterly and directly contrary to the known laws and statutes and freedom of this realm;

And whereas the said late King James the Second having abdicated the government and the throne being thereby vacant, his Highness the prince of Orange (whom it hath pleased Almighty God to make the glorious instrument of delivering this kingdom from popery and arbitrary power) did (by the advice of the Lords Spiritual and Temporal and divers principal persons of the Commons) cause letters to be written to the Lords Spiritual and Temporal being Protestants, and other letters to the several counties, cities, universities, boroughs and cinque ports, for the choosing of such persons to represent them as were of right to be sent to Parliament, to meet and sit at Westminster upon the two and twentieth day of January in this year one thousand six hundred eighty and eight, in order to such an establishment as that their religion, laws and liberties might not again be in danger of being subverted, upon which letters elections having been accordingly made;

And thereupon the said Lords Spiritual and Temporal and Commons, pursuant to their respective letters and elections, being now assembled in a full and free representative of this nation, taking into their most serious consideration the best means for attaining the ends aforesaid, do in the first place (as their ancestors in like case have usually done) for the vindicating and asserting their ancient rights and liberties declare

That the pretended power of suspending of laws or the execution of laws by regal authority without consent of Parliament is illegal;

That the pretended power of dispensing with laws or the execution of laws by regal authority, as it hath been assumed and exercised of late, is illegal; . . .

That levying money for or to the use of the Crown by pretence of prerogative, without grant of Parliament, for longer time, or in other manner than the same is

or shall be granted, is illegal; . . .

That the raising or keeping a standing army within the kingdom in time of peace, unless it be with consent of Parliament, is against law;

That the subjects which are Protestants may have arms for their defence suitable to their conditions and as allowed by law; . . .

AN ACT FOR PUNISHING OFFICERS OR SOLDIERS WHO SHALL MUTINY OR DESERT THEIR MAJESTIES' SERVICE

Whereas the raising or keeping a standing army within this kingdom in time of peace, unless it be with consent of Parliament, is against law; and whereas it is judged necessary by their Majesties and this present Parliament that during this time of danger several of the forces which are now on foot should be continued and others raised for the safety of the kingdom, for the common defence of the Protestant religion and for the reducing of Ireland; and whereas no man may be forejudged of life or limb, or subjected to any kind of punishment by martial law, or in any other manner than by the judgment of his peers and according to the known and established laws of this realm; yet nevertheless it being requisite for retaining such forces as are or shall be raised during this exigence of affairs in their duty an exact discipline be observed, and that soldiers who shall mutiny or stir up sedition or shall desert their Majesties' service be brought to a more exemplary and speedy punishment than the usual forms of law will allow.

II. Be it therefore enacted . . . that from and after the twelfth day of April in the year of our Lord one thousand six hundred eighty-nine every person being in their Majesties' service in the army, and being mustered and in pay as an officer or soldier, who shall at any time before the tenth day of November in the year of our Lord one thousand six hundred eighty-nine excite, cause or join in any mutiny or sedition in the army, or shall desert their Majesties' service in the army, shall suffer death or such other punishment as by a court-martial shall be inflicted.

III. And it is hereby further enacted and declared, that their Majesties, or the general of their army for the time being, may by virtue of this Act have full power and authority to grant commissions to any lieutenants-general or other officers not under the degree of colonels from time to time to call and assemble court-martials for punishing such offences as aforesaid. . . .

VI. Provided always, that nothing in this

Act contained shall extend or be construed to exempt any officer or soldier whatsoever from the ordinary process of law.

VII. Provided always, that this Act or anything therein contained shall not extend or be any ways construed to extend to or concern any the militia forces of this kingdom.

VIII. Provided also, that this Act shall continue and be in force until the said tenth day of November in the said year of our Lord one thousand six hundred eighty-nine, and no longer. . . .

J. S. Omond

15. PARLIAMENT AND THE ARMY

Although the Civil Wars had been fought over the question of the respective powers and prerogatives of parliament and the crown, neither the victory of the parliamentary forces in 1649 nor the Restoration of the monarchy in 1660 really settled the dispute. It was only in the three decades following the Restoration climaxed by the Glorious Revolution of 1688 that the constitutional relationship between the two branches of the government was worked out, to the advantage of parliament. Parliament thus gained a large measure of control over the armed forces of the country, usurping what had formerly been considered to be the exclusive preserve of the monarch. How parliament was able to accomplish this is described in the following passage from *Parliament and the Army* by Lt. Col J. S. Omond.

The death of Oliver Cromwell on September 3rd, 1658, removed the power which had controlled the destinies of England, both at home and abroad, during a critical period of her history. He had governed the country by his reliance on the army ever since the battle of Worcester seven years before. The country was tired of military rule, and a gradual desire for the re-establishment of the monarchy was growing up. Richard, his son, who succeeded him as Lord Protector, had not the force of character, nor probably the ability, to cope with the situation which developed with great rapidity in the course of the next twelve

months. A new Parliament met at the beginning of 1659, and the members supported him hoping that he would be less dependent on the army, less amenable to its wishes, more inclined to listen to their counsels, and less easily swayed by the fear of military violence. However, as Whitelock records, "the soldiers began to speak high and threatening." A quarrel between Richard and the army soon arose over a request from the officers that Fleetwood, who was his brother-in-law, should be their commander and independent of the authority of the Protector. Fleetwood was nominated as commander, but Richard

From J. S. Omond, *Parliament and the Army* (Cambridge, 1933), pp. 11–34, abridged. Reprinted by permission of the Cambridge University Press.

insisted that he must act as Lieutenant-General under the Protector. Parliament supported him in this view as a means of upholding the control of the army by the civil authority. In April, the soldiers forced him to dissolve Parliament. His resignation followed on May 25th, and the Protectorate was at an end.

The military party next attempted to govern by themselves. The first step taken before Richard Cromwell's resignation was to restore the remains or Rump of the Long Parliament which Oliver Cromwell had thrown out in 1653, but it was found that this remnant of a Parliament was most tenacious of its rights. The members told the officers "that the Parliament expected faithfulness and obedience to the Parliament and Commonwealth." Before anything could be done to settle the points in dispute, a rising in favour of Charles, the eldest son of the late King, took place in Cheshire. Lambert suppressed this outbreak. On his return to London, Parliament refused to agree to the conditions proposed by the officers, and members were prevented by troops from entering the House. The attitude assumed by the army in these disputes was that violence to Parliament might be used if the army considered that Parliament was in the wrong, "which gives the army a superior authority, and an inspection into the proceeding of Parliament." The army had come to despise civilians because they were civilians. It endeavoured to govern without any civil authority. Taxes were only collected with difficulty. Quarrels divided the army, and the attempt at military government was a complete failure. The Rump was recalled for the second time in December and resumed its sittings.

Meanwhile, north of the Tweed, the army was not so violently affected by political considerations as the troops nearer to London and had taken no part in the setting-up and knocking-down of Parliaments. It was commanded by General George Monk, who had fought with Cromwell at Dunbar in 1650 and had been left in command in Scotland at the time of the battle of Worcester. After a period of service at sea,

Monk had returned to Scotland and reduced that country to submission. By 1658, Cromwell was uncertain of Monk's real attitude to the Protectorate, and the Commander-in-Chief in Scotland became "the object of all conjectures." When Richard Cromwell succeeded his father, Monk recommended a reduction of the army and the assembly of both Houses of Parliament. When, in October, 1659, Lambert and his supporters established a Committee of Safety, with Fleetwood at its head, Monk is reported to have said to his troops:

The army in England has broken up the Parliament. Incapable of rest, it is determined to invade all authority, and will not suffer the nation to arrive at a lasting settlement. . . . I think it is the duty of my place to keep the military power in obedience to the civil. It is the duty of us all to defend the Parliament from which you receive your pay and commission.

Monk's army was primarily a military force and everybody who disagreed with him had been gradually removed from its ranks.

After a period or delay while the situation in England was developing, he crossed the Border with some seven thousand men on January 1st, 1660, and reached London about a month later. The Rump was still sitting and wished him to coerce the City of London, which had refused to pay any taxes as it was without representation in that Parliament. Monk, however, forming the opinion that the Rump was detested on all sides, declared himself in favour of a freely elected Parliament. A dissolution was voted, and the newly elected House of Commons was filled with supporters of the Stuarts and a Monarchy. It was the natural turn of the tide. Men of all classes were weary of rule by army methods, and looked to the restoration of the old system as a means of escape from the tyranny of a military autocracy and from the recent forms of civil government which had proved to be but useless experiments.

In response to an invitation to return to this country as King, Charles, who was then resident in Holland, issued the Declaration of Breda, where Monk had gallantly led a storming party of Goring's regiment some twenty-three years earlier when he was a soldier of fortune on the continent. Amongst other undertakings, Charles offered to satisfy the army in regard to arrears of pay. The Declaration was accepted by both Houses of Parliament, and on May 29th, Charles entered London amidst the plaudits of a rejoicing population. The re-establishment of government by King, Lords and Commons was due to a large extent to the deep-seated popular fear of, and objection to, military rule, aided by acute divisions in the counsels of the military hierarchy. By the conciliatory terms of the Declaration, the new King had expressed his intention of governing with the aid of Parliament and not against its wishes as his father had claimed the right to do. Nevertheless, as matters developed, it seemed as if he desired to secure his throne by the retention of a strong, permanent force. It was not surprising, perhaps, that he should wish to do so. His father had failed to appreciate the parliamentary point of view. Charles II may well have thought that if he could control an army, he would ensure his own safety. Moreover, his life had been largely spent in France where the King was absolute and had well-organised and powerful military forces at his beck and call. Doubtless, Charles had absorbed ideas about the kingly office which consorted badly with the views held in this country, even by those who had been most responsible for his restoration to the throne of England.

When he became King, the New Model Army of the Civil War was still in existence. Parliament's wish was to disband that army and to trust to the militia, which was administered by the Secretary of State with the local assistance of the Lords-Lieutenant, who enjoyed the patronage of the force. Its officers were country gentlemen. Its members were the non-martial, peace-loving inhabitants of the urban and rural districts. Parliament's distrust of the army was profound. It still feared that it might be used as a weapon for the coercion of the country. It was loath to give to the King the control of a force which would look to him for its pay and privileges. It was jealous of the army commanded, as it would be, by the King. Parliament distrusted the army and believed in the militia.

Whatever Charles' original intentions may have been, he was wise enough to accept and act upon the advice tendered to him by Edward Hyde, afterward first Earl of Clarendon. It was agreed that the army raised by Parliament was to be dissolved by acts of Parliament, money being raised to pay off the troops. But, whatever Parliament's aversion to a standing army may have been, disturbances in London, the threat of trouble in Scotland, and the necessity of throwing a garrison into Tangiers, prevented the total disbandment of all the then existing regiments. The King was allowed to keep garrisons in certain fortified places and to retain some of the regiments which had helped the cause of the Restoration. He seized the opportunity which these difficulties afforded, and raised the strength of the troops before long to some five thousand men. This body was the nucleus of an army which was further increased to a strength of sixteen thousand by the end of his reign. . . .

* * *

His brother, James, who was fifty-two years of age when he succeeded to the throne in 1685, had taken part in four campaigns with Turenne and two with the Spaniards. He was interested in military affairs and had reorganised the Board of Ordnance on a system which was largely adopted in later days by the Duke of Wellington. He had no confidence in the militia which was the only military force then recognised by law and wished to see it set aside. He desired to maintain and augment the regular army which had been strengthened in the preceding year by the arrival home of the garrison from Tangiers and of six regiments from Holland. The Duke of Monmouth's rebellion in the West of England and the attempted rising headed by the Duke of Argyll in Scotland no doubt emboldened him to approach Parliament with a request for assistance in the support of the increased standing army. His revenue was not large enough to meet the extra charges involved, and naval expenditure was absorbing considerable sums. The army was still regarded, more especially in the House of Commons, as a body associated with all the evils of the last half-century. It was thought to be an instrument of oppression. It was held up to obloquy as a weapon of the tyrant, whether he be King or Protector. The days of the Major-Generals were not forgotten. When Parliament met, opposition to the increases in the army was aroused by the King's request for means with which to meet the additional charges. It mattered not to the members that the King's supporters pointed out how incompetent the militia was, and how much superior a military force would be if it were a properly trained and disciplined body of men. The members of the House of Commons preferred to rely on a hastily enrolled militia rather than on a standing army, the mere thought of which filled them with consternation and alarm. They protested against the continual employment of officers who had not subscribed to the conditions imposed by the Test Act, even if the King declared that he could depend on those officers. James asked Parliament for £1,400,000. Parliament voted him £700,000, but for no specific purpose. The country was alarmed at his high-handed action in employing officers who did not subscribe to the rites of the Anglican Church. Protestant refugees who had fled from France after the Revocation of the Edict of Nantes by Louis XIV had spread tales of what might follow in the train of an army controlled by Roman Catholics. The protests were not confined to the members of the House of Commons. Viscount Mordaunt, afterwards third Earl of Peterborough, a man who was to come to greater prominence during the war of the Spanish Succession, said in a debate in the Upper House that the evil which they were considering was neither future nor uncertain. A standing army existed. It was officered by Papists. They had no foreign enemy. There was no rebellion in the land. For what then was this force maintained except for the purpose of subverting their laws and establishing that arbitrary power which was so justly abhorred by Englishmen? The King was unmoved by the opinions expressed in either of the Houses of Parliament and, refusing to part with the officers concerned, prorogued Parliament the following day. It was not summoned again during his reign.

From that time onwards, the sequence of events marched rapidly towards the inevitable conclusion in a country which was determined not to submit to an armed tyranny. Some thirteen thousand to sixteen thousand soldiers were quartered at the camp at Hounslow in the hope that they would overawe London. Efforts made by the King to get the officers and men to promise to secure the repeal of the Test Act met with little or no support. In Ireland, the King's Deputy, Tyroconnel, was allowed to expel Protestant officers and men from the army to make room for Roman Catholics, and no Protestants were allowed to enlist. Desertions from the Hounslow camp increased, and some deserters were hanged on a conviction by a court packed by the King's orders. In fact, the army was breaking in the King's hands, and there was no Mutiny Act in existence by which discipline could be enforced.

At last, the camp at Hounslow was given up, and the troops were dispersed to quarters in various parts of the country. . . . The King had decided to reorganise his army, and had arranged for a number of battalions which had been raised in Ireland to be brought over to England. Irish recruits were sent to this country to fill up the vacancies in the English regiments.

It was these events, and certain other circumstances with which we are not concerned, that determined some of the Whig and Tory leaders to put themselves into communication on June 30th, the day after the acquittal of the Bishops, with William, Prince of Orange, inviting him to land with an armed force to defend the liberties of England. On October 16th, 1688, after making arrangements for the conduct of the affairs of Holland during his absence and fitting out the expedition, the Prince embarked at Helvoetsluis, but was driven back by contrary winds. He set sail again on November 1st. A following wind carried him further to the west than he intended to go, and he was pursued by the British fleet. The wind changed, drove the English ships back up the Channel, and enabled William to effect a successful and uninterrupted landing four days later at Torbay. After a fruitless attempt to oppose his army to that of the Prince of Orange, in the course of which he was deserted by a proportion of his troops, James II left England in December.

On his arrival in London, the Prince of Orange summoned a Convention of the Estates of the Realm, at which, among other subjects, the future status of the army was discussed. . . .

The problem of the army, with which the Convention was faced, was not simple enough to be settled by a series of executive acts. It was puzzling and intricate. Within living memory, the nation had had experience of military government. It had not forgotten the weakness of a system under which the army governed Parliament. It was now suffering from the effects of an even more recent attempt by the Crown to make the army its servant. An adjustment between these two extremes was essential. It required the introduction of a delicate compromise in the constitutional system of the country which would allow neither the Sovereign nor Parliament to claim and establish supremacy in the management and control of the army. The Convention met in January, 1689, and a committee, of which the chairman was Somers, drew up the Declaration of Right. It enumerated fourteen grievances, including the statement that "the raising or keeping a standing army within the kingdom in time of peace,

unless it be with the consent of Parliament, is against the Law." At a later period, history was repeated when the Assembly of Massachusetts passed a resolution to the effect that the establishment of a standing army in the colony in time of peace was an invasion of natural rights and a violation of the constitution. There were other important statements in the Bill of Rights, in which the terms of the Declaration of Right were afterwards enacted, but the salient feature, from an army point of view, was the foregoing declaration that the consent of Parliament was required if any army was to be maintained in this country.

The year 1689, in which a member of Parliament announced that he considered "redcoats" to be among "the curses of the nation," witnessed the passing into law of a measure of first-rate importance to the army and to its future relations with the civil authority. The circumstances are well known, but must be repeated here. A regiment was ordered to march to Harwich for embarkation for service in Holland. On reaching Ipswich, it mutinied and declared in favour of James II. It set out for the north but was overtaken at Sleaford, in Lincolnshire, by a force of Dutch cavalry, to whom it surrendered. Something had to be done to cope with such a situation, as it was obvious that William III could not depend on troops whose disposition was so uncertain. There was no Mutiny Act, and the existing law gave no powers to the Sovereign by which he could maintain authority over the army. The question was brought before the House of Commons and, as a result, the first Mutiny Act was passed. It declared that standing armies and courts-martial were unknown to English law, and enacted that no man mustered for the service of the Crown should desert the colours, nor mutiny against his commanding officer. The Act was only to be operative for a period of six months. It empowered the King to deal with military crimes which did not fall within the compass of the civil law. This Act placed the army on a constitutional basis and regulated the position of the Crown in regard to the raising and maintenance of a standing army. It stated in the terms of the Declaration of Right, that it was illegal to raise or keep such an army without the consent of Parliament, and declared that

whereas it is judged necessary by Their Majesties and this present Parliament that, during this time of danger, several of the forces which are now on foot should be continued, and others raised for the safety of the kingdom, for the common defence of the protestant religion, and for the reducing of Ireland.

Prior to the passage of this measure, military law had only been called into being in the event of war. As no army existed in peace, there was no need to have a special code of law with which to govern it. In the event of war, the Sovereign or the Commander-in-Chief issued articles of war for its government. Parliamentary jealousy of a standing army had always opposed the grant of any special powers to the Crown in case it should be interpreted as a recognition of the existence of the force. A new orientation was given to the policy of Parliament in relation to the army by the settlement made when William and Mary came to the throne, which approved the maintenance of an army provided the annual vote for men was passed by Parliament. The provision of means to uphold discipline, in the force so approved, followed as the next logical step in the development of the constitutional relationship between the Crown, Parliament, and the army. The declaration in the Bill of Rights, in regard to the necessity of Parliament's concurrence in the maintenance of a standing army, was repeated annually in the preamble of the Mutiny Act up to the year 1878.

* * *

Parliament had thus established a standing army, and secured for itself certain rights in regard to it, which had hitherto been definitely considered as among the royal prerogatives or had occupied a vague and uncertain position between the Sovereign and Parliament. From this time onwards, the principal means of asserting Parliament's authority were based on the declared illegality of maintaining a standing army unless sanctioned by Parliament. The authority for its retention was renewed periodically, and was combined with the power of voting a definite number of men for a limited time with such financial supply as would enable that number of men, and no more, to be retained in military service for that time. This arrangement of the consitutional aspect of the question was probably the best that could be devised in the midst of the crisis with which the country was faced, and it still remains the keystone of the relationship between Parliament and the army. . . .

16. THE LEVÉE EN MASSE

The French Revolution came about because the more enlightened members of the upper and middle classes desired to effect a certain number of reforms in a social and political organism which was proving unable to cope with the demands of an increasingly complex world. These essentially moderate men who began the Revolution had by the summer of 1792 lost control of it to the more radical elements in the country, the Jacobins. They sought not merely a reform of the existing order of things but rather a fundamental reconstruction of French society in the name of liberty, equality, and fraternity. As a necessary prelude to this great undertaking, the Jacobins had abolished the monarchy, executed the king, and proclaimed France a Republic. Their plans for a new France involved a revolutionary reshaping of the military institutions which had been inherited from the Old Regime. The new revolutionary army would not be a group of men set apart from society and living in accordance with their own particular code, as had been the old royal army. It would be an emanation of the French people, inspired thereby with the most fervent patriotism. The decree reprinted below calling for the *levée en masse* aimed at nothing less than enrolling the whole French nation for the defense of the fatherland against those foreign foes who sought to crush the Revolution. No matter how imperfectly this goal was realized, the decree represented the first explicit statement of what has come to be known in the twentieth century as "total war."

Decree Establishing the Levée en masse 23 August, 1793

1. Henceforth, until the enemies have been driven from the territory of the Republic, the French people are in permanent requisition for army service.

The young men shall go to battle; the married men shall forge arms and transport provisions; the women shall make tents and clothes, and shall serve in the hospitals; the children shall turn old linen into lint; the old men shall repair to the public places, to stimulate the courage of the warriors and preach the unity of the Republic and hatred of kings.

2. National buildings shall be converted into barracks; public places into armament workshops; the soil of cellars shall be washed in lye to extract saltpeter therefrom.

3. Arms of caliber shall be turned over exclusively to those who march against the enemy; the service of the interior shall be carried on with fowling pieces and sabers.

4. Saddle horses are called for to complete the cavalry corps; draught horses, other than those employed in agriculture, shall haul artillery and provisions.

5. The Committee of Public Safety is charged with taking all measures necessary for establishing, without delay, a special manufacture of arms of all kinds, in harmony with the *élan* and the energy of the French people. Accordingly, it is authorized to constitute all establishments, manufactories, workshops, and factories deemed

necessary for the execution of such works, as well as to requisition for such purpose, throughout the entire extent of the Republic, the artists and workmen who may contribute to their success. . . .

7. No one may obtain a substitute in the service to which he is summoned. The public functionaries shall remain at their posts.

8. The levy shall be general. Unmarried citizens or childless widowers, from eighteen to twenty-five years, shall go first; they shall meet, without delay, at the chief town of their districts, where they shall practice manual exercise daily, while awaiting the hour of departure. . . .

11. The battalion organized in each district shall be united under a banner bearing the inscription: *The French people risen against tyrants.*

12. Such battalions shall be organized according to established decrees, and their pay shall be the same as that of the battalions at the frontiers.

13. In order to collect supplies in sufficient quantity, the farmers and managers of national property shall deposit the produce of such property, in the form of grain, in the chief town of their respective districts.

14. Owners, farmers, and others possessing grain shall be required to pay, in kind, arrears of taxes, even the two-thirds of those of 1793, on the rolls which have served to effect the last payment. . . .

18. The present decree shall be conveyed to the departments by special messengers.

17. THE REPRESENTATIVES ON MISSION

The position of the armed forces in any revolutionary regime is always somewhat ambiguous. They are supposed to defend the revolution against all its foes, foreign and domestic, but as was seen in the case of the New Model Army, by the fact that they are the one powerful and relatively stable body in an extremely unstable situation, they present a constant threat to the regime. A revolutionary government thus must take every possible precaution to insure its control over the armed forces. The Committee of Public Safety, which was in effect the government of France during the most desperate period of the Revolution, the summer and winter of 1793–1794, sought to maintain its control through the institution of Representatives on Mission. These Representatives, who were generally chosen from among the ranks of the National Convention, the revolutionary legislature, were charged with specific missions and given extraordinary, if temporary, powers in order to carry them out. Part of what was expected of a Representative on Mission is stated in the following selection, drawn from a contemporary document.

Plan of Work, Surveillance, and Correspondence Proposed by the Committee of Public Safety for the Representatives of the People appointed to the Armies of the Republic.

The National Convention has appointed representatives of the people to serve with the armies. They are to be invested with unlimited powers in order that there may be established between the frontiers and the interior of the country the most vigorous rapport. Further, they will set in motion all branches of the Republic, the armies as well as the navy, to achieve the same goal. . . . They will animate the government in all its parts with the same

From *Recueil des Actes du Comité du Salut Public*, Vol. IV, ed. F. A., Aulard (Paris, 1891), pp. 23–43, abridged. Translation by the editor.

spirit. . . . They will raise the courage of the defenders of the fatherland and they will make certain that discipline is observed. . . . They will inquire about the state of supplies, munitions, and provisions in the ports and fortified places, and about the means of attack and defense. . . . They will visit the camps, the armies, the fortified places, and above all the hospitals, in order to provide an example of courage in danger, . . . and devotion to their country. They will coordinate the authority of the administrative bodies, the genius of our industry and our commerce, and the energy of all Frenchmen in order to multiply the means and resources of the state. . . . They will swiftly extend and spread the influence and the authority of the National Convention. It is through a vigorous rapport with the Convention, by giving witness to a singleness of purpose and a uniformity of action in the exercise of the powers which have been delegated to them that the representatives of the people will affirm the unity and indivisability of the Republic and lead people to appreciate its necessity and its advantages. . . .

One of the essential duties of the representatives of the people is to come to a common understanding with the generals. . . . The generals must not feel that the surveillance exercised by the representatives of the people is motivated by distrust or anxiety. They must see them only as citizens who have been invested with great powers in order to provide a strong reinforcement for their efforts, and who are there to support them with their influence and to increase the confidence of the people in them. . . .

The representatives of the people must observe the character and the natural aptitudes of each general. They must study the principles according to which they make war, their tactics, their movements, and their actions in general. The soul of a republican hero opens to such confidence and disdains dissimulation and slyness.

It is necessary that great confidence be placed in each general, and that he sense this and be convinced of it. He must be allowed a great measure of liberty and independence of action, if he is, as we wish him, to conceive of great designs and successful plans.

The representatives of the people by their conduct vis-à-vis the generals will promote the boldness and the elevation of their plans and their enterprises. They will notice all that may be great, useful, and sound as well as that which may be merely audacious and foolhardy. The generals must see the representatives of the people as acting to support them in all that they undertake for the defense of the Republic and the success of its arms.

The representatives of the people will also observe the actions of the generals in command of the divisions, the brigades, and all the officers of the armies. They will make certain . . . of their zeal, and their exactitude in conforming with the intentions of the people. . . .

If there are still to be found among the generals, officers, and non-commissioned officers of every rank Frenchmen unworthy to bear the name, who are not absolutely devoted to the maintenance of equality and the Republic, the representatives of the people will suspend them and will have them replaced according to the manner prescribed by law, . . . They will order the retirement of officers who are suspect; they will be empowered to confine them provisionally, and to command them to retire to a distance of twenty leagues behind the frontiers and away from the armies.

They will immediately inform the Committee of Public Safety of the motives which determined the suspension of these officers and which are of a nature to require secrecy, while they will inform the National Convention of their reasons when such publicity will not harm the Republic or will not aid the guilty persons and their accomplices.

The representatives of the people will fraternize with the soldiers of the fatherland. They will visit them frequently and they will inflame their zeal. They will cause them to realize the advantages to be derived through discipline, for it is this which renders armies invincible, which makes them terrible to the enemy, . . . which teaches them to rally in the midst of a retreat, which sustains their courage, which . . . prevents routs and defeats. The representatives of the people will . . . receive their complaints. They will enlighten the soldiers and will inquire about their needs. They will let them know of the concern and interest shown by the National Convention over everything pertaining to the army. . . .

The representatives of the people will remind Frenchmen of the oath they have sworn to maintain the unity and indivisibility of the Republic and the integrity of its territory. . . .

The Committee of Public Safety believes that to have the representatives of the people sharing the fatigues of the soldiers of the fatherland and presenting themselves under all conditions will be a splendid example to them and most likely to convince the army that the National Convention wishes to share its labors and its dangers. The fact that a great number of representatives of the people have conducted themselves in this way and are still doing so has produced the best possible effects. . . .

The representatives of the people must be familiar with the total manpower resources of the army. They must make certain that the muster lists are exact. . . . A list of battalions with the names of their officers was all that a despotic government, fatuous and indolent, required. The strength of an army does not consist in the number of its battalions, but rather in the number of soldiers ready for action.

The representatives of the people will devote their full attention to the examination and the verification of the first muster, and they will then keep exact track of all the changes which may take place in each division, or even in each battalion. They will exercise surveillance over all the musters which follow. Although they may henceforth count on the civic devotion of all the officers, they should not for an instant lose sight of the duties that have been imposed upon them through the surveillance with which they have been charged. . . .

They will order commanding officers to make frequent inspections of the linen, the shoes, the clothing, and the weapons of their soldiers. . . .

They will keep an exact record of the services and of the outstanding actions of the soldiers from every branch. They will proclaim these actions at the moment of the musters and will present these soldiers to the army or to their division.

They will note the position and the movements of the army and they will keep a close record of them.

They will note and will encourage the astonishing progress that has been made by the French artillery.

They will be sure that they are being kept informed concerning the provisioning of powders and cartridges. . . .

They will have reports drawn up on the materiel for encampments.

They will examine the quality of what is being furnished to the army, its real value and its price. They will make inquiries about the markets and they will submit to searching examination the conduct of the suppliers and military contractors. They will eliminate the unimpeded brigandage that has been committed until now and they will bring light to bear on the squandering of public funds. . . .

Cities and fortified towns have . . . their resources and their particular needs. The representatives of the people will give them their most serious attention. They will know how to distinguish those which are capable of sustaining a siege. . . . One should think of putting into a defensive state only the places which are to stop the enemy and to support a siege. . . .The places that are defensible are known. It is towards these places that the attention of the representatives of the people should be drawn. . . .

In the case of towns which are threatened

with a siege, the representatives of the people will make certain that the public authorities, both civilian and military, have warned the citizens to provide themselves with the necessary provisions. They will require that the administrative bodies and the general councils of the communes expel all persons who are suspect, all those to whom certificates of civic devotion have been refused, those whose civic behavior provides reason to suspect them of being in correspondence or collusion with the enemy, or of being able to stir up trouble and disorder in a place during the siege. . . .

The representatives of the people will go to their destinations invested with the highest trust and unlimited powers for the carrying out of the mandate which has been given them. They will display great strength of character. They must realize that great responsibility is the inescapable consequence of great power. It will be through their energy, their courage, and above all their prudence that they will achieve success and glory.

(signed) The members of the Committee of Public Safety—

Guyton, Barère, Bréard, Delmas, R. Lindet, Danton, Delacrois, Treilhard, Cambon.

18. SAINT-JUSTE ON THE ARMY OF THE REVOLUTION

The implacable fervor and fanatical zeal of the true Jacobin found their most perfect personification in Robespierre's young colleague in the Committee of Public Safety, Saint-Juste. The selections below, taken from one of his speeches before the Convention and from his orders to the Army of the Rhine, to which he was assigned as Representative on Mission, give some indication as to what the Jacobins understood to be the nature of the revolutionary army and revolutionary war.

Speech of 10 October 1793 on the necessity of the government being revolutionary until the peace

Today when the Republic has twelve hundred thousand men to provide for and the people to save, today when it is a matter of proving to Europe that it no longer lies within its power to reestablish over us the authority of a tyrant, you must render the government able to support you in your plans and able to strengthen the national economy and further public happiness. . . .

Up until now there have been at the head of our armies only imbeciles and rogues. Your Committee of Public Safety has purged the headquarters, but all the officers may still be accused of not paying much attention to their duties. They do not study the art of how to conquer. They give themselves up to debauchery. They absent themselves from their units when the time comes for training or for fighting. They command in haughty fashion and therefor feebly. The veteran soldier laughs at the stupidity of the ones who lead him, and that is why we suffer defeats.

Today we lack military laws and institutions which are suitable to the Republic which we are in the process of founding. In a period of innovation all that is not new is pernicious. The military art of the monar-

From the *Oeuvres complètes de Saint-Juste*, Vol. II (Paris, 1908), pp. 84–86, 108–153, abridged. Translation by the editor.

chy no longer suits us. We have a different kind of men and different enemies. The power of a people, their conquests, their military and political splendor depend on one single point, on one particular military institution. Thus the Greeks owed their military glory to the phalanx, while the Romans owed theirs to the legion which overcame the phalanx. The phalanx and the legion should not be looked upon simply as units consisting of a certain number of men. They signified a certain order of combat, a military constitution.

Our nation is possessed of a unique character. Its military system ought to differ from that of its enemies. For if the French nation is terrible in its ardor and its fighting ability and if its enemies are ponderous, cold, and sluggish, its military system must be founded on impetuousness.

If the French nation has been impelled into this war by all the strong and generous passions, love of liberty, hatred of tyrants and oppression, and if on the contrary its enemies are mercenary slaves, automatons without passion, the system of war of the French armies must stress shock tactics.

The same sense of activity must permeate all parts of the military machine. The administration of the army must reenforce discipline.

The administrative departments of the army are full of brigands. Forage for the horses is stolen. Battalions are lacking cannons, as well as the horses to move them. There is no orderly hierarchy, for everyone steals and holds everyone else in contempt.

The time has come to remedy these many abuses if you wish the Republic to be firmly established. The government must not only act in a revolutionary manner towards the aristocrats, it must also do so with regard to those who rob the soldier, who corrupt the army by their insolence, and who, through the dissipation of public funds, lead the people back to slavery and the realm to dissolution. At the origin of all these evils are the depravity of some and the frivolity of others.

Proclamations of Saint-Juste and Le Bas as representatives of the people on mission to the armies of the Rhine

> Strasbourg — 3rd day of the 2nd month of the 2nd year of the Republic, one and indivisible. (24 Oct. 1793)

We have arrived and we swear, in the name of the army, that the enemy will be vanquished. If there are people here who are traitors, or even who are indifferent to the cause of the people, we bring with us the blade which is to strike them down. Soldiers, we come to avenge you and to give you chiefs who shall lead you to victory. We are resolved to seek out these men and to reward them, to exalt true worth and to prosecute all crimes, whoever may have committed them. Courage, brave friends of the army of the Rhine. Good fortune will henceforth be with you and you will be triumphant in liberty.

All chiefs, officers, and other agents of the government are, within three days, to give satisfaction to the just complaints of the soldiers. And at the end of this time, we ourselves will hear these complaints and we will give examples of justice and severity such as this army has not hitherto seen.

Saint-Juste, Le Bas

To the general in chief of the army of the Rhine

> Strasbourg, 9th day of the 2nd month of the 2nd year of the Republic, one and indivisible. (30 Oct. 1793)

General, you will give the order to all general officers to sleep and eat in their tents at the head of their brigades and divisions.

Saint-Juste, Le Bas.

71

I. The Military Forces of the Dynastic State

From the representatives of the people, dispatched on an extraordinary mission with the army of the Rhine, to the municipal authorities of Strasbourg.

Strasbourg, 25 brumaire, 2nd year of the Republic, one and indivisible.

Ten thousand men are without shoes in the army. You must remove the shoes of all the aristocrats in Strasbourg within the day, and tomorrow by ten o'clock in the morning, the ten thousand pairs of shoes must be on their way to headquarters.

Saint-Juste, Le Bas.

Saint-Juste to Hoche

Strasbourg, 25 brumaire, year 2

General,

Within a few days, there must not be a Prussian left, not an enemy to carry back to his own country the news of Alsace. It is up to you to demonstrate whether you are capable of delivering a noble stroke. Enflame your army. . . .

The representatives of the people with the army of the Rhine,
Saint-Juste.

Letter to Hoche

Bitche, 12 frimaire, year 2 of the Republic, (2 Dec. 1793)

At Kayserlauten,[1] you have taken on a new obligation. Rather than one victory, there must be two. It appears that the enemy has dug himself in very deeply. You should do the same as he at Rentel, Samehil, and Anweiller, on the heights of which there must be built redoubts and batteries. It was a wise measure you took in having the gorges of Pirmasens fortified. We have sent intelligent men there so that the work may be speeded up. Issue further orders to the end that the country may be made impassable. . . . Let no difficulties halt you in setting up your batteries. There does not exist an obstacle which does not arouse the courage of an intelligent, reflective man. . . .

We advise you, if the enemy should advance on Zweibrucken, to await him there, but at the same time to attack him always, without letting him anticipate you. That is the way to build up courage and hope among the soldiers. You have everything to fear if he attacks you.

To the highest possible degree, coordinate your movements with those of all the divisions on your right. . . . The whole line must strike at the same time, and strike without letting up, without permitting the enemy a moment's respite. All those who command these combined movements must be friends. . . .

Saint-Juste, Le Bas

[1] Scene of an unsuccessful attack of the army under Hoche. [Editor's note]

Robert R. Palmer

9. THE MILITARY ACHIEVEMENTS OF THE COMMITTEE OF PUBLIC SAFETY

In the summer and early autumn of 1793, the French Republic appeared doomed. Large areas of the countryside were in armed revolt against the revolutionary government in Paris while on the frontiers the armies were falling back against the advancing Allies. In this moment of supreme crisis, the Republic and, with it the Revolution, were saved primarily through the exertions of the Committee of Public Safety. Using every means at its disposal, the Committee relied on patriotic oratory as well as the guillotine to coerce, and ultimately to inspire, the French nation in the defense of the Revolution. The following selection which recounts the military achievements of the Committee of Public Safety is drawn from the already classic study of that group, *Twelve Who Ruled*, by Professor Robert R. Palmer.

The *levée en masse*, decreed by the Convention on August 23, was to be the means by which the Republic fought the war. The word *levée* means either a "levy" or a "rising." All France was to rise spontaneously in a wave of patriotic enthusiasm. Young and unmarried men were to join the armies, others to work at the manufacture of munitions; women were to act as nurses or to make tents and clothing; children also were to labor, and men past their active years were to deliver patriotic speeches, stirring up hatred of kings and arousing loyalty to the Republic. The idea of this national rising came from the Hébertists. Many others including Robespierre at first doubted its value, fearing that it represented only the desperation of anarchy. And indeed, it would have produced little more than a mad convulsion, had the country remained in what Robespierre called the wreckage of government.

It was the Committee of Public Safety that turned the *levée en masse* into a true national levy, an organized mobilization of the human and material resources of the country. Carnot and the others made the idea their own; they framed the decree and saw it through the Convention; and their chief concern in the next few months was to execute its manifold provisions.

For the first time the world saw a nation in arms. War became the struggle of a whole people—or at least was carried through on that principle, for in sober fact the whole people was hardly more eager to go to war in the France of 1793 than in the Europe of 1914 or 1939. Henceforth the old-fashioned idea of war was doomed. Before the Revolution wars had been clashes between governments or ruling families, fought by relatively small armies of professional soldiers. Many people suffered, but the people as such was not vitally concerned. The French Republic introduced a new system. When governments become the people's governments, their wars become the people's wars, and their armies the armies of the nation. . . .

The Republic had about 500,000 men under arms at the end of the summer. They were grouped in eleven armies, each named after the scene of its proposed operations.

Reprinted from *Twelve Who Ruled* by Robert R. Palmer, pp. 59–60, 79–86, 96–97, abridged, by permission of Princeton University Press. Copyright 1941 by Princeton University Press.

Four of the largest were stationed on the northern border, those of the Rhine, the Moselle, the Ardennes, and the North. Over these eleven armies there was no centralized military command, not even a general staff, but only the Ministry of War and the Committee of Public Safety. The revolutionists were afraid to make one general too strong.

The troops were in want, and to all appearances were undisciplined and demoralized. Few people, either in the ranks or in Paris, had much confidence in the higher officers; for the experienced ones were not republicans, and those who were politically suitable were seldom trained for responsible positions. The officers reciprocated by having little trust in their men. A core of the old professional army remained; but there were thousands of volunteers who, having enlisted in the excitement of revolutionary patriotism, often had aggressive political ideas; and thousands of conscripts, unwilling to serve and hard to train in the prevailing atmosphere of liberty; and, as time passed, thousands of recruits raised by the Levy in Mass, a mixed throng of young men under twenty-five, of all shades of political opinion.

Generals complained—and it was not only aristocratic generals who did so—that their men were impossible to control. Soldiers broke hours, sat idly in cafés, joined the local Jacobin societies, formed political cells of their own, read the radical newspapers from Paris, quarreled with each other over politics, corresponded with the Paris Commune, reported their superiors to the travelling representatives on mission. Careless of their equipment, they would abandon valuable cannon without making an effort to save them, thus wasting the substance of the Republic. If an engagement were lost, there was always danger of panic, led by the newer men, who were not brigaded with veterans but formed units of their own. Should there be a small success, the troops were inclined to relax prematurely, think unnecessary the further efforts that their officers called for, refuse to deliver a finishing blow, and sometimes, in

the shortage of provisions, break up into marauding bands. One French village, redeemed from the "satellites of despots," saw its food, beds, assignats and all other valuables vanish before the onslaughts of its liberators. Lawlessness prevailed especially in the Army of the North, after Custine, an ex-nobleman, was relieved of the command.

If the troops were undisciplined it was in part because they thought themselves free men. The hordes of the Republic were very different from the hosts drawn up against them. The armies of Austria, Prussia, England, Holland, Spain and Sardinia were alike in one respect: they were all composed of two classes that could not mix, a vast concourse of rustics and of unfortunates lifted from the streets of towns (even of serfs, in some of the German regiments), and a small film of hereditary aristocrats, gently bred people who gave the orders. In the French armies every man from drummer-boy to commander-in-chief took care to address everyone else as "citizen." The familiarity that thus ensued was not altogether a military advantage; but it made the Frenchman feel that a gulf divided him from his abject opponents.

The French army was a nursery of patriotism. Not all were patriots when they joined it; but the bewildered or sullen recruit could not resist forever the influence of the more emphatic personalities, nor could he, if a normal man, long belittle a cause for which he was obliged to risk his life. He heard everywhere the great words Liberty and Equality, the Republic and the Nation, the rolling thunder of the "Marseillaise" and the lighter strains of the "Carmagnole." He saw the tricolor every day at his barracks, and again in the battlefield where it fused into his moments of most tense excitement and seemed to protect him in the hour of mortal danger. He would observe also, if a man of sense, his sergeants receiving commissions and his lieutenants rising to be generals; and while his attitude to officers thus created might not always be respectful, he could at least reflect that the men who led him were men of his own kind.

Unruly but patriotic, undisciplined but enthusiastic, discouraged by defeat and by the ineptitude and colorlessness of its generals, extremely political but inclined to take a low view of politicians, the army in August, like France itself, was a formless and fluctuating mass, a new and unknown quantity in eighteenth century calculations, potentially something that might revolutionize Europe, but as yet no one knew exactly what.

The Committee of Public Safety organized the army as it organized, or tried to organize, everything else. With respect to the army it acted chiefly through Carnot.

Carnot is the one man of the Twelve who today is a French national hero. He is also one of the figures about whom controversy rages. Modern conservatives, in admitting him to the national shrine, like to believe that he was not at heart a revolutionist. They represent him as a painstaking patriot who did his duty while the world tumbled about him, surrounded by ferocious Terrorists and suckers of human blood, obliged against his will to cooperate with radicals whom he despised. Carnot the republican disappears in Carnot the organizer of victory.

In truth, however, Carnot was a republican, a radical and a revolutionary, not as brutal as Collot, to be sure, nor as doctrinaire as Saint-Just, but a man who believed that the glory of the Revolution lay more in the principles that it announced than in the battles that it might win. He never went to the Jacobin club, though he was a member; he rightly believed that the Jacobins often wasted their time in futile recrimination. . . . He was not subject to complexes, phobias or obsessions; he had no delusions of grandeur; he was as free from messianic ideas as any ardent revolutionist could be. He was not a party leader, and so, like Barère, he survived many changes of régime. He was indeed rather innocent in politics, a fact of which shrewder heads were in time to take advantage.

Carnot was ably assisted by the Minister of War, Bouchotte, who transacted much of the routine business. Bouchotte occupied a somewhat ambiguous position. He was repeatedly attacked for being insufficiently revolutionary, yet during his ministry the War Office became a hive of Hébertists and extremists. The Committee considered him indispensable and defended him publicly. Bouchotte had both administrative ability and constructive intelligence. He was a good judge of military talent. He could draw up and execute far-reaching plans. Under his orders the French army first used balloons; and it was he who built the first "telegraph" from Paris to Lille, a series of semaphores placed on hilltops which reduced to a few minutes the time needed for communication between the two cities. On this matter he had the full support of Carnot, who encouraged the inventor, and who, on August 25, transmitted 166,240 livres to Bouchotte to pay the costs.

The Committee kept watch over the armies either through Bouchotte's agents, who after September 11 were obliged to report directly to the Committee once a week, or for more important affairs through itinerant members of the Convention, who outranked all generals in the field. Sometimes the Twelve dispatched one or more of their own number. Prieur of the Marne and Saint André made a rapid tour of the northern armies in August. Couthon left shortly after their return to carry through the reconquest of Lyons. Usually, however, the Committee worked through ordinary representatives on mission. . . .

The main problem with the army, as Carnot saw it, was the problem of personnel. To this even the question of supply was secondary. Above all else, the government had to be sure that the armed forces were fighting on its side. It was necessary, therefore, to liquidate most of the older officers, and to carry on a vigorous propaganda among the troops, who, though generally revolutionary in their ideas, were not necessarily much attached to the Mountaineers who ruled in Paris.

According to Jacobin estimates, almost a thousand nobly born officers still remained, despite the waves of emigration of preceding years. These men were for the most part patriotic enough, in the sense of wanting to defend France against spoliation by foreigners. But they were rarely patriots in the Jacobin sense. The Revolution had long since gone beyond any program that they favored. They were prone, therefore, to engage in conspiracy or to lose interest in the war, not being eager to win victories for a government which they thought was ruining the country. They resented, moreover, being spied on by their enlisted men and ordered about by civilians in colored sashes. Custine, arrested on July 22, was put to death on August 27. The other generals were demoralized, fearing to assume responsibility when failure might mean the guillotine.

The purging of the army officers was one cry that could rally all the factions in Paris, the panacea from which all politicians promised a restoration of confidence. It was, however, not easy to carry out. Bouchotte went at it wholeheartedly, but with such caution as national urgency and Jacobin agitation would permit. He was aware that denunciation often sprang only from jealousy, petty irritation or personal vengefulness. He knew also that to dismiss officers wholesale, when successors were hard to find, might easily be suicidal. He therefore temporized; as late as September 7 he had only reached the point of removing officers who persisted in wearing the uniform of the Bourbons. Shortly after, as one of the many consequences of the Hébertist uprising, all officers of noble birth were suspended without more ado. On November 4 the Committee of Public Safety, feeling that the problem had become routine, turned over to the Committee of General Security the task of watching over the loyalty of the officers, and transmitted to that body its bulky records on the subject. . . .

The Republic now faced a tremendous interrogation mark. In a world where generalship had been the business of aristocrats, could a régime that denounced aristocracy conduct a successful war? Was it possible to find commoners who could lead armies? Could the middle class, which had replaced the aristocracy in so many other ways, now replace it on the battlefield? If it could, then aristocracy, as known before the Revolution, would have lost still another reason for existence. If not, democratic ideas would remain a dream.

The right men were soon found. Representatives on mission sometimes commissioned promising young officers tentatively as generals, like medieval kings knighting the valiant on the field. It was thus that Bonaparte became a brigadier at the end of 1793. Sometimes the agents of Bouchotte, acting through local patriotic clubs, sent in glowing reports to the War Office. Bouchotte and Carnot digested and compared these reports, confirmed appointments, rectified mistakes. Somehow they discerned the men of ability amid the vapors of patronage, favoritism and suspicion. It may be doubted whether any other government, in an equal time, has matched their record, for before the end of 1793 they raised to the rank of general (among others) Bonaparte, Jourdan, Hoche, Pichegru, Masséna, Moreau, Davout, Lefèvre, Perignon, Serrurier, Augereau and Brune. One of these became an emperor, eight others marshals of his empire; the remaining three (Hoche, Pichegru, Moreau) rose to be distinguished commanders under the Republic.

These twelve were all new men. Their average age in 1793 was thirty-three—four years less than that of the twelve who made up the Committee. A few were well enough born to have been officers in the Bourbon army. None, however, could have attained high rank under the old régime. They were among the first to profit from the removal of class barriers from their careers. . . .

With the enlisted men the management of personnel took the form of propaganda to build up loyalty to the government. Never before, except possibly in some religious wars, had a government gone to such lengths to assure its solidarity with the men who did its fighting. There was no such problem in the enemy armies, where common soldiers were seldom politically conscious and were indeed usually illiterate. The soldiers of the Republic—aroused by a new sense of freedom, feeling themselves to be citizens, aware of possessing rights (did not the Declaration say so?), half of them able to read, most of them until recently civilians, many of them volunteers—would not, like professionals, deliver their full powers merely at a word of command, but had also to have an idea of why they were fighting and to believe that the war was conducted for their own good.

Few allegations therefore are more doubtful than the theory of some modern French nationalists, who maintain that the Republican armies were not politically minded, and fought simply for the glory of France and the frustration of foreigners, while chatterers and cutthroats reigned in Paris. The armies were by no means likely to underrate the glory of France, but it was the new France, not the old, that aroused their emotions. They were nationalistic, but the "nation" in those days was a word of challenge to the old order.

Bouchotte and the War Office, under direction of the Committee, spent every effort to keep up revolutionary enthusiasm among the troops. Their agents were in every camp. The government took the side of enlisted men against officers, and of the volunteers against the decaying professional regiments. Between June and the following March, with funds assigned to him by the Committee, Bouchotte inundated the armies with 15,000 subscriptions to Paris newspapers. He virtually subsidized Hébert by buying up, and sending to the front, thousands of copies of Hébert's vitriolic paper, the *Père Duchesne.* He circulated 400,000 copies of the Constitution and its accompanying Declaration of Rights. Carnot himself eventually founded and edited a special journal to be read by soldiers.

The representatives on mission, . . . had many tasks, but none was more important than their work as evangelists. They carried out the gospel from Paris. They preached hatred of tyrants, detestation of aristocrats, rigor toward suspects, dark threats for the lukewarm and the faint-hearted. They appealed to the soldier's attachment to the broad changes brought in by the Revolution, and from this vague feeling tried to create something more concrete and more impassioned—loyalty to the Republic. And they sought to identify, in the soldier's mind, the Republic with the Mountain, the purged Convention, and the Committee of Public Safety.

Ramsey W. Phipps

20. THE ARMIES OF THE FIRST FRENCH REPUBLIC

Where Professor Palmer would attribute the astounding success of the French armies in the years after 1793 to the herculean labors of the Committee of Public Safety and to the new energies released within the people by the Revolution, the late Colonel Ramsey Phipps of the British Army takes a different view. It is his contention that the armies of the French Revolution were successful only to the degree that they adhered to the time honored canons of military discipline and organization. Col. Phipps argues that almost every ideologically inspired effort to intervene in purely military matters ended in disaster for the French. The following selection is drawn from the first volume of his *The Armies of the First French Republic*.

English soldiers, sprung from a race trained in public meetings, beginning with the Parish Councils, know pretty much what to think of Parliamentary spouters. To the French Private, as to most of his class in the nation at this moment, the New Jerusalem had descended on Paris. In the ranks, as in the cottages, there long existed a pathetic belief in the virtuous aims of the foolish and sanguinary party that had seized the reins of government in France. It was hard not to credit the denunciations against the officers which were showered from Paris with such authority; and when defeat came it was so consoling to believe that some treachery had been at work. The men were assured that the reign of Love and Equality had begun. If no effects were visible, surely that must be the fault of some rebel or traitor? Nor was it one shock only which the army had to bear from emigration. One commander, Marshal Bouillé, had gone over to the enemy on the failure of the King's flight to Varennes. Next another, Lafayette, left his army almost in presence of the enemy and crossed the frontier. Then Montesquiou, commanding

in the south, followed this example. The first act we know of the future Marshal Davout was when he fired on the Commander-in-Chief of the main army of the Republic, Dumouriez, the successor of Lafayette, then engaged in an attempt to overthrow the Government in conjunction with the enemy. Small wonder if men looked in each other's faces to ask, "Are you a traitor?" Matters were made worse by the decree which for a time drove from the army those Nobles, such as Davout and Grouchy, who had remained faithful to the Republic. From this cause, and from the emigration, the changes amongst the officers were enormous. Between 1791 and 17th July 1792 five hundred and ninety-three Generals had been replaced.

Fortunately enough good sense remained to prevent the regulars being altogether submerged. Although here and there some Republican spouter of patriotic sentiments found his way to command, the hard test of war found such men so wanting that they had to be replaced, and fortunately the slayers were apt to turn on their own instruments. No doubt the army, if left to it-

From Ramsey W. Phipps, *The Armies of the First French Republic* Vol. I (Oxford, 1926), pp. 20–25, abridged. Reprinted by permission of the Clarendon Press, Oxford.

self, would have rectified the confusion, but the natural growth of discipline and organization was delayed by the action of the Convention, which placed it entirely under the civil power.

After certain essays, on 30th April 1793 it decreed the system of the *Représentants en mission*. Establishing eleven armies, it sent Representatives to them, generally four to each. These men were given the fullest powers. . . . Alongside every commander was placed a sort of Committee with full powers over him.

To wield an army with effect a commander requires full power and the confidence of his troops, but the Representatives and the Ministers were jealous of all authority except their own. When a commander grew popular with his troops, he became an object of suspicion to these watchers and, if he could not be denounced, he was shifted to another force, so that he could be the more easily dealt with. When a sort of half approval is given to the sanguinary means by which such men as Saint-Just "restored discipline" in the army, it is forgotten how discipline came to be so relaxed. One of the crimes which sent Custine to the scaffold was his attempt to restore discipline in his Armée du Nord. When his successor, Houchard, was arrested, he was at once sent to the common prison, evidently to degrade him as much as possible. . . .

These men might have done much good, as indeed some did, by working with the commanders and assisting them in matters within civil cognizance. Unfortunately they too often aspired to command. Ordering impossible or fatal movements, interfering with each detail of command, seeing treason in everything, indiscriminately inflicting death, and what was worse than death, disgrace, these men dazed the Generals and deprived rank of all prestige. Bewildered, half murmuring, the troops saw Generals that had led them to victory hurried to the scaffold. Had any General won continued success and gained sufficient hold over his men, the wild disorder caused by the Rep-

resentatives would soon have ended. Unfortunately the desertion of so many Generals and the defeats of others, often caused by the Representatives, robbed the commanders of proper power. . . .

One crime of the commanders often was not really defeat but that they had attacked the work of the army officials. Men of vigour, such as Dumouriez and Custine, could not see with equanimity the ignorance, sloth, and carelessness of the officials on whom the welfare of their men depended. Few things are so comforting as the ardour and knowledge with which Napoleon attacked such officials. He, almost alone amongst Sovereigns, possessed regimental experience, and shooting a few commissaries was ever his suggestion to a commander in difficulties about supply. But the days of Napoleon were yet far off and at this period the officials had a terrible instrument of defence ready to their hand. The officer who complained of them must be a bad patriot, and for him broad and smooth lay the road to the scaffold. Little knowledge of human nature is required to understand that the Republican system of killing unsuccessful commanders, far from spurring on the survivors, did but dispirit and confound the successors of the murdered Generals. Once in command of an army, a General soon found how much his will was limited by the interference of the Representatives with him, as well as by the disorganization and defects of the army itself. Realizing his difficulties, he saw the gulf before him. Death if he halted to reshape his forces, Death if he attacked and were defeated; whilst, as Houchard found, even victory might not save him. "Victory or Westminster Abbey," a glorious success or a splendid grave, were in the thoughts of Nelson as he swept on the enemy's line. A felon's fate, a dishonoured grave and execrated name, were in the minds of the commanders of the Republic. Those who believe that it was the guillotine that drove Generals to victory must remember that the commanders were not executed as blunderers, but as traitors.

Standing on the frontier, the soldiers of France faced her enemies. Those they did not fear. What they did dread was the foe in rear. In the stress of defeat, in the anxious hour of waiting, even in the very moment of victory, the hand they loathed might be laid on them. Then followed the dreary journey to the capital, the squalid imprisonment, often amidst jeering aristocrats, finally the mock trial, sure to end in death, if not in insult worse than death. The man who had hoped to leave at least an honoured name to his children too often died in the belief that his sons would be taught to shrink from his memory.

Albert Sorel

21. THE EMERGENCE OF THE ARMY AS A POLITICAL FORCE

The Revolution destroyed or seriously damaged all the ideals and institutions upon which public order and political authority in France had been founded, with one important exception, the army. As each succeeding group of revolutionaries found themselves unable to replace these ideals and institutions with any others which might be acceptable to the mass of Frenchmen, the Revolution began to flounder. It was into this incipient power vacuum that the army moved almost naturally, as the only institution able to command the support of the great majority of Frenchmen, even if this support was on occasion achieved through coercion. The following account of how the army came to act as the political arbiter in France is taken from the majestic study by the great French historian Albert Sorel *L'Europe et la revolution française*. The process here depicted may be compared with what took place in England during the Civil War.

It was in the winter of the year III, 1794–1795 that they [the armies] displayed in the highest degree their energy, their worth, and their courage. They were henceforth definitively organized and constituted as a body, and they had acquired an esprit de corps. Their chiefs were heroes and because of that heroism the soldiers admired them and became attached to their persons. . . . A military ideal little by little replaced the civic ideal in the minds of the better disciplined troops. This was a consequence not only of the discipline itself but also of the war that was being waged.

By crossing the frontier, the troops assumed a new character. They were invading the lands of the enemy in order to liberate the territory of their own country, and they believed that they were fulfilling a duty and committing a just act. . . . They were the instrument, sharp and bloody as it might be, of civilization and progress. This was something that they felt instinctively, but this instinct even though noble, bore within it less abnegation and much more pride than did previously the simple, primitive patriotism, pure abnegation and pure devotion, of the great popular levies of national defense. . . .

The generals remained republican, but their ambition drove them to raise themselves to the front ranks of that republic

From Albert Sorel, *L'Europe et la revolution française*, Vols. IV & V (Paris, 1885–1904), Vol. IV, pp. 379–381, 469–473; Vol. V, pp. 12–15, abridged. Translation by the editor.

which they had defended, to whose territory they had added, and for whose subsistence they provided. Through their negotiations with enemy generals and through the administration of occupied or subject countries, almost unconsciously they became intrigued with political affairs. It is not insignificant that a man such as Hoche tried his hand at governing provinces and handling people. In discovering for himself that he was a politician and a statesman, he saw new fields opening up to his genius. Just because this ambition was in the highest degree noble, sincere, and patriotic, its aim was more elevated, seeking the welfare of the Republic. . . . Such were the heroes of the first rank. There were others who sought only glory, but who pursued it passionately. They endeavored to keep the war going so as to provide further opportunities to obtain this glory. Then there were the legions of adventurers who thought only of brilliant display and riches. In the intervals between battles they advanced their cause by political intrigue. Some of them were quite remarkable soldiers, such as Pichegru. . . .

In 1795, most of the chiefs were still doubtless animated by the great wave of civic enthusiasm that had carried them to the frontiers and supported them during the ordeal of the Terror. They would all have signed the admirable letter which Jourdan addressed to his troops after the coup d'état of Prairial: "The army must behave under the present circumstances as it has every time that similar events have taken place. That is to say, having been placed on the borders of the country to combat the enemies from without, it does not concern itself with what is taking place at home and it is confident in its belief that the good citizens who are there will succeed in silencing the royalists and anarchists. . . ." But along with these sentiments from the heroic age, there were to be seen developing here and there in the ranks as well as at headquarters, those instincts which presaged the advent within the armies of the political age. The officers and

men of the 127th demi-brigade wrote to the Convention after the insurrection of Prairial[1]: "Legislators! . . . If detachments from the victorious armies are needed to defend the National Convention, speak, legislators! We shall fly to your assistance. The spreaders of sedition will triumph only by marching over our corpses. . . ."

The most ardent republicans were the first to draw the armies into political affairs, to order them to intervene. The Convention called them to its defense. It urged them to sign republican petitions and to vote for the new constitution. . . .

Such an intervention, which had seemed sacrilegious to the revolutionaries when it was carried out by the royal army and aimed at them, to block their path, now appeared to be legitimate, for it was aimed at defending them in their fortress and carried out by *their* army. In truth, since 1789 force had always been the deciding factor in every crisis, but until Thermidor it had been the organized force of the people. After Prairial it was the regular army. Once the army had entered political life it did not withdraw. The Directors were unable to find within themselves nor around them any other means of government. They adopted this means then, which suited them moreover by its simple and brutal nature. They tried only to attenuate its effects, or at least to blind themselves to its consequences. The Directors thought that they were averting these consequences by forming an army that was *theirs*, commanded by chiefs who were at their disposal. . . .

While making the soldier the arbiter of public affairs, they could not permit him to reason, for if he thought about things instead of blindly obeying, his train of reasoning might lead him to conclusions that were contrary to the aims of the Directors. The soldier, this simple soul, in the midst of his uncertainty as to where his duty lay, might be induced to conform to the opinion of the people as it had been legally ren-

[1] Uprising on May 20, 1795 by the people of Paris against the Convention. Put down by military force. [Editor's note]

dered in elections by the majority of citizens. . . . It was essential that the men in the ranks be of the same mind as their officers, and it was still more essential that the generals, who in the moments of crisis represented the supreme political weapon, renounce for themselves to have any political views. Otherwise the temptation might come to them to take advantage of the force that was at their disposal for the benefit of a royal pretender, or quite simply for their own benefit. Caesar, Cromwell, Monk were three ghosts which never ceased to haunt this government which at the same time had condemned itself to raise up Caesar, Cromwell and Monk.

But this dreary contradiction which was to bring about the ruin of the Directory and with it the Republic did not stop here. Although the Directors wanted this army to be available, they did not want it to be actually present, or even too close. It was necessary to keep it occupied, . . . to distract it from politics when there was no call for it, and so there had to be war. The war was also necessary to provide for the army, because the Republic did not have the means. More significant still, the army through the moneys raised in the conquered countries transformed these peoples, who were supposed to be liberated, into tributaries and thus became the chief source of supply for the treasury. France, which was without industry or public credit, . . . in which commerce had ceased, was incapable of paying the enormous taxes which the upkeep of a huge army and the prodigalities of a democratic government required. The tax-payer, when he paid, did so only in paper money which was no longer worth anything. Gold and silver, which alone counted, could only be obtained from abroad. Thus, the whole reality of power lay in the hands of the army. . . .

It was unlikely that these armies, . . . would assume a disinterested attitude concerning political affairs in which they had the decisive voice, or with regard to the conquests they had made or the tribute they had procured. They had become the

soul of the nation. All that remained of the energy, the enthusiasm, the pride of 1792 had found refuge within the armies. The people, weary of useless speeches and saturated by inert laws, turned away from the discussions in the legislative councils, which exercised no effect over the government of the country, and towards the armies which knew how to act, to cause things to happen, and which still provoked those great throbs of excitement which had become a necessity since the start of the Revolution.

As had their role within the Republic, so had the nature of the armies been strangely modified. The war had lost its unique character, that of a holy war, which it had taken on between 1792 and 1794, between Valmy and Fleurus. With the conquests that the armies had made. . .perspectives changed. Doubtless there still remained from the primitive spirit of the Revolution and from the French temperament something humane and chivalrous which made the conquests seem less harsh, but with so many tempting opportunities, . . . ambition was revived, along with greed and a desire to make one's fortune. The generals remained republican, but the particular conception they held of the Republic evolved through conquest and the war. . . .

The soldiers were aware of their importance within the Republic. They began to wonder where they were being led and who was leading them, as well as what was being done with *their* conquests. They looked to the rear, to Paris. Their vocation was no longer patriotic and quasi-mystical, but rather purely and simply martial. If the great mass of them were in the army because conscription obliged them to be there, there were many for whom the army had now become a glorious profession in which was to be obtained rank, honors, and even riches. There were a multitude of young men who could see no other career opening for them, to whom the times had given a taste for adventure, in whom had been developed physical strength, moral energy, and ambition. . . .From the

Revolution, they still preserved, in the words of Stendhal, "that excessive scorn, which was practically a sense of hatred for the behavior of the kings against whom they were fighting, . . . the belief that Frenchmen alone were reasonable beings. In our eyes, the inhabitants of the rest of Europe who were fighting to preserve their chains were only pitiful imbeciles or knaves who had sold out to the despots who were attacking us." Nowhere was the Roman ideal of the Republic more ardently maintained than in the armies. . . .The soldiers continued to claim and to believe themselves to be republican, but at the same time, they affected to scorn the lawyers, the talkers, and government by the demagogic leaders.

The Directors did not have to exert themselves very much if they wished to launch the army in an attack on parliament. It was enough to declare that the lawyers were conspiring with Pitt and the émigrés to bring about a return of the monarchs and the humbling of France. But in delivering the lawyers up to the soldiers, the Directors were delivering themselves as well, since in the estimation of the army, they were parasites of the same order within the Republic. The soldiers conceived of the Republic as something created in their own image, as being glorified by them and led from triumph to triumph for the splendor and happiness of France. . . . For reasons of prestige the Directors would always have to associate a general with themselves and with their policies, but they would soon become disillusioned with one, only to delude themselves about another immediately after. They were never able to find any means of getting rid of the favorite of the moment except by disgracing him, which made of the favorite a malcontent and perhaps even a rebel. Alternately, they would call the army into the affairs of state and then come to fear it, make much of the generals and then hate them, deliver power over to them and then quibble with them as to how it should be exercised, place all their hopes in them and then work against

them, . . .assert in haughty tones the supremacy of civil authority and then exercise that supremacy by means of the sabers of these same generals. Little by little, they thus made a series of capitulations, surrendering to the military, with rage in their hearts and lost to all shame, both themselves and the whole Republic. . . .

All this could only end with a general taking over the government of France. One idea dominated the minds of all Frenchmen: To enjoy the fruits of the Revolution in a glorious peace, that is, internal order, intelligent governmental administration, guarantees of security and work, the Civil Code, and the boundaries of the nation at her natural frontiers. France would belong to the person who could fulfill these demands. It would be a victorious general, for only through such a one could the victory be obtained that was necessary for peace to be imposed on Europe, and the double prestige accruing from these victories and from the peace would be the only things that would permit any government to dominate the various factions. . . . The Directory in conjunction with the two legislative councils was only organized anarchy, while the conquest of the natural frontiers meant systematized war. War and anarchy led inevitably to a military dictatorship for a nation that wanted order and victory.

With a precarious government and in a society which was still in convulsions, the army constituted the only organized force. . . . The army was profoundly national and everyone who fought in it identified his own cause and his own ambitions with the independence of the Republic and the consolidation of the Revolution. Nowhere was anyone at the same time. . .less Jacobin and less royalist. The soldiers were against the royalists, who by reestablishing the Old Regime would despoil the officers of their ranks and the whole army of its prestige, while the Jacobins, once in power, would have reduced the supremacy of the army by subordinating it to the civil authorities. . . .The republicans had made of the soldiers the arbiters of power within the state. It was natural for them to seek to possess that power for themselves. . . .

Their accession had been foreseen. As early as 1790 Rivarol had said: "Either the king will have an army, or the army will have a king. . . .Revolutions always end with the sword: Sulla, Caesar, Cromwell." In 1791, one of Mirabeau's secretaries who espoused some of his master's views wrote: "Seeing that the present dynasty has inspired nothing but distrust, people will prefer the authority of some successful soldier or of a dictator created by chance." In the same year Catherine the Great wrote: "Caesar will come. . . . Do not doubt it." And in 1794: "If France gets out of this, she will be possessed of more vigor than ever. She will be as obedient as a lamb, but a man is required, of superior ability and courage. . . ." Finally in 1795, the Duke of Richelieu declared: "By the nature of things, France will have a king, but this king will not be of the house of Bourbon." . . .

Force of circumstances carried to power a general, but it could not determine which general would be the one. . . .Among those who by their services to the Republic had been placed in the front ranks, one could imagine several choices. None had rendered greater services than Carnot, but if he had been the "Organizer of the victory," he was neither a victor nor a conqueror. . . .With Hoche one would have seen in power a spirit of enterprise, pride and shrewdness; . . .with Bernadotte, diplomacy; with Pichegru, a taste for intrigue. . . .

These are only empty and idle diversions. History does not admit fictions. The fact is that Hoche died before the moment was ripe, Pichegru went astray amidst his plots. . . and Bernadotte. . .was satisfied to be left as Prince of Sweden. The Committee of Public Safety itself designated who was to be the dictator. . . . It arranged for Bonaparte the means of entry. It was only a coincidence perhaps, but Bonaparte wished to succeed in life, and so he went to Paris to seek an opportunity. The Revolution was filled with them. If he had not met Barras, . . .if there had been no 13 Vendamaire, he would have found other men and other circumstances from which he would have profited. The reasons for which he was employed by the Committee of Public Safety were fortuitous; those which led him to gain mastery within the Republic were not.

22. THE RISE OF NAPOLEON BONAPARTE

While in France, after the fall of Robespierre, the revolutionary fervor of the Convention subsided into the corruption of the Directory, the army continued to spread the Revolution beyond the frontiers of France. In each of the lands conquered by these seemingly invincible soldiers, the ideas of the Revolution penetrated as well, acting as a dissolvent of traditional institutions and time honored ways. In this great epic of conquest, many brilliant careers were made and none more than that of a young general of artillery, Napoleon Bonaparte. Few generals have known better than Bonaparte how to inspire devotion in the men under his command, none how to exploit his conquests to his own political advantage. The following selections, which are drawn from the dispatches and orders of his Italian Campaign of 1796–1797, demonstrate the way in which he used his military genius, along with the rhetoric of the Revolution, in an effort to create a personal following within the army and even among the conquered peoples, thereby preparing for himself a political career. When the French people, wearied by the corruption, the incompetence, and the political instability of the Directory, looked to the army to impose a degree of order upon the country, Bonaparte was ready to answer their call.

Bonaparte's Proclamations to the Army of Italy

27 March and 26 April, 1796
(7 Germinal and 7 Floréal, Year IV)

Soldiers, you are naked, ill fed! The Government owes you much; it can give you nothing. Your patience, the courage you display in the midst of these rocks, are admirable; but they procure you no glory, no fame is reflected upon you. I seek to lead you into the most fertile plains in the world. Rich provinces, great cities will be in your power. There you will find honor, glory, and riches. Soldiers of Italy, would you be lacking in courage or constancy?

Soldiers:

In a fortnight you have won six victories, taken twenty-one standards, fifty-five pieces of artillery, several strong positions, and conquered the richest part of Piedmont; you have captured 15,000 prisoners and killed or wounded more than 10,000 men.

Heretofore you fought for sterile rocks, made famous by your prowess, but useless to the *Patrie*; today, by your accomplishments you equal the armies of Holland and the Rhine. Destitute of everything, you have supplied everything. You have won battles without cannon, crossed rivers without bridges, made forced marches without shoes, camped without brandy and often without bread. Soldiers of liberty, only republican phalanxes could have endured what you have endured. Soldiers, you have our thanks! . . .

The two armies which but recently attacked you with audacity are fleeing before you in terror; the wicked men who laughed at your misery and rejoiced at the thought of the triumphs of your enemies are confounded and trembling.

But soldiers, as yet you have done nothing compared with what remains to be done. . . .

. . . Undoubtedly the greatest obstacles have been overcome; but you still have battles to fight, cities to capture, rivers to cross. Is there one among you whose courage is abating? . . . No, . . . All of you are consumed with a desire to extend the glory of the French people; all of you long to humiliate those arrogant kings who dare to contemplate placing us in fetters; all of you desire to dictate a glorious peace, one which will indemnify the *Patrie* for the immense sacrifices it has made; all of you wish to be able to say with pride as you return to your villages, "I was with the victorious army of Italy!"

Friends, I promise you this conquest; but there is one condition you must swear to fulfill — to respect the people whom you liberate, to repress the horrible pillaging committed by scoundrels incited by our enemies. Otherwise you would not be the liberators of the people; you would be their scourge; . . . Plunderers will be shot without mercy; already, several have been. . . .

Peoples of Italy, the French army comes to break your chains; the French people is the friend of all peoples; approach it with confidence; your property, your religion, and your customs will be respected.

We are waging war as generous enemies, and we wish only to crush the tyrants who enslave you.

To the People of Lombardy[1]

H.Q., Milan
30 Floréal, Year IV (19 May, 1796)

The French Republic, which has sworn hatred towards tyrants, has also sworn brotherhood towards the peoples. This

[1]This and the following letter are reprinted from *Letters and Documents of Napoleon, Volume I, The Rise to Power*, by John Eldred Howard, pp. 116–117, 121–122. Copyright ©by John Eldred Howard, 1961. Reprinted by permission of the Oxford University Press, Inc. and Cresset Press Ltd.

principle, sanctified in the Republican Constitution, is that of the army.

The despot who has so long held Lombardy enslaved has done great evil to France; but Frenchmen know that the people do not support the cause of kings. The victorious army of an insolent monarch must doubtless spread terror among the nation it has conquered; a republican army, forced to wage war to the death against the kings, swears friendship to the peoples whom its victories free from Tyranny.

Respect for property and for persons; respect for the religion of the people: these are the sentiments of the Government of the French Republic and of the victorious army in Italy. The clearest proof is the good discipline it has kept since its entry into Lombardy.

If the victorious French seek to treat the people of Lombardy as brothers, these owe them a just return.

The army has to continue its victories; it has to drive the despot who held Lombardy in chains out of the whole of Italy. The independence of Lombardy, which should bring it happiness, depends on the success of the French; it must aid them.

To assure their march the troops need provisions which cannot be drawn from France, which is so far away; they must find them in Lombardy, whither their conquests have led them. The laws of war assure this; friendship should make haste to offer it.

Twenty millions of francs must be contributed by the various provinces of Austrian Lombardy; the needs of the army require them. . . . That is a very small contribution for such fertile lands, above all in view of the advantage which should ensue for them. The assessments might have been carried out by agents of the French Government; that would have been legal. But the French Republic does not so intend; it delegates it to the local authority, the State Congress. It does no more than indicate a basis: this contribution, which must, in the first place, be spread among the provinces in the same proportion as the taxes were levied which Lombardy paid to the Austrian tyrant, should fall upon the rich, the truly well-to-do, and on the ecclesiastical bodies, those who for too long have believed themselves privileged and have succeeded in evading every tax; the indigent classes must be spared. . . .

BONAPARTE. SALICETI

To the Executive Directory

H.Q., Lodi

25 Floréal, Year IV (14 May, 1796)

I have just received the mail which left Paris on the 18th. Your hopes are realized, for at this moment the whole of Lombardy belongs to the Republic. Yesterday, I sent a force to invest the castle of Milan. Beaulieu is at Mantua with his army; he has flooded all the surrounding country. He will succomb there, for it is the unhealthiest part of Italy.

Beaulieu still has a numerous army, having begun the campaign with much superior forces. The Emperor is sending him reinforcements of 10,000 men, who are on the march.

I think it would be most unwise to divide the Army of Italy into two, and it is equally against the interests of the Republic to put two different generals here.

The expedition to Leghorn, Rome and Naples is no great matter; it should be carried out by divisions in echelon, so that we could, by a counter-march, appear in force against the Austrians and threaten to envelop them at the least movement.

That needs not only a single general, but also that nothing shall interfere with his movements and operations. I have carried on this campaign without consulting anyone; I should have done no good had I had to come to terms with the viewpoint of another. Lacking everything, I have got the better of far superior forces because, in the belief that I had your confidence, my movements have been as rapid as my thought.

If you place all kinds of fetters on me; if I must refer each step to the Government Commissioners; if they have the right to change my dispositions, to take away or send me troops, look for no good result. If you weaken your strength by dividing your forces, if you break the unity of military thought in Italy, I must tell you with sorrow that you will have lost the finest opportunity of bringing Italy under your rule.

In the present situation of the Republic in Italy, it is essential that you have a general in whom you have complete confidence. If it is not I, I shall not complain but shall deport myself with ever more zeal to earn your regard in whatever post you may place me. Each one has his own way of making war. General Kellermann has more experience and will do it better than I; but the two of us together will do it very badly.

I can render important services to our country only if I have your complete and absolute confidence. It needs much courage to write you this letter, for it would be so easy to accuse me of ambition and pride; but I owe you the recital of all my feelings, for I cannot forget that you have always given me evidence of your regard.

The various divisions are occupying Lombardy. When you receive this letter we shall already be on the march, and your reply will probably reach us near Leghorn. Your decision in this affair will be more decisive for the outcome of the campaign than 15,000 reinforcements that the Emperor might send to Beaulieu.

BONAPARTE

Godefroy Cavaignac

23. THE FRENCH REVOLUTION AND THE REFORM OF THE PRUSSIAN ARMY

The efficacy of the military institutions of Revolutionary and Napoleonic France was proven time and again on the field of battle. A state could afford to ignore the French example only at its peril, as Prussia discovered in 1806 in the wake of the Battles of Jena and Auerstadt. Decisively defeated and all but annihilated as a political entity, Prussia, under the impulse of a small band of dedicated men, set out to reform her political and above all her military institutions. Taking from the French those military ideas and institutions which had proven most effective, in particular universal conscription, and adopting and reconciling them to the realities of the Prussian political situation, these reformers forged a new army with which Prussia returned to the war in 1813, to play a decisive role in bringing about the downfall of Napoleon. An account of this great achievement and its implications for the later history of Europe is given in the following selection from *La Formation de la Prusse Contemporaine*, by the French politician and historian, Godefroy Cavaignac.

It had been the chief reason for Prussia's existence, to embody at the heart of Germany the idea of the modern state, the concept of a state thoroughly equipped for the carrying out of social ends. . . .The same profound causes which had led the Prussian state to emerge in the midst of the fragmented Germany of the eighteenth century, drove it to forge for the enslaved Germany of 1812, the instrument of its imminent liberation. The events which had taken place over the past twenty years indicated to Prussia the manner in which this might be accomplished.

The achievements of the French Revolution, by revealing new sources of national energy and popular strength led people everywhere to seek the development of this strength in the extension, in the nationalization of military service. . . . The example provided by the various insurrections in Europe also had a decisive influence on those European states which were anti-Napoleonic. The wars in the Vendée, the Tyrolean uprising, and above all the insurrection in Spain, which permanently checked the invincibility of Napoleon, exercised a considerable moral influence by proving how strong national sentiment could be when it was pushed to the point of sacrifice. . . . Thus everything that had happened within the past twenty years, the military successes of the Revolution, the resistance that it had encountered, the uprisings which had halted Napoleon, all showed that military force would henceforth have to be sought in the heart of the nation. One saw little by little spreading and prevailing the idea of compulsory military service, involving the whole nation.

The establishment of universal military service was in the development of the Prussian state a decisive and essential

From Godefroy Cavaignac, *La Formation de la Prusse contemporaine* (Paris, 1898) Vol. II, pp. 310–311, 389–402, abridged. Translated by the editor.

achievement. It is thus worth comparing the great legislative measures at the start of the War of Liberation with the similar ones that the aggressive designs of Europe imposed on the French Revolution. . . .

The legislative measures which in 1813 readied the army of liberation in Prussia and the decrees by which in France the revolutionary armies were organized and constituted present in their overall aspect. . . certain striking analogies and a kind of parallelism. . . .

The situations were in certain respects comparable. In both cases the nation was carried away by one of those ardent movements which suspend the whole social life of a people, although the origin of the two movements, and the ideas which instigated them were very different. In both cases, the community as a whole was roused to safeguard its independence, and its intellectual patrimony against foreign powers. These wars were no longer prolonged and listless affairs, in which vigorous action was paralyzed by a multitude of vacillations, and in which, by the conventions which surrounded these wars, destruction was limited, . . . Nations driven to the defense of their own cause would no longer tolerate anyone trying to restrain them or to prevent them, because of some convention or other, from the unlimited utilization of all the resources at their command.

In both cases, the men to whom effective responsibility for leading the movement had fallen were convinced that the salvation of the threatened nationality depended on an eruption of the energies of the people. This conviction on the part of the Prussian patriots stemmed from the great example supplied by the French Revolution, and it was graven in their minds. The writings of Gneisenau allow no doubt on this point.

But in both France and Prussia, the great undertaking to guarantee the independence of the nation, as well as its effective organization, conflicted with the still dominant intellectual currents of the eighteenth century and with the universal disrepute into which the traditional military system had fallen. It is well known how vigorous this sentiment was among cultivated Germans at the beginning of the century. It had been proclaimed by Kant and even admitted by Scharnhorst. It was no less alive in France at the start of the Revolution. . . .

But the force of events were in singular fashion to unsettle this philosophical humanitarianism, this pacific and bourgeois optimism. It had first become evident for the French in the era of the Revolution and it was now becoming evident for the Germans of 1813, that a well constituted and organized military system, and sometimes even war with all its hardships, were the necessary guarantee of the welfare of society and, in particular, those aspects of it which are most dear to the philosophical spirit. Reality with its laws of iron demanded of the idealists of intellectual Germany as it had of the humanitarian philosophers of the Revolution, a vast effort aimed at safeguarding the nation and defending its moral and material interests.

The old style armies with their inherent weaknesses, with the panoply of abuses, defects, and disrepute that they carried with them, were no longer sufficient for this great task. The Germans, having had to endure a practical demonstration of this truth, were that much more aware of it. The solution in both countries appeared to be the same. The nation as a whole would rise up to defend its dearest possession, in one case that liberty which it had just won, in the other the independence it had just lost. But in neither country were people willing, at first, to fuse the national army which had been raised up in a surge of enthusiasm and the old army of the line, which they considered as being scarcely more than a suspect band of mercenaries.

In France as in Prussia, the distinctions maintained with so many precautions, because of the fears and the ulterior motives of the legislators, did not take long to disappear. They were carried away in the midst of the national effort to which all were devoted and in which all energies were merged. In France, the *amalgame* was more complete, more rapid. The army of the line and the national army were for a moment distinct, but the unity of the revolutionary army was quickly established. The national army appeared to have absorbed the old permanent army, but because of the prolongation of the war, it soon took on in its turn the characteristics of a permanent military organism. Within a few years, the revolutionary army had become the imperial army.

In Prussia, although it was first thought to limit the Landwehr to the defense of each province, Landwehr battalions were soon called upon. . . to fight alongside of the old battalions of the line. . . . But this fraternity of arms did not result in the suppression of the individuality of the Landwehr. At the end of the war, there was still an army of the line and a Landwehr. There had taken place neither a merging of the two bodies, nor an amalgamation. . . .

In sum, at a first superficial glance the French and the Prussian systems appear to be quite similar. But a closer examination reveals fundamental divergences between them.

In France, the decrees of the revolutionary assemblies provided no clear statement of the idea that there existed a universal obligation with regard to military service. When Dubois-Crance for the first time formulated before the Constituent Assembly the fundamental principle underlying the theory of compulsory military service, that all citizens are equally liable to serve, to pay the *impôt de sang*,[1] the Constituent rejected it without hesitation. . . . Later, even the Convention voted down the principle of compulsory military service the first time that it was presented.

Nevertheless, the hour came when necessity finally had to be recognized, but even when the Convention accepted it, the principle was not to be applied in a regular and systematic way. Rather, it was swallowed up in the momentary and disorderly confusion of the *Levée en Masse*. . . . The

[1] Literally, blood-tax. [Editor's note]

decrees of August 1793, by which were organized the masses of effectives for the revolutionary armies, proclaimed for the first time that military service was to be a universal obligation, subject to no restrictions and with no provision for the procurement of substitutes. But the Committee of Public Safety conceived of and presented this measure of "permanent requisition" only as a momentary effort. . . . For as long as the Revolution lasted, the efforts necessary for national defense had this air of being a voluntary surge, something spontaneous, rather than an obligation that was regularly and systematically imposed.

Once the crisis seemed to have been surmounted in the wake of the great national outburst, the idea of universal, compulsory military service did not remain in the laws of the country. . . . In the general reorganization of society which followed the great turning point in the Revolution, and in which the new military institutions were given so large a place, the system of recruitment, nationwide conscription based on the drawing of lots, was set up with a provision for the procurement of substitutes.

It was by no means the same in Prussia. The idea that there was a universal obligation for military service was evident from the start. In all the projects that were drawn up after the defeat of 1806, this was manifestly the fundamental idea of the Prussian patriots. In their eyes the nation that was now threatened could only be saved through the efforts of all its citizens. It was the duty of all to participate in the great work of national defense and that obligation must be inscribed in the law. . . . The universal obligation for military service was not only a legislative principle, it was from 1813 on a palpable reality.

Thus, from the beginning in this parallel development of analogous institutions, the fundamental difference between the two peoples was to be clearly seen: one accustomed to rely more on a spontaneous élan, to which all freely gave their consent; the other, on that constraint which the modern state imposes on all its citizens for the accomplishment of the common goals of the whole society.

Prussian historians have gone too far, however, when they insist on seeking out in the ancient origins of the Prussian state the principle of universal compulsory military service. An ordinance of Frederick-William I proclaimed it as early as 1733, but it was little more than the enunciation of a Platonic principle. All the ordinances of the eighteenth century did not prevent the army of Frederick II from being an army of mercenaries. It was only in 1813 that the universal obligation for military service became part of the customs of the country, but it became a definitive part of them at that point. It really formed the basis for the legislation of 1813. The relative ease with which Prussia adopted the principle points up one of the significant features of the Prussian people, a people accustomed over a long period of time to rely on themselves, and imbued with the necessity of undergoing for the achievement of common goals whatever sacrifices, even harsh ones, the community demands. In this case, for the formation of a new army, the people accepted these sacrifices that much more easily, since their submission to the supremacy of the landed nobility was of long standing, and since this landed oligarchy was by its whole tradition a military caste.

But, in the principle of compulsory military service there is more than simply the idea of a harsh sacrifice, accepted by the whole citizenry for the defense of the nation. By the very force of things, the idea of democratic equality was also introduced.

It is true that the Prussians in 1813 were far more prone to see in their new military legislation the idea of a sacrifice made out of a sense of social duty in the interests of the community, and not any measure promoting equality. . . . Nevertheless, compulsory service, from the moment that it was genuinely required, introduced, in spite of everything . . . a principle of democratic equality into the military institutions of Prussia. And when the crises which had shaken the whole of Europe were terminated, when peace and calm had returned to the continent, it happened that old monarchical Prussia, with its feudal landed class, with its social hierarchy, emerged from the upheaval endowed with a mode of recruitment the principles of which were more in keeping with the spirit of the new century than that of revolutionary France. This was a decisive factor for the history of the nineteenth century.

II. *The Armed Forces of the National State*

The national state which took shape during the course of the nineteenth century was a far more formidable political organism than the dynastic state from which it had evolved. European society in the centuries preceding the French Revolution had been relatively simple in structure, with the great mass of the population made up of self-sufficient peasants living at a bare subsistence level. To all intents and purposes, they did not enter the political process except as a docile group to be exploited in the interests of the state. Government functioned almost exclusively in terms of the aims and aspirations of a small ruling elite and the making of state policy was thus a comparatively simple affair. When, under the impact of the democratic ideas disseminated through the French Revolution, government came to be understood as involving the aims and aspirations of a whole society, the making of state policy became less simple. Concurrent with this democratization of the political process, there was another phenomenon evolving which was inexorably changing the shape of European society and, along with it, the European state.

The Industrial Revolution created vast new sources of wealth, it quickened the pace of technological progress, and it led to the growth of huge urban agglomerations. It also necessitated a tremendous increase in the scale of the state. Within a stable, self-sufficient rural society, the maintenance of order and the regulation of internal affairs are simple matters, demanding little in the way of government. It is different with an expanding industrial society. There the social and economic complexities of an urban way of life require that the government perform an ever increasing variety of functions. The rapid growth in the population of Europe during the nineteenth century also worked to increase the scale on which the state now had to operate. Whatever the form of government, this expansion in the scope and the complexity of the civil imperative in an increasingly democratic, industrial society meant that the power of the national state would dwarf anything seen in previous centuries. The accelerating process of social and economic change also had a profound effect on the military needs of the European states.

Europe in the nineteenth century was potentially able to devote a far larger proportion of the energies of society to military endeavor than had hitherto been possible. Technological progress in both agriculture and industry was such that it was becoming feasible to think of enrolling, at least temporarily, the whole young manhood of a country for war, and thus to move from the rhetorical flourishes of the decree on the *levée en masse* to its actual realization. The huge increase in the potential size of the war effort demanded concomitant changes in the permanent military institutions of the national state, as provisions now had to be made for training most of the eligible men of military age and for their mobilization at the outbreak of hostilities. At the same time, technological advances and the introduction of a variety of new weapons signified that the conduct of war would be a far more complex and difficult matter than in the past. Gone were the days when the task of an officer did not go much beyond making sure his men knew how to march in step, to maintain straight ranks, and to load and fire in unison. Before the century was over, an officer, and at a fairly low rank in the military hierarchy, would have to become a specialist in the management of violence, violence which would be expressed through an articulated and subtle mechanism. To be an officer was coming to demand a high degree of professional training and constant application. The officer corps was thus being made into a professional caste with its own particular institutional interests, quite apart from the interests of the state and society it served.

The first state to perceive and to react to the military implications that were inherent in the social, economic, and political forces of the new century was Prussia. The twin catastrophes of Jena and Auerstadt had been more than simply a defeat for Prussian arms. They had called into question the very principles upon which the Hohenzollern polity was founded. In the years immediately following, a dedicated band of reformers led by Stein and Scharnhorst sought to recast the bases of both the army and Prussian civil society, in such a way as to break down the old barriers between them and to instill within the passive and obedient subjects of the king a feeling of identification with the aims of the state. They saw the creation of a sense of citizenship within the Prussian people, coupled with a fundamental reform in the organization of the army, as the most effective means of revitalizing the state for the great task of overcoming their French conquerors and of guaranteeing Prussia's place in the future as a great European power.

With regard to the reform of the army, they were particularly successful, possibly because their aims were limited and the programs to be undertaken concrete, with only incidental ideological overtones. In addition to instituting a regular system of conscription (see selection 23), thus imparting military training to a large part of the male population, the reformers also set up the institutions whereby these masses of men could be most efficiently mobilized and utilized in case of war. For this system to function the officer corps had to have been trained in certain skills and to have mastered a considerable body of specialized knowledge. War, in short, was ceasing to be considered as an art, mastery of which was a matter of innate genius, and was becoming instead a science whose basic principles could be analyzed rationally and whose techniques could be taught. For the study of this new military science and its dissemination to a select intellectual elite, the *Kriegsakademie* was founded. The practical application of this growing body of knowledge was effected through the newly reorganized and reinvigorated General Staff. Furthermore, entrance into the Prussian officer corps was now to depend on certain educational criteria. Noble birth alone was no longer sufficient, as it had been in the days of

Frederick the Great, to assure one the possession of the qualities needed to make a good officer. This did not, in fact, lead to any marked changes in the social composition of the ruling military caste, which still continued to be recruited primarily from among the Junkers, but they were nevertheless obliged to meet a minimal intellectual standard if they wished to wear a uniform.

It was the ideal of the men of the Stein and Scharnhorst era not only to reform the existing armed forces but also to use the military needs of the state as a means of instilling within the educated classes a sense of active participation in the larger interests of the kingdom. To that end they instituted the *Landwehr,* a kind of militia recruited in particular from the middle class. The reformers saw the *Landwehr* as serving on an equal basis with the units of the regular army in time of war and thereby working to bridge the gulf which had always separated the civilian and military elements in Prussian society. In this as in their other hopes of building a more liberal political order in Prussia, the reformers were thwarted. The old military autocracy was restored, albeit on a more efficient basis, in the general reaction following the defeat of Napoleon. The *Landwehr* was never provided with adequate funds or training and the gulf between military and civil society remained as broad as ever, with the army serving above all as an instrument for the maintenance of social order.

For a moment, during the Revolution of 1848, it did seem as if the dreams of the reformers might yet be realized. Rocked by the unexpected vigor of the resistance of the people of Berlin and momentarily confused at the uncertain attitude of the monarch, the army retreated before the insurrection, leaving the populace in control of the city. Within a few months, however, both the king and his soldiers had recovered themselves and had reestablished royal authority in Berlin. In the wake of the revolution, the vacillating and inconsistent Frederick William IV granted his subjects a constitution, possibly to forestall further upheaval. Royal authority was not really impaired by this constitution, for even though a parliament with considerable rights and powers was called into existence, the crown's exclusive prerogatives over the army and its independent position within the state were not touched. It was the aspiration of the middleclass majority in the lower house of parliament to have a voice in military affairs and it was the absolute refusal of the king to countenance such pretensions which led to the great constitutional conflict of the years 1860–1866. The conflict was resolved in favor of the crown through the rude yet subtle policies of Otto von Bismarck.

Called to the post of Minister President in 1862, Bismarck proceeded to disregard the fact that parliament had refused to vote the military budget and to order the revenues necessary for an enlargement and reorganization of the army collected anyway. He then used this renovated army as an instrument to effect the unification of Germany in a way most advantageous for the interests of the Prussian state and its traditional ruling military caste. By force of arms, the other German states were brought into union with Prussia. In thus fulfilling the most cherished hopes of the nationalistic Prussian middle classes, he overwhelmed their constitutional scruples (see selection 24).

Although Bismarck was not a soldier and had a well founded distrust of the political judgment of the Prussian officer corps, he nevertheless had an acute appreciation for the role of force, as represented by the army, in politics, both domestic and international. He was therefore determined to allow the other rival elements within the body politic as little a share in discussing military matters as possible. The provisions of the German Constitution of 1871 which concerned the armed forces of the state reflected that determination (see selection 25). The continuing independence of the army from all effective parliamentary control signified that the German Empire, like the Kingdom of Prussia before it, was still a military autocracy for all its constitutional trappings. Rather than being satisfied with the high degree of autonomy they already enjoyed, the military authorities constantly sought ways to increase it. This was by 1914 to create serious political and even constitutional strains (see selection 26).

In the two decades during which Bismarck held the levers of power, the remarkable political mechanism he had fashioned worked well enough. When the young William II, having succeeded to the throne in 1888, dismissed the old Chancellor two years later, the defects in the system began to become apparent. Totally lacking Bismarck's acumen in matters of state, William had an exalted vision of his power and his prerogatives as Emperor. He was constantly reminding his subjects that he believed the one indispensible support of the throne to be the army, possessing which he might govern as he thought best (see selection 27). Where Bismarck had done his utmost to maintain the subordination of the military to the constituted authority, as vested in his own person, William, in his foolish infatuation for all things military, allowed his soldiers an increasingly large voice in deciding questions of foreign and domestic policy which were quite outside of their sphere of professional competence. That the views of a reactionary military caste could be so easily imposed on the government of a modern industrial society was indicative of the weaknesses in the Bismarckian system.

The role of the military in the political evolution of France in the nineteenth century differed noticeably from what it was in Prussia. Much of the explanation for this difference is to be found in the peculiarities of the seventeenth and eighteenth century history of each state. In Prussia both state and civil society had been brought into existence primarily in response to the needs of the army. During the nineteenth century, as state and society began to function in terms of a more purely civil imperative, their evolution was nevertheless circumscribed by what the crown and the ruling military caste considered to be their institutional interests, and by extension, the safety and welfare of the country. In France, on the other hand, the tradition of the army since the days of Le Tellier had been one of rigid obedience to the preexisting civil power as represented by the crown. If during the French Revolution the military had come to play a decisive role in politics, it was because of the power vacuum created by the decay and collapse of the traditional political and administrative institutions. Their reestablishment by Napoleon brought about a restoration of the old sense of subordination in the army. It was accentuated by the conditions of nineteenth century French political life.

Given the incessant changes of regime in nineteenth-century France, the military quickly came to see that their institutional interests could best be protected by abstaining from all political activity and by observing the strictest neutrality in the constant strife of opposing factions and philosophies. A necessary corollary to this attitude was that the soldiers serve each regime with an equal sense of impartiality, their loyalty being given not so much to the regime in question, but rather to the idea of the state or the nation which was momentarily embodied in it (see selection 28). So deeply convinced were the military as to the necessity of passive obedience to whatever powers that be and of absolute political neutrality, that in the 1872 debates over the military franchise the most vociferous and adamant opponents of giving soldiers the vote were those officers who sat in the National Assembly (see selection 29). In return for their abstention from the great social and political quarrels which were the nineteenth century legacy of the Revolution, the soldiers expected their most vital personal and professional interests to be respected. Such a guarantee was provided when in 1834 during the July Monarchy a law on the status of an officer was enacted. By its terms an officer's rank became his property, something of which he could be deprived only through due process of law. He was thus protected against arbitrary, politically motivated reprisals on the part of the government.

Relations between the army and each of the four successive regimes under which France was governed from 1815 to 1870 were facilitated by the fact that all of them, with the possible exception of the short-lived Republic of 1848, were to some degree authoritarian in spirit. All of them placed great stress on the need to maintain social and political order. Between these regimes and the army there was thus a fundamental similarity of outlook. Such a sense of compatibility was less likely to exist in the case of the regime founded in 1870, for in the following decades the political personnel of the Third Republic became progressively more democratic in their philosophy of government and in the policies they thereby advocated. It may be argued that the existence of a large, powerfully organized standing army, and the fears which it almost automatically inspired, hampered the evolution of effective democratic institutions in France (see selection 30). A large percentage, perhaps a majority, of the officer corps came from those groups within French society which were avowedly anti-republican. Nevertheless, the tradition of military aloofness from politics was by now so deeply ingrained that it functioned even with regard to a democratic regime. At no time did the army become involved in any overt actions against the Republic. When the government, frightened and angered by the attitude of the army during the Dreyfus affair, sought by a variety of unorthodox and unethical measures to "republicanize" the officer corps (see selection 31), the military, although severely wounded in their most vital professional interests, as well as in their pride, did not desert their tradition of absolute obedience to the powers that be. Indeed, by 1914 they had come to see it as the one essential prerequisite to the moral cohesion of the army and therefore its effectiveness as a fighting force.

World War I provided awesome evidence as to the military power inherent in a modern industrial society. Military specialists in countries such as France and Germany had foreseen the state's growing ability to mobilize a far larger proportion of its population than was ever possible before, and had made their plans accordingly. They had, however, been incapable of envisaging a conflict which would come to demand the commitment of something approaching the total resources, physical, fiscal, and spiritual, of the nations involved. This was to be a conflict where, as David Lloyd George has pointed out, the outcome depended as much on the resilience and morale of the home front as it did on the men in the battle line (see selection 33). Very few in the years before 1914 had any conception of the tremendous capacity for organized and sustained violence that was inherent in the nation state, and it only revealed itself in the tactical and strategic stalemate which developed on the Western Front following the Battle of the Marne. The responsible political leaders and the military experts saw no way out of the stalemate except to throw in ever larger forces, more men and more materiel, in an effort to overwhelm the enemy by sheer weight. The cost of such a style of warfare was staggering.

The first person to realize what this war might involve in terms of materiel and to take any significant steps to deal with the problem was the German industrialist Walther Rathenau. Within a few days of the outbreak of hostilities, he had convinced the military authorities that certain measures would have to be taken to husband Germany's economic resources in case of a prolonged conflict. By dint of his energy, foresight, and administrative skill, virtually the whole economic life of Germany was with remarkable speed coordinated and directed toward the war effort (see selection 32). It was somehow appropriate that the German state, whose political and social evolution had been so largely dictated by military considerations, should be the first of the belligerents to grasp, almost instinctively, the implications of what was to be known as total war. The German experience contrasts significantly with that of Great Britain.

Because of the lack of a strong military imperative over the past two and a half centuries, British statesmen and soldiers found it extremely difficult to readjust their thinking to something as gigantic as World War I. In the early days of the war, Lloyd George met with tremendous inertial resistance from the War Office as he sought ways to remedy the desperate shortage of munitions in the British units in the field (see selection 33). By the same token, it was not until 1916 that the British government finally deserted traditional reliance on voluntary enlistments and resorted to conscription to fill the manpower needs of the army.

Yet for all their seeming inefficiency and their initial inability to comprehend the magnitude of the conflict, in the long run the democratic governments of France and Great Britain proved more able to mobilize the energies of their peoples for war than did those of the more traditionally militaristic states. In Germany, where the peculiar requirements of the ruling military aristocracy had stunted the growth of a healthy political life and the development of a vigorous political elite, civil leadership proved unequal to the extraordinary demands of total war. The military in the person of General von Ludendorff found themselves impelled to supply the political initiative which neither the Chancellor,

Bethmann-Hollweg, nor the Emperor could provide (see selection 34). Although a man possessed with tremendous force of character and a driving will, Ludendorff was too rigid in his outlook, too prone to see the total war effort in solely military terms, to succeed (see selection 35). By way of contrast, in both Great Britain and France, the normal play of the political process, somewhat altered by war-time pressures, brought forth dedicated and forceful civilian leaders, who possessed both tenacity of purpose and political skill. Clemenceau in France and Lloyd George in Britain managed to galvanize and inspire their peoples in ways that Ludendorff could never emulate. The quality of its political leaders was by no means a negligible factor in the victory of the Allied cause.

Every European government declared war in 1914 with the classic aim of employing military means to promote some rational and limited policy of state. Such, however, was the scale on which modern industrial society was now capable of waging war, and such was its capacity for organized and sustained violence, that in a very real sense the responsible leaders of the belligerent powers soon lost control of the conflict. They now fought simply to win, for nothing that any state could hope to attain through victory, short of the impossible and irrational goal of absolute hegemony over the vanquished, was possibly commensurate with what the war was costing. In the process of achieving a purely military decision, the belligerent powers exhausted the physical and spiritual capital on the basis of which a remarkably stable and effective political and social order had been built over the past four centuries. How this old order was to be replaced was not apparent in the immediate aftermath of the war.

THE PRUSSIAN ARMY AND THE FOUNDING
OF THE GERMAN EMPIRE

Herbert Rosinski

24. THE PRUSSIAN ARMY, 1815-1870

Despite the catastrophic defeat of 1806 and the heroic efforts of such reformers as Stein and Scharnhorst, the essential nature of state and society in Prussia underwent few fundamental changes during the era of the French Revolution and the Napoleonic Wars. The Prussian reformers, for all their splendid aspirations, were unable to do any more than restore and revitalize the political and social organism which had been created by the great Hohenzollerns. They could not transform it. Prussia was to remain during the first half of the nineteenth century what it had been in the eighteenth century, a military absolutism whose real reason for existing was to support the army. The situation of that army and its effect on the political evolution of both Prussia and Germany is described in the following passage from *The German Army,* by Herbert Rosinski.

In Prussia and throughout the whole north of Germany political life after 1815 subsided into stagnation for nearly thirty years, and the centre of the internal political struggle shifted for a time to the smaller South and Central German territories. There, in the diets established in most of these states in the years after the Napoleonic Wars, liberalism began its onslaught upon the Standing Army. While the extremists denounced these "mercenary hordes" in terms so wild and extravagant as to be merely ridiculous and demanded their radical abolition in favour of a popular militia, the more sober elements concentrated upon an attempt to subject them to an oath on the constitution and the abolition of such marks of special status as military jurisdiction. The struggle for these demands for many years met with little success, but in the spring of 1848, when the powers of reaction overnight crumpled up before the half-tragic, half-fantastic intermezzo of the Revolution, their realization at last seemed to be within reach. In prac-

tically all German states the troops were sworn in on the constitutions, a popular militia was conceded in many cases, and in one state, Baden, the standing army itself was "democratized." The National Assembly in Frankfurt in its deliberations on the future federal consitiution envisaged the extension of the Prussian "Landwehr" system to the whole of Germany, the coordination of all individual armies in a federal force, and their swearing in on the federal constitution.

The breakdown of this revolution put an end to all these dreams and left the first round in the struggle with the governments. In the period of reaction that followed the concessions made were annulled and resistance, where it was attempted in Saxony, Baden and the Palatinate, broken by the Prussian army. It was only a dozen years later, after that reaction in its turn had exhausted itself, that the second, and far more serious, struggle broke out in Prussia.

There Frederick William IV, the brilliant

From Herbert Rosinski, *The German Army* (London, 1939), pp. 85–93. Reprinted by permission of the Hogarth Press.

but erratic son of Frederick William III, after yielding at first to the revolution had, thanks to the unswerving loyalty of the army, more royalistic than the king himself, in the end emerged completely triumphant and re-established his authority practically unimpaired. The constitution, which he imposed rather than granted in 1850 as an outward concession to the spirit of the age, did not restrict the royal power in any serious respect. The diet or Landtag was indeed granted the right to vote the budget, but the cabinet remained responsible to the king, not to the Landtag, and therefore independent of any parliamentary vote of censure. The extra-parliamentary basis of the royal power, the fact that the army was the king's and only the king's, was after the attempt to tamper with it in 1848 expressly safeguarded in the constitution. Article 46 established the king's undivided and uncontrolled power of command, while Article 108 excluded any attempt to impose upon the army an oath on the constitution. Thus when the forces of the opposition after an eclipse of nearly a decade returned to the attack, their struggle to establish parliamentary control and reduce the military monarchy of the Hohenzollern to the status of the constitutional régimes of the West concentrated upon this central pillar of the royal power.

The concrete issue over which the conflict finally broke out was the attempt of the new regent, Prince William, who in 1858 had assumed the regency for his brother, to remedy the profound defects in the Prussian military system revealed by the mobilization of 1850. Since its institution in 1815 the "Landwehr System" had never been adapted to the growing man-power of the country, with the result that its yearly contingent of recruits still stood at 40,000 at a time when the population had risen from 11 to 18 millions, and the class yearly available for conscription to some 155,000. In these circumstances universal conscription had become almost a farce: men who had once been conscripted and trained were called up for service long after they

had passed their military prime, while thousands of much younger men, who had escaped conscription, were left at home. This inadequate exploitation of the country's man-power was the more intolerable since militarily the "Landwehr" had failed to fulfil Boyen's high expectations. The more mature outlook of the "Landwehr" men, upon which he had counted to offset their lack of youthful elasticity, had merely served to accentuate their lack of discipline and nonmilitary spirit, while its officers, chosen up to the grade of captain mainly from the ranks of the "one-year volunteers," could not in any way compare with the regular officers of the line. The result was that the "Landwehr," on the various occasions when it had been called to the colours, had proved completely unequal to the demands made upon it, and by its intimate combination with the Standing Army threatened to impair the latter's efficiency as well.

To remedy this state of things, the Prince Regent saw no other way than to abolish the dualism of Standing Army and "Landwehr" altogether, by constituting the former the "army in the field," and transforming the latter into a reserve, entrusted with secondary duties in its rear. To that end the Standing Army was to be greatly strengthened, both by being considerably enlarged and by being allotted five, instead of hitherto only two, classes of reservists, while the "Landwehr" was to be cut down from seven to four classes, embracing the men from 29 to 32 years of age.

In 1859 Prussia mobilized nine army corps during the Franco-Austrian War, calling some 55,000 married men to the colours, while some 150,000 younger men escaped service. The Prince Regent upon demobilization proposed on his initiative to retain the skeleton corps of the Landwehr regiments just formed, and he submitted to the Landtag the project of a law authorizing an increase of the yearly contingent from 40,000 to 63,000 men and the establishment of thirty-nine new regiments. As the Minister of War, von Bonin, hesitated to assume the responsibility for such far-reaching measures, he was replaced by Albrecht von Roon, an officer of great talents and even greater strength of character, whom the Prince Regent had known well for many years.

To the Prince Regent and his collaborators the issue appeared a simple technical problem: the restoration of the military strength of Prussia by means best adapted to that purpose; unfortunately their project seemed to the Liberal majority controlling the Landtag to contain political implications which immediately aroused their apprehension and opposition. Since the Wars of Liberation, the "Landwehr" had been the favourite child of Liberalism. Legend had magnified its very creditable achievements in that struggle, until in the popular imagination it completely outshone the Standing Army. In contrast to the latter, which was regarded with suspicion as the instrument of the ruler and of reaction, the "Landwehr" was acclaimed as the true "citizen force"; its officers' corps, drawn chiefly from those classes which formed the backbone of the Liberal movement, was felt to be a guarantee against the possibility of its being misused as an instrument of internal repression. To cut down this popular element of the army in favour of the stronghold of reaction, which after 1848 had been ruthlessly purged of all officers sympathizing with the popular movement, roused the misgivings of men who felt themselves on the threshold of a new struggle for the establishment of parliamentary control.

Consequently the Landtag made its acceptance of the plan dependent upon a reduction of the period of service from three to two years, and, when that was refused, rejected the law itself; as a compromise it voted the money necessary for reorganization provisionally for one year. The following year it repeated the procedure, adding the rider that a new military law regulating the situation should be submitted by the Government in the next session.

In the new parliament, however, the radical elements predominated and, when the Government again refused to consider the restriction of military service to two years, the Landtag cut the appropriation out of the budget altogether, thus raising the fundamental issue, whether the king's prerogative entitled him to undertake the reorganization without the authorization of a law and the appropriation of the necessary funds by the Landtag. On that latter point even Roon felt doubtful and therefore had been inclined to compromise on the question of service, so as to avoid an acute conflict, but the king—Prince William had succeeded his brother in the autumn of 1861—remained adamant; in his eyes the whole work of reorganization stood or fell with the three years' service; not that he considered it impossible to train a man in less time, but in his opinion only such a prolonged training could inculcate in him discipline and military spirit. Thus the conflict over the reorganization of the army had developed into a fundamental trial of strength between the Crown and the Landtag. The leaders of the Landtag hoped to force from the king the recognition of the minister's responsibility to the Landtag and a change of the constitution of the Upper Chamber, the "Herrenhaus." In the Government's camp the extreme reactionaries hoped that some incautious move in the Landtag would give them the opportunity to call in the troops and overthrow the constitution by force. Detailed plans for the concentration of 50,000 men with one hundred guns in and around Berlin had been worked out and sealed orders delivered to all military commanders. The king himself, a man of the most profound sense of honour, a devout Christian, incapable of tampering with the oath he had sworn on the constitution, was far from such ideas, but he felt that in instituting the reorganization he had been acting within his rights as commander-in-chief; perplexed to find even his cabinet doubtful, he saw no other way out of the situation than to abdicate and let his son, later Emperor Frederick III, the son-in-law of Queen Victoria, who was known for his liberal sympathies, make his peace with the new age. At that critical moment, Roon in a famous telegram summoned his friend Bismarck, then Prussian Ambassador to Napoleon III, to Berlin and induced the hesitating king to grant him an interview. In that remarkable conversation in the little palace of Babelsberg, midway between Berlin and Potsdam, Bismarck declared himself ready to carry on the government and the work of reorganization in the teeth of the Landtag opposition, if necessary to the scaffold, and the king thereupon declared that in those circumstances he felt it his duty to fight on. By an ingenious expedient Bismarck overcame his colleagues' constitutional qualms; he argued that, when king and parliament could not agree, there occurred a deadlock for which the constitution contained no provision, and he entered upon his desperate struggle with the infuriated Landtag.

The reorganization of the Prussian army, which could not have been completed without his intervention, put Bismarck in the saddle and allowed him to end the internal conflict by appealing to the external success which he had been able to achieve by means of it. Within four years of his taking up the reins of government the Prussian army was rejuvenated, homogeneous, efficient; it had won the old German duchies of Schleswig-Holstein from the Danes, had decided the hundred years old Austro-Prussian rivalry in Germany on the battlefields of Bohemia, and had united the whole of the former German Empire north of the Main in the "Norddeutscher Bund." On the eve of that success Bismarck was far too wise and realistic to follow the advice of the reactionaries and use his success to smash the liberal movement; on the contrary he made his peace with the Landtag, by officially demanding from it indemnity for the money spent without its consent, a gesture of reconciliation that met with full response from the new national-liberal movement, which during those days separated itself from the intransigent radicals.

Four years later the Prussian army, now increased by contingents from the South and Central German states, which in 1866 had fought on the side of Austria, brought back from the battlefields of France not only Alsace-Lorraine, but the unity of all Germany, with the exception of the German parts of Austria, and the imperial Crown. . . .

25. BISMARCK ON THE ARMY AND PARLIAMENTARY LIBERALISM

Although the Prussian army served as the instrument by which the unification of Germany was accomplished, the man chiefly responsible for this great achievement, Otto von Bismarck, was not a soldier, but rather a politician, probably the greatest his nation has ever produced. Bismarck was always acutely aware of the realities of political power. He thus recognized that the prerogatives of his monarch, and along with them the favored position of his class, the Junkers, within Prussia, and later within Germany, rested on their control of the armed forces. The following four selections, taken from his parliamentary speeches over a period of four decades, show Bismarck's constant concern with the place of the army within the state. In the first of these speeches, he lauds the role of the army in defending the particularist traditions of the Prussian monarchy against the aspirations of the nationalistic German liberals who, following the Revolution of 1848, met at Frankfurt to draw up a constitution for a unified German state.

SPEECH BEFORE THE SECOND HOUSE OF THE PRUSSIAN PARLIAMENT
SEPTEMBER 6,1849.

Who was it that upheld all that was worth upholding in Germany? Certainly not the Frankfurt Assembly. . . . What saved us was just that thing which a moment ago I called the specifically Prussian element. It is the traces of that pure blooded Prussianism, which has been so strongly anathematized and which survived the Revolution: the Prussian army . . . the fruits gathered over long years, of the intelligent Prussian administration and of the vivifying reciprocal action, which in Prussia, exists between the king and his people. It is the old Prussian virtues of honor, fidelity, obedience, and bravery, with which our whole army is imbued from the officer corps, and which forms its backbone, down to the rawest recruit.

This army feels no sense of enthusiasm over the tricolor flag of the Frankfurt Assembly. Within the army you·will find as little need as among the rest of the Prussian people for national regeneration. It is satisfied with the Prussian name, proud of it. These troops follow the black and white banner,[1] not the tricolor, and it is under this black and white flag that they will joyfully die for the fatherland. Since March 18, 1848, we have come to know the tricolor as the battle flag of our adversaries. . . .

The people from which this army springs, of which this army is the truest representation, . . . this people in no way feel the necessity of their realm being dissolved in that licentiously corrupt south German fermentation. Their loyalty is not to be bound to any federal presidency, which is a mere scrap of paper, nor to a council of sovereigns in which Prussia has

[1]The colors of the Prussian royal house. [Editor's note]

This and the following speech may be found in *M. de Bismarck, Député, 1847–1851* (Paris & Berlin), pp. 130–131, 364–371, abridged. Translation by the editor.

only a sixth of the votes. Rather, their loyalty attaches itself to our living and free monarchy, to the King of Prussia, the heir of his forefathers. . . .

We are Prussians and we wish to remain Prussians. I know that by these words I express the profession of faith of the majority of my compatriots, . . .

SPEECH DELIVERED BEFORE THE SECOND HOUSE OF THE PRUSSIAN PARLIAMENT; MARCH 11, 1851

As can be seen in the following selection and also in the last one, Bismarck always sought to keep military matters out of parliament. Not only was he convinced of the incompetence of the civilian legislators to deal with technical military questions, he was also suspicious of their motives, believing that the liberals wished a larger voice in these matters so as to restrict the power of the crown for their own selfish factional ends. In this particular case Bismarck is defending the officer corps against the Budget Commission of the Prussian Parliament, which wished to reduce their pay as an economy measure.

Our commission has proposed that many reductions be made in the military budget. If these propositions are adopted by us and thus become the resolution of the Second House, it is essential that the other two authorities participating in the legislative process be convinced that this resolution is sound, so that the law fixing the budget may be voted. . . .

I am certain that it is to the interest of his Majesty's government not to let people believe that there is even the shadow of a possibility that the funds for . . . this or that body of troops, and therefore the organization, and ultimately, even the existence of the army, may be dependent on the resolutions of only one of the two houses in the legislature. . . .

Then too, we must mollify the government which is justifiably dubious as to whether we are in possession of a fuller knowledge of the facts than the Minister of War, and thus more competent to judge the matter at hand. It wonders if an assembly composed of civil servants and lawyers, of . . . mayors and university professors is really in a position to pass sound judgment on how the Landwehr cadres may be best organized, or on the

casting of cannons and the boring of field pieces, or on the building of fortifications, or on the possibility of defending Torgau with or without Fort Zinna. . . .

We do not have a superabundance of officers. The recent mobilization demonstrated that if with the officers we now have it was possible to provide adequately for the needs of the army, it was uniquely because their sense of duty, reenforced by their sense of honor, had been aroused to the highest pitch, and because they displayed the greatest energy. It would seem to me that this is not the time to cut down on any of those advantages which might encourage young men from the cultivated classes, such as are always to be found in Prussia, who have the desire. . . to place at the disposal of the king their services and their lives, in return for a meagre salary but much honor. Not only should we not discourage these young men from choosing the career of an officer, we should also try to convince their fathers — for fathers calculate dispassionately — to consecrate their sons to military service. . . .

It is the spirit of the officer corps that will always determine that of a whole army. . . . Unfortunately, my opinion in this matter finds its confirmation in the sad year of 1806, when the senility and disconcertment of the higher ranking officers were sufficient to demoralize an army which was in itself of very high quality. There is further proof of my view in the army of Frederick the Great, where our officers created good Prussians out of adventurers recruited from every country.

The officer corps has a particular importance in a country where the term of service is as short as it is in Prussia. In those provinces where there are very few men who reenlist and where few become N.C.O.'s, the officer corps is the sole foundation of the army. This same body also functions essentially as the skeleton of the whole Landwehr system.

I would not want these words to be interpreted as meaning that I believe the disappearance of any brilliant material prospects for the future would have any effect on the Prussian officer corps and that honor alone would no longer be sufficient to make them do their duty and more than their duty. I am only trying to show how great a portion of that gratitude which we owe to the army — gratitude which everyone admits — belongs specifically to the officer corps.

We are beholden to them especially. . . that Prussia could be saved from anarchy. We owe to them the fact that we are able today to sit peacefully in this chamber and to discuss a reduction in their salary.

These are the things that we owe to this officer corps, who were not to be led away from the thorny path of duty by either the humiliations of March 1848 . . . or by the derisive insults heaped upon the "trade" as it was called. . . .and which knew no other duty for itself than to be faithful and obedient to its king and war lord, and to uphold within the army the spirit that it had inherited from our fathers. . . . Therefore, gentlemen, let not the first fruits of your gratitude towards the army be a reduction in the level of its pay!

SPEECH OF JUNE 14, 1882

The constitutional conflict of the 1860's, to which Bismarck refers in the following selection, pitted him against the liberal majority in the Prussian parliament. The issue over which they fought was control of the army. The conflict was resolved through Bismarck's use of the army to effect the unification of Germany, all of which permitted him to taunt the liberals that military force was far more effective politically than their nationalistic oratory.

The conflict came about because the majority of the Lower House placed themselves in opposition to the spirit and the mission of the Prussian people and the German nation. The truth of the matter is that it was the King, with his projected laws for the reorganization of the army, who really represented and defended the national cause, and that the King was fought purely and simply out of a desire to erect a system of parliamentary domination, and for reasons of factional tactics.

These same gentlemen say that from the beginning they have acted in the interests of and worked for the German state, and that if ultimately it has been reestablished, it is to them that the credit must go, for it was they who were the first to conceive of the idea. This pretension to priority is unfounded. Who is there then among us, in

This and the following speeches may be found in *Les discours de M. le Prince de Bismarck*, Vol. X, pp. 325–326, and Vol. XIV, pp. 53–58 (Paris & Berlin, 1882 and 1887). Translation by the editor.

1813 and 1815, as well as throughout the whole of the period since then, who has not wished for the creation of the German state? At most a few reactionaries of such an extreme type that I myself have scarcely known a single one. As for myself, I can supply from my former days (prior to the Revolution of 1848), before the annoyance I felt because of the barricades might have influenced me, more than one example attesting to the fact that I had always before my eyes a restoration of the German nation. With regard to these gentlemen who today pretend that they were the ones who brought it into existence, although they may have always had the prior wish in their hearts, I myself set about the *practical* task of satisfying these wishes and putting them into effect.

You did just the opposite of what any clear and practical mind judged was necessary to bring about the reconstruction of the German state. Anyone with even the vaguest notion about the principles of politics must have understood that without the Prussian army, and a strong Prussian army, the German national idea could not be realized, any more than it could without the King of Prussia having accepted it. The task was not one of pronouncing discourses at the tribune, haranguing people who were already convinced. Rather, it was a matter of winning the acquiescence of the King of Prussia to those measures which alone were practical and decisive, and of providing the King with an army that was strong enough for him to be able to make himself the executor of the great work required by the needs of the nation. No such idea occurred to any of you gentlemen. In 1862, each one of you could have been minister in my place and would have met with a more cordial reception from the King than I, for in that period he looked upon me as being too reactionary to be immediately accorded his full confidence. But which one of you seemed to have the least idea of the practical problems involved? Who then was it that desired Prussia to have a strong army? You tried to reduce to nothing that army, to destroy it, to make of it a militia with a term of service of two years, if not shorter. If we were to scrutinize the speeches of the era, we would see that it was the American military system, the militia, that was invoked in them. Do you really believe that we could have accomplished what we did with such a system?

Gentlemen, you went about things in the wrong way. You misconstrued the whole affair. . . . You fought and disparaged that which could have served your cause, the Prussian army. You hated the officer and showed yourselves to be hostile to him. . . . Read the newspapers of the period. You will see how in their pages the army was vilified, the army which alone, all things considered, was and has remained the upholder of the national idea. Throughout that whole period, the speeches of the professors and the writings of the journalists were on one side, the military on the other, while what was said concerning my person was very flattering for me: "One can see in a glance," someone said of me, "that he is only a Prussian officer in mufti." I accepted that description with gratitude. Although I have nothing of the Prussian officer about me except the uniform, to be possessed of his ideals would raise me higher, if I may say so, on the wave of patriotism than any parliamentary attribute that I here exercise.

SPEECH OF JANUARY 11, 1887

In the following selection, Bismarck expounds on the military rights of the crown as set forth in the German Constitution of 1871. The Septennate was a law by which the size of the army was set for a period of seven years, thus depriving parliament of the occasion to discuss military questions on an annual basis.

Looking toward the expiration of the present Septennate, the question is always raised: What is to be considered as the law, if there has been a disagreement between the two elements in the legislative process over the law on the effective strength of the army, such as should be enacted in conformity with article sixty of the Constitution? . . . Would the army then cease to exist? You yourselves cannot pretend to believe such a thing.

In such a case, those provisions of the Constitution, which were modified by the law enacted in accordance with the terms of article sixty, would again go into force. That law which is founded on article sixty establishes . . . the highest permissible figure for the number of men in service, a figure beyond which the Emperor cannot go. According to the law presently in effect, this limit will remain extant until next year, 1888. Once the said law has expired and if a new one is not enacted, far from the figure being lowered or the army vanishing, on the contrary the highest permissible figure for the number of men in service will rise to the level allowed by article fifty-nine of the Constitution, which states that every German capable of bearing arms must spend three years under the colors. . . .

Nor is there in this particular case any possibility of using the annual law on the budget to accomplish your ends, for in the fourth and last paragraph of article sixty-two it is expressly stated that

In fixing the Budget for the army expenditures the basis shall be the statutory organization of the Imperial army as founded upon this Constitution.

Thus, if a figure for the effective strength of the army is not ultimately set according to article sixty of the Constitution, you cannot, as a consequence of this, refuse the government right to establish a budget of expenditures without yourselves behaving in an unconstitutional fashion.

If an agreement cannot be reached which is acceptable to the Bundesrat[1] with regard to the defense of the German Empire, the resulting situation would in no way mean that the army will disappear. On the contrary, the imperial powers to the fullest possible extent would quite simply go into effect again. It was to make certain of the cooperation of the Reichstag in this matter that article sixty was drawn up and a law was promised which was to set. . . the effective strength of the army at a figure which the Emperor could not exceed. He is in this way obligated until 1888 and is so only through the stated law. On this question, you may consult all the legal treatises that are sympathetic to your particular political opinions. . . .You will find that the participation of the Reichstag in this matter and its rights relative to the size of the army rest uniquely on there continuing to be a law which will be made by virtue of article sixty, a law which allows him less than what he is fully entitled to by the Constitution.

If, in this conflict, you insist on being of a different opinion from the Bundesrat, your opinion, according to the terms of the Constitution, can lead to no positive results. You would compromise yourselves in an absolutely unnecessary way in a ques-

[1]The Federal Council, as opposed to the Reichstag, or parliament. [Editor's note]

tion where, because constitutional law is against you, you are impotent to make your wishes prevail.

You have not read the Constitution if you can let yourselves believe that you have the power to establish the size of the army annually by budgetary means. . . .

I do not understand, gentlemen, why you feel the need to provoke the crises which are bound up in this question any more frequently than they would occur according to the septennial compromise. We do not feel this need. We do not wish any crisis or any conflict. We intend to be satisfied with the compromise presently in force, but we will not let ourselves be pushed any further than this compromise. We are absolutely satisfied with the Septennate in its entirety. . . and on that we will not give an iota.

The German army is an institution which cannot be dependent on the changing majorities of the Reichstag. Who will guarantee that a majority that is as heterogeneous in its composition as the present one will be durable? It is an absolute impossibility that the size of the army be dependent on the makeup and the disposition of the Reichstag.

Without our German army, . . . without the necessity for a common defense against attacks from without, the whole confederation, upon which the German Empire rests, would never have succeeded in being established. Always keep this in mind whenever you would wish to trample under your feet that which is the essential element in the existence of the Confederation, . . .for we all wish to be protected, all of us and your constituents too, you may count on it!

The attempt that has been made . . . to make the existence of the army dependent on changing majorities, . . . in other words, thus to change the Imperial army, such as we have had until now into a parliamentary army, an army over whose existence it is no longer his Majesty the Emperor, but rather Messrs. Windthorst and Richter[1] who keep watch. This attempt will not succeed. . . .

Did you doubt. . . that we would appeal to the voters to learn if it is really their will that the defensive strength of Germany depend . . . every year on the vote of parliament?

It is an impossibility that it be the will of the German people that. . . their security, which is founded on their army, must depend on parliamentary majorities, which change every year. . . .

You cannot in any case expect of his Majesty the Emperor that today, in his ninetieth year, he disavow and be willing to lend his hand to the destruction of the work to which he has consecrated the last thirty years of his life: the creation of the German army and the German Empire. If you believe this, if in some fashion you convince us by your behavior that you are indeed aiming at such a goal, if you do not, by your prompt and complete adoption of our project, calm the fears of the states represented in the Bundesrat concerning the defensive strength of Germany, then we prefer to continue this discussion under more auspicious circumstances, by taking it up again with another Reichstag than the one I see before me.

[1]Two of Bismarck's most determined adversaries in the Reichstag. [Editor's note]

Gordon A. Craig

26. THE PRUSSIAN ARMY IN THE GERMAN EMPIRE

In the German Empire as created by Bismarck, the whole functioning of the state was subordinated to the needs of the army. Nevertheless, the military, always scornful and suspicious of the civil element in society, persistently sought to reenforce their preeminent situation and to increase their independence vis-à-vis the other organs of the state. In the following selection taken from his splendid study *The Politics of the Prussian Army*, Professor Gordon Craig describes the unfortunate political and military effects of this attitude on the part of the army.

As a result of the extension of Prussian hegemony over all of Germany, the military powers of the Prussian ruler had been greatly expanded. When the constitution of the North German Confederation was adopted in 1867, King William was named *Bundesfeldherr* and given complete power of command over the armies of the member states. Four years later, when the empire was established, this command was widened to include the troops of all German states except Bavaria, whose army in time of peace remained subordinate to the king of that state and was administered by the Bavarian Minister of War, although, in time of war, it too passed under Prussian command.

It was the contention of most German conservatives, and virtually all military officers, that—apart from the special arrangements made to satisfy Bavarian *amour propre*—the king-emperor's authority over the national military establishment was subject to no limitation: that his right, for instance, to effect far-reaching changes in the organization of the army, which had been so hotly contested in the constitutional struggle, was now beyond question.

They pointed out that the fourth paragraph of article 63 of the imperial constitution stipulated that "The emperor determines the peace-time strength, the structure and the distribution [*Einteilung*] of the imperial army." Jurists were apt to argue, however, that this provision was, at least in part, dependent on article 60 of the constitution, which provided for an imperial law governing the peace-time strength of the army. The scope of the emperor's powers under article 63, they contended, would necessarily be determined by the measures taken to implement article 60.

The issue was not joined until 1874. Up to that time the size of the army was governed by the so-called "iron law" of 1867 which provided for an army equivalent to 1 per cent. of the population, supported by an automatic annual grant of 225 thaler per man. Originally scheduled to expire in December 1871, this law was extended for an additional three years. It was apparent, however, that implementation of article 60 could not be postponed beyond 1874 and that a fundamental decision would have to be made.

Given their belief in the unlimited nature

From *The Politics of the Prussian Army* by Gordon A. Craig, pp. 219–232, 238–243, abridged. © 1955 by Gordon A. Craig. Reprinted by permission of Oxford University Press, Inc.

of the royal power of command, it was clear that the army authorities would demand a perpetuation of the iron law or something very much like it. The emperor himself was convinced that his recent triumphs in the field had proved the validity of the position he had taken during the constitutional conflict, and he was determined that parliament must now be denied any effective influence over the army. With his full approval, then, his military advisers drafted, for submission to the imperial Reichstag in 1874, a law setting the size of the army at 401,659 men, this figure to be considered permanent in time of peace until such time as there should be a "declaration of a further legal modification." Future modification, however, would depend upon government initiative. It was all too clear that the army was seeking to remove the strength of the army from the sphere of parliamentary debate and, since this would make the grant of funds an automatic matter, to emasculate the Reichstag's budgetary powers in so far as they applied to the army.

Neither Bismarck's parliamentary skill, however, nor the prestige of Helmuth von Moltke was sufficient to carry the bill in its original form through the Reichstag. . . .

The government was, indeed, saved from complete defeat only by the timely intervention of Bismarck who, from his sick bed, arranged a compromise with the majority leaders of the National Liberals which was ultimately accepted by the greater part of the other opposition groups. In accordance with this the strength of the army was set at the figure requested by the government, but only for a period of seven years, at the end of which it had to be renewed by the Reichstag. This so-called *Septennat* was finally approved late in April, but not without some bitter opposition speeches which showed that the old wounds had been reopened. . . .

The emperor had assented to the amended version of the bill with disappointment and, apparently, with some resentment against Bismarck for his willingness to make concessions. But, as he wrote to Roon in May, "really in our time seven years are almost half a century when one thinks of the seven years from 1863 to 1870! In this way we have the army organization intact for seven years and, after seven years, we will perhaps find ourselves *before*, or even *after*, another war; if not, then the population will have grown and we will have to increase the recruits by one per cent. . . ." Even so, the emperor was alarmed by the tone of some of the parliamentary speeches and by the evident desire of certain deputies to pry into the internal affairs of the army, and his alarm was shared by members of his military entourage. It was probably the fear that, in future budget debates, the Reichstag might insist on discussing such matters as personnel problems and promotions that led to the adoption, in the years after the defeat of 1874, of a very complicated defensive technique against such parliamentary pretensions. In brief, this involved the systematic removal of all matters of command and personnel policy from the jurisdiction of the one officer who regularly appeared before the Reichstag and who could be considered accountable to it for military affairs: namely, the War Minister.

Ever since the beginning of the constitutional system in Prussia the lot of the War Minister had been a hard one. As an officer he was bound by his personal oath of loyalty to his king and was expected to defend the royal power of command; as a minister of state he was bound by his oath to the constitution and was expected to countersign royal orders which affected the army and to bear responsibility for them before the *Landtag*. Conflicts of loyalty were frequent and the possibility of resolving them to the mutual satisfaction of king and *Landtag* remote. But, if the position of the War Minister in the Prussian system was difficult, it became, in the words of one critic, "monstrous and against all reason" under the empire. In the first place, there was no imperial War Minister, partly because, in a strictly legal sense, there was no imperial army but only an army made up of contingents from the separate states, and partly because, with the exception of Bismarck, there were no imperial ministers, the heads of the different departments of the government being secretaries of state under the Chancellor's supervision. In effect, Bismarck himself was the imperial War Minister, for he bore the ultimate responsibility for military affairs before the Reichstag. But the Chancellor had no real control over the internal workings of the army, whereas the Prussian War Minister had authority over all the armed forces of the empire (with the exception of the Bavarian army) and supervised such common military institutions as the General Staff, the Division of Personnel (which was part of the Prussian War Ministry, although administered by the Chief of the Military Cabinet), the schools and the *Kriegsakademie*, and the logistics and supply departments. In reality, if not in law, he was now more an imperial than a Prussian official; and, in the discussion of military affairs before the Reichstag, he, rather than Bismarck, generally represented the government. Because he did so and because he continued to countersign orders affecting the contingent army, the Reichstag regarded him as being responsible to them and directed questions at him which bore upon every aspect of the army's affairs. In a strictly legal sense he was not bound to answer such questions; in practice it was always difficult, and sometimes inexpedient, to refuse. Even a man of such determination as Roon had not always succeeded in distinguishing between questions bearing upon the forces of the empire (which he could answer) and questions dealing with the Prussian army (which he could not) or between administrative matters (which he could discuss) and command questions (which the emperor considered none of the Reichstag's business). Roon's successor, General von Kameke, affected liberal political views and, in the parliamentary halls, he was inclined to be more compliant than Roon.

To certain of the highest officers in the army the very existence of a constitutional War Minister had always seemed to represent a threat to the military prerogatives of the king. Edwin von Manteuffel, for instance, had always felt this way, and between 1857 and 1865, he had used all the powers of his curiously dual position—as Chief of the Military Cabinet, he was simultaneously head of the Division of Personnel in the War Ministry and chief of the bureau which handled the sovereign's military correspondence—to withhold from the War Minister information which might find its way to parliament. Thus he had generally refrained from transmitting to the minister royal communications to the commanding generals or orders on matters of military command which he had drafted, unless specifically instructed to do so by the king; and he had striven also, although with incomplete success, to remove all personnel matters—selection, promotion, decorations, punishments, and the like—from the War Minister's jurisdiction.

The Chief of the Military Cabinet after 1871 was General E. L. von Albedyll. In 1862, after twenty years of field service, Albedyll had been transferred to the Division of Personnel in the War Ministry, and there he had worked under Manteuffel until that officer was made Governor of Schleswig in 1865. For Manteuffel Albedyll had affection and veneration; he absorbed Manteuffel's principles as his own, and he frequently consulted him after he himself had become Chief of the Military Cabinet. The eighteen years during which he stood at the elbow of the king-emperor may, indeed, be considered a kind of continuation of the Manteuffel régime; and, during them, Albedyll achieved his predecessor's ambition of removing the most vital matters of military administration from the effective control of the War Minister. . . .

[*In the first months of 1883 Albedyll and the future Chief of the General Staff, the extremely ambitious Alfred von Waldersee, were able to exploit a particularly virulent parlia-*

mentary debate over military questions in the interests of greater independence for the army. At their behest, the Emperor drastically reduced the powers of the Minister of War. In March 1883 an order was issued which removed all matters pertaining to military personnel from the Ministry of War and transferred them to the Military Cabinet. Two months later, the Chief of the General Staff was given the right of direct access to the Emperor, which effectively removed from the authority of the Minister of War the most vital questions concerning military command and the preparation of the army for war. The prerogatives and the responsibility of the Minister of War were now limited to matters of military administration and finance.]

Writing in his diary at the end of March, Waldersee paid tribute to the adroitness of the Chief of the Military Cabinet. "The wholly satisfactory solution. . . ," he wrote, "is entirely to the credit of Albedyll who — with the approval, but at the same time the very careful abstention, of the Chancellor — handled the difficult matter very skilfully and has thereby earned great merit in the army and the fatherland." From his old mentor Manteuffel Albedyll also received praise for having destroyed the pernicious French theory that "the War Minister is *quasi* chief of the army." But it is doubtful whether congratulations were really in order. What Albedyll had really done was to destroy the administrative unity which the army had enjoyed since the days of Scharnhorst and Boyen, and, in doing so, he had introduced a degree of interdepartmental rivalry that had been unknown before 1883. The War Ministry, the Military Cabinet, and the General Staff had become mutually independent agencies, but it was virtually impossible to define the limits of their spheres of competence and, between 1883 and 1914, disputes were frequent, acrimonious, and damaging to the efficiency of the army. . . .

The primary purpose of the changes of 1883 had been to render ineffective parliamentary attacks on the army. But the method employed had been so clumsy that

it tended to defeat its own purpose. The War Minister had now been given the thankless task of turning away all questions on any but purely administrative and financial matters with the argument that he neither possessed knowledge of, nor had the authority to discuss, these matters. It was hardly to be expected that the Reichstag would be satisfied with this. . . . The Reichstag was quick to see that the War Minister had been rendered impotent, and the realization goaded the opposition parties on to new attacks on the army and, especially, on the agency which they rightly considered to be responsible for the minister's loss of power. In all of the military debates after 1883, the Military Cabinet was made a special target for parliamentary abuse, being described as another of those camarillas which had exercised such baleful influence in Prussian history as a symbol of encroaching absolutism. Moreover, to a much greater extent than ever before, the deputies began to turn their serious attention to the actual policies of the Military Cabinet with regard to such things as selection and promotion, and the results of their investigations convinced them that the army was engaged in a deliberate plot to thwart social and political progress in Germany. . . .

The ruler who came to the imperial throne at the end of 1888, after the brief reign of Frederick III, William II, was not without good qualities; it was generally agreed that he was intelligent, warmhearted, and ambitious to win the respect and love of his subjects. But his intelligence was accompanied by scorn for the opinions of others; his warm-heartedness too often took the form of favouritism; and his ambition was qualified neither by patience nor prudence. . . .The part of his youthful training which had made the greatest impression on him had been the military; but, rather than developing in him a true understanding of military problems, the chief effect of this had been to turn him into a kind of perennial Potsdam lieutenant, whose love for uniforms was so inense that he is reported to have insisted on wearing full admiral's regalia to performances of *The Flying Dutchman*, who dined to *Ilanenmusik,* and who preferred military companions, military manners, and military advice to any other. . . .

There can be little doubt that William's desire to act according to the principle *sic volo, sic jubeo,* his inflated conception of the royal power of command, his contempt for the constitution, and the violence of his reaction to any sign of independence on the part of the Reichstag were strengthened by the fact that he rarely moved outside this narrow military circle. It may be true, as Eulenburg wrote, that there were more donkeys than foxes in royal headquarters. But among the emperor's confidants were men like Chief of the Military Cabinet Hahnke (1888–1901) and Chief of the General Staff Waldersee (1888–91) — men ambitious for personal power and impatient with the restrictions placed upon them by the constitutional system. If William's thoughts frequently turned, after political and social problems began to crowd in upon him, to the thought of a radical solution of all of German's ills by a military *coup d'état,* this was due in large part to the influence of his military entourage. The members of William's private *Tabakskollegium* had no doubt that forcible dissolution of the Reichstag and the crushing of socialism would be a feasible military operation — General von Gossler referred to it as a *Kinderspiel* — and Waldersee was generally considered to be the man who would direct it. And if, despite the violence of William's private and public utterances, these plans came to nothing — thanks to the fundamental indecisiveness of William's character and, also, to the stubborn resistance of Bismarck's successors Caprivi and Hohenlohe[1] — the emperor's military advisers were nevertheless influential in creating and perpetuating a state of such tension between the government and the Reichstag that a complete breakdown of the constitutional system seemed always imminent.

[1]Chancellors from 1890 to 1894 and from 1894 to 1900 respectively. [Editor's note]

This they did by sniping from behind the *coulisses* at responsible ministers who sought a *modus vivendi* with the Reichstag and by denigrating them before the emperor in such a way as to weaken his confidence in them.

This was particularly irresponsible conduct in view of the fact that a good working relationship with parliament was more important for the army now than it had been even in the 70's and 80's. The days in which it had seemed desirable to permit the Reichstag to discuss the peace-time strength of the army as rarely as possible were now dead and beyond recall. In the spring of 1887 Bismarck had fought a long and bitter battle with the Reichstag for a new *Septennat* setting army strength at 468,409 non-commissioned officers and men, and he had forced new elections rather than consider a proposal which would have allowed the deputies to debate the size of the army every three years rather than every seven. It had been a hollow victory. No sooner had the new law been pushed through than it was generally considered to be inadequate. A new bill, reorganizing the reserves, had to be brought before the Reichstag in December 1887 and, in 1890, another one, raising army strength to 486,983. After the lapsing of the Reinsurance Treaty with Russia in 1890, the subsequent *rapprochement* of France and Russia and the rapid arming of the new partners, further increases became essential. In 1892 Waldersee's successor as Chief of the General Staff, Count Schlieffen, wrote to his sister: "Our special enemies (Denmark not included) have almost double our strength. The relationship is something like 5:3. . . . For me there is no doubt that this question cannot be put aside if Germany is not to collapse utterly. All men capable of service must be trained." But all men could not be trained without new increases and reforms and this meant new appeals to the Reichstag for authorization and for funds.

Such appeals were made with increasing frequency between 1890 and 1914, and even the parties which were normally friendly to the army were unhappy about the mounting debt made necessary by constantly heightened military expenditure — especially since the army's demands were soon supplemented by requests from the navy as well. The ministers who were primarily responsible for winning the assent of the Reichstag — the Chancellor and the War Minister — would have had a difficult time in any circumstances. But their task was made doubly difficult by constant criticism, on the part of the emperor and his military suite, of the tactics they employed to gain their objectives, and by bitter opposition by the *Hauptquartier* to anything that seemed to be a concession of the parliamentarians.

27. WILLIAM II ON THE MILITARY PREROGATIVES AND DUTIES OF THE GERMAN EMPEROR

By terms of the Constitution of 1871, the German Empire was governed as a semi-absolutist state. Military affairs were the almost exclusive domain of the Emperor and parliament was effectively removed from any real control over the army. As long as semi-absolute power was in the hands of a politician of Bismarck's acumen and as long as the German people were still enthralled by the great achievement of national unification, there was little discontent at this state of affairs. But Bismarck was dismissed in 1890 by the young Emperor William II, who thereafter governed in his own name. His quasi-mystical attitude toward his role as Emperor and his tendency to insist on his military prerogatives are revealed in the following passages. That a modern industrial state was ruled by a monarch who thought of himself above all as a soldier and whose basic source of political support was an army officered primarily by a reactionary rural aristocracy was hardly a healthy situation.

THE ADDRESS OF WILLIAM II TO HIS RECRUITS IN 1891 AS REPORTED IN THE *NEISSER ZEITUNG*

Recruits! You have now before the consecrated servant of the Lord and before His altar, sworn fealty to me. You are still too young to understand the true meaning of what has just been said; but be diligent now and follow the directions and instructions given you. You have sworn loyalty to me; that means, children of my guard, that you are now my soldiers, you have given yourselves up to me, body and soul; there is for you but one enemy, and that is my enemy. In view of the present Socialistic agitations it may come to pass that I shall command you to shoot your own relatives, brothers, yes, parents — which God forbid — but even then you must follow my command without a murmur.

The German Emperor as Shown in His Public Utterances, ed. Christian Gauss (London, 1915), pp. 74–75.Reprinted by permission of Charles Scribner's Sons.

THE ARMY TO WORK FOR PEACE

On the tenth anniversary of his accession, the Kaiser addressed the Prussian Life Guards at Berlin:

"With deep sorrow did I take up the crown; on all sides men doubted me: on all sides did I encounter misconceptions. One thing alone had confidence in me, one thing alone believed me—it was the army, and supported by it, and relying upon our God as of old, I undertook my heavy office, knowing well that the army was the main support of my country, the main pillar of the Prussian throne, to which God's decree had called me. So then I turn first of all to-day to you and express to you my congratulations and thanks in which I, at the same time, include with you all your brothers in the army. I am firmly convinced that during the last ten years, by the self-sacrificing devotion of officers and men, by its loyal, devoted work in peace, the army has been maintained in that splendid condition in which I received it from the hands of my late grandfather. During the next ten years we will continue to work together in loyal association, with unquestioning fulfilment of our duty, with the old unwearied industry, and may the main pillars of our army ever be unassailed; these are bravery, sense of honour, and absolute, iron, blind obedience. That is my wish which I address to you and with you to the whole army.

CABINET ORDER TO THE PRUSSIAN ARMY

JANUARY, 1901

To My Army:

To-day, at the celebration which commemorates the two-hundredth anniversary of our taking over of the royal power of Prussia, my thoughts are directed first of all to my army. In Prussia the King and the army belong indissolubly together. This close personal relationship between me and every single one of my officers and soldiers rests upon a tradition that dates back 200 years. The spirit which from the time of Frederick the Great has been fostered in the army by all the Kings, the spirit of honor, of fidelity to duty, of obedience, of courage, of chivalry has made the army what it is and what it ought to be, the sharp, reliable weapon in the hand of her Kings for the protection and the blessing of the Fatherland's greatness.

To serve the Fatherland at the head of the army, that is my will and that also was the foremost wish of all my predecessors. It is to their care that the army owes its power and the consideration which it enjoys. For 200 years she has proven true the sentence of the great King: "The world does not rest upon the shoulders of Atlas any more securely than the Prussian state upon the shoulders of the army!" It has sealed with its blood its love and gratitude for its Kings!

For all this I thank the army deeply. I thank it for the devotion which it has unselfishly shown me and my house year in and year out, in its unceasing service for the Fatherland. So long as this spirit binds the army to its Kings, so long we need fear no storms; and Prussia's eagle will proudly pursue its lofty and undeflected flight for the good of Prussia, for the good of Germany! May God grant us this!

WILLIAM, I. R.

BERLIN ROYAL PALACE.

The first selection is from the German Emperor, *et al.*, *Germany's War Mania* (New York, 1915), pp. 87–88. Reprinted with permission of Dodd, Mead & Co. The second selection is from *The German Emperor as Shown in His Public Utterances*, ed. Christian Gauss (London, 1915), pp. 169–171. Reprinted by permission of Charles Scribner's Sons.

Raoul Girardet

28. THE ARMY IN THE STATE, 1815-1870

To protect the army against the perils of French political life in the nineteenth century required that the soldiers themselves revise, consciously or unconsciously, certain of their fundamental assumptions with regard to such matters as discipline, obedience, loyalty, and military honor. In the following passage, taken from the remarkable study *La société militaire dans la France contemporaine* by Professor Raoul Girardet of the Institut des Sciences Politiques in Paris, some of the reasons for this basic change in the French military ethos are examined.

The revolutions of the nineteenth century were too numerous and too varied for the army to have let itself be drawn into them, without running the risk of complete and rapid disintegration. To assert its absolute disinterest with regard to political matters was doubtless the only way in which the army could be certain of preserving its coherence and even of continuing to remain in existence. . . .

For the soldier who had now become something of a civil servant, the old traditional values of personal fidelity, in the sense of being personally attached to a man, a principle, or a cause, lost a great part of their meaning. . . . Neutrality, or more precisely, passivity in political questions became one of the essential dogmas of the new military ethic. The soldier had only one duty to bear in mind, a simple duty, but one allowing neither exception nor compromise: "To uphold the law of his country. . . .", that is to say, to maintain, protect, and defend the existing institutions and the state in its present forms. There was no longer even any possibility of doubt, internal debate, or conflict of conscience. In the event of a political upheaval,

when everything around him was collapsing and giving way, the soldier would "seek refuge under his flag," which is to say, he would follow the orders of his superiors, who at each successive level of the military hierarchy had only to refer to the man above them, until ultimately they reached the decisions of the Minister of War of the moment. Thus the political loyalty of the army was to be at the same time both revocable and constant. It would be affixed to none of the changing forms of political authority, but rather to the very essence of that authority. . . .

It is to be noted that the attitude of the army in this regard was very similar to that of all the great administrative organisms that had been born in the Napoleonic period. The army officer acted in no way different from the magistrate, the tax inspector, the teacher, or the engineer in the Department of Public Works. In this respect, all French civil servants in the nineteenth century shared a common psychological trait. The idea of the state ultimately came, in their eyes, to be completely separate from the person of the sovereign or the constitutional form of the regime. A purely

From Raoul Girardet, *La Société militaire dans la France contemporaine, 1815–1939* (Paris, 1953), pp. 119–114, abridged. Reprinted by permission of Librairie Plon. Translation by the editor.

selfish preoccupation with the pursuit of one's own career, with being promoted, and finally with attaining one's pension as smoothly as possible worked to reinforce this conception of a public service, unchanging and permanent, through all the different forms of government. And it is a fact that this unconditional willingness on the part of all the civil servants to serve each successive regime assured nineteenth century France a remarkable administrative continuity, despite her permanent political instability. . . .

No matter how closed in was the world of the army, no matter how isolated it was within the nation, the military could not remain totally indifferent to the various influences which surrounded them. . . . There can be no doubt that most officers were in sympathy with a strong government. Its precise form was less important than that it show energy, that it know how to command and to make itself obeyed, being more concerned about its own authority than about respect for public liberties.

But this fact must be noted: the army was not at the source of any of the upheavals or revolutions in the political history of nineteenth century France. The military were far from having played as important a political role as might have been expected in so confused and so constantly upset an epoch. Furthermore, it should be noted that within that French society of the last century, a society torn by partisan strife, the army was never deeply divided against itself. It was never split along factional lines. Only under exceptional circumstances were certain of its elements to rise up violently against each other. In fact, between 1815 and 1870 it became increasingly more aware of its unity and endeavored to strengthen its cohesion. It would seem that the great surges of public opinion that so furiously wracked the country hardly touched the gates of the barracks. As soon as one entered the world of the army, ideological conflict, the clash of opposing tendencies and systems softened and diminished, losing their violence, their intensity, and even their significance. . . . The several regimes of nineteenth century France might exhibit varying degrees of sympathy towards the army; the military might evince a variable enthusiasm towards these regimes; they might even give witness with regard to some of them of certain mental reservations. Still, it must be admitted that the army as a whole served them all with a spirit of equal docility and equal submission. . . .

The first years of the Bourbon Restoration, years in which were liquidated a long period of civil strife, obviously marked a certain confusion in the political attitude of the army, a certain wavering in the affirmations of its loyalty. It stands to reason that the restored Bourbon dynasty could not count on being very popular among the former officers of the Empire, who having been retired on half pay in 1815, were reinstated in 1818, and who thereafter made up the largest part of the cadres. Too many grudges had been built up in 1814 and 1815. The White Terror[1], . . . the harshness and the injustice of the post-Napoleonic purge, the systematic reinstatement of the émigrés, all of that represented memories that were too recent and too sad. . . . It is also understandable that the government of the Restoration felt some mistrust towards these veterans of the Imperial epoch. . . . Within the interval of two months and in two neighboring countries, Italy and Spain, the army had taken the initiative in vast revolutionary movements. In France itself, it is known that some ten military conspiracies were uncovered more or less simultaneously, at the end of 1821 and the start of 1822, in the opposite ends of the country, at Belfort, Saumur, Nantes, and Toulon. . . .

But one must question if these elements had any real importance within the whole of military society. It would be, in truth, to

[1]The efforts by the reactionary, royalist elements in 1814 and 1815 to extirpate anyone connected with the Revolution. [Editor's note]

paint a totally false picture of the general political attitude of the army during the Restoration if one bestows too much attention on the conspiracies of 1821 and 1822. . . . Limited to a few garrisons, easily suppressed, the military plots of the Restoration involved in reality only a very small fraction of the cadres and were simply characteristic of a period of transition and adaptation. Less than a year after the execution of the four sergeants of La Rochelle, the army under the command of the Duke of Angoulême crossed the frontier into Spain to reestablish Ferdinand VII as absolute monarch, without there being recorded the least defection and in spite of the objurgations of all the liberals. . . .

During the Revolution of 1830, the troops of the Paris garrison . . . held out against the riot for two whole days, July 27 and 28, in the streets of a city that was almost entirely hostile, under a burning sun, and without food, all this despite their evident lack of enthusiasm for the cause they were defending. The first defections, which were moreover limited to two regiments, only took place in the course of the day of July 29, when the game could already be considered as having been lost politically. The army had absolutely nothing to do with the fall of the restored Bourbon dynasty. . . .

Without doubt, the new dogma of absolute political passivity was still far from being definitively accepted and completely admitted by all. Following the triumph of the Parisian insurrection of July 1830, disturbances, scenes of disorder and indiscipline in numerous garrisons, marked the transition from one regime to another. Noncommissioned officers, the most turbulent element in the army . . . were to be seen haranguing and expelling those of their chiefs who were suspected of loyalty to the fallen dynasty. Certain officers, retired on half-pay, tumultuously returned to active service. Some 2000 officers, who were faithful to the old conception of military honor and bound to the ancient principles of personal devotion to the sovereign, resigned their commissions. . . .

The period of disorder was, in any case, of very short duration. Calm was quickly restored. On May 1, 1831, the anniversary of Saint Philip, the festival of the new sovereign was warmly celebrated in every barracks. According to General La Motte-Rouge, "On May 1, 1831, the enthusiasm in the army was the same as that of August 15 under the Empire, August 25 under Louis XVIII, or November 4 under Charles X, that is to say the enthusiasm of the soldier who has nothing to do with politics. He drinks the health of his sovereign because the sovereign is the chief of the army, the chief to whom he has sworn an oath of fidelity. He is the keystone in the social edifice which the soldier has been ordered to defend against internal enemies as well as those from without." This was the assurance of a devotion which was not to be belied for the eighteen years that the July Monarchy lasted. . . .

Various elements contributed perceptibly to increasing the prestige of the regime in the eyes of the army. At the beginning of the reign, it is unquestionable that improvements were made in the material situation of the officers. Above all the soldiers responded to the magnetism and the personal authority of the princes of the royal family. The Duke of Orleans was passionately interested in everything military, while the Duke of Aumale fought in the African campaigns. . . . There can be no doubt that the Orleans family was able to win that honest popularity with the great mass of the army that the sovereigns of the Bourbon dynasty could never claim.

Thus the attitude of the army before the Revolution of 1848 and the fall of the bourgeois monarchy was all the more significative of the decisive progress which had been achieved within the minds of the soldiers by the new military ethic. . . . In the provincial garrisons and in Africa the report of the events of February 1848 was greeted with stupor, despondency, and very often indignation. However, and this is the remarkable thing, no one thought to oppose by force this new but unloved regime. As for the July Monarchy whose disappearance was regretted by all, no one showed the slightest inclination to try to restore it by force of arms. Despite their ill-humored protestations, there were no discussions among the military as to whether the fait accompli should be accepted or not. Loud and ostentatious adhesions to the Republic. . . were rare and severely judged. But on the other hand, contrary to what had happened in 1830, no one thought to resign his commission. The Duke of Aumale, who was at the time Governor General of Algeria, enjoyed great and indisputable prestige among his officers and men, but if he had wanted to attempt anything by force of arms, no one would have followed him. . . . Irreproachable in his conduct as a soldier and a functionary, in accordance with the narrow definition which the era had come to attribute to these terms, the prince himself, in fact, by retiring set the example of obedience and submission before the new "legal" authority. Such an attitude would have been unthinkable two centuries or even fifty years before. That a prince of the blood royal believed that it was his duty to forego all resistance in the face of the riot which brought down his dynasty, and that he was unanimously praised for this gesture by his loyal supporters and his companions in arms, all this was still another decisive indication of the complete reversal of a whole system of values, of the triumph of a new conception of military honor, and of the new role of the soldier within political society.

The advent of the Second Republic marks, however, the start of an exceptional period of three or four years during which the army came out of the political retirement in which it had remained since 1815. It was a highly eventful period, one which saw the army intervene in a decisive fashion in the struggle between the different factions, and in which the military were to know the temptations of public life. At the end of it, they were the ones who held the fate of the regime in their hands. In this complex period, however, if one is to understand the psychology of the soldiers of the epoch in its veritable terms, it is essential that their behavior be defined with more precision and a greater sense of nuances than is usually done, and that the traditional simplifications be treated with caution. . . .

The army bowed to the results of the February Revolution, but born of a riot, the Republic none the less seemed to represent the triumph of. . . that whole revolutionary rabble which the military had been taught to scorn and to kill. Further, there was as the consecration of its defeat, the disarmament of the troops in Paris after the February days and the purge of the high command undertaken by the Provisional Government (thirty-seven generals placed on the inactive list in April 1848). This all represented so much abusive harassment, aimed at humiliating and lowering the dignity of the military. Everything about the new regime seemed intended to wound the deepest feelings of the army. The disarray of the popular demonstrations, their tumult and their anarchic excitement shocked the army's sense of what was proper and its respect for strict order and discipline. . . . The social tendencies which were now becoming apparent exasperated these men who were almost exclusively of bourgeois or peasant origin, and who were complete strangers to the world of the workers and thus perfectly ignorant of its problems. The rhetoric of the politicians in power, the grandiose phrases on which they became intoxicated, and the impression of sterile agitation that was to be gained so often from their behavior, finally ended by arousing the ridicule and derision of a group in which a taste for action and the use of force were part of its professional attributes, and for which the term "lawyer" was one of the traditional forms of scorn. . . .

Still, the army was led to intervene decisively in the political struggles of the period, not so much because it was impelled by its sentiments, its particular sympathies or antipathies, but rather because of the pressure of events and above all because of the entreaties of various factions. The terrible days of June 1848 provided the first occasion for the military to assume an absolutely exceptional situation within the national life. The army crushed the uprising in the working class districts and thus saved the regime and along with it social order. A general, Cavaignac, became for a while the chief of the Provisional Government, invested with quasi-dictatorial powers. A relatively large number of his comrades, and among them the most illustrious . . . left their commands to take their places in the Legislative Assembly. In particular . . . there arose throughout the whole of French conservative society a tremendous burst of enthusiasm and gratitude towards the army. . . .

Then the very evolution of the regime acted to increase the political importance of the army and ended by allotting it an absolutely preponderant role. It was commonly known by the end of 1848 that the Republic was quite probably doomed. The main question was how its succession would be settled. The Legislative Assembly, in which a conservative majority predominated, leaned towards a restoration of the monarchy, but the President of the Republic, Louis Napoleon Bonaparte, who had been triumphantly elected on December 10, 1848, openly aspired in his own interests to reestablish an imperial regime. The question was whether in some way the army would associate itself with the ambitions of the Prince-President, or would assist the Assembly in repulsing them. In this conflict between the two great constituted authorities of the country, the executive power as against the legislative, a conflict which extended through the years 1850 and 1851, the support of the army turned out to represent the necessarily decisive element. This support was solicited by both sides, and in the very name of the obedience that they owed the legally constituted power the military could not escape or refuse to take part. Harassed and borne along by forces which overwhelmed him, the soldier found himself called upon to be the arbiter of the situation. Whether he wished it or not, the future of the country had come to depend on his intervention. It was a paradoxical revenge for an army that had been so humiliated in 1848. Less than three years later, it had become the prize in the struggle between the factions and the means by which their contest would be decided. On December 2, 1851 it would be the bayonets of the Paris garrison which would assure the victory of Louis Napoleon and the brutal downfall of the republican regime. . . .

However it may have appeared, the coup d'état of Louis Napoleon was far from being a *pronunciamiento* in the exact sense of the word. Although it was the essential instrument in the operation, the army, as a matter of fact, took neither the initiative nor the responsibility for it. Under the circumstances, it did no more than submit in docile fashion to the orders of its direct chief, the President of the Republic, the head of the executive power and master of the armed forces according to the provisions of the Constitution of 1849. And nothing would be more false than to believe that in other respects it leapt unanimously and without reservations into the adventure. Very typical in this respect were the difficulties that the Prince-President met when it was a question of recruiting the military personnel necessary for the coup d'état. . . . In order to insure the success of the coup, he had to embark on a long and patient preliminary operation, introducing cells of adherents into the higher echelons of the army and within the Paris garrison in particular, eliminating his opponents, . . . circumventing the indifferent, and above all, placing in the vital positions those who were resolute and devoted.

But finding these resolute and devoted elements was extremely difficult. Having had no luck with the senior officers in the army, Commandant Fleury, who was the aide-de-camp to the Prince and who played an essential role in the military preparation for the coup d'état of December 2, had to turn to his former comrades of the African army, that is to say, to a younger generation of officers, who were more ardent, audacious, and avid. Traversing the Algerian garrisons at the start of 1851, Fleury was greeted by many word of mouth assurances of sympathy, . . . but he obtained scarcely more than one formal pledge, that of Saint-Arnaud. At the time Saint-Arnaud was an obscure brigadier general, but he was anxious to play a more important role, and his *condottiere* spirit was weighed down by only a few scruples. . . .

Once the operation had succeeded, it is certain that the great majority of soldiers greeted with enthusiasm . . . the fall of the Republic and the coming to power of Louis Napoleon Bonaparte. Doubtless there were a few who were refractory. They were to be found, by and large, in the highest ranks. . . . But even those who disapproved of the coup d'état bowed before it without either resisting or protesting. Moreover, by bringing to the army war, honors, and glory, the imperial regime fulfilled all the hopes that had been placed in it. One must, however, emphatically note that the army was after 1851 accorded no special influence in the conduct of the great matters of state. Although of military origin, the government of the Second Empire was in no way a government by the military. Neither within the realm of foreign policy nor in that of domestic affairs was there to be seen any intervention by the soldiers, or even any very significant pressure from them. It was outside the military sphere that were taken the great decisions of the reign. On the morrow of the coup d'état, the army found itself removed once again from the political life of the nation. It returned to its essential calling and became again a passive instrument in the hands of the government, the simple agent for carrying out its decisions. When on September 4, 1870, another Parisian uprising brought about the overthrow of that regime to whose establishment the army had contributed so much and by whom it had been covered with prestige, none of the military raised their voices to defend it or drew their swords to stand by it. The decisive role played by the army in the agony and the fall of the Second Republic should in no way lead one to forget the main features of the political psychology of the French soldier ever since the first years of the July Monarchy. . . .

From the early days of the Restoration down to the fall of the Second Empire, a few military chiefs might occasionally succumb to the blandishments of politics. The army as a whole might sometimes let itself be carried away by certain currents of opinion and display more or less plainly certain sympathies or certain tendencies; but, and this is the essential point, none of the great upheavals of the century had its origin in the garrisons or in the barracks. The military never deliberately . . . sought to impose upon the country their own chosen laws, government, or regime.

29. DEBATE ON THE POLITICAL RIGHTS OF THE FRENCH SOLDIER

The professional soldier in nineteenth-century France tended to have a profound aversion for politics. Not only did he concur in the general belief that the political life of the country would be more healthy if the army kept to a strictly military sphere; he also believed that France's military security would be more certain if political questions were kept out of the army. To this end, the legislators who wrote the Conscription Law of 1872, which reintroduced into France the principle of universal military service, went so far as to deprive the soldier of the vote. The motives underlying this seemingly extreme point of view may be seen in the following selections, taken from the parliamentary report on the law and from the debates which preceded its enactment.

FROM THE REPORT ON THE PROPOSED CONSCRIPTION LAW

In prescribing by article five, that no man, while in uniform, will go to the polls, the law is taking its stand on the grounds of discipline.

We do not intend to deal with any points that will be treated in an electoral law. Our only aim is to remove all causes of discord and insubordination from within the ranks of the army. In effect, it is not desirable that soldiers, who must be obedient to their hierarchical superiors for the accomplishment of military goals, should on a given day find themselves their equals, perhaps their adversaries, without, however, ceasing to be under their orders.

Further, the political opinions of a soldier may be affected in a most regrettable way by what has taken place on active duty.

Then too, in order to avail themselves of this right as it is presently instituted according to the existing laws, it would be necessary for the men in a given regiment to form as many little isolated groups as there are departments from which they originate. The soldiers making up each little group would have to discuss and come to an understanding with each other. In order to inscribe on their ballots the names of men about whom they know nothing, they would have to seek information outside the barracks or the camp, information which, moreover, electoral agents are only too eager to supply them; and God knows what political ideas and principles they often teach. . . .

For us, gentlemen, it is one of the most striking proofs of the discipline, the good sense, and the strength of the army, that it has known how to resist the dangerous agitation and the baleful doctrines which have for the last few years sought to take possession of it.

For the army itself, it is thus a bad thing to permit the men who belong to it the right to vote. But it is no less harmful for the government, whatever its form, and for society.

The votes of the military, as you know, are not thrown into the ballot box on election day and mixed in with those of other citizens. They are counted apart, and according to whether the votes of the military

From the *Annales de l'Assemblée Nationale* (1872), Vol. VIII, p. 98, and Vol. XII, pp. 64–70, abridged. Translation by the editor.

have been favorable to such and such a party, or such and such a political personage, public opinion, without taking the trouble to inquire into the real reasons for their voting in a particular way, can go astray trying to read into the results electoral motives which simply are not there.

Thus, the right to vote for men in uniform contains many serious drawbacks, quite apart from its dangerous effect on discipline.

Let us leave the army to its pure and beautiful mission; those who make it up should have only to concern themselves with becoming ever more proficient in their art, their particular craft. Let us not give to the army a political role; it belongs to the country as a whole, and it is in this that its grandeur lies: Let us not bring it down to the dimensions of the parties.

DEBATE OVER ARTICLE FIVE OF THE CONSCRIPTION LAW

Edouard Millaud: Presenting the extreme republican view

Gentlemen, in republican governments and even in free countries where the republican form of government does not exist, . . . the army does not stand on one side and the nation on the other; there is an absolute fusion, . . . there is unity. One does not separate the citizens from the soldiers. The soldiers are citizens and the citizens are soldiers. . . .

We must not have a permanent army, fashioned to the needs of Caesarism; we must have a national army, an army that is veritably French, and as a consequence, one that is inspired by duty and the love of justice. . . .

I believe that we must accord the vote to every soldier, not only because it is a right but because it is to our best interests. . . .

It is to our best interests because it appears to me more terrible, more baleful to have the nation at the mercy of the army than to give to the army the right to vote. The thing that I fear is that the army is not imbued with a civic sense. It is as if this army does not feel itself to be entirely in touch with the nation, as if each soldier does not possess a conscience which is able to resist the suggestions of his chiefs. . . .

It must not be possible for the chief to say: I will watch over the interests of all. . . . It is wrong, if it is a question of

electing a deputy who will have to decide whether to go to war or not, that the soldier have grounds for complaining that he did not participate in the appointment of this deputy. It is wrong that those who are elected by the nation are, in fact, elected by only a part of it. . . .

We must not forget that in our time war has become harsh and difficult, and that it requires great patience during whole months, that the soldiers are obliged to spend a long time in the field sleeping on the ground and marching under a heavy pack. . . . In order to put up with so many hardships, they have need of strength, moral courage, and, in a word, the titles and the rights of a citizen. If you will not make citizens of them, they will be able, by dying for France during the war, to show that they are Frenchmen, but after the war how will they manifest this quality? Only by their right to vote. . . .

As a consequence, I believe that the Assembly must maintain the present law, by the provisions of which the soldiers vote with their respective units. We do not have to fear that this will be a cause of indiscipline for our army. . . .

General de Cissey, Minister of War

This provision of the law in no way suppresses the civic rights of the soldier. As soon as he returns home, he will regain his full rights and he will vote just as any other citizen. But the soldier under arms can only be the soldier of the law; he must remain a stranger to all parties and to all political strife; he must represent force in the service of the law.

General Ducrot, fervent royalist and spokesman for the army

I do not wish that soldiers called to the colors be permitted to vote, because that would endanger the moral authority that the chiefs must have over their subordinates. . . .

The vote is an element of discord and disunion which we do not need. In order to have an army that is truly solid and capable of accomplishing great things, it is necessary before anything else that its chiefs know how to acquire an incontestable

moral authority over their subordinates. . . .

This moral authority will be achieved, when having understood the extent of their duty, they give evidence to their subordinates of that solicitude, that kindness, that affection, I would even say that respect, which is deserved by men to whom are entrusted the destinies of the fatherland and upon whom the chiefs base their own hopes for success and glory.

Then, gentlemen, their subordinates will repay these generous sentiments with respect, with obedience, and with confidence. It is in this way that a solid army is achieved, for a union is established between the officers and men. In the words of Marshal MacDonald, the soldiers have been "sewn" together. That our soldiers may indeed be "sewn" together, we must thrust away all elements of discord and disunion.

David Thomson

30. THE ARMY UNDER THE THIRD REPUBLIC

The Third Republic, which emerged in the wake of the overthrow of Napoleon III during the Franco-Prussian War, proved to be the most durable political regime France has known since the Revolution of 1789. Nevertheless, because there was always a large element within the country who wished to see the Republic replaced by a stronger and more authoritarian regime, its chances for survival, especially during the first three decades of its existence, often seemed problematical. To what degree the army was associated with this strong anti-republican minority is open to debate, but it is the contention of Professor David Thomson of Cambridge University that the authoritarian spirit of the military presented a real obstacle to the development of effective democratic institutions in France.

Military defeat, invasion and occupation of the northern provinces, the loss of Alsace and Lorraine, and the exaction of an indemnity of five thousand million (five milliard) francs as well as the costs of German occupation, all brought home very vividly to

every Frenchman the new danger on France's northeastern frontier. By mobilizing national spirit at home and national credit abroad, Thiers managed to pay off the indemnity in full by 1873; and by persuading Bismarck in 1872 to link instal-

From David Thomson, *Democracy in France* (London and New York, 1946), pp. 147–161, abridged. Reprinted by permission of the Oxford University Press. Book published by the Oxford University Press under the auspices of the Royal Institute of International Affairs.

ments of payment with instalments of evacuation, he got the last German troops off French soil by September 1873. Already France had begun to overhaul her military machine.

Military service for five years for all men between twenty and forty was made compulsory by Thiers's law of 1872. Evasion of personal service, common under the Second Empire, was made much more difficult. Technical weapons and fortifications were vastly improved. Credits of 500 million francs for the improvement of national defence were readily voted annually by the National Assembly, and after it by the Chamber. France threw herself into a frenzy of military preparation. But was it only for national defence? Was it not rather for a war of *revanche,* a vast national reprisal on the traditional enemy beyond the Rhine, recently grown so monstrous and threatening? Both answers were freely given. And the efforts of Bismarck to keep France without allies, and incidents such as the great war scare of 1875 which inflamed opinion just when the Republic itself was being constitutionally defined, seemed to betoken another Franco-German struggle within a few years. . . .

The present argument is concerned only with the effects of this constant, looming shadow of war on the working of democratic institutions, and the shaping of democratic ideas, in the Third Republic. Its first effect was clearly to rally opposing parties and classes, and to compel them to work together by reason of a common external pressure and a clear national danger. The Right-wing parties were ultra-nationalist. . . . So, too, were the Left-wing parties. . . . Gambetta's record of waging *la guerre à outrance* in 1870, and the enthusiasm of Republicans of every shade for military reorganization, provided all parties with a basis of agreement. There was at first no pacifism on the Left, though there might be rather more thunder on the Right. . . .

The greatest force driving a wedge between parties on the issue of national defence measures was Republican fear of Caesarism. Conscription laws which placed French manhood at the disposal of the General Staff for a total of twenty years during times of emergency, when that General Staff was so closely connected with clericalism and Monarchism by sympathy, family, and professional training, could never be regarded with equanimity by good Republicans. The obvious remedy was to Republicanize the military command. But efforts to do this never succeeded —and indeed the greatest of them precipitated the worst military-political crisis which the Republic had to face until the supreme crisis of Dreyfus. It was fear of Caesarism which produced the most sensational attempt at Caesarism—Boulangism. The circumstances of the dramatic rise and fall of General Boulanger show clearly the dilemma of the Republicans.

In January 1886 Boulanger became Minister of War in the third ministry of Freycinet—the stoutest of Republicans and the former collaborator of Gambetta in the writing and publication of *La République française.* The appointment was made on the special recommendation of Clemenceau, with whom he was on excellent terms. The reforms of the Army, long planned and discussed but hitherto little practised, which Boulanger proceeded to carry out with energy, were admirably Republican. The change from the old professional army to the new democratic force based on universal conscription demanded more intelligent discipline, better material conditions, more care for morale. These demands he implemented fully. He even purged the Army of prominent Royalist officers like the Duc d'Aumale himself, uncle of the Orleanist pretender to the throne. At his first great review at Longchamps on Bastille Day 1886 he was acclaimed as a popular idol—the darling of the people, who was giving them a people's army and an inspiring example of Republican leadership. He became the hero of revues as well as of reviews, and the music-halls sang his praises. No one since Gambetta had succeeded so well in capturing the imagination and the hearts of the common people. A *mystique* of Boulangism grew up. He was popular partly because his new model army meant the chance of *revanche*. And there lay the sting.

The idea of *revanche* was dying, amidst the seductive colonialism of Jules Ferry. But it was dying only in certain minds, and amid positive distractions from the old obsession. Paul Déroulède and his League of Patriots existed to keep it alive. By 1886 they had come to despair of the old politicians, and turned to demanding the revision of the constitution as the prerequisite for a prepared *revanche.* They also turned to Boulanger as their greatest hope. When Bismarck himself, in his Reichstag speech of January 1887 named Boulanger as the greatest obstacle to good relations between France and Germany, any remaining doubts were dispelled. General Boulanger became "General Revanche." And he was led to sponsor the cause of revision of the constitution: revision in the direction of a far stronger and more directly popular executive. Thrown out of office when the ministry fell, in May, he was relegated to a military command in Auvergne, and thenceforth was ready to conspire in order to regain his coveted ministry.

His chance came with the Wilson scandal of 1887 — one of those sudden dramatic revelations of political graft in high quarters which so often precipitated political crisis in the parliamentary Republic. Daniel Wilson, the son-in-law of Jules Grévy, the venerable President of the Republic since 1879, was discovered to have carried on a prosperous traffic in decorations and honours from the Élysée itself. The scandal also involved General Thibaudin, one of the few sound "Republican Generals" who had been a Minister for War. . . . In the prolonged political crisis which ensued, and which involved the resignation of both ministry and President, the forces hostile to the Republic looked to Boulanger as an ally. Both Monarchists and Bonapartists began to pay court to him. When the Government dismissed him from the Army, he had but one course left by which to pursue his growing ambitions: popular agitation and

the use of violence. Thanks to the eager support of both extreme Left and most of the Right, and to the lavish financial help of the Royalist Duchesse d'Uzès, he was elected in several constituencies at once. The climax came in January 1889 when he stood for Paris itself — traditional home of Radicalism and democratic Republicanism. He was elected by 245,000 votes, and a *coup d'état* was staged. But Boulanger's nerve seems to have failed at the last moment — or else his incorrigible frivolity and laziness gained the upper hand. He did not march on the Élysée, preferring the attractions of his mistress, Madame de Bonnemain. The Republic was saved by little effort or virtue of its own.

But the Government, given breathing-space as by a miracle, acted quickly. . . . The new Prime Minister, Tirard, and his Minister of the Interior, Constans, took action against the League of Patriots, and planned to bring Boulanger to trial before the Senate, as the High Court. Boulanger, successfully scared, fled to Brussels on the appropriate date of April 1. Two years later he shot himself on the grave of his mistress, and provoked from Clemenceau the comment that he "died as he had lived, like a subaltern. . . ."

But the problem of an Army which might produce a Caesar remained unsolved. The real paralysis of government on the night of the Paris election had been due to the virtual certainty that the Army of the Republic could not be counted upon to oppose the popular military hero. The parliamentary politicians, ever jealous of a rival power within the State challenging "the Republic one and indivisible," had learnt that it was well to keep generals unpopular, and thoroughly divorced from Radical reputations which might put demagogic ideas into their heads. Bonaparte himself had been a good "Republican" general. But how then could the High Command be Republicanized? Perhaps only by having an anti-militarist as Minister for War. But even this device was not to prove very effective. . . .

The Boulangist crisis was the first stage

in the Right becoming peculiarly nationalist. Until then, it had even been accused of being anti-nationalist, of subordinating French national interests to those of the Church, and ultramontanism had lent colour to these charges. Now it had emerged as the supporter of a peculiarly aggressive form of nationalism, and the Left had moved into the posture of opposing militarist men and ideas, and had been led to attack even the idea of *revanche* when it appeared a weapon or an excuse for Caesarism. The Dreyfus affair marked the main stage in this reversal of party positions as regards national security and the Army. . . .

The charge of espionage brought against Captain Dreyfus, a Jewish officer, was readily accepted by the military tribunal and he was duly sent to Devil's Island. This success was equally naturally followed by a concerted drive to expel all Jews and Protestants from the armed forces of France. It was a drive engineered and carried out by the clericalist, ultra-nationalist members of the General Staff. Only gradually did it become clear that the isolated case of Dreyfus was but one item in a vast conspiracy against the Republic: a truth which dawned only when the document which had condemned him came to be strongly suspected of being a forgery. The upheaval in the French Army, occasioned by charges and counter-charges, gradually attracted wider public attention. Each new revelation in the vast and sensational scandal roused public opinion to still more feverish unrest. The recent scandals connected with parliamentary politicians were forgotten in this greater and more intriguing scandal concerning the Army itself. And the issues raised soon clarified into fundamental issues regarding the very nature of democratic society itself. A new *mystique* was born: the *mystique* of civilianism.

As the Dreyfus affair dragged on, the issue of the guilt or innocence of Dreyfus sank into the background, and the general defence of the military and nationalist leaders came to rest not on the thesis that Dreyfus was guilty, but that even if he were inno-

cent, it was better that one man should suffer than that the whole prestige of the French Army should be undermined in face of the enemy. This involved a challenge to the democratic creed, to the sacredness of individual rights and the sanctity of justice. It evoked, in reaction, a full-dress restatement of civilian ideas and the necessity for all order and security to be based upon justice and truth. The courageous act of the great novelist, Émile Zola, in publishing *J'accuse* in January 1898, raised the controversy to a level of dignity and moral greatness which it had not previously known. Setting forth his list of charges in detail, and explaining that he harboured no personal grievance or even knowledge of the military leaders accused, he deliberately incurred legal penalties as, in his own words, "a revolutionary means of hastening the explosion of truth and of justice." Jules Guesde, the Socialist leader, declared Zola's letter "the greatest revolutionary act of the century." The trial of Zola and his publisher in the *Cour d'assises*, defended by Clemenceau, became a political debate of the highest quality. . . .

The social forces which rallied to the defence of Dreyfus and of civilian democracy are significant: they reveal the nature of the fundamental social cleavage which the incidents of the affair exposed. In addition to leading Radicals like Clemenceau and Socialists like Jaurès; and in addition to prominent literary figures like Zola and Anatole France; the main classes from which the Dreyfusards drew their support were the teaching profession and the universities, already deeply imbued with the anti-clerical spirit of the *École normale*, the lower middle-classes, similarly anti-clerical and anti-militarist in outlook, and the industrial workers of the larger towns, whose Socialistic brand of Republicanism was aroused by the affair. To the negative emotions of anti-clericalism and anti-militarism was added the moral faith, so vital to modern French democracy, that no social order could endure unless it was based on justice to the individual and respect for human personality regardless of race or creed.

127

When the forces of the older aristocracy, the service leaders and clericals, the authoritarians and the higher *fonctionnaires,* found themselves opposing this faith as well as defending clericalism and militarism, they were doomed. Yet the clash of forces, the clash of revolutionary and counter-revolutionary forces, was not resolved without prolonged political and parliamentary crisis, involving moments of real danger to the Republic itself. . . .

31. GENERAL ANDRÉ ON THE POLITICS OF OFFICER PROMOTION

By the end of the nineteenth century, relations between the army and the state in France had come to be based on the assumption that there was a specific military sphere of competence within which the soldiers were to have a high degree of autonomy. The politicians would not meddle in strictly military affairs and it went without saying that the soldiers kept out of politics. The Dreyfus Affair, which wracked French political life in the closing years of the nineteenth century, subjected this assumption to a severe strain. The politicians began to question whether a necessarily authoritarian military establishment did not after all represent a real danger to the democratic institutions of the Third Republic. This fear is reflected in the following selection taken from a speech in November 1904 before the Chamber of Deputies delivered by General Louis André, the Minister of War of the moment. He here defends the government's policy of using political rather than military criteria in deciding which officers were to be promoted. By consciously seeking to influence the political attitudes of the soldiers, the government was radically reversing what had come to be the accepted assumptions of civil-military relations in France. In so doing it brought about a steep decline in both the morale and the military effectiveness of the army.

When on May 28, 1900 I had the honor to be received by M. Waldeck-Rousseau,[1] who called upon me to accept the office of Minister of War, a rather long conversation ensued between us. He told me of the grievous preoccupations which perturbed him and of the grave, incessant worries which were causing him a continual insomnia and concerning which he wished to make me his confidant.

His preoccupations were centered on the subterranean endeavors that were taking place with the aim of inducing the army to set itself up as an adversary of the

[1]Premier of France between 1899 and 1902. [Editor's note]

civil authorities . . . and we recalled to each other the alarming symptoms of recent years. . . .

In the first place, there were the grave military incidents that took place in the course of the Dreyfus Affair, such as when an effort was made to lead some regiments to the Elysée during the funeral of Felix Faure, and the fact that certain of the military were manifestly hesitant in the course of that adventure as to where their duty lay. Such as when the President of the Republic was returning from Versailles to Paris, following his election, and was booed by the crowd in the presence of his

From the *Annales de la Chambre des Députés* (1904, session extraordinaire), pp. 269–278, abridged. Translation by the editor.

military escort, who let their indifference be openly seen. . . . Such as the affair at Auteuil, where insult to the President was replaced by a brutal and odious assault . . . and where in the crowd which was encouraging the attacker we had sadly to note the presence of officers in mufti. . . . Such as the obscene insults addressed to the President of the Republic by the officers of a regiment which had to be transferred in its entirety. . . .

These were alarming symptoms. . . .

At that period, following the initiative of M. Waldeck-Rousseau, the republicans placed their confidence in me because they were aware of the danger.

I expected a struggle, open resistance that I would have to overcome! Well, not at all! There was neither struggle nor open resistance. Rather, I met that sort of resistance that one may call the force of inertia. It was evident in the complaisance of certain chiefs, who were always ready to excuse the reprehensible acts of their subordinates for the very honorable reason that a chief must cover his inferiors, and in their obstinate insistence not to inform me of such acts. . . .

Any of these acts which have come to my knowledge have been curbed. A certain number of them have been made public. . . . But there are others, and there are a great number of them, which are known of only within the circles in which they took place. . . .

The republicans who hear what I have to say will draw from it the conviction that there is no reason to think that our task of republican action is yet finished. . . .

After a long period in the course of which republican officers obtained practically nothing, and in which officers hostile to the government obtained everything, I have found it just that one be able to give satisfaction to republican officers. . . .

In my estimation, I had a narrow duty to carry out in the examination which I made of the rights to promotion, and that was, strictly military qualifications being equal, to take into account their more or less correct attitude vis-à-vis our political institutions.

And since I speak of correct attitude, this is how I understand it and have ordered it taught in our military schools:

"An officer must not commit any political acts. . . . To serve the government of France is simply to do his duty."

To this I added: "To love our republican institutions, to assert republican principles in his conduct is not to commit a political act."

I further added that "every manifestation opposed to the Republic in the outward actions of an officer is contrary to his duty for then he commits a political act.". . .

I have indicated the problem that was posed for me and the goal that I pursued.

To achieve it, certain information was necessary. Gentlemen, do not believe that these pieces of information reached the Ministry of War under the present state of affairs. If the officer corps had been inspired by an absolutely correct attitude in this matter, the Minister of War would have been completely informed and would have found in their reports all the necessary data to draw the correct conclusions. Everything would have been easy.

It has not been so. . . . I have been incompletely informed by the usual hierarchical channels. . . .

All these facts proved that a minister who wished to have no doubts as to the data that he might need in order to be able to differentiate between one officer and another, would have to apply himself to the task of bringing together every possible piece of information concerning those whom he is called upon to judge. . . .

First and foremost, I thought that the sources ought to be of a very diverse nature so that they would be complete and would verify each other mutually. Moreover. . . only information that had been absolutely confirmed was to be taken into consideration, even by means of an investigation, if necessary. . . .

By virtue of an agreement between Waldeck-Rousseau and myself, information was furnished by the Ministry of the Interior from the beginning of my term of office. . . .

Numerous recommendations were addressed to me by politicians and I called upon them for assistance. At the moment of my entry into office I very overtly requested all republican members of parliament . . . who might have useful information with regard to officers who were known personally to them, that they furnish me with it. . . .

In addition, generals and colonels came to me to make their professions of republican faith in my office. They gave me information concerning their direct subordinates. . . . Officers themselves wrote to inform me of their sentiments. . . . Since 1902, in consequence of a circular from the President of the Council of Ministers, information has been requested from the prefects. . . .

I will be telling nobody anything very new when I state that information emanating from parties hostile to the Republic has often influenced officer promotion. . . . Thus, I subjected to a detailed examination the officers' dossiers, whenever they passed through my hands. . . . Whenever I found that in a report his republican opinions had been imputed to an officer, I wished to preserve that report . . . in order to seek to make amends in so far as I was able, for any delay that he may have undergone in his promotion because of it.

I thought that if there were information still in existence in the Ministry of War, emanating from parties hostile to the Republic, I could accept it along with the other information with which I had provided myself, and on the condition that I had it verified, . . . by information coming from republican associations. . . .

All the decisions that I have taken are based on this verified information. I say

now and will repeat it: I have never been inspired in this matter by anything but a sense of equity and you may be certain that never have I placed on the promotion table or in the competition for the Legion of Honor—as I have been accused—officers who do not fulfill the regularly required conditions. . . .

I assert—and I take you all as witnesses—that I have never given in to any kind of pressure no matter from where or from whom it came.

I have sought, all other qualifications being equal, to give preference to republican officers, and I have sought to take into account to the degree that it was possible, the delays in their careers that their opinions may have caused them. In this order of ideas I have not been able to do all that I would have wanted, and the republican party might, perhaps in this respect, find that I have been neither swift enough nor gone far enough. I have been accused of having held back officers who were noted as reactionary; I might more justly be reproached for not having given to republican officers all the compensation they had a right to expect.

When I assumed the office of Minister of War at the behest of Waldeck-Rousseau, who knew well the state of the army and who was aware of the difficulties that I was going to encounter and of the time that would be necessary for me to overcome them, he recommended that I move slowly and methodically. In my conduct, I have conformed to his views. . . .

I beg you to believe that I did not mount this rostrum to defend my ministerial portfolio. . . . I remain at my post in order to defend the Republic there—and there to defend and to reassure republican officers . . . and also those officers who are now being won over to the Republic.

32. **WALTHER RATHENAU ON THE INDUSTRIAL MOBILIZATION OF GERMANY**

In total war, the whole resources of a nation—military, economic, and spiritual—are committed to the conflict. This phenomenon, which had been foreshadowed as long ago as the French Revolution, finally came into existence in the trench stalemate which followed the Battle of the Marne. As the belligerent powers progressively committed their entire energies to trying to break the deadlock, the war took on gigantic dimensions. This sudden increase in the scale and the scope of the war caught most of the responsible civilian and military leaders unawares. One man who did foresee what was coming from the moment war was declared was Walther Rathenau, head of the great German electrical firm, A.E.G. By dint of his foresight Germany organized her industrial resources for the war effort far in advance of any other combatant power. In this effort, he received the full cooperation of the military authorities. Despite her inferiority in manpower and a blockade which systematically deprived her of foodstuffs and raw materials, Germany was thus able to hold out far longer than might reasonably have been expected. In the following selection, taken from a speech he delivered in 1915, Rathenau recounts what he was able to accomplish.

The object of my paper is to report to you a new departure in our economic warfare which has no precedent in history, which will have a decided influence on the war, and which in all probability is destined to affect future times. In its methods it is closely akin to communism and yet it departs essentially from the prophecies and demands resulting from radical theories. It is not my purpose to give an account of a rigid system based on theories, but I shall relate how this system grew out of our actual life, first taking concrete form in a small group, then affecting ever widening circles, and finally bringing about a complete change in our economic life. Its visible result is a new department attached to the War Office which places our whole economic life in the service of the war. . . .

When on August 4 of last year England declared war our country became a beleaguered fortress. Cut off by land and cut off by sea it was made wholly self-dependent; we were facing a war the duration, cost, danger, and sacrifices of which no one could foresee.

When three days had passed after England had declared war I could no longer stand the agony. I called on the Chief of the War Department, Colonel Scheuch, and on the evening of the same day I was kindly received by him. I explained to him that I was convinced that the supply of the absolutely needed raw materials on hand could probably last only a limited number of months. Colonel Scheuch shared my opinion that the war would be one of long duration, and so I was forced to ask him, "What has been done and what can be done to avert the danger that Germany will be strangled?"

Very little had been done in the past, but

Excerpted from *Fall of the German Empire, 1914–1918*, Volume II, edited by Ralph Haswell Lutz, Hoover War Library Publications, No. 2, with the permission of the publishers, Stanford University Press. Copyright 1932 by the Board of Trustees of the Leland Stanford Junior University; copyright reviewed 1960 by Ralph Haswell Lutz.

much has been done since the interest of the War Department has been aroused. Returning home deeply concerned and worried I found a telegram from von Falkenhayn, then Minister of War, asking me to come to his office the next morning. . . .

Our discussion lasted the greater part of the forenoon, and when it was ended the Minister of War had decided to establish an organization, no matter whether great or small, provided it had authority and was efficient and able to solve the problem which we were facing. In that moment the Prussian Minister of War was bold enough to take upon himself the responsibility for a decision which meant the turning-point in that matter which I am discussing here.

I was about to take leave, but the Minister detained me by making the unexpected demand that I should undertake to organize the work. I was not prepared for this; I asked for time to think the matter over, but my request was not granted; I had to consent, and a few days later I found myself installed at the War Office.

The *Kriegs-Rohstoff-Abteilung* (War Raw Materials Board) was established by ministerial decree. There were to be two directors: a retired colonel, a man of great experience, representing the War Office in matters demanding expert military knowledge; and myself, whose duty it was to create the organization. We were located in four small rooms, working with the assistance of a secretary whose practical experience was of great value. . . .

The first problem was the question of available supplies. It was necessary to ascertain the period of months for which the country was provided with the indispensable materials. Any further action depended on that. Opinions received from the great industries were quite contradictory.

Having asked the authorities if statistics might be furnished, I was informed that such statistics might be worked out but that it would probably take six months to do so. When I stated that I must have them within a fortnight because the matter was urgent I was assured that that was quite impossible. Yet I had to have them; and I had them within fourteen days. . . .

At first we were concerned with only a small number of materials. The whole fields of foodstuffs and of liquid fuel were excluded; included was everything called "raw materials." The official definition gave the following interpretation: "Such materials as are needed for the defense of the country and which cannot be produced within the country at all times and in sufficient quantities." At first hardly more than a dozen of such indispensable materials were enumerated; the number, however, increased from week to week and has now passed the hundred mark.

So far we had but little data, but we had a foundation to work on. We had learned to what extent the country was supplied, and by degrees we began to see the problem in its entirety. But we did not yet know how the problem was to be solved. . . .

The very fact that the problem was not understood caused many difficulties. Up to the present the German people believe that the supply of raw materials takes care of itself. The food question is being discussed all day long; the question of raw materials is hardly mentioned. Even now it is hard for us to realize what the situation was at the beginning of the war. For the first six months no one had any idea what we were trying to do. . . .

We were forced to advance slowly, step by step. Yet I may say that, after all, all authorities have supported us, that the people have finally come to understand that our organization is able to take up any problem, however difficult it may be, and can find new ways to solve the problems.

But the beginning was difficult. . . .

The first question was to establish a legal basis. . . . It was necessary to establish and formulate new and fundamental ideas upon which the reorganization of our economic life could rest. The term "sequestration" (*Beschlagnahme*) was given a new interpretation, somewhat arbitrarily, I admit, but supported by certain passages in our martial law. At a later period our interpretation was sanctioned by law.

"Sequestration" does not mean that merchandise or material (Ware) is seized by the state but only that it is restricted, i.e., that it no longer can be disposed of by the owner at will but must be reserved for a more important purpose (or, that it must be put at the disposal of a higher authority). The merchandise must be used for war purposes only: it may be sold, manufactured, shipped, transformed; but no matter what is done to it, it always remains subject to the law that it must be used for war purposes only.

At first many people found it difficult to adjust themselves to the new doctrine. We were often told that we had made the great mistake of not confiscating everything. I do not mention this assertion with the idea of contradicting it, for it needs no contradiction. If we had requisitioned the goods of even a single branch of industries, e.g., of the metal industries (that is to say, if we had requisitioned all copper, tin, nickel, aluminum, antimony, wolfram, chrome) we should have become owners of millions of lots of goods and every day innumerable inquiries would have been received demanding to know what was to be done with this or that parcel of goods? Is it to be rolled, drawn, or cast? Who is to get it? There is much demand! On the other hand, all manufacturing would have come practically to a standstill until such a time as all goods could have been reapportioned. And the responsibility of accounting for goods worth many milliards of marks would have rested on us.

The interpretation formulated by us for the term "sequestration" has stood the test and will remain a potent factor in our economic warfare. The new doctrine, however, entailed grave dangers. For when goods are sequestered, peace industries must come to a stop. A manufacturer of metal goods whose store of metals has been sequestered no longer can manufacture peace articles; he must depend on war work. His whole plant and his machinery, his methods, and

his products must be readjusted. He has to begin all over again. Our industries underwent a terrible period of trial and hardship, especially those in the field of metallurgy, chemistry, and the textile materials. . . .

But the crisis is past. For two months we gave the industries a certain amount of leeway, though with a heavy heart. Who could tell whether or not the release of a single ton of saltpeter would decide the fate of a battle or of a beleaguered fortress? But somebody had to take the responsibility and we have not shirked doing it.

Within two months German industrial life was readjusted. It was done quietly, without a breakdown, with self-confidence and energy, and with magnificent efficiency. That, gentlemen, speaks highly for the German industries and must never be forgotten. Not France, nor England, nor the United States, nor any of our enemies or our quasi-enemies will ever do the same.

So much regarding sequestration. Its effect was the reorganization of our industries. And now I approach the second factor.

We were aware that our economic life had to be remade. We knew that new forms and methods must be found for the distribution of materials. But how was that to be done?

The army and the navy must retain absolute freedom to do business with whom they choose. We could not tell them: you will receive orders from us as to with whom you may deal. On the other hand, the concern receiving orders from the Government must be furnished the needed material. New agencies had to be created for gathering, storing, and distributing the material circulating in a new form through the arteries of German commerce. A new system had to be created, that of the Kriegswirtschafts-Gesellschaften (War Industries Boards). Today we are as accustomed to them as if they had been handed down from time immemorial. But at first they appeared so paradoxical that, even in our intimate circle, otherwise so harmonious, there was difference of opinion as to the possibility and practicability of this new organ.

On the one hand, it meant a step in the direction of state socialism. For commerce was no longer free, but had become restricted.

On the other hand, it meant the attempt to encourage self-administration of our industries. How were such contradictory doctrines to be made to agree?

With more or less benevolence we have been afterward informed what course we ought to have taken: we should not have founded companies but should have added to the existing government apparatus. Today criticism has become silent. If anyone is still skeptical let him go to the War Metal Board or to the War Chemical Board. If he sees the beehive, thousands of men at work, a constant stream of visitors, if he watches the amount of correspondence, of shipments, and of payments, he will realize that this work could not have been done within the framework of government administration; it had to be left to professional experts and to self-administration.

The system of war boards is based upon self-administration; yet that does not signify unrestricted freedom. The War Raw Materials Board was established under strict government supervision. The boards serve the interests of the public at large; they neither distribute dividends nor apportion profits; in addition to the usual organs of stock companies, a board of governors and a supervising committee, they have another independent organ, a committee of appraisement and distribution, made up of members selected from various chambers of commerce, or of government officials. This committee serves as intermediary between the stock companies, representing capitalism, and the Government—an economic innovation which may be destined to become generally accepted in future times.

Their duty is to amass raw materials and to direct the flow of supply in such a way that each manufacturing concern is furnished the needed materials in quantities corresponding to the orders it receives from the Government and at prices fixed for such materials.

* * *

On April 1, 1915, I was able to turn over the department to the Prussian War Office as a going concern, working smoothly. I was greatly pleased when the majority of my co-workers stayed with the Government. Under the direction of my successor, Major Koeth, the department has grown enormously. Many new organizations have been added and the whole system has been perfected. Judged by its personnel and by the extent of its work, it is, with the exception of the War Office and the Ministry of Railways, equal to any governmental department in Prussia. It differs from them all in that it has grown up within eight months. It is served by a staff of more than five hundred officials, the raw-materials companies employing in addition, together with their branch organizations, a staff of several thousands.

When His Excellency von Falkenhayn came to Berlin this spring and asked after the state of our supplies, I was in a position to tell him: As far as the essentials are concerned our supplies are sufficient; the outcome of the war is not threatened by a lack of raw materials.

A similar statement was made by the Chancellor in the Reichstag. In certain fields our supply is absolute, i.e., our productive capacity equals the consumption; in others it will suffice as long as the war may last, and that depends on our enemies. In certain fields we have also undertaken to supply our allies.

The English blockade has failed. More than that, England has suffered. England's greatest worry is, at the present time, her unrestricted free trade. England is able to buy and she does buy, yet she fears every purchase made by her subjects in foreign countries. For every purchase, whether it be tea or saltpeter, endangers her economic balance. Every purchase must be paid for and as full payments cannot be made by wares (many of her industries formerly working for the export trade are now engaged in the manufacture of ammunition), every purchase means that English money flows into foreign countries.

German commerce circulates within the country. This state of our economic life was forced upon us, but we have adjusted ourselves to it. In some respects it has harmed us. But it has also strengthened us in that we now enjoy the whole benefit of the cycle. Our goods are produced within our boundaries and they are consumed within our boundaries. Nothing goes beyond these boundaries unless it be the cannon ball hurled by our artillery. Whatever the state consumes is paid for by the state in cash. The money thus paid is returned to the state in the form of bonds and once more enters into the cycle. The state has become a commercial unit.

33. DAVID LLOYD GEORGE ON BRITISH DEMOCRACY IN TOTAL WAR

Great Britain, unlike Germany, was slow in mobilizing both her manpower and her industrial resources for total war. Indeed, the English government initially met with great initial resistance from the competent military authorities, as it tried in the autumn of 1914 to improvise ways of meeting the increasingly desperate shortage in munitions. It was through his successful efforts to resolve the munitions crisis that David Lloyd George made his reputation as a wartime leader, becoming Prime Minister more or less on the strength of this accomplishment. Yet in spite of its relative slowness in mobilizing the industrial resources of the nation for total war, the seemingly cumbersome machinery of British democracy in the end demonstrated its efficacy. The democratic political systems of Britain, and of France, somehow proved more able to tap the spiritual and moral resources of their peoples than did the supposedly more efficient German militarist autocracy. In the following passage, drawn from his *War Memoirs*, Lloyd George discusses these two different but related aspects of total war.

The Munitions Crisis

The outbreak of war found this country totally unprepared for land hostilities on a Continental scale. Our traditional defence force has always been our Navy, and this weapon has been kept efficient and ready at all times. But our Army, mainly used for policing our widely scattered Empire, was a small, highly trained force of professional soldiers, excellent for their normal tasks, but lacking both the numbers and the equipment for large-scale fighting against European armies.

Unhappily, too, the War Office was hampered by a traditional reactionism. Its policy seemed ever to be that of preparing, not for the next war, but for the last one or the last but one. The Boer War found us still in the mentality of the Crimea, and the Great War caught our military thinkers planning for the next war under the conditions of the Alma in so far as these were modified by the irrelevant experiences of the African veldt. Unfortunately, they only remembered the lessons that were better forgotten because they were inapplicable, and forgot all the experiences by which they ought to have profited because they were a foretaste of the methods of future warfare. . . .

From David Lloyd George, *War Memoirs* (Boston, 1933), Vol. 1, pp. 112–148, Vol. VI, pp. 330–346, abridged. Reprinted by permission of The Beaverbrook Foundations.

It was not so much a question of unpreparedness at the outbreak of war. No one before the War contemplated our raising armies aggregating hundreds of thousands of men for any war in which we were ever likely to be engaged. Our military arrangements with France never went beyond the dispatch of an Expeditionary Force of six divisions to support the French armies on their left flank. When the Cabinet decided to appeal for volunteers they only asked for a recruitment of 100,000. What followed that appeal exceeded the most sanguine anticipation. When the German armies overran Belgium and broke the French front, marching up to the gates of Paris, the youth of Britain rolled up in such numbers that the whole idea of our contribution to the War was changed by this uprising of indignant valour. The Cabinet, excited by the spectacle to a fit of audacity, raised the limit of enlistment to 500,000. The flood did not take long to overflow even that limit.

No blame can, therefore, be attached to the War Office or its responsible heads for failing to have in store, at the outbreak of the War, a reserve of equipment and munitions for the hitherto undreamed-of-forces we were compelled to raise and put into the field. But they cannot be held guiltless of mental obtuseness in their neglect to keep abreast of modern development in pattern of munitions and machinery for munition production, and still more of a most pitiable breakdown of initiative in facing the new task which confronted them, of bringing munition production up to the standard demanded by the actual conditions of warfare as they soon manifested themselves in the campaign of 1914.

Modern warfare, we discovered, was to a far greater extent than ever before a conflict of chemists and manufacturers. Manpower, it is true, was indispensable, and generalship will always, whatever the conditions, have a vital part to play. But troops, however brave and well led, were powerless under modern conditions unless equipped with adequate and up-to-date artillery and mortars (with masses of explosive shell), machine-guns, aircraft and other supplies. Against enemy machine-gun posts and wire entanglements the most gallant and best-led men could only throw away their precious lives in successive waves of heroic martyrdom. Their costly sacrifice could avail nothing for the winning of victory.

This question of munitions supply, thus, emerged as the crucial issue of the War. Before long it became clear that unless we could solve it, and solve it promptly, we were doomed to certain futility in this War. . . .

Let me state at the outset that neither at the outbreak of war nor at any subsequent period in its course was the provision of munitions hampered by failure to furnish the money for their purchase or production. On the contrary, I repeatedly made it clear that as far as the Treasury was concerned no obstacle would come from that quarter in providing every supply that could possibly aid us to victory. If the choice were between spending gold or British lives, I was ready to take the responsibility of calling on the nation to yield its last coin, provided it were wisely and effectively spent. Nor did the country itself ever hesitate to support this attitude.

On the 5th of August, 1914, the day after the declaration of War, the House of Commons was invited by me to vote an initial sum of £100 million towards the cost. I let the War Office know that it could have whatever funds it needed to expedite supplies, and in September I took the further step of definitely setting aside a sum of £20 million and earmarking it as a fund to be drawn on to finance extensions of factories and works for the production of munitions. . . .

But although a financial *carte blanche* had thus been offered to the responsible authorities for all measures necessary to supply munitions, and although the needs of our troops at the front were urgent and terrible, the shortage of munitions continued and increased. The War Office neglected to utilise to the full its powers to remedy the lamentable shortage from which our armies were suffering so severely.

Admittedly the authorities were faced with an unprecedented situation. To cope with it, measures equally unprecedented were necessary. The gravamen of the charge against them is that they completely failed to show the resource and flexibility of mind requisite to grapple with that situation and to improvise those exceptional measures. The only defence they have been able to produce is the plea that the demands on them were out of all proportion to previous experience; that they strove to meet them through their traditional channels of supply; and that those channels became choked in the effort. But that was obvious from the outset. Their task should have been to increase those sources of supply in ways available to us as one of the three greatest and most resourceful and adaptable manufacturing countries in the world. Any powers they sought for the purpose would instantly have been accorded to them by Parliament. They not only failed to do this; they put all kinds of obstacles, both at the outset and later on, in the way of everyone who tried to help them, or relieve them of some part of their burden.

Up to the beginning of the War the normal routine was for the Minister of War as the instrument of Government to decide what operations he would sanction. The Commander-in-Chief would notify him of his requirements for carrying out those operations. On the basis of this information the Master-General of Ordnance would decide what stores must be obtained, and would in turn inform the Director of Army Contracts, who would approach the recognised armament firms, and refer their quotations for consideration to the Financial Secretary of the War Office. After due discussion, a contract would eventually be placed. . . .

The War Office had always dealt direct with the Government Arsenals and a certain small circle of contractors only, and could not bring itself to launch out into dealings with a wider circle. The taking in

hand of an array of new and untried firms and the organisation of them for munitions production would beyond question have been a serious and unprecedented responsibility. The Ordnance Department recoiled from that risk.

When, therefore, prominent industrialists all over the country clamoured to be of assistance. and made offers to supply military stores and munitions, the War Office did all it could to keep them at bay. Complaints reached me that they were treated as if they were greedy suppliants for profitable war contracts. The general policy of the War Office was to give these would-be helpers a list of the traditional contracting munition firms, and invite them to approach these firms with offers to sub-contract for supplies. It must be borne in mind that these firms were already working at full pressure, choked with orders from the War Office for not only their maximum output, but for whatever extended output they could hold out any hope of developing. It was obvious that their overworked staffs would neither have the time to organise a large system of subsidiary firms, nor the inclination to share some of their best skilled men to train workers in other concerns in the processes of munition manufacture; and furthermore, they would naturally be none too eager to teach other firms which might thereafter develop into awkward rivals and competitors with themselves in days to come. In peace-time there had been between Admiralty, War Office and foreign orders only barely sufficient orders for armaments to go round, and few guessed how long it would be before peace returned. . . .

The policy of the War Office relieved it of the dreaded responsibility for the control of work from these outside firms, but at the cost of interposing between the crying needs of our front line on the one hand, and the vast manufacturing capacity of Great Britain on the other, the narrow bottle-neck of a handful of overworked firms, far too busy with their own tasks to undertake the gigantic duty which the War

Office sought to thrust upon them, of organising the whole potential productive capacity of the country for munitions manufacture.

The military organisers appear to have been handicapped by that ingrained distrust, misunderstanding and contempt of all business men (not on the War Office register) which was traditionally prevalent in the Services; and doubtless the business men on their side were — to say the least — puzzled by their contact with the military mind and army manners. . . . Doubtless there were many incompetents and exploiters among those eager applicants for orders. But a filter of red tape was ill adapted to sift them out and still retain the really efficient business men, who are often the first to recoil, perplexed and disgruntled, at such treatment. The good men and the rubbish alike failed to squeeze through the fine and resistant mesh. Meantime the War Office, aware that it was not in sight of obtaining the gigantic supplies required by the front line, spent much time begging the soldiers not to use up shells so quickly. . . .

It was not perhaps obvious at first to everyone how vital this question of munitions was, or how urgent and grave it was to become. The eyes of the nation during those early months were set more upon the spectacular massing of our man-power, and the enrolment of the first million of the new Army. Indeed, this public attitude caused an accentuation of the difficulty, for vast numbers of highly skilled workers, whose technical ability was of the first importance for increasing the output of munitions, were swept by the torrent of public enthusiasm or driven by the undiscriminating taunts of their neighbours into the ranks of these recruits. But it was clear to some of us that the arming and equipment of our forces would be no less essential than their numbers, and far harder to attain. And when the first warning echoes of the shortage in France began to be heard, and rumours of the congestion in our munition firms at home came to our ears, we felt that special action must be taken to deal with the matter.

In September I urged the appointment of a special Committee of the Cabinet to look into the question of guns, shells and rifles. At first, Lord Kitchener resisted so strongly that the Cabinet turned down the proposal. He was held in such awe at this date that his colleagues did not dare challenge his authority. Eventually, however, early in October, I prevailed upon the Cabinet to appoint a Committee to examine the question of our munition supplies, and to advise as to means of increasing production and expediting deliveries. . . .

This Committee met altogether six times between the 12th of October, 1914, and the 1st of January, 1915, and took the initiative in some of the more important questions of policy and procedure which arose. . . .

In spite of the recommendation of the Cabinet Committee that it was advisable to mobilise the engineering resources of this country more fully for the production of munitions, the War Office adhered to its dependence on the established armaments firms. Had the War been "over by Christmas," then the official policy might have carried us through. Although Lord Kitchener, on December 4th, 1914, in one of the very few interviews he granted to the Press, spoke of the possibility that the War would last three years, the authorities at the War Office responsible for the supply of munitions were slow to envisage the character and the probable duration of the struggle. . . .

This failure to realise the scale of warfare to which we were committed, and the corresponding scale of armament and munition output that would be required, was characteristic of the War Office during those early months. When it was discovered in December that the deliveries of gun ammunition promised by the main contractors were not coming forward, it was not inferred that the scheme of production was at fault. The contractors' estimates had been too sanguine; the sub-contractors had broken down over unforeseen difficulties.

These failures were, indeed, taken by the War Office to be proof of the fundamental soundness of their contention that the technical difficulties of armament work were likely to defeat the inexpert manufacturer, and could only be tackled by the established firms.

Some Reflections on the Functions of Governments and Soldiers Respectively in a War

Every prolonged war has at one stage or another produced differences and disputes between the civilian Government and the Generals in the field. The only exceptions are those where autocrats themselves commanded their own armies. Where success tarries disappointment ensues and disappointments lead to disagreements. It is also inevitable that there should be argument as to reinforcements and supplies between those who have to use them and those who have to furnish them. No country has unlimited resources at its command, and a wise Government faced with a formidable enemy will mobilise its strength to the best advantage. In this respect Governments cannot delegate their primary responsibility. But whilst Governments and Generals ought to realise each other's difficulties they are naturally more imminently conscious of their own. One point of view is more constantly present to the Government — the General, on the other hand, has the other point of view always in front of him. Where Governments have several armies in the field, each under a separate command, they are confronted with the additional problem of distributing their resources between these various units. If the fight is on sea as well as on land, Governments must decide what proportion of the strength of the nation they ought to devote to each respectively. Governments have the entire responsibility for the home front. That front is always underrated by Generals in the field. And yet that is where the Great War was won and lost. The Russian, Bulgarian, Austrian and German home fronts fell to pieces before their armies collapsed. The averting of that great

and irrevocable catastrophe is the concern of the Government. Great care must be taken of the condition and susceptibilities of the population at home, who make it possible to maintain, to reinforce and to equip armies. All the suffering is not in the trenches. The most poignant suffering is not on the battlefield, but in the bereft hearths and hearts in the homeland. If in addition to the anguish of grief women have to witness the pinched faces and waning strength of their children there will soon be trouble in the nation behind the line, and if men home on leave have to carry back these unnerving memories to the trenches their will to fight on is enfeebled. That is what accounted for the sudden breakdown in the German resistance in November, 1918. The ration allowance for each British household was cut down to the lowest minimum compatible with health. Anything lower would have made trouble. But there was no privation. In Germany and Austria children died of hunger. The ration of the British soldier was maintained at its excellent maximum to the end. The food allowance of the German soldier was cut down to an unappetising and insufficient minimum. But the feeding and clothing of a population of over 45,000,000 and of three to four millions abroad takes some doing. That was the care of the Government. Generals thought we were spending on this problem a good deal of energy and man power which ought to have been devoted to strengthening their armies. Millions of the picked young men of the nation were placed at their disposal. More than half these millions were either killed or wounded, too often in the prosecution of doubtful plans or mishandled enterprises. Generals demanded more millions not only to fill up gaps thus caused but to further increase the numbers under their direction. The Government had other responsibilities to discharge which also required the services of able-bodied men. It was for the Government to determine apportionments. Out of this discussion came suspicions and resentments which poisoned good will and whole-hearted coöperation.

Ought we to have interfered in the realm of strategy? This is one of the most perplexing anxieties of the Government of a nation at war. Civilians have had no instruction, training or experience in the principles of war, and to that extent are complete amateurs in the methods of waging war. It is idle, however, to pretend that intelligent men whose minds are concentrated for years on one task learn nothing about it by daily contact with its difficulties and the way to overcome them. . . .

Questions of policy were also essential to a wise handling of the question of man power. It was for the military to estimate the numbers they needed, but there were other Departments making similar demands and it was for the Government to weigh the relative importance of those demands and to decide how many they could and should allocate to each. It is just like the claims each Government Department presents to the Treasury for the coming financial year. The aggregate always exceeds what the finances of the nation can afford. The Government decide what to allow, what to reject, or how much to cut down in claims which are in themselves justifiable. This is a domain of strategy in which the Government must be supreme. An extra 200,000 men at the front would not have converted the Passchendaele fiasco into a triumph, but it might have lost the War by disorganising the services that kept the nation from the hunger and penury that destroyed Germany and Austria.

The psychological blunders perpetrated by Germany afford many illustrations of the shortsightedness of subordinating considerations of statesmanship to immediate military exigencies. Strategy must take cognisance of both. There is the occupation of Belgium. It was not sound strategy because it was a political blunder. It brought the British Empire into the War. . . . The provocation which brought America into the War was another political blunder, for which the soldiers were primarily responsible. The insistence on taking too many men from food and war production because they were needed at the front was yet another. All these issues enter into strategy and in determining them statesmen must have their say as well as soldiers. In some of them statesmanship is the most important element and statesmen ought to have the final decision — after giving due weight to everything soldiers may have to urge from their point of view.

But there is a region where the soldier claims to be paramount and where the interference of the statesman seems to him to be an impertinence. There is the question of whether a great battle which may involve enormous losses ought to be fought — if so, where and at what time. The second question is whether a prolonged attack on fortifications (practically a siege) which is causing huge loss of life without producing any apparent result ought to be called off. Should Governments intervene or leave the decision entirely to the soldiers? . . .

Generally speaking, the argument of the high Commands in the War for its sole claim to decide military policy was put far too high by them and their partisans. War is not an exact science like chemistry or mathematics where it would be presumption on the part of anyone ignorant of its first rudiments to express an opinion contrary to those who had thoroughly mastered its principles. War is an art, proficiency in which depends more on experience than on study, and more on natural aptitude and judgment than on either. It is said that medicine is an art based on many sciences. But compare the experience acquired by a doctor in the course of his practice with that of the professional soldier. A physician fights a series of battles with the enemy every day and every year of his professional life.

That experience adds to his mastery of the art to which he has dedicated his abilities. The same observation applies to law and to politics. The lawyer and the politician, before they reach the age at which our

Generals took over the command of our Armies in the War, are already the veterans of a myriad fights. In these incessant struggles they have been confronted with highly skilled adversaries. A soldier may spend his lifetime in barracks or colleges without a day's actual experience of the realities with which he will have to contend if war breaks out. On August 4th, 1914, not one of our great Commanders had encountered an enemy in battle for 12 years. Even then the experience they had acquired in the only war in which they had taken part had no relevance to the problems of the World War. On the South African veldt horsemanship counted more than drill. A fox hunter was more useful than a machine-gunner. The aeroplane and the tank were unknown and unthought of. . . . All the men who filled the highest commands in our Army in France were veterans of the Boer War. It is not too much to say that when the Great War broke out our Generals had the most important lessons of their art to learn. Before they began they had much to unlearn. Their brains were cluttered with useless lumber, packed in every niche and corner. Some of it was never cleared out to the end of the War. For instance, take their ridiculous cavalry obsession. In a war where artillery and engineering and trench work were more in demand than in any war in history we were led by soldiers trained in the cavalry. Haig was persuaded to the end of the War that a time would come when his troopers would one day charge through the gap made by his artillery and convert the German defeat into a headlong scamper for the Rhine. Needless to say, that chance never came. Generals were in every essential particular inadequately prepared for the contingencies which confronted them in this War. . . .

In the most crucial matters relating to their own profession our leading soldiers had to be helped out by the politician. I have already given in detail an account of the way the Generals muddled the problem of munitions. They did not possess the necessary understanding of the probable character of the War to foresee that it would be a war which would consume a prodigious quantity of shot and shell. What they ordered was of the wrong kind. They preferred shrapnel to high explosive because the former was more useful in the Boer War. What they provided was on the assumption that the War would be conducted in the open field. When it developed into a war of deep digging they did not realise that in order to demolish those improvised ramparts it was essential to equip an army with thousands of guns of a calibre heavier than any yet trundled into the battlefield. A fortress with its flanks extending from the North Sea to the Swiss mountains and held by millions of men and masses of cannon and machine guns was a nightmare they never contemplated in their most disturbed slumbers. It took them months to adapt their strategy to this novel and unforeseen portent. They did not realise that the machine gun and the hand grenade would practically take the place of the rifle. Politicians were the first to seize upon the real character of the problem in all these respects and it was they who insisted on the necessary measures being taken — and taken promptly — in order adequately to cope with it. It was politicians who initiated and organised these measures. In doing so, at each stage they had to overcome the rooted traditions, prejudices and practices of military staffs. It was politicians who insisted upon the importance of providing sufficient and suitable transport facilities behind the line on a great scale in order not only to bring up supplies, but to increase the mobility of the Army along the whole front. It was civilians, chosen by politicians, who reorganised and developed these facilities. It was politicians who foresaw that any attempt to break through the immense fortifications thrown up by the enemy on the Western Front would involve enormous carnage and a prolongation of this destructive war. It was they who urged the finding of a way round on the most vulnerable fronts. It was politicians who urged the importance of making the best use of the magnificent and almost inexhaustible fighting man power in Russia and the Balkans by providing them with the necessary equipment to play their part in attacking the enemy on his Eastern and Southern Fronts. It was amateurs who discovered the tank, easily the most formidable of our weapons and it was they who invented and urged the use of one of the most serviceable machines of the War, the Stokes mortar. It was a civilian who invented the hydrophone which located the deadly submarine and enabled us to hunt it down in the pathless depths of the sea.

Let anyone read the history of the War with care and then conjecture what would have happened if the ignorant and cold-shouldered civilian had not insisted on coming to the rescue of the military and the discharge of those functions which in peace and war constituted an essential part of the duties and responsibilities of the latter. I have not perused a military history which recognises fairly and generously the contribution rendered to the achievement of victory by the unwelcome intervention of the amateur untrained in military colleges or parade grounds.

Looking back on this devastating War and surveying the part played in it by statesmen and soldiers respectively in its direction I have come definitely to the conclusion that the former showed too much caution in exerting their authority over the military leaders. They might have done so either by a direct and imperative order from the Government or by making representations followed, if those were not effective in answering the purpose, by a change in the military leadership. The latter method of procedure would no doubt have been the sounder and wiser course to pursue had it been feasible. The difficulty, however, all Governments experienced was in discovering capable commanders who could have been relied upon not only to carry out their policy but to do so efficiently and skilfully. . . . There was no conspicuous officer in the Army who seemed to be better qualified for the Highest Command than Haig. That is to say, there was no outstanding General fit for so overwhelming a position as the command of a force five times as great as the largest army ever commanded by Napoleon, and many more times the size of any army led by Alexander, Hannibal or Caesar. I have no doubt these great men would have risen to the occasion, but such highly gifted men as the British Army possessed were consigned to the mud by orders of men superior in rank but inferior in capacity, who themselves kept at a safe distance from the slime which they had chosen as the terrain where their plans were to operate.

34. LUDENDORFF ON THE FAILURE OF THE GERMAN HOME FRONT

The most notable military figure to emerge in Germany during World War I was Erich von Ludendorff. An unknown staff officer at the start of the war, he was by 1918 virtual Commander-in-Chief of the German armies and in effect the head of the German state. That he was able to achieve such a position of eminence is certainly tribute to his ability and to his force of character. Ludendorff, more than anyone else in either the government or the army, recognized the need to mobilize the psychological and spiritual resources of the nation for total war. When the government proved incapable of undertaking this immense task, Ludendorff, as the most forceful figure in the army, which had always been the most important single institution in the German state, assumed the responsibility. In the following selections from his war memoirs, Ludendorff justified the measures he was obliged to take as head of the military dictatorship which ruled Germany from 1916 to 1918.

The armies and fleets fought as they had fought in days past, even though numbers and equipment were mightier than ever before. What made this war different from all others was the manner in which the nations supported and reinforced their armed forces with all the resources at their disposal. Only in France, in 1870–71, had anything of the kind been seen before.

In this war it was impossible to distinguish where the sphere of the army and navy began and that of the people ended. Army and people were one. The world witnessed the War of Nations in the most literal sense of the word. The great powers of the earth faced one another in united concentrated strength. And not only between the armed forces did the combat rage along those huge fronts and on distant oceans; the very soul and vital force of the enemy were attacked in order to corrode and paralyze them. . . .

This world-wide War of Nations made enormous demands on us Germans, on whom its whole overwhelming burden fell. Every individual had to give his very ut-

most, if we were to win. We had literally to fight and work to the last drop of blood and sweat, and with it all maintain our fighting spirit and, above all, our confidence in victory—a hard but imperative necessity in spite of the dearth of food which the enemy inflicted upon us, and the onslaught of his propaganda, which was of amazing force, if unobtrusive.

Our army and navy are rooted in the nation as is the oak in German soil. They live upon the homeland, and from it they draw their strength. They can keep, but cannot produce, what they need, and can only fight with the moral, material, and physical means which the country provides. These means make victory possible—faithful devotion and unselfish self-sacrifice in the daily contest with the miseries of war. They alone could secure Germany's final success. With them our country waged the titanic conflict against the world, even allowing for the assistance of our allies and the exploitations of occupied territories as far as the laws of land warfare permitted.

The army and navy had thus to look to

From *Ludendorff's Own Story*, Vol. 1, pp. 2–9, Vol. II, pp. 64–65, by Erich von Ludendorff. Copyright 1920 by Harper & Brothers. Reprinted with the permission of Harper & Row, Publishers.

the homeland for its constant renewal and rejuvenation in morale, numbers, and equipment.

It was essential to maintain the morale and war spirit of those at home at the highest pitch. Woe to us if they should fail! The longer the war lasted the greater were the danger and the difficulties, and the more imperious grew the demands of the army and navy for spiritual and moral reinforcement.

The very last resources, both in men and material, had to be made available, and devoted to the prosecution of the war.

These were enormous tasks for the country. The homeland was not only the basis on which our military power rested, and which must therefore be carefully safeguarded; it was the life-giving source which had to be kept clear, lest it lose anything of that virtue wherewith it steeled the nerves and renewed the strength of the army and navy. The nation was in need of that inner spiritual strength which alone enabled it to reinforce the army and navy. The power of the nation and that of the armed forces were so intermingled that it was impossible to separate them. The fighting efficiency of the forces before the enemy depended absolutely upon that of the people at home.

That meant that at home every one must work and live for the war in a way that had never been known before. It was the duty of the Government, and especially the Imperial Chancellor, to direct and foster that spirit. . . .

Soon after we were summoned to assume the supreme command, and had time to consider the situation in all its bearings, the Field-Marshal and I laid our views as to the requirements of the army and navy before the Imperial Chancellor, and discussed the problems which they raised for the country. We called upon him to co-operate in prosecuting the war, and were buoyed up with hope in spite of the menacing aspect of the situation.

The Government had welcomed our appointment to the supreme command. We met the authorities with frank confidence. Soon, however, two schools of thought, represented by their views and ours, began to come into conflict. This divergence of view was a great disappointment to us and vastly increased our burden.

In Berlin they were unable to accept our opinion as to the necessity of certain war measures, or to steel their wills to the point of magnetizing the whole nation and directing its life and thought to the single idea of war and victory. The great democracies of the Entente achieved this. With an iron will, Gambetta in 1870–71, and Clemenceau and Lloyd George in this war, enrolled their peoples in the service of victory. Our Government failed to recognize this inflexible purpose, and the definite intention of the Entente to destroy us. It should never have doubted it. Instead of concentrating all our resources and using them to the utmost in order to achieve peace on the battle-field, as the very nature of war demands, the authorities in Berlin followed a different path: they talked more and more about reconciliation and understanding, without giving our own people a strong warlike impetus at the same time. In Berlin they believed, or deceived themselves into believing, that the hostile nations were longing to hear words of reconciliation and would urge their governments toward peace. So little did they understand the mind of our enemies, both people and governments, their strong national feeling, and unbending will. In Berlin they had learned nothing from history. They only felt their own impotence in face of the enemy's spirit; they lost the hope of victory, and drifted. The desire for peace became stronger than the will to fight for victory. The road to peace was blocked by the will of the enemy, whose aim was our destruction; in seeking it the Government neglected to lead the nation by the hard road to victory.

The Reichstag and the people found themselves without that strong leadership which, generally speaking, they longed for, and slid with the government down the slippery way. The tremendous questions arising out of the war were more and more thrust on one side, for people's minds were occupied with questions of internal politics and thoughts of self. This meant the ruin of our country. . . .

General Headquarters urged the view that it would be time enough for us to lay down our arms and think about understandings when human nature had undergone a change; otherwise we were bound to suffer. The palm of peace is no defense against the sword. As long as human beings, and, above all, our enemies, remained the same as mankind has ever been, Germany, and in any event the Field-Marshal and I, as the responsible military commanders, must retain our hold of the sword and keep it sharp. It was, therefore, our serious duty, in dealing with the Government, to insist on the necessary war measures being carried out, and to try to infuse into it that degree of determination which we thought was required.

In all questions General Headquarters addressed itself to the constitutional authorities. The war required rapid and far-reaching decisions at any moment, and thus stimulated that quality of resolution on which it was always making demands. In Berlin the old peace routine held sway. Replies, even to the most important questions, often did not arrive for weeks. In consequence of this extraordinary dilatoriness on the part of the Berlin authorities, and of their failure to grasp the necessities of the war, the tone of our correspondence at times became somewhat acrimonious. This we regretted, but we were consumed with justifiable impatience. Immediate action was called for, since it was often a question of averting some irreparable disaster.

In peace-time the Imperial Government was supreme. The Foreign Office considered itself above all criticism. The Government departments only gradually accustomed themselves to the idea that on the outbreak of war a new authority, General Headquarters, had come into being, which

not only shared the responsibility with the Imperial Chancellor, but bore such an enormous proportion of it that it had necessarily to try to make up for their inertia by displaying greater energy on its own part. . . .

The Government went its own way, and, as regards the wishes of General Headquarters, neglected nothing which it considered essential. But much was left undone that had been insisted on as urgently necessary for the prosecution of the war.

Right after war broke out, General Headquarters was obliged to take action in connection with several matters which were really the sphere of other authorities. The press, the censorship, precautions against spies and sabotage at home, dealing with revolutionaries — all these wide fields were left to the unaided efforts of the military authorities, to the detriment of the conduct of the war. Uncertainty as to their powers and lack of personnel checked the initiative of the authorities concerned. Their strong sense of responsibility urged the General Staff to creative work. It was better able to meet the requirements in personnel than other departments, particularly from among officers of the reserve on leave with previous training. And so the direction of this work fell into the hands of the General Staff. The execution, however, often remained in the hands of the home authorities. The line of demarcation, within which these authorities considered themselves to be solely responsible, was not clearly defined. Friction was unavoidable. This would have been avoided by that resolute leadership at home for which General Headquarters often asked.

* * *

The path of our internal development had not afforded scope for the growth of strong personalities. It was quite striking to see how the officer class, the members of which were always thought to be the most narrow-minded, had produced men of decision, while the civil official class, on the contrary, had, unfortunately, so conspicuously failed in this respect. Men who were prominent in public life kept out of the way, and followed their own professions. There may have been men of strong character in the Reichstag who could have guided the destiny of the country. The party system prevented their coming to the front. We were poor in men. Our political system had not produced new creative brains, and by its barrenness it pronounced its own sentence.

Arthur Rosenberg

35. THE DICTATORSHIP OF LUDENDORFF, 1916-1918

The following account of the military dictatorship, at the head of which Ludendorff ruled Germany for the last two years of the war, is taken from *The Birth of the German Republic*, by the noted German historian Arthur Rosenberg. Sympathetic to the socialist cause, he is for obvious reasons harsh on Ludendorff and his efforts to win a total victory. Yet Rosenberg also is less inclined to condemn Ludendorff as an individual than the basic weakness of the civilian institutions in Germany which under the stress of war collapsed, thus creating the power vacuum into which he had to move.

On August 29, 1916, under pressure of the feeling in the nation and the army, the Emperor was forced to relieve von Falkenhayn of his command. This day marked the downfall of the Bismarckian Empire and the beginning of the German Revolution. Nobody else could be appointed to Falkenhayn's vacant post except Field Marshal von Hindenburg. He brought with him to the Great General Head-quarters, General Ludendorff, who had been his Chief of Staff in the east. The change in personnel at once brought about a complete change in the authority of the army commands. The Supreme Army Command, which was famous throughout the whole world during the later years of the war, came into being. According to the Bismarckian Constitution, however, the Supreme Command of the German army rested solely in the hands of the Emperor, who in giving his commands could avail himself of the advice of the Chief of the General Staff. The Chief of the General Staff was responsible to the Emperor for the exact execution of the Imperial commands and for the proper administration of the army, in the same way as a regimental commander is responsible to a general or, in civil life, a cashier to his employer. If the Emperor was not satisfied with the conduct of the Chief of the General Staff, he either deprived him of his post or through a public manifestation of his displeasure induced him to proffer his resignation. The Chief of the General Staff had under him a number of assistant staff officers of whom one — by no means the most important — was the Quartermaster-General. Such was the organization as it existed in accordance with the German Constitution in the German Great General Head-quarters until August 1916.

The first sign of an alteration in the organization of the Great General Head-quarters was the creation of an extraordinary dual command. It was common knowledge that the victory won by General von Hindenburg in the east had been

From Arthur Rosenberg, *The Birth of the German Republic* (London, 1931), pp. 123–134, abridged.

planned by General Ludendorff. The nation and the army alike demanded that the entire conduct of the war should be placed in the hands of Hindenburg and Ludendorff. Hence Ludendorff accompanied the Field Marshal to the Great General Head-quarters, where, as Chief Quarter-Master-General, he was given a new and unprecedented post. In this capacity General Ludendorff shared with Hindenburg the full responsibility for the conduct of operations. Thus the Emperor came to have two Chiefs of the General Staff. As a matter of fact, however, the division of work resulted in Hindenburg's taking into his own hands the Supreme Command with, as his Chief of the General Staff, Ludendorff who, as he had done formerly in the east, drew up the plans to which Hindenburg lent his authority. In assenting to this reorganization of the Great General Staff the Emperor in reality abandoned the Supreme Command which he had until then at least formally retained in his own hands. After August 1916 the Emperor's authority over the German army became an empty formality.

The basis of Ludendorff's dictatorship was the entirely new interpretation — an interpretation entirely foreign to all the traditions of the German army — which he put upon his "responsibility." It was not merely that Ludendorff understood by "responsibility" the duty of a subordinate towards his superior, but rather that he interpreted his position as though it were that of a Minister responsible to Parliament. Thus, for example, when the Imperial Chancellor pursued a policy that, in the opinion of Ludendorff, was mistaken and even injurious to the conduct of the war, Ludendorff declared that he could not assume the "responsibility" for such a policy and proffered his resignation. The result was that it was the Imperial Chancellor who resigned and not Ludendorff. By a skilful use of this form of blackmail, which he called his "responsibility" or his "dislike of assuming the responsibility," Ludendorff not only forced the Emperor to give way to him in military matters but also in all decisive political questions.

General Ludendorff enjoyed the complete confidence of Field Marshal von Hindenburg. If Ludendorff proffered his resignation, Hindenburg did likewise. It was, however, impossible for the Emperor to relieve Hindenburg and Ludendorff of their commands. The Imperial authority had sunk so far, and that of the two Generals had risen so high, that William II was helpless as against Ludendorff. If in 1917 the Emperor had attempted to get rid of Ludendorff, a "Ludendorff" crisis would very quickly have become an "Emperor" crisis. It was only in October 1918, when the Quartermaster-General himself formally admitted that he had lost the war, and thereby in a sense announced his abdication as dictator, that it became possible to deprive him of his post. . . .

Ludendorff even claimed the right to name the Imperial Chancellor. Bethmann-Hollweg was dismissed because Hindenburg and Ludendorff refused to work in collaboration with him. . . .

Ludendorff not only refused to suffer any Imperial Chancellor who was not welcome to him, but he extended his dictatorial supervision to Ministers and Secretaries of State. When von Kühlmann, who was Secretary of State for Foreign Affairs, delivered in June 1918 a speech in the Reichstag with which the Supreme Command was dissatisfied, he was dismissed at Ludendorff's desire. Moreover, the Supreme Command reserved to itself the right to define Germany's war aims. When the peace negotiations between Germany, Russia, the Ukraine and Rumania were initiated, Ludendorff insisted that the Emperor should formally permit the participation of the Supreme Command notwithstanding the fact that, according to the Constitution, the Imperial Chancellor alone was responsible for the conclusion of peace. The rivalry between the Supreme Command and the Imperial Chancellor brought into being a situation that was contrary to the Constitution. Nevertheless, the attitude of Germany in the peace negotiations at Brest-Litovsk, and with Rumania, was determined by General Ludendorff.

The Supreme Command also interfered in all questions of domestic policy in so far as it was interested in them. At that time in Germany hardly anything happened that could not in some form or other be traced back to the Supreme Command. Its excuse for interference in Labour questions, food supplies, Trade Unions, raw materials, &c., was the fact that these all came under the heading of war industries. If no direct ground for interference was present, Ludendorff declared that his reason for interfering in a domestic issue was "that it had an unfavourable effect upon the morale of the army." The pressure brought to bear on the Emperor by the Supreme Command far exceeded anything in the nature of authoritative advice in military and political questions. William II was even forced to propose to General Ludendorff the names of those whom he wished to appoint to positions at Court. . . .

It is quite clear that in such a state of affairs it was no longer possible to talk of a monarchical government in Germany. The Constitution of 1871 had been in fact thrown aside. Nevertheless, General Ludendorff quite sincerely looked upon himself as loyal to the Emperor. At the same time he demanded of the Emperor that he should only do that which was right and necessary, and only retain in his service suitable and competent men. But it was General Ludendorff himself who decided what was to be done and in whom confidence was to be placed; and he demanded of William II that he should assent to these decisions. It was thus that the Carolingian Mayors of the Palace treated the Merovingian Kings.

William II was not ignorant as to the state of affairs, and looked upon Lundendorff's dictatorship as a grave personal humiliation. As in the past so now William II poured out his heart in marginal comments on the documents that were laid before him. Yet what a difference existed between the pre-war Imperial marginal comments with their proud and harsh expressions characteristic of an autocratic ruler and the depressed, embittered observations in 1917 and 1918! In January 1918, for example, a report from Field Marshal von Mackensen in Rumania, in which he set forth his views on the situation in the Balkans and on Austro-German relations, was laid before the Emperor. William II wrote in the margin that Mackensen's views "wholly coincide with my own. Up to the present, however, I have been unable to gain a hearing for them from the Chief of the General Staff." . . .

In those days William II judged the political situation in Germany somewhat as follows: "On the one side stands the all-powerful Supreme Command. On the other the majority of the Reichstag and certain Ministers who, relying on the support of the Reichstag, seek to overcome the authority of the Supreme Command. Neither party bothers about the Emperor, who himself can do nothing to improve matters." And that was the same William II who in 1890 could dismiss a Bismarck from office, and who had formerly wished to trample underfoot everything that stood in his path! In Ludendorff he had found his master. The Emperor was "ignored" by every one. Bismarck was revenged. . . .

It is true that General Ludendorff never sought to make himself the ruler of Germany. When in August 1916 he found himself placed in the Supreme Command by the desire of the army and the nation, he ruthlessly interfered whenever he deemed it to be necessary without worrying himself very much about his fitness to so do; and when he found that his will had become all-powerful he accustomed himself to govern. If Ludendorff had been an English or French General, or even a Prussian General under William I, he would never even have dreamt of interfering in politics. Fate, however, brought General Ludendorff to power at the very moment at which the Imperial Government, in the sense of the Constitution of 1871, had ceased to exist, and a new form of government had not yet come into being. Ludendorff the Politician is the stop-gap between two periods in German history and, from a moral standpoint, it would be wrong to condemn him for having played this role. That Ludendorff was a strategist of the first order is unquestionable. Great soldiers, however, are seldom statesmen. As a politician Napoleon was as great a failure as Caesar. Hannibal, by his — from a political standpoint — mistaken invasion of Italy, largely helped to bring about the downfall of Carthage. Moltke the Elder never attempted to interfere in politics.

In August 1916 Ludendorff possessed neither political capacity nor experience. Hence in non-military questions he allowed himself to be influenced with the greatest ease if only the person or the measure proposed fitted in in general with his train of ideas. He seized upon the advice given him by clever individuals and proceeded to put it into practice with his own peculiar tenacity and his immense authority. Ludendorff indeed defended himself from the charge of being a reactionary by pointing to his work for the wounded soldiers and for the promotion of building and the creation of settlements. At the same time it was incomprehensible to him that a workman could possess an independent judgement in politics. Nor could he understand why it was that the working class was influenced by the appalling want of the later years of the war to adopt views on the subject of war aims which did not coincide with his own. He was prepared to adopt the most ruthless measures against strikers. In no circumstances was any concession to be made to any wish put forward by a striker. In a letter to the Minister for War on February 18, 1918, Ludendorff voiced his belief that it would be possible in the future to settle disputes "in general without the employment of force." "Nevertheless it is necessary," he added, "to be prepared for all eventualities, and it is for this reason that I have consented to leave the desired troops in Germany." In

the same letter Ludendorff advised the Minister for War to place all factories under military control. "Military control is naturally only a temporary expedient. It appears, however, to be specially effective in that the workmen once more gain the impression of an over-riding authority which has power over them and is prepared to afford the utmost protection to those who desire to work — these are always by far the greater majority among the workmen." Strikes in time of war were high treason. The guilty should be tried by court martial to avoid their being given mild sentences. It followed that suitable Judge-Advocates-General should participate in such trials as Presidents of the Courts and Crown Prosecutors. If the Ministry of War had not sufficient energetic officers for this purpose, Ludendorff declared his readiness to come to its assistance with suitable officers withdrawn from the army at the Front. . . .

Thanks to his military training Ludendorff in social questions was an even more die-hard Conservative than Bismarck. The army, the landed proprietors, and the industrialists were in his eyes the chief elements in the nation. He was always open to proposals coming from industrial circles. He shared completely in Bismarck's ideas on the subject of a forcible suppression of Social Democracy — that is to say, of an independent political public opinion in the working class. The difference between them was that Bismarck, in order to be able to hold down the workers, sought by every means in his power to prevent Germany from being involved in war. Ludendorff, on the other hand, developed his plan of campaign against the Social Democrats in the midst of the most frightful war in which the German nation had ever participated — a war which demanded the most tremendous sacrifices from the working class that comprised the majority of the German people. Such a policy could only lead to a catastrophe. . . .

III. *Army and State in an Age of Totalitarianism*

The effect of World War I on European society went far beyond what could be calculated in terms of human lives lost and property destroyed. Probably more serious yet less immediately apparent was the psychological and spiritual damage wrought by the war. Over a period of some four centuries, European society, for all its dynamism and capacity for change, had possessed a real underlying continuity and had functioned in accordance with a series of remarkably stable ethical and cultural norms. The fundamental element in this system of values was the concept of the worth of the individual. To the degree that any social or political institution might be required to restrict the liberty or the autonomy of a person, it was for the accomplishment of a rationally defined, limited goal. Even a state as oppressive as Tsarist Russia in the nineteenth century never pretended to the right to control a man's whole existence, spiritual as well as physical, thereby utterly destroying his sense of individuality. Nor did any state until the twentieth century possess the technical means to attempt anything so frightening in its magnitude.

For a person to believe himself an autonomous individual and to be able in a rational fashion to envisage and realize his own particular goals, he must feel reasonably secure within his own mind and with regard to the world around him. This in turn depends to a large degree on there being order and stability in his everyday existence and in society as a whole. Such stability and order were just the qualities most lacking during World War I and during the years of chaos and upheaval following the war. Men taken as individuals felt an acute sense of helplessness amidst the collapse of the old institutions and ideals. Only when organized as a group did they now seem able to accomplish anything. As a result, people almost instinctively embraced any system of values which might rationalize this radical new awareness of their own impotence. Moreover they were ready to accept any program of social and political action which might again provide some sense of purpose to their disoriented and distracted lives. The new mass movements which came to power in the 1920's and 1930's did just that. All that they demanded of a man was that he cease to consider his own prosaic concerns as being of any importance and that he submerge himself completely in the movement. In return, he was given a new vital purpose in life, that is, to work for the realization of the glorious, messianic goals of the group.

These mass movements once again seemed to provide human existence with meaning, and to give to men a simple, straightforward set of values by which to live. Insofar as men's actions furthered the aims of the movement, they were to be understood as morally or ethically valid. No other standard of judgment was considered relevant.

To perceive and define the goals of the movement, as well as the policies best suited to achieve them, was the task of the leader and the ruling elite. It was the function of the state to mobilize the total energies of the people for the carrying out of these policies. By the fact that everything was to be judged only in terms of the needs and the aims of the movement, the state as its chosen instrument had absolute and unlimited power over the life of every person. This is perhaps the most significant feature of what has come to be called totalitarianism. Under a totalitarian system the liberty and the autonomy of the individual were no longer merely restricted in the interests of achieving a limited, rational policy of state. Rather they were now annihilated in order to further the pursuit of an unlimited, irrational vision. In the aftermath of the war, almost all the belligerent nations to some degree rebelled against the old, but now seemingly irrelevant, political and social verities. It was, however, in such states as Russia and Germany, where the psychological blow of defeat came as the shattering culmination to the other strains of war, that the propensity to a totalitarian solution was most marked.

For all the essentially irrational and revolutionary nature of these new regimes, the permanent apparatus of state to which they fell heir and upon which they were obliged to rely for the administration of their respective peoples, at least initially, functioned according to traditional, rational norms. Many within the new ruling elites were conscious of this seeming anomaly and sought ways to render the methods of government more compatible with the ultimate goals of the movement. This was particularly evident with regard to the military institutions of the totalitarian state, and it was in Russia in the months following the Communist take-over that the idea was given its most explicit formulation.

As befitted the armed forces of the new revolutionary regime, the Red Army was originally to be recruited from among the most class-conscious elements of the working classes. During the Civil War force of circumstances soon drove the regime to resort to more traditional military methods and even to the use of former Tsarist officers in the ranks of the Red Army (see selection 36). With the victory of the Bolsheviks in the Civil War and the definitive establishment in Russia of the new social and political order, it became feasible to experiment with more revolutionary theories of military organization (see selection 38). Either because of pressures generated by the internal evolution of the Soviet regime, or because of the peril implicit in the rise of Nazi Germany, the experiments with these new theories remained only tentative. Two decades after the Revolution, the shape of the military institutions of the Soviet Union did not differ much from those of other states (see selection 39).

The place of an army organized according to traditional military canons within a totalitarian regime devoted to the realization of a utopian ideology,

was highly ambiguous. Rational considerations of national security were less likely to determine the attitude of the state toward the army than the irrational fears and visions of the ruling elite. Because the army did not function in terms of these same imperatives, they naturally suspected it of being a disloyal, and therefore a dangerous, element in the state. Although they could not afford to abolish or even radically to reorganize the army as an institution, they could nevertheless destroy every soldier whose ideological devotion was not absolutely above suspicion (see selection 40). The ostensible reason for the implementation of such a policy during the Great Purges of 1936–1938 was the military security of the Soviet state against its external foes (see selection 41). In actual fact, Stalin and his cohorts, acting from political motives, seriously impaired the effectiveness of the Red Army just on the eve of its ultimate trial, the war against Germany (see selection 42).

Unlike Russia, Germany did not succumb to a totalitarian regime as an immediate consequence of her defeat in World War I. Indeed, for a decade and a half the government of the country was republican and parliamentary in form, although the reality of German political life under the so-called Weimar Republic was considerably less edifying than its liberal and enlightened constitution might indicate. Real political power in republican Germany was not to be found in parliament, but rather with those groups who had held it under the Bismarckian Reich—the industrialists, the landowners, the bureaucracy, and possibly most surprising of all, the military. Drastically reduced as it may have been through the Treaty of Versailles, the army continued to function under the direction of its traditional leaders. Despite the defeat and the downfall of the monarchy, they were able to preserve a sense of continuity going back to the days of Frederick the Great.

Whatever their pretensions to a special privileged place within both state and society, the German, as well as the Prussian, military had always maintained a sense of deference and subordination toward constituted authority. The obedience formerly rendered to the monarchy was now given, although with less enthusiasm, to the Weimar Republic. In the estimation of General von Seeckt, its brilliant chief from 1920 to 1926, no other course of action was compatible with either the honor of the army or its best interests (see selection 43). For its part, the Republic, enjoying only the most uncertain and insecure of mandates, and recognizing the essential role of the army in the maintenance of order, was content to leave the military authorities almost full autonomy in the management of their own affairs (see selection 44). Indeed, in the making of general military policy, such was the willingness of the government to defer to the opinions of the army chiefs that it may well be argued the army exercised an influence within the state as great as at any time in its history. The entente between the Weimar Republic and the army, and the high degree of independence enjoyed by the latter, were founded on a rational appreciation by both of their own particular interests and those of the country.

Born of a shattering defeat and then immediately saddled with the onus of accepting the humiliating Treaty of Versailles, the Weimar regime never generated much enthusiasm or even respect among the great mass of the German

people. Its authority already weakened by the circumstances of its birth, the Republic was then obliged to deal with the social and economic chaos created first by the hyperinflation of 1923, and then the Great Depression of 1930–1933. Under the strain of this last prolonged crisis, the parliamentary system broke down, leading ultimately to the collapse of the Republic. Disillusioned by the events of the past fifteen years and disoriented by the failure of the old political and social formulas, the German people turned to anyone promising them a way out of their despair. Adolf Hitler and the Nazis came to power in January 1933 because they offered a program which at one and the same time seemed to fulfill the longings of the psychologically and economically dispossessed and to reassure the propertied classes against the perils of working class unrest. Along with the other traditional conservative groups in German society, the military gave their tacit consent to the Nazi take-over, confident that they still held the ultimate reins of power within the state.

Having come into office as Chancellor in perfectly constitutional fashion in January 1933, Hitler quickly obtained legal parliamentary assent to govern unconstitutionally. He then proceeded to use the full power of the state to revolutionize German society and to reorganize it along totalitarian lines for the implementation of his own messianic racial vision. The fundamentally irrational nature of Hitler's program, particularly with regard to foreign policy, soon alarmed the army. Organized to carry out the limited and rational mission of defending the frontiers of the country against enemy attack, and possibly to advance these frontiers where the risk was not too great, they recoiled at the Nazi goal of seemingly unlimited conquest in the East. Although they clearly foresaw the probable consequences of this policy, the soldiers were incapable of stopping Hitler. Playing on their tradition of obedience to constituted authority and their oath of allegiance to him (see selection 45), and at the same time over-whelming their possible objections by his brilliant early successes in foreign policy, Hitler reduced the military to complete subservience (see selection 46). Whatever their antipathy to the Nazi movement, the soldiers found themselves acting as Hitler's accomplices and thus saddled with some degree of responsibility for the disaster which befell Germany (see selection 48).

Since the Nazi regime expected absolute loyalty and unthinking obedience from all its servants, Hitler was angered at the evident lack of enthusiasm on the part of the military chiefs for his grandiose schemes of conquest. In one sense this confirmed the belief of such men as Ernst Roehm, Hitler's old comrade, that military institutions stemming from a former era and suited to the needs of now outmoded regimes were out of place in the revolutionary Nazi state. Roehm was executed in the Blood Purge of 1934 for too strongly advocating that the armed branch of the party of which he was head, the S.A., replace the army. During the war, and particularly toward its end, the S.S. under Heinrich Himmler seemed to be attempting to do the same thing. Hitler, for all his anger at and distrust of the old Prussian officer corps, never quite dared to forego their unsurpassed technical ability. As the war, which Hitler had launched and which the military had conducted with their usual skill, began to appear irremediably lost, a small band within the army, going against all the traditions

of the officer corps in the hope of staving off the final catastrophe, unsuccessfully tried to assassinate him and to overthrow the Nazi regime (see selections 46 and 47). It was the last gesture of a few rational men against the demands of an irrational system.

In France, unlike what happened in Russia and Germany, the decades after World War I did not witness any drastic changes in the structure of society. The victory of France in 1918 obscured the awful toll exacted by the war, and indeed would seem to have confirmed the essential soundness of her political and social institutions. It was not until the sudden collapse of 1940 that it was revealed how thoroughly they had been sapped. Even then, the reaction was neither so extreme nor so generalized as in Germany and Russia. The Vichy state came into being in a regular and constitutional fashion, as the Third Republic, in effect, voted itself out of existence.

Although the Vichy regime may well have been authoritarian in spirit, it was not totalitarian. Rather than calling for a radical rejection of liberal ideals and institutions in the name of some revolutionary, utopian vision, the leaders of the Vichy state rooted their political philosophy in certain concepts deep in the French conservative tradition. There was thus something vaguely familiar about Vichy in the eyes of the French people, despite its "modern" fascist trappings. In any case, the military, along with the great mass of Frenchmen, rallied to the new regime not so much out of ideological conviction as because they believed it to be the legally constituted government of the country. More indicative of the breakdown in the old principles of French political life than the adherence of the military to this new semi-fascist state, were the actions of a little band of soldiers and sailors who, under the leadership of General de Gaulle, refused to recognize its authority (see selections 49 and 50).

During the nineteenth and first half of the twentieth centuries, ideological and political differences among the servants of the French state, and particularly among the soldiers, had been resolved, or at least reconciled, through a theory of strict discipline. In faithfully and obediently serving the regime of the moment, no matter how great his aversion toward it, a soldier could by that token believe he was also serving the permanent interests of France. When De Gaulle, on patriotic and ideological grounds, called upon the military to reject the authority and to disregard the orders of the Vichy government, he was going against one of the essential principles upon which the cohesion and stability of the French army had been founded. One result of this revolutionary act was that the French soldiers and sailors between the years 1940 and 1942 found themselves facing two competing authorities, each one claiming the right to his undivided allegiance (see selection 51). Following the Allied invasion of North Africa, the Germans occupied the whole of Metropolitan France and thus put an end to the existence of Vichy as a theoretically independent sovereign state. This allowed a large part of the French army, particularly those units stationed in Africa, to join with the forces under General de Gaulle and to reenter the war against the Axis on the Allied side. Its unity was thus restored. Nevertheless the army continued to suffer a profound malaise stemming from the collapse of 1940 and the resulting Vichy-Gaullist split.

In the aftermath of the Allied victory, the old republican institutions were restored. Despite the bright hopes of many that there would be a radical and vigorous new departure, a political system which had shown an increasing inability to resolve the problems besetting the country and whose authority had declined sharply as a consequence, was simply resurrected more or less intact. In the decade and a half following World War II, the Republic demonstrated even less resilience and stability than it had in the years leading up to 1939, yet it was faced with a whole new set of problems, in particular the dissolution of the French colonial empire. Subject to a multitude of conflicting pressures, the weak and unstable Fourth Republic was unable to evolve a coherent, effective policy with which to meet the demands of the colonial peoples for self-government. The Republic apparently lacked either the means or the determination to suppress their revolutionary aspirations by force, while at the same time, it was unwilling to satisfy them. For lack of a better policy, the government therefore assigned the army the mission of combatting these colonial insurrections in the forlorn hope that somehow a viable solution would emerge. Their morale already tried by the events of World War II, the soldiers now found themselves obliged to fight a seemingly endless series of small-scale yet costly campaigns, which, having been provided with neither sufficient means nor a coherent policy to implement, they could not win. Frustrated and angered by what they felt to be the indifference of those at home, the military became increasingly alienated from civil society (see selection 52).

The war in Indo-China and then in Algeria was waged less against a clearly defined body of enemy troops than against the revolutionary aspirations of a whole people. To regain their allegiance, military means alone were not enough. These had to be integrated with and supplemented by a program of political, social, and economic reform. Inexorably, by the very nature of the military mission assigned to them, that is, to crush the rebellion, the soldiers found themselves impelled to assure the natives that France would never leave them and that she would better their lot. When in 1958 the military saw the government proposing a policy which they believed would lead to eventual Algerian independence, the anger and the frustration of the past two decades came to a head. Joining with the European population of Algeria, the army revolted against the government. The Fourth Republic, lacking any very widespread or deep support among the French people, could not muster sufficient force to suppress the uprising. Its unceremonious collapse brought to power a new regime under General de Gaulle (see selection 53).

The Algerian uprising of May 1958 represented a general repudiation by the army of the authority of the civil government. One would have to go back in French history to the early days of the reign of Louis XIV and the Fronde to find anything comparable, for the Bonapartist *coups de'état* of 1799 and 1851 involved small cliques of ambitious soldiers rather than the whole army. Paradoxically enough, it was General de Gaulle, the prime beneficiary of the revolt, who more than anyone else provided a modern precedent for the army's claim to decide for itself how far it was bound by the policies of a given government. Now as chief of state he in turn had to deal with an insubordinate soldiery.

More and more convinced that De Gaulle intended to have France desert Algeria, army units stationed there were on two separate occasions involved, both directly and indirectly, in armed uprisings meant to force him to change his program (see selection 54). The failure of both attempts would seem to have brought to an end the incursion of the military in the political sphere and to have contributed greatly to reestablishing the authority of the civil government in France.

SOVIET RUSSIA: THE ARMY OF THE
REVOLUTIONARY STATE

36. THE FOUNDING OF THE RED ARMY

In much the same manner as the more fervent Jacobins at the height of the French Revolution, the Bolsheviks sought to create a radically new kind of military establishment, one which would be in both its principles of organization and its doctrines of war a true embodiment of the working class revolution. Thus, as the first selection indicates, the Bolsheviks considered working class volunteers to be the only ones worthy of shouldering the military burdens of the revolutionary state.

Within a few months the Bolsheviks were forced to turn to conscription to meet the growing military emergency which was created by the concerted efforts of the anti-revolutionary elements in Russia, allied with foreign powers, to crush them. Even so, the revolutionary government did not contemplate arming the bourgeoisie. Rather they intended to use them for other tasks in the great struggle ahead. The order instituting conscription is given in the second selection.

The desperate situation of the Bolsheviks in the Civil War robbed them of all opportunity to experiment with their revolutionary theories of military organization. They were to find, as had their Jacobin counterparts 125 years before, that to wage war effectively required more than sheer revolutionary zeal. Thus the Bolsheviks sought military talent wherever it could be found. Former Tsarist officers were incorporated into the Red Army either voluntarily or by force, with their families made to stand hostage for their good behavior. In the third selection, Trotsky, Commissar for War in the Bolshevik government and the real driving force behind the Red Army, declares that these former Tsarist officers, whatever their social origins, are to be treated with all due respect so long as they fight for the cause of the working class revolution.

With their military units commanded by men of such disparate origins, many of them potentially unreliable, the Bolsheviks were obliged to take steps to insure

From Erich Wollenburg, *The Red Army* (London, 1938), pp. 249–255. Reprinted with the permission of Martin Secker and Warburg, Limited.

the loyalty of the Red Army, through the institution of the military commissars. Here too they were acting in a manner analogous to the Jacobins of the French Revolution. Like the Representatives on mission, the military commissars were meant to see that the men in command of the Red Armies carried out the orders of the revolutionary government to the letter. In the fourth of the following selections, the duties of the military commissars are given along with their prerogatives vis-à-vis the officers commanding their respective units.

THE SCHEME FOR A SOCIALIST ARMY

Decree issued by the Council of People's Commissars on January 15, 1918

The old army was a class instrument in the hands of the bourgeoisie for the oppression of the workers. The seizure of power by the workers and propertyless persons renders necessary the formation of a new army. The tasks of this new army will be the defence of the Soviet authority, the creation of a basis for the transformation of the standing army into a force deriving its strength from a nation in arms, and, furthermore, the creation of a basis for the support of the coming Socialist Revolution in Europe.

I

The Council of People's Commissars has decided to organize the new army as a "Red Army of Workers and Peasants" on the following basis:

1. The Red Army of Workers and Peasants will be formed from the class-conscious and best elements of the working classes.

2. All citizens of the Russian Republic who have completed their eighteenth year are eligible for service. Service in the Red Army is open to anyone ready to give his life and strength for the defence of the achievements of the October Revolution, the Soviet Power and Socialism. Enlistment in the Red Army is conditional upon guarantees being given by a military or civil committee functioning within the territory of the Soviet Power or by Party or Trade Union committees or, in extreme cases, by

two persons belonging to one of the above organizations. Should an entire unit desire to join the Red Army, its acceptance is conditional upon a collective guarantee and the affirmative vote of all its members.

II

1. The families of members of the Red Army of Workers and Peasants will be maintained by the State and receive, in addition, a monthly supplement of 50 roubles.

2. Members of soldiers' families who are incapable of work and have hitherto been supported by the aforesaid soldiers will receive further support in accordance with the local cost of living, as determined by the local Soviets.

III

The Council of People's Commissars is the supreme head of the Red Army of Workers and Peasants. The immediate command and administration of the Army is vested in the Commissariat for Military Affairs and in the Special All-Russian College therein contained.

The President of the Council of People's Commissars:

V. ULYANOV-LENIN.

The Commander-in-Chief:

N. KRYLENKO.

The People's Commissars for War and the Fleet:

DYBENKO, PODVOISKY.

The People's Commissars:

PROSHYAN, SAMOISKY, STEINBERG.

For the Bureau of People's Commissars:

VLADIMIR BONTSCH-BRUYEVITCH.

SCHEME FOR COMPULSORY MILITARY TRAINING

Published in No. 83 of the "Isvestia" of the All-Russian Central Executive Committee of the Soviets, April 26, 1918

The liberation of mankind from the burden of militarism and the barbarity of war between nations, is one of the basic tasks of socialism. The aims of socialism are universal disarmament, perpetual peace and the fraternal co-operation of all races inhabiting the world.

These aims will be accomplished when power is transferred to the hands of the workers in all powerful capitalist countries, when all means of production have been taken out of the hands of the exploiters and made over to the workers for the common good, and when a communist order of society has created a firm basis of human solidarity.

At present Russia is the only country in which the State authority is vested in the workers. The imperialist bourgeoisie is still in power in all other countries. Its policy is directed towards the suppression of Communist Revolution and the enslavement of all weak races. The Russian Soviet Republic is surrounded by enemies on all sides and must therefore create a powerful army, under the protection of which the communistic transformation of the country's social order may be accomplished.

The Republic's Government of Workers and Peasants has set itself the immediate task of enrolling all citizens for compulsory labour and military service. In this work it has encountered obstinate resistance from the bourgeoisie, who refuse to renounce their economic privileges and are trying to recapture the reins of government by means of conspiracies, insurrections, and treasonable agreements with foreign imperialists.

To arm the bourgeoisie would be tantamount to provoking a continuous internal war within the ranks of the army and so crippling the army's strength for war against external foes. The usurious, exploiting portion of society which is unwilling to assume the same rights and duties as the rest must not be allowed to obtain arms. The Government of Workers and Peasants will find means to impose on the bourgeoisie in some form or other a part of the burden of the defence of the Republic, which has been forced by the crimes of the possessing classes to endure these heavy trials and necessities.But in the immediate transition period military training and the bearing of arms must be restricted to workers and peasants who employ no outside labour.

Citizens between eighteen and forty years of age who have undergone the prescribed military training will be registered as liable to military service. They are required to answer the first summons of the Government of Workers and Peasants to fill up the cadres of the Red Army, which have been formed of devoted soldiers, ready to sacrifice themselves for the freedom and independence of the Russian Soviet Republic and the International Socialist Revolution.

Male citizens of the Russian Federated Soviet Republic are liable to undergo military training:

(1) During school age, the lower limit of which will be determined by the People's Commissariat for Education.

(2) During the preparatory age, from sixteen to eighteen years.

(3) During the age of obligatory military service, from eighteen to forty years.

Female citizens will be trained only with their own consent, in accordance with the general practice.

N.B. — Persons whose religious convictions forbid the use of arms will be liable only to forms of training that exclude the use of arms. . . .

TROTSKY ON THE ENROLLMENT OF
FORMER TSARIST OFFICERS IN THE RED ARMY

The frequent and often unjustified attacks on military specialists from the former officers' cadres now working for the Red Army have produced, in some units of the command, an uncertain and harrowing atmosphere. On the other hand, former officers who are now on government duty behind the front are wary about moving into the Red Army because of the prevailing distrust towards them, artificially fanned by unbalanced elements in the Soviet ranks. These facts create obvious and serious damage to the armies in the field.

I therefore feel it necessary to issue the following declaration:

A general hostility to former regular officers is alien to both the Soviet Power and to the best units on active duty. Every officer who wants to defend our country against the invasion of foreign imperialists and its Krasnov and Dutov agents is a welcome worker for the cause. Every officer who wants to and can co-operate in forming the internal structure of the army and thus help it to achieve its objectives with a minimum loss of workers' and peasants' blood, is a welcome collaborator with the Soviet power, has a right to be respected, and shall be respected in the ranks of the Red Army. . . .

The Soviet power knows full well that many thousands and tens of thousands of officers who graduated from the schools of the Old Regime and were brought up in a bourgeois-monarchist spirit cannot accustom themselves at once to the New Regime, understand it or respect it. But during the thirteen months of Soviet power it has become clear to many, many officers that the Soviet regime is not an accident; it is a regularly constituted structure, based on the will of the working millions. It has become clear to many, many officers that there is now no other regime capable of securing the freedom and independence of the Russian people against foreign intervention.

The officers who, guided by this new awareness, honestly join our ranks, will find full oblivion there for the crimes against the people in which they took part because of their old upbringing and their insufficiently developed political and revolutionary consciousness.

In the Ukraine, in Krasnov's army, in Siberia, in the ranks of the Anglo-French imperialists in the North, there are not a few former Russian officers who would be willing to submit to the Soviet Republic if they did not fear a drastic punishment for their previous activities. To them, the repentant apostates, applies what we said above about the general policy of the Workers' and Peasants' Government: it is guided in all its actions by its revolutionary objectives, not by blind vengeance, and it opens its doors to every honest citizen willing to work in the Soviet ranks.

From *Basic Writings of Trotsky*, edited by Irving Howe, pp. 121–122. © Copyright 1963 by Random House, Inc. Reprinted by permission.

ORDER OF THE PEOPLE'S COMMISSAR FOR WAR, APRIL 6, 1918

Regulations for War Commissars

A War Commissar is a direct political representative of the Soviet Government with the army. His post has a special significance. Commissars' posts will be assigned only to irreproachable revolutionaries who have the ability to remain incarnations of revolutionary duty at critical moments and under the most difficult circumstances.

The War Commissar's person is inviolate. An insult offered to a War Commissar engaged in the performance of his duty or any act of violence committed against a War Commissar will be deemed equivalent to the greatest of crimes against the Soviet Power of the Republic. It is the duty of a War Commissar to prevent the army from showing disrespect to the Soviet authority and to prevent army institutions from becoming nests of conspiracy or employing weapons against workmen and peasants. A War Commissar takes part in all the activities of the commanding officer to whom he is attached; these two persons must receive reports and sign orders jointly. Validity is ascribed only to those orders of a War Soviet which bear the signature of at least one Commissar in addition to that of the commanding officer.

All work must be done under the eyes of the Commissar. The only work which he does not undertake is the special military leadership, which is the task of the military expert with whom he co-operates.

Commissars are not responsible for the appropriateness of orders given for purely military, operative purposes. The entire responsibility for these falls on the military commander. The Commissar's signature to an operative order implies that he guarantees the said order to be one dictated by purely operative (and not counter-revolutionary) reasons. If a Commissar cannot approve of a military order, he must not veto it, but must report his opinion of it to the War Soviet immediately superior to his own. A Commissar may prevent the execution of a military order only when he has justifiable grounds for belief that it is inspired by counter-revolutionary motives.

An order receives the force of law when it has been signed by a Commissar, and must then be executed at all costs. It is the Commissar's duty to see that all orders are carried out to the letter, for which purpose he is invested with all the authority and all the means of the Soviet Power. Commissars who connive at the non-execution of orders will be forthwith removed from their posts and prosecuted.

Commissars must maintain intact the connection between the institutions of the Red Army and the central and local organizations of the Soviet Government, and assure the support of these organizations to the Red Army.

Commissars must see that all ranks of the Red Army do their duty conscientiously and energetically, that all money expenditure is economical and under the strictest control and that the greatest care is taken of all the war property of Soviet Russia. . . .

From Erich Wollenburg, *The Red Army* (London, 1938), pp, 255–257. Reprinted with the permission of Martin Secker and Warburg, Ltd.

D. Fedotov White

37. THE MILITARY COMMISSARS

Even though they appeared to represent an outside political element within army circles, the military commissars actually played a vital role in the creation and the early development of the Red Army. Not only did they supply a necessary liaison between the revolutionary government and its forces in the field, they also acted as a cohesive factor within the individual units in the early days before the Red Army was forged in the heat of battle. In the following selection, taken from D. Fedotov White's *The Growth of the Red Army*, the work of the military commissars is described and their accomplishments assessed.

The order of the People's Commissar for War dated April 6, 1918, was the first document issued by the central Soviet authority to define the functions of military commissars.

The order stated that the military commissars were the immediate political organ of the Soviet Government in the army and that the commissars were to be appointed from "irreproachable revolutionaries, able to remain the embodiment of the revolution under the most difficult circumstances." . . . The commissars were instructed to take part in all forms of activities of the military specialists and were to receive jointly with the latter all reports and letters. Theirs was the duty to countersign all orders. Only orders so countersigned were to be considered valid. At the same time the responsibility for the efficacy of the purely military — operation and combat — orders was left to the commanding personnel. The commissars' signature on such orders merely meant that there was no reason to suspect a counter-revolutionary motive behind the intentions expressed in the order. At the same time the commissars were made responsible for the prompt execution of all orders.

. . .Among the duties of the commissars was the liaison service between the Red Army establishments and the central, as well as local, institutions of the Soviet Government. They were responsible for obtaining effective co-operation of the latter with the Red Army.

The highest ranking military commissars (at the time of the issuance of the order, those of the Supreme Military Council) were to be appointed by the Soviet of the People's Commissars, those of the District and Regional Councils by the Supreme Military Council in agreement with the respective local soviet.

The selection of these early commissars seems to be somewhat haphazard – the one at the cavalry corps "made appearances only to obtain from the medical officers prescriptions for alcohol under the guise of medicine, and spent his time getting drunk and running after loose women." . . .

I. Petukhov, in his book on party organization and party work in the Red Army, considers that because of the acute antagonism between the Red soldiers and the old army officers appointed to command them during the early days of the Red Army, the first thing the commissars had to accom-

Reprinted from *The Growth of the Red Army* by D. Fedotov White (Princeton, 1944), pp. 74–79, abridged, by permission of Princeton University Press. Copyright 1944 by Princeton University Press.

plish was to overcome that antagonism. Petukhov says: "As between the commander (who only a few days before had been "in faith and truth" serving the Czar) and the Red soldiers, there hung a "precipice," the rôle of the commissar, as the political organ of the Soviet Government in the army, had to be reduced to the establishment of the necessary bond of confidence between them."

Trotsky in 1918, in outlining the rôle of the commissar in the army, said: "The military specialists will direct the technical end of the work, purely military matters, operation work and combat activities. The political side of the organization, training and education, should be entirely subordinated to the representatives of the Soviet régime in the person of its commissar." . . .

Beginning with the earliest days of their work, the commissars were drawn into propaganda and agitation activities. They also had to take interest in the so-called "cultural-enlightenment" work in the Red Army. Clubs and libraries were established in the Red Army, and served to circulate government-inspired newspapers and books. These were supplemented by discussions and lectures on political subjects, sponsored in many cases by the commissars. . . .

It would be erroneous to suppose that the commissars in the army from the very beginning were all Communists. The statute establishing the institution of the military commissars merely insisted that they should be recruited from "irreproachable revolutionaries" reflecting thus the heterogeneity of the personnel which was already performing the functions of local political control in the Red armed forces.

It is obvious that as the functions of the military commissars developed so as to embrace not only the supervision of the actions of the commanding personnel, but also the direction of the political work of the Communist party in the Red Army, none but Communists became eligible for these posts. . . .

The gradual extension of the scope of activity and influence of the military commissars found an expression in a note drafted by Trotsky in the fall of 1918. "There do not exist and did not exist any orders telling the commissar 'thou hast no right to interfere in any dispositions whatsoever of the commanding personnel.' . . . The sphere where the commissar has least 'rights,' is the domain of operations, of command. . . . But nobody ever prohibited the commissar from expressing his opinion regarding operation problems, giving advice, controlling the execution of an operation order, etc." This "liberal" interpretation of the order of April 6, 1918, was followed by the remark, that on his own part, the commander also has a right to take an interest in political work: "a good commander cannot fail to take an interest, as the state of political work has a tremendous influence on the fighting efficacy of the unit."

One may see in these remarks a trend toward the interpenetration of the fields of activity of the commissar and the commander, toward the synthesis of these originally opposed elements of Red Army leadership. . . .

It is quite natural that such energetic "muscular Communists" would antagonize various groups in the Red Army. There is evidence that some of the commissars went very far in extending their authority in the fields of military administration and supplies. Some of them began to issue orders of their own in these spheres of activity without the signature of the commander. The youthful Commander of the Soviet Armies, Tukhachevskii, already a Communist at the time, complained that such orders were issued by commissars and members of the Revolutionary Military Council of his army. . . .

. . . The undoubtedly ardent and earnest political enthusiasm of the commissars of the early days gradually (at least among a large section of them) ran into channels entirely unforeseen by its originators. The ancient rhythm of army life was seemingly in conflict with the rôle of an observer and

political auditor. The energetic young Communists cast for this rôle were men of action. The combat, the planning of strategic maneuver, the administrative details of a detachment, held a strong allure for them during the war. The "political enlightenment" and even political work among the greenhorn Communists in the ranks, who were fumbling with the basic tenets of Marxism, was a tame pastime in comparison with the "glory" of the battlefield, and the exercise of authority in the everyday life of the camp.

In other words, a curious conflict suggests itself here: that between the new-fangled institution breaking up the sacrosanct principle of unity of military leadership and the general *gestalt* of army life. While the Red Army was still an inchoate body composed of elements mechanically thrown together, the institution of commissars had its place and useful function. As soon as these elements grew into the chemical structure of the army, the crystal of the commissar institution did not fit into its new shape. It is as if the institution of commissars had only a very limited span of life and that its cycle had run its course by the end of the Civil War. As soon as the Red Army had become a regularly organized armed force, commanded by men welded into it by the fire of battle, the commissar had no place in it. . . .

38. THE SCHEME FOR A SOVIET MILITIA

> With the victory of the Red Army in the Civil War becoming increasingly certain, the Bolshevik government was able to contemplate a reorganization of the Soviet military establishment that would be more in accordance with strict revolutionary principles than had hitherto been possible. It was orthodox Marxist theory that a militia system, once it had been fully implemented, would be far more effective militarily than any system founded on a standing army. In the following selection, taken from the declarations of the Ninth Congress of the Communist Party of the Soviet Union in 1920, are outlined the principles by which the militia was to be organized.

Scheme for the Transition to the Militia System

(1) The approaching end of the Civil War and the favourable change in the international situation of Soviet Russia make it necessary for us to remodel our military forces in accordance with the country's urgent economic and cultural needs.

(2) On the other hand it is necessary to affirm that the Socialist Republic can by no means be regarded as out of danger so long as the imperialist bourgeoisie holds the reins of government in the most important countries in the world.

The imperialists are losing ground, and at any moment the course of events may impel them to undertake further warlike adventures against Soviet Russia. Hence the necessity for maintaining the defences of the Revolution at the required standard.

(3) The transition period, which may be long and wearisome, must effect a reorganization of the armed forces which will give the workers the necessary military training while withdrawing them from productive labour as little as possible. Only a Militia of Red Workers and Peasants, based on the territorial system, can conform to these requirements.

(4) The essence of the Soviet militia sys-

From Erich Wollenburg, *The Red Army* (London, 1938), pp. 258–259. Reprinted with the permission of Martin Secker and Warburg, Ltd.

tem must be the closest possible association of the army with the processes of production, so that the man-power of certain defined industrial areas will also form the man-power of certain defined military units.

(5) The militia formations (regiments, brigades, divisions) must be territorially adapted to the territorial distribution of industry in such a way as will permit the industrial centres and their surrounding agricultural belts to constitute the bases of the militia formations.

(6) The organization of the Workers' and Peasants' Militia must be based on cadres well equipped in all military, technical and political respects to serve the needs of the workers and peasants continually trained by them. These cadres must be able at any given moment to call up the workers and peasants from their militia district, incorporate them in the military machine, arm them and take them into action.

Leon Trotsky

39. THE REVOLUTION BETRAYED

As the chief organizer and animator of the Red Army, Leon Trotsky did more than anyone else to save the Russian Revolution during the more desperate moments of the Civil War. Following Lenin's death in 1924, Trotsky lost out to Stalin in the struggle for power and was eventually exiled from the Soviet Union. As brilliant a writer and polemicist as he was a military organizer, Trotsky spent the rest of his life until his assassination in 1940 expounding upon the ways in which the Revolution had been perverted and otherwise betrayed by Stalin. In the following selection, taken from his book, *The Revolution Betrayed*, he discusses the unfortunate evolution of the Red Army in the 1930's. In Trotsky's estimation, the Soviet government, instead of working to create a truly revolutionary army, was actually resurrecting a military establishment that differed very little from that of any bourgeois regime.

The great French Revolution created its army by amalgamating the new formations with the royal battalions of the line. The October revolution dissolved the tzar's army wholly and without leaving a trace. The Red Army was built anew from the first brick. A twin of the Soviet regime, it shared its fate in great things and small. It owed its incomparable superiority over the tzar's army wholly to the great social revolution. It has not stood aside, however, from the processes of degeneration of the Soviet regime. On the contrary, these have found their most finished expression in the army. . . .

. . . In what degree do the Soviet armed forces at the end of the second decade of their existence correspond to the type which the Bolshevik party inscribed upon its banner?

The army of the proletarian dictatorship ought to have, according to the program, "an overtly class character—that is, to be composed exclusively of the proletariat and

From Leon Trotsky, *The Revolution Betrayed* (New York, 1937), pp. 209–210, 215–225. Reprinted with the permission of Merit Publishers and Weidenfeld & Nicolson Ltd.

the semiproletarian layers of the peasantry close to it. Only in connection with the abolition of classes will such a class army convert itself into a national socialist militia." Although postponing to a coming period the *all-national* character of the army, the party by no means rejected the *militia* system. On the contrary, according to a resolution of the 8th Congress (March 1919): "We are shifting the militia to a class basis and converting it into a Soviet militia." The aim of the military work was defined as the gradual creation of an army "as far as possible by extra-barrackroom methods—that is, in a set-up close to the labor conditions of the working class." In the long run, all the divisions of the army were to coincide territorially with the factories, mines, villages, agricultural communes and other organic groupings, "with a local commanding staff, with local stores of arms and of all supplies." A regional, scholastic, industrial and athletic union of the youth was to more than replace the corporative spirit instilled by the barracks, and inculcate conscious discipline without the elevation above the army of a professional officers' corps.

A militia, however, no matter how well corresponding to the nature of the socialist society, requires a high economic basis. Special circumstances are built up for a regular army. A territorial army, therefore, much more directly reflects the real condition of the country. The lower the level of culture and the sharper the distinction between village and city, the more imperfect and heterogeneous the militia. A lack of railroads, highways and water routes, together with an absence of autoroads and a scarcity of automobiles, condemns the territorial army in the first critical weeks and months of war to extreme slowness of movement. In order to ensure a defense of the boundaries during mobilization, strategic transfers and concentrations, it is necessary, along with the territorial detachments, to have regular troops. The Red Army was created from the very beginning as a necessary compromise between the two systems, with the emphasis on the regular troops.

In 1924, the then head of the War Department wrote: "We must always have before our eyes two circumstances: If the very possibility of going over to the militia system was first created by the establishment of a Soviet structure, still the tempo of the change is determined by the general conditions of the culture of the country —technique, means of communication, literacy, etc. The political premises for a militia are firmly established with us, whereas the economic and cultural are extremely backward." Granted the necessary material conditions, the territorial army would not only stand second to the regular army, but far exceed it. The Soviet Union must pay dear for its defense, because it is not sufficiently rich for the cheaper militia system. There is nothing here to wonder at. It is exactly because of its poverty that the Soviet society has hung around its neck the very costly bureaucracy.

One and the same problem, the disproportion between economic base and social superstructure, comes up with remarkable regularity in absolutely all the spheres of social life, in the factory, the collective farm, the family, the school, in literature, and in the army. The basis of all relations is the contrast between a low level of productive forces, low even from a capitalist standpoint, and forms of property that are socialist in principle. The new social relations are raising up the culture. But the inadequate culture is dragging the social forms down. Soviet reality is an equilibrium between these two tendencies. In the army, thanks to the extreme definiteness of its structure, the resultant is measurable in sufficiently exact figures. The correlation between regular troops and militia can serve as a fair indication of the actual movement toward socialism.

Nature and history have provided the Soviet state with open frontiers 10,000 kilometers apart, with a sparse population and bad roads. On the 15th of October, 1924, the old military leadership, then in its last month, once more urged that this be not forgotten: "In the next few years, the creation of a militia must of necessity have a preparatory character. Each successive step must follow from the carefully verified success of the preceding steps." But with 1925 a new era began. The advocates of the former proletarian military doctrine came to power. In its essence, the territorial army was deeply contradictory to that ideal of "offensivism" and "maneuverism" with which this school had opened its career. But they had now begun to forget about the world revolution. The new leaders hoped to avoid wars by "neutralizing" the bourgeoisie. In the course of the next few years, 74 per cent of the army was reorganized on a militia basis!

So long as Germany remained disarmed, and moreover "friendly," the calculations of the Moscow general staff in the matter of western boundaries were based on the military forces of the immediate neighbors: Rumania, Poland, Lithuania, Latvia, Esthonia, Finland, with the probable material support of the most powerful of the enemies, chiefly France. In that far-off epoch (which ended in 1933), France was not considered a providential "friend of peace." The surrounding states could put in the field together about 120 divisions of infantry, approximately 3,500,000 men. The mobilization plans of the Red Army tried to insure on the western boundary an army of the first class amounting to the same number. In the Far East, under all conditions in the theater of war, it could be a question only of hundreds of thousands, and not millions. Each hundred fighters demands in the course of a year approximately seventy-five men to replace losses. Two years of war would withdraw from the country, leaving aside those who return from hospitals to active service, about ten to twelve million men. The Red Army up to 1935 numbered in all 562,000 men — with the troops of the G.P.U., 620,000 — with 40,000 officers. Moreover, at the beginning of 1935, 74 per cent, as we have already said, were in the territorial divisions, and only

26 per cent in the regular army. Could you ask a better proof that the socialist militia had conquered — if not by 100 per cent, at least by 74 per cent, and in any case "finally and irrevocably"?

However, all the above calculations, conditional enough in themselves, were left hanging in the air after Hitler came to power. Germany began feverishly to arm, and primarily against the Soviet Union. The prospect of a peaceful cohabitation with capitalism faded at once. The swift approach of military danger impelled the Soviet government, besides bringing up the numbers of the armed forces to 1,300,000, to change radically the structure of the Red Army. At the present time, it contains 77 per cent of regular, or so-called "kadrovy" divisions, and only 23 per cent of territorials! This shattering of the territorial divisions looks too much like a renunciation of the militia system — unless you forget that an army is needed not for times of peace, but exactly for the moments of military danger. Thus, historic experience, starting from that sphere which is least of all tolerant of jokes, has ruthlessly revealed that only so much has been gained "finally and irrevocably" as is guaranteed by the productive foundation of society.

Nevertheless, the slide from 74 per cent to 23 per cent seems excessive. It was not brought to pass, we may assume, without a "friendly" pressure from the French general staff. It is still more likely that the bureaucracy seized upon a favorable pretext for this step, which was dictated to a considerable degree by political considerations. The divisions of a militia through their very character come into direct dependence upon the population. This is the chief advantage of the system from a socialist point of view. But this also is its danger from the point of view of the Kremlin. It is exactly because of this undesirable closeness of the army to the people that the military authorities of the advanced capitalist countries, where technically it would be easy to realize, reject the militia. The keen discontent in the Red Army during

the first five-year plan undoubtedly supplied a serious motive for the subsequent abolition of the territorial divisions.

Our proposition would be unanswerably confirmed by an accurate diagram of the Red Army previous to and after the counterreform. We have not such data, however, and if we had we should consider it impossible to use them publicly. But there is a fact, accessible to all, which permits of no two interpretations: at the same time that the Soviet government reduced the relative weight of the militia in the army to 51 per cent, it restored the cossack troops, the sole militia formation in the tzar's army! Cavalry is always the privileged and most conservative part of an army. The cossacks were always the most conservative part of the cavalry. During the war and the revolution they served as a police force—first for the tzar and then for Kerensky. . . . Collectivization—introduced among the cossacks, moreover, with special measures of violence—has not yet, of course, changed their traditions and temper. Moreover, as an exceptional law the cossacks have been restored the right to possess their own horses. There is no lack, of course, of other indulgences. Is it possible to doubt that these riders of the steppes are again on the side of the privileged against the oppressed? Upon a background of unceasing repressions against oppositional tendencies among the workers' youth, the restoration of the cossack stripe and forelock is undoubtedly one of the clearest expressions of the Thermidor!

A still more deadly blow to the principles of the October revolution was struck by the decree restoring the officers' corps in all its bourgeois magnificence. . . .

In September 1935, civilized humanity, friends and enemies alike, learned with surprise that the Red Army would now be crowned with an officers' hierarchy, beginning with lieutenant and ending with marshal. According to Tukhachevsky, the actual head of the War Department, "the introduction by the government of military titles will create a more stable basis for the development of commanding and technical cadres." The explanation is consciously equivocal. The commanding cadres are reinforced above all by the confidence of the soldiers. For that very reason, the Red Army began by liquidating the officers' corps. The resurrection of hierarchical caste is not in the least demanded by the interests of military affairs. It is the commanding position, and not the rank, of the commander that is important. Engineers and physicians have no rank, but society finds the means of putting each in his needful place. The right to a commanding position is guaranteed by study, endowment, character, experience, which need continual and moreover individual appraisal. The rank of major adds nothing to the commander of a battalion. The elevation of the five senior commanders of the Red Army to the title of marshal, gives them neither new talents nor supplementary powers. It is not the army that really thus receives a "stable basis," but the officers' corps, and that at the price of aloofness from the army. The reform pursues a purely political aim: to give a new social weight to the officers. Molotov thus in essence defined the meaning of the decree: "to elevate the importance of the guiding cadres of our Army." The thing is not limited, either, to a mere introduction of titles. It is accompanied with an accelerated construction of quarters for the commanding staff. In 1936, 47,000 rooms are to be constructed, and 57 per cent more money is to be issued for salaries than during the preceding year. "To elevate the importance of the guiding cadres" means, at a cost of weakening the moral bonds of the army, to bind the officers closer together with the ruling circles.

It is worthy of note that the reformers did not consider it necessary to invent fresh titles for the resurrected ranks. On the contrary, they obviously wanted to keep step with the West. At the same time, they revealed their Achilles' heel in not daring to resurrect the title of general, which among the Russian people has too ironical a sound. In announcing the elevation to marshals of the five military dignitaries —choice of the five was made, be it remarked, rather out of regard for personal loyalty to Stalin than for talents or services—the Soviet press did not forget to remind its readers of the tzar's army, its "caste and rank worship and obsequiousness." Why then such a slavish imitation of it? In creating new privileges, the bureaucracy employs at every step the arguments which once served for the destruction of the old privileges. Insolence takes turns with cowardice, and is supplemented with increasing doses of hypocrisy.

However surprising at first glance the official resurrection of "caste and rank worship and obsequiousness," we must confess that the government had little freedom of choice left. The promotion of commanders on a basis of personal qualification can be realized only under conditions of free initiative and criticism in the army itself, and control over the army by the public opinion of the country. Severe discipline can get along excellently with a broad democracy and even directly rely upon it. No army, however, can be more democratic than the regime which nourishes it. The

source of bureaucratism with its routine and swank is not the special needs of military affairs, but the political needs of the ruling stratum. In the army these needs only receive their most finished expression. The restoration of officers' castes eighteen years after their revolutionary abolition testifies equally to the gulf which already separates the rulers from the ruled, to the loss by the Soviet army of the chief qualities which give it the name of "Red," and to the cynicism with which the bureaucracy erects these consequences of degeneration into law.

The bourgeois press has appraised this counterreform as it deserves. The French official paper, *Le Temps,* wrote on September 25, 1935: "This external transformation is one of the signs of a deep change which is now taking place throughout the whole Soviet Union. The regime, now definitely consolidated, is gradually becoming stabilized. Revolutionary habits and customs are giving place within the Soviet family and Soviet society to the feelings and customs which continue to prevail within the so-called capitalist countries. The Soviets are becoming bourgeoisified." There is hardly a word to add to that judgment.

Leonard Schapiro

40. THE GREAT PURGE

The Great Purges of 1936–1938 stand out as one of the most mysterious and dramatic episodes in the history of the Soviet Union. During the purges the majority of those who had led the Revolution and who had subsequently occupied the most important posts in the apparatus of state and party, the so-called Old Bolsheviks, were tried, condemned, and executed as traitors. In the process, many of the leading military figures were also eliminated. Some of the possible underlying reasons for the purges, as well as their effect on the Red Army, are discussed in the following selection by the noted student of Soviet Affairs, Leonard Schapiro.

The arrests and executions which decimated the Red Army during 1937 and 1938 must be seen against the background of what was going on at the time in Russia in general, and within the Communist Party in particular. For by 1937 the majority of all men in the forces and the overwhelming majority of officers were Party members. Hence there existed a likelihood that the policy applied to the civilian Party would in the end be applied to the military Communists.

Between 1929 and 1938 a series of assaults were made on the whole of Russian society. During the first five of these years—the period of the first Five-Year Plan—the main victims were peasants and civilian Party members. The peasants were arrested and deported in millions for resisting collectivization; while the Party was repeatedly purged by expulsions as part of Stalin's policy of eliminating real or suspected supporters of Trotsky. After 1935 there began the waves of arrests and executions which removed from the scene the great majority of the older Communists who had helped to make the Revolution. At the same time many members of the intellectual and professional classes also disappeared.

The first phase had served to discredit, but not to annihilate, all political opponents, and also to promote to key positions within the party apparatus new men whom Stalin trusted to support him. The second phase seemed—in so far as a rational explanation can be given to what can only be regarded as a form of madness—to have been aimed at the physical destruction of all actual or potential opponents; together with their supporters.

The purge of the Army took place almost entirely during this second phase. In spite of the large peasant element in the Red Army, the military Communist organization seems to have been considered sufficiently loyal to Stalin's agricultural policy to escape purging on anything like the scale suffered by the civilian Party. For example, in 1929 only 3–5 per cent. of the military Communists were purged, as compared with 11.7 per cent. for the Party as a whole. In 1933 the figures were 4.3 and 17 per cent. There can, however, be no doubt that many

From *The Soviet Army*, © 1956 B. Liddel Hart, pp. 65–72, abridged. Reprinted with the permission of Harcourt, Brace & World, Inc., and Weidenfeld and Nicolson, Ltd.

commanders were seriously concerned about the appalling effect on the morale of their troops caused by the ruthless collectivization policy. Some of the more influential, such as Blücher in the Far East, were able to assert themselves sufficiently to wrest concessions from the Government in favour of the peasant troops under their command and of their families. There may well have been protests and complaints. But there is no evidence that this understandable concern for morale among the officers ever reached the state of undermining the loyalty of the Army as an instrument on which Stalin could rely to enforce his policy. . . .

After 1935 a marked change could be observed in the demeanour of the senior Army officers. The Red Army was rapidly expanding, in the face of the gathering threat of war caused by Hitler's rise to power. With this expansion grew the officers' sense of their prestige and assertion of their right to more elbow-room in a society which had, on the whole, since the end of the Civil War, treated them with scant respect. The restoration of military ranks on 22nd September 1935, and the creation of the first Marshals, gave great impetus to this new sense of freedom. The same decree also conferred on all commanders, except junior commanders, the important privilege (or so it must have seemed in 1935) of immunity from arrest by civil organs without a special authorization in each case by the Peoples' Commissar for Defence. Other privileges followed, including important material concessions. In some cases senior commanders demanded with success the removal of political deputies whom they disliked. In others they successfully interfered with the political deputies' curriculum of training in ideological matters. In April 1936 the formation of Cossack units was permitted, and a Cossack Corps was in existence by 1937. The free Cossack tradition was, of course, little in tune with the rigorous dictatorship to which the country was subjected. (The

Cossack Corps was disbanded during the purge.)

None of these signs was more than a straw in the wind. None of them remotely approximated to rebellion or disloyalty in the ordinary sense of these terms. But to a dictator, ready and able to make his own position trebly sure by the most ruthless means, even such moderate signs of freedom may have begun to look like a threat to his position. Moreover, in 1937 one-fifth of the Red Army officers were veterans of the Civil War, many of them ex-officers or ex-non-commissioned officers of the old Imperial Army. Almost all the highest commands were occupied by these veterans. Few of them owed their positions to Stalin, and none had any special reason to show loyalty to him as against any other faction that might have formed within the Communist leadership.

According to one account there were some signs that support for Bukharin was growing in 1936 among the senior army leaders. By this time Bukharin, though still a member of the Central Committee of the Communist Party, had been edged out of all influence in the political machine. But he was known to be critical of Stalin and his methods. His advocacy of progress by evolution, rather than by force, held an especially strong appeal for many of the older Communists who were appalled by Stalinism in practice. There is therefore little reason to doubt that there were many senior officer Communists who were in sympathy with Bukharin. At a meeting of the Central Committee of the Party in the autumn of 1936 a large majority voted against Stalin and against Ezhov, then head of the Security Service, and in favour of Bukharin. Ezhov accused Bukharin of being an agent of the Gestapo. Bukharin replied accusing Stalin of a plot to seize sole power with the aid of Ezhov. According to the account referred to above, all the senior officers on the Central Committee supported the majority against Stalin, with the exception of Voroshilov and Budenny. Those who thus opposed Stalin included Tukhachevsky, Gamarnik, Blücher, and several more who were subsequently liquidated.

However, even if some of the senior officers thus ventured into open support of Bukharin, they were apparently quite unable to hinder Stalin's subsequent action to destroy Bukharin and all those who could remotely be suspected of supporting his views. More accurately, there is no evidence whatever that they tried. By January 1937, Bukharin and his principal supporter, Rykov, were under arrest. In the same month there was an ominous sign that some action was brewing against the Army leaders, when the Commander-in-Chief, Tukhachevsky, and the former military attaché in London, Putna (who was shot at the same time as Tukhachevsky), were referred to, in the course of the show trial of Communist leaders, as having been in contact with agents of Trotsky. In February Bukharin and Rykov were expelled from the Party. A vast new wave of arrests followed upon a campaign for vigilance against "enemies of the right." On 3rd March Stalin, in a speech at the Plenum of the Central Committee, dropped a strong hint of what was to come when he spoke of the harm that a few spies on the Army staff could do. By April Tukhachevsky was being openly cold-shouldered.

In May the political commissar system — that is to say, the system of dual command according to which every military order must be countersigned by a political commissar — was reintroduced at the highest levels of command. This system had been progressively abandoned after 1924, and by 1934 had been entirely replaced by the single-command system, with the political deputy responsible only for political matters. The reintroduction of the system first adopted after the revolution suggested that a crisis was imminent.

On 11th June 1937 the arrest was announced of Marshal Tukhachevsky and of the following senior officers: Yakir and Uborevich, both commanders of military districts; Primakov, deputy commander of a military district; Kork, head of the War College; Feldman, head of the Administration of Command Personnel; Eideman and Putna. Gamarnik, head of the political directorate of the Army, was stated to have committed suicide when faced with arrest. The trial of those arrested, according to the announcement, was to take place the same day in secret. . . .

On the following day, the condemnation and execution for treason of all the eight arrested commanders was announced. This was the beginning of a wave of arrests, and in many cases of executions, which continued almost uninterruptedly for the rest of 1937 and throughout 1938. The arrests, which fell with equal severity on both military and political officers, affected much more heavily in proportion the higher command. The great majority of the Civil War veterans were removed — though there were exceptions such as Shaposhnikov or Konev, or old cronies of Stalin such as Voroshilov and Budenny.

The following figures taken from a recent study agree in the main both with earlier estimates and with Japanese intelligence estimates: 35,000 victims in all, or about half the total officer corps; three out of five marshals; thirteen out of fifteen army commanders; fifty-seven out of eighty-five corps commanders; 110 out of 195 division commanders; 220 out of 406 brigade commanders. All eleven vice-commissars of War; seventy-five out of eighty members of the Supreme Military Council, including all the military district commanders as at May 1937. In percentage of ranks: 90 per cent. of all generals, and 80 per cent. of all colonels. . . .

Was there a conspiracy or a revolt? The evidence at present available is against it. The time for a conspiracy to put Bukharin in power and to oust Stalin was 1929 or 1930, while Bukharin was still a force in politics, not 1936 or 1937, after collectivization had been completed. The natural moment for a spontaneous revolt to save Bukharin would have been at the end of 1936, not June 1937, when he was already doomed. The normal method of dealing with a conspiracy is by a sudden swoop without warning. The arrests of June 1937 were, as shown above, nothing of the kind, though they may have appeared so at the time in the West. Accounts by *émigrés* of a conspiracy are scrappy, unconvincing, and contradictory. Not a jot of evidence has emerged from the German archives—for example, at the Nuremberg trials, or in German memoirs published since the war. . . .

If there was no conspiracy by the army commanders, what was the reason for the purge—if indeed a reason can be found for a holocaust on a scale which bears the imprint of madness? Some light may be thrown on the question by considering the main results which flowed from the purge.

First, the effect was to remove virtually the whole upper crust of senior officers, mostly veterans of the Civil War, and in many cases ex-officers of the Imperial Army. They had, it is true, almost all joined the Communist Party, and had not openly opposed collectivization. But many of them were known critics of collectivization; and their outlook, like that of so many old Communists, was often out of tune with Stalin's ruthless measures. Thus, from the point of view of a dictator bent on making his position secure beyond possible doubt, their removal may have appeared as a valuable prophylactic measure.

Secondly, the places of those removed were filled by the rapid promotion of young promising Communist officers. Unlike those whom they displaced, these new men owed everything to Stalin. To the Civil War veterans, Stalin was at best an equal. To the new men he was the architect of their careers in a rapidly expanding Army. Again, to a dictator who placed his own security in the forefront, the creation of such a prætorian guard of young officers may have appeared a very desirable end.

Lastly, the removal of the old officers eventually led to the development of mod-

ern military doctrine. This took place largely under the influence of Shaposhnikov and his pupils—men like Antonov, Vasilevsky, or Zhukov. Up to 1937 the dominant influence on doctrine was that of Tukhachevsky, and of others who were victims along with him. It would be wrong to attribute to Tukhachevsky all the failings of Soviet military doctrine up to 1937. For example, he was the first to urge two of the doctrines which became cardinal during the war: the need for overwhelming artillery support in attack, and for the use of tanks in a mass, and not merely in close support of infantry. On the other hand, it was true that Tukhachevsky's doctrine was in part vitiated by his enthusiastic adherence to Communist theory. He maintained, for instance, that the Red Army had no need for reserves, since it would find allies among the oppressed masses wherever it advanced.

But even if it is conceivable that the purge was in part motivated by a desire to infuse new blood into the dominant military doctrine, it would be quite wrong to suggest that the removal of Tukhachevsky led immediately to a reform in this field. Thus, the early disasters of the Red Army in 1941 were directly attributable to the failure to work out in advance the proper deployment of forces for defence in depth; and enormous tank losses were sustained as a result of initial failure to use tanks *en masse,* and by employing them, as Halder described it "a little everywhere."

The initial setbacks in Finland and the initial breakdown in face of the German attack in 1941 must in part be attributed to disorganization caused by the purge. The subsequent recovery of the Red Army showed that it contained reserves of military talent capable, given time, of making it a highly effective machine. That the purge gave the impetus to this development by the rapid advancement of new men may have been the case. But it is impossible to say that the mass arrests were either a necessary or an economic method of achieving this. The desire for one or all of the three results enumerated above may have contributed to Stalin's decision to launch his attack on the Army in June 1937.

But, to be seen in its true perspective, the military purge must be viewed as part of the process that was taking place in the country as a whole. Seen in this light, the temptation to look for rational explanations ought perhaps to be resisted. For, when once terror had been let loose on so vast a scale among the Party, intellectual and professional *élite* generally, the logic of common caution may well have made it seem imperative to Stalin that the Army should not be allowed to remain the only part of society immune from his assault.

41. MARSHAL VOROSHILOV ON THE STATE OF THE ARMY IN 1939

In the speech of Marshal Klimenty Voroshilov before the Eighteenth Congress of the Communist Party, selections from which are reprinted below, one may find stated the official Soviet view as to the relationship between the party, the government, and the army. According to Voroshilov, it was only through the purges that the ideological purity of the army could be maintained and along with it the security of the state.

Comrades, I have told you about the changes that have taken place during the past five years in the organization, armament and technical equipment of our army. Our army has completely changed as regards quantity, and especially as regards quality.

I have said nothing about the personnel, about our men, commanders, commissars, political workers, engineers, sappers, surgeons, quartermasters, in a word, about the human element of our army which in the long run decides everything and actually determines the fighting strength and military power of the Workers' and Peasants' Red Army.

Without men, technique is dead. Technique in the hands of men who understand it and have mastered it is a great force.

Cadres decide everything. That is beyond question. That is why the Party Central Committee and the Government have devoted, and are devoting, so much attention to increasing the number of our own, genuinely Soviet military cadres, people with a high sense of military duty and su-

premely devoted to their country and to the great cause of Lenin and Stalin. Much attention is being devoted to educating and perfecting our cadres both in political and in specialized military knowledge. We have all the cadres we need and of the right quality. They are steadily developing in all respects in step with the development of our great country and army. It is just these people, just these cadres that make our Red Army a first-class army, invincible in the power of its organization, armament and military efficiency, and unique in its spirit and political and moral strength.

When the Red Army was being purged of the scoundrels who had betrayed their state and their colours, the fascists and other imperialist aggressors raised a frenzied outcry claiming that our military cadres had been weakened and that as a result the fighting efficiency of the Red Army had suffered, and so on in a similar strain.

Comrade Stalin has made perfectly clear the true reasons for all this howling of our enemies. We are not playing the game,

From *The Land of Socialism, Today and Tomorrow: Reports and Speeches of the Eighteenth Congress of the Communist Party of the Soviet Union* (Moscow, 1939), pp. 283–284, 290–298, abridged.

don't you see, in rooting out the secret agents and spies from the ranks of our army, where this scum had been sent by foreign espionage services. It would have been nicer for the fascist rulers and their servitors if vile traitors like the Tukhachevskys, Yegorovs and Orlovs and similar corrupt scoundrels were allowed to continue operating in our midst, betraying our army and country. It would have been far more convenient, of course, for the instigators of world wars to carry on their sinister work having their own reliable agents in foreign armies. After all, it is easier for a burglar to break into a house if he has an accomplice inside to let him in. . . .

The Red Army is a unique army the like of which is unknown in history. It was created by the first people to defeat its enemies in the struggle for social emancipation.

The specific features of the Red Army are described in the words of Comrade Stalin:

> The first and principal feature of our Red Army is that it is the army of the emancipated workers and peasants, the army of the October Revolution, the army of the dictatorship of the proletariat. . . .
> The second feature of our Red Army is that it is an army based on the fraternity of the nations of our country, an army that emancipated the oppressed nations of our country, an army that is defending the liberty and independence of the nations of our country. . . .
> And, lastly, a third feature of the Red Army: it is the spirit of internationalism, the international sentiments which imbue our whole Red Army.

This definition of the specific features of our Red Army given by Stalin is the guiding principle of all the Party's educational and political work in the Red Army. It is on these three precepts that the political life and morale of men and commanders rest. . . .

A special responsibility for this work lies on the military commissar.

The political apparatus of the army, that is, the military commissars, political guides and political workers of all kinds, has been considerably enlarged in the interval be-

tween the Seventeenth and the Eighteenth Congresses. On January 1, 1934, we had fifteen thousand political workers; today the army has thirty-four thousand, an increase of 126 per cent.

As a result of the purge of the Red Army of traitors, spies and treasonable elements, and the purge of the political apparatus itself of such putrid and treacherous scum, the role and importance of the political apparatus, and of the military commissar in the first place, has been considerably enhanced. And the sense of responsibility of the whole political personnel for their work has grown.

The political personnel of the Red Army have been largely renewed in the past few years. Thousands of fine young men, members of our Party, honest, devoted and capable workers, have been advanced from the lower ranks to various responsible posts.

These are some of the finest people in the Party organization of the army; these are active people who are supremely devoted to the cause of Lenin and Stalin, and who in the past two or three years have shown themselves to be real Party men, fighters for the purity of the ranks of the Party and for the might of the Red Army. It is they who, together with the whole Party organization and with the support of all honest non-Party men and commanders, have with an iron broom swept the army clean of traitors and scoundrels, so that it is now stronger and politically more closely welded than ever before. These political workers, in conjunction with all the active Party and Y.C.L. members in the army, are carrying on important educational work, raising the political level of our army with the object of preventing the appearance within it not only of treacherous and treasonable elements, but of all sceptics, malcontents and other dross who in the long run grow into, and are bound to grow into, real traitors and agents of our class enemies. . . .

The Workers' and Peasants' Red Army is of the same flesh and blood as its people and shares the interests of the whole country. Under the leadership of the great Party of Lenin and Stalin, it is waging a struggle for the new, communist society, and at the first call of the Party, at the orders of its Government, it will stand in defence of its country, its people and the socialist state.

The Red Army, guided by its Party and non-Party Bolsheviks — its commanders and military commissars — and thanks to its powerful Party and Y.C.L. organizations and its efficient political work, has always a good grasp of home and foreign affairs. It is always keenly responsive to all events in the home and foreign affairs of the country.

Comrades, our army has grown up with the people and has fought side by side with the people; it fought and completely defeated all its class enemies, domestic and foreign, in the Civil War. Many of the finest people of our Party, fighting in the ranks of the Red Army, laid down their lives for the cause of the people, for the cause of Lenin and Stalin.

In these past few years, when the army was being thoroughly reorganized and re-equipped and becoming an ever stronger and more mighty force of the Soviet state, the despicable traitors of the Trotsky-Zinoviev-Buckharin gang tried, by treason to the colours and betrayal of the interests of the people and the state, to destroy our army from within, to treacherously enfeeble it and to make its defeat certain in time of war.

This suppurating ulcer has been lanced. The Red Army was rapidly and thoroughly purged of all this filth.

Comrades, the Red Army is a tremendous force. The men, commanders and political personnel of our army represent a monolithic collective body welded together by the Marxist-Leninist ideology. The Red Army is ready at any moment, like one man, to perform its sacred duty as defender of the state where labour is victorious, is eager and willing, as one man, to sacrifice life itself for the great cause of Lenin and Stalin. . . .

42. KHRUSHCHEV ON THE MILITARY CONSEQUENCES OF THE PURGES

According to Nikita Khrushchev, the poor performance of the Red Army in the opening days of the German invasion was directly attributable to the faulty leadership of Stalin. In particular, he blames Stalin for wrecking the efficiency and the discipline of the army through the purges. The selection is taken from Krushchev's famous 1956 "Secret Speech" on the crimes of Stalin as it is reprinted in Bertram Wolfe's *Khrushchev and Stalin's Ghost.*

On the eve of the invasion of the territory of the Soviet Union by the Hitlerite Army, a certain German citizen crossed our border and stated that the German armies had received orders to start the offensive against the Soviet Union on the night of 22 June at 3 o'clock. Stalin was informed about this immediately, but even this warning was ignored.

As you see, everything was ignored: warnings of certain Army commanders, declarations of deserters from the enemy army, and even the open hostility of the enemy. Is this an example of the alertness of the chief of the party and of the state at this particularly significant historical moment?

And what were the results of this carefree attitude, this disregard of clear facts? The result was that in the first hours and

From Bertram Wolfe, *Krushchev and Stalin's Ghost* (New York, 1957), pp. 172–176. Reprinted with the permission of Frederick A. Praeger, Publisher.

days the enemy destroyed in our border regions a large part of our Air Force, artillery and other military equipment; he annihilated large numbers of our military cadres and disorganized our military leadership; consequently we could not prevent the enemy from marching deep into the country.

Very grievous consequences, especially in reference to the beginning of the war followed Stalin's annihilation of many military commanders and political workers during 1937–1941 because of his suspiciousness and through slanderous accusations. During these years repressions were instituted against certain parts of military cadres beginning literally at the company and battalion commander level and extending to the higher military centers; during this time the cadre of leaders who had gained military experience in Spain and in the Far East was almost completely liquidated.

The policy of large-scale repression against the military cadres led also to undermined military discipline, because for several years officers of all ranks and even soldiers in the party and Komsomol cells were taught to "unmask" their superiors as hidden enemies.

It is natural that this caused a negative influence on the state of military discipline in the first war period.

And, as you know, we had before the war excellent military cadres which were unquestionably loyal to the party and to the Fatherland. Suffice it to say that those of them who managed to survive despite severe tortures to which they were subjected in the prisons, have from the first war days shown themselves real patriots and heroically fought for the glory of the Fatherland; I have here in mind such comrades as Rokossovsky (who, as you know, had been jailed), Gorbatov, Maretskov (who is a delegate at the present Congress), Podlas (he was an excellent commander who perished at the front), and many, many others. However, many such commanders perished in camps and jails and the Army saw them no more.

All this brought about the situation which existed at the beginning of the war and which was the great threat to our Fatherland.

It would be incorrect to forget that, after the first severe disaster and defeats at the front, Stalin thought that this was the end. In one of his speeches in those days he said: "All that which Lenin created we have lost forever."

After this Stalin for a long time actually did not direct the military operations and ceased to do anything whatever. He returned to active leadership only when some members of the Political Bureau visited him and told him that it was necessary to take certain steps immediately in order to improve the situation at the front.

Therefore, the threatening danger which hung over our Fatherland in the first period of the war was largely due to the faulty methods of directing the nation and the party by Stalin himself.

43. GENERAL VON SEECKT'S 1920 ORDER TO THE GERMAN ARMY

Despite the catastrophic defeat suffered by Germany in 1918 and despite the provisions of the Versailles Treaty reducing its size to 100,000 men, the German army, or Reichswehr, continued to play a preeminent role in the life of the German state, even under a republican regime. It was the aim of the leaders of the Reichswehr, and in particular the Chief of the High Command, General Hans von Seeckt, that the traditions and the spirit of the army be preserved against the day when the Versailles Treaty would no longer be operative. Seeckt believed that the strength and the unity of the army could only be assured if the military kept aloof from the intense and often violent party struggles that characterized German political life after 1918. The basis for this policy was laid in the days following the overthrow of the monarchy in the bloodless revolution of November 1918, when the High Command agreed to give its support to the new provisional republican government in return for a promise that it would respect the vital interests of the army. As far as Seeckt was concerned, the army was to oppose any attack on the Weimar Republic, even it was made in the name of the monarchy to which he and most officers were still loyal.

In the General Order reprinted below, Seeckt reminds the military of their duty to the Republic. This order was issued following the Kapp Putsch of March 1920, an abortive coup d'état, in which a number of extreme reactionaries, including several high ranking officers, attempted to overthrow the Weimar Republic and to establish a more authoritarian regime. By adhering to the policy which Seeckt here advocated, the Reichswehr was able to preserve its cohesion and unity, and incidentally, to have a far greater influence on national policy, than if it had openly taken sides in the political struggle.

Berlin, April 18, 1920
Chief of the Army Command
No. 95, Chief

This is a crucial hour for the officers corps of the Reichswehr. Its behaviour in the immediate future will determine whether the officers corps will retain the leadership in the new army. At the same time it will be determined whether the Reichswehr will succeed in preserving the values of the past for an active present and a bright future. The very existence and the prosperity of the state are closely connected with the Reichswehr. . . . We must contribute to the reconstruction and do our part. . . . This recognition is lacking in many places; and I observe unrest, distrust, insecurity. We shall not get ahead that way. If we do not succeed in reestablishing the old ties of confidence, I do not see any chance for improvement. That does not refer to officers only, but to all parts of the army. Everyone has the duty to maintain, and where it has been lost to rebuild the confidence between Reichswehr, government and high command of

From Alma Luckan, "Kapp Putsch—Success or Failure," *Journal of Central European History*, Vol. VII, No. 4. Reprinted by permission.

the army, and also between enlisted men and officers, and between the civilian population and the Reichswehr. . . .

A number of indications make me realize that many members of the Reichswehr are not aware yet of the situation in which we find ourselves as a result of the events in March, and that we now have to bear the consequences of what . . . political short-sightedness has perpetrated. It is the tragic outcome of such deeds that the innocent many have to suffer for the guilt of the few. I do not deny that military obedience is an excuse for the majority of the misdemeanors, but we must neither overlook nor deny the fact that a number of irresponsible actions occurred in our own ranks, and they require rectification. . . . I mean under misdemeanors . . . above all the cases of gross insubordination and brutal excesses which have occurred in some part of the army. I have no intention of either tolerating or forgetting such occurrences. . . . We do not intend to inquire into personal opinions, or start proscriptions, but we shall examine . . . each individual case, . . . There is no intention on the part of the responsible authorities of changing the principles upon which the organization of the Reichswehr rests. All ranks of the Reichswehr will be open to anyone; the choice of leaders will be made as before, on the basis of qualification and character.

Any kind of political activity in the army will be prohibited. Political quarrels within the Reichswehr are incompatible with both the spirit of comradeship and with discipline, and can only be harmful to military training. We do not ask the individual for his political creed, but we must assume that everyone who serves in the Reichswehr from now on will take his oath seriously.

Those who do not condemn the unfortunate attempt made during the month of March at overthrowing the government,

and those who still believe that a repetition would end in anything but new misfortune for our people and for the Reichswehr, should decide on his own that the Reichswehr is not the place for him.

When I hear others judge the situation and complain of the hardships it imposes upon us, I notice a lack of comprehension as to the real cause of our misfortune: the treaty of Versailles. That holds true above all of the uncertainties in the organization of our army. We should not allow further dissemination of the opinion that has unfortunately been spread by many that . . . the highest military authorities are not trying everything possible to bring about an improvement in the situation. We also must refute the misconceptions spread by the same groups that there is any possibility of avoiding the immediate reduction of the army to 200,000 men. We are trying with all means to preserve this number beyond June 10th. . . .

We are filled with gratitude and admiration for our comrades in Thuringia, Saxony and in the Ruhr for having done their duty, and filled with regret for the heavy losses they have suffered, we express the hope that the fighting against our own people will soon come to an end.

I have accepted the command of the army with full confidence in the officers' corps. I have lived for and with the army for 35 years. What is left of my strength belongs to the army. No one is more appreciative deep down in his heart of the suffering and troubles of everyone of you. We shall conquer these difficulties as so often before if we remain united. . . .

This order is to be read to all officers and after reading the order a report is to be made by the commander of each army district to the Ministry of Defense. The enlisted men are likewise to be informed of this order.

signed: v. Seeckt

Harold Gordon

44. THE REICHSWEHR AND THE GERMAN REPUBLIC

The bases on which the Weimar Republic and the army established a fruitful modus vivendi are discussed in the following passage drawn from Professor Harold Gordon's exhaustive study *The Reichswehr and the German Republic*.It is his thesis that despite the many reasons they had for cooperation there were unfortunately strong elements of distrust on both sides which limited this accommodation between them and contributed to the ultimate downfall of the Weimar regime.

The Reichswehr was born in the turmoil of the German Revolution of 1918–1919. Though its birth was in many ways a response to the desire of many Germans to see the reestablishment of orderly processes of government and life, the emergence of the new army must be attributed chiefly to one factor: the alliance between the new government authorities and the leaders of the Imperial Army. These two elements —the political leaders of the German Republic and the military leaders of the old army—were united upon a common objective, the restoration of political and social order.

In cooperation, the Socialists and the soldiers gathered together a force which prevented the complete disintegration of Germany. The military leaders by themselves would have been helpless to stop the growing chaos; the Republicans would have been lost without a force to defend them against their foes. In collaboration they created a situation in which the leaders of the Republic could establish the foundations of a new polity.

Despite the many accusations to the contrary, the leaders of the Reichswehr and of the Weimar Republic collaborated with remarkable success throughout the period in question, despite the widely differing ideological bases of the various governments and despite the prevalence of monarchist feeling in the Reichswehr. President, Reichswehrminister, and senior generals were always in general agreement on military policy, and the majority of the Cabinet generally proved itself amenable to the decisions reached by these leaders. Occasional disputes arose upon individual points, but they were usually settled upon a give-and-take basis, with the Reichswehr sometimes successful and sometimes unsuccessful in pressing its point. The leaders of the army tried to influence policies which might affect military interests, but did not proceed to the point of insubordination in their efforts.

On two occasions—during the Kapp Putsch and during the Bavarian crisis of October-November 1923—General von Seeckt differed from the opinions of his civilian superiors as to the military measures necessary to suppress a rebellion. In the first instance, he disagreed with the Minister on the advisability of fighting the Kappists in Berlin, and resigned—although he had not been given a direct order to march. In the second case, he persuaded the President of the wisdom of further de-

Reprinted from *The Reichswehr and the German Republic* by Harold Gordon (Princeton, 1957), pp. 425–430, by permission of Princeton University Press. Copyright ©1957 by Princeton University Press.

lay, in hopes of averting bloodshed. In neither case is there any indication that he acted from sympathy for the rebels or that he was exceeding his official prerogative of disapproving a proposed course of action which in his opinion would have disastrous consequences. He did not threaten the government in either case with the disaffection of the army. In the first instance, he simply exercised his right — and duty — to withdraw rather than carry out a policy which he personally believed fraught with danger to the nation (a precedent which was later followed by Colonel General Beck in 1938, when he resigned from his position as Chief of the General Staff as a protest against Hitler's plans for large-scale military adventures). In the second instance, the disagreement was resolved by his success in convincing the President of the correctness of his views.

The only case of unwarranted military interference in matters concerning the government of the Reich was at least partly the direct result of the personal political ambitions of General von Seeckt. In 1923, he helped to overturn the Stresemann government not only by the legitimate expression of his distrust of Stresemann at the request of the President, but by working against Stresemann within the latter's own political party. Later, only circumstances prevented Seeckt from committing a similar indiscretion when he prepared a campaign for the Presidency. However, the sudden death of President Ebert resulted in the shipwreck of his plans and saved him from himself. Aside from these two instances, the senior military leaders were careful not to exceed their competence. They lobbied for governmental and party acceptance of Reichswehr policy; but they did not interfere in party politics as such. In the question of the army's dealings with Russia, while the Reichswehr technically exceeded its formal competence, its actions were known and approved by the Presidents and Chancellors of the Reich and therefore do not constitute opposition to or insubordination toward the government, despite the an-

noyance of the Foreign Office at such unconventional competition.

On lower levels, however, the Reichswehr was much less successful in dealing with the Republic. The difficulties which arose in this respect were partly the result of the party allegiance of many of the Prussian state officials — who as members of the Majority Socialist Party were often hostile to the Reichswehr — and partly the result of the clumsiness, hauteur, and tactlessness with which many higher troop commanders handled the civilian populace during periods when martial law was in effect. These same qualities also made trouble during normal dealings with civilian officialdom. Commanding generals sometimes displayed an appalling ignorance of their powers under martial law and, still more, of the political repercussions of many of their actions. Further difficulties arose in the pre-1921 period as a result of the delegation of broad judiciary powers to battalion-level officers, many of whom were completely untrained for the military-political task assigned to them. Misunderstandings, unnecessary friction, and, on some occasions, summary execution of alleged rebels resulted from this situation, and helped to alienate broad groups of the population from the Reichswehr, or, at the least, made reconciliation with these groups far more difficult than it need have been.

A further difficulty arising from the domestic situation was the isolation of the Reichswehr from significant elements of the population, an isolation which was expressed in the overt hostility of large segments of the urban working class and considerable numbers of the intelligentsia, as well as in the lack of interest in things military which characterized most middle-class liberals. The isolation of the Reichswehr from these groups was reflected in the comparatively low representation of these groups in the ranks and in the Officer Corps as well as by their hostility or indifference toward military aspirations and activities.

The higher military authorities recognized this problem and deplored its existence. Their attempts to remedy it were, however, unsuccessful, partly because of the mechanics of the military system — especially the long term of service — but primarily because of traditional attitudes within the army and within the groups which the army hoped to attract. Working-class youths usually had insufficient education to qualify for commissions, and, in any case, having absorbed a pacifist tradition reinforced by active dislike and distrust of the army, they had no desire to serve in any capacity, even if the term of service were drastically reduced. Some youths from liberal middle-class families were also pacifist by inclination and training. Far more, however, were repelled by the generally conservative nature of the Officer Corps, especially when this factor was coupled with the austerity, discipline, sacrifices, and low pay characterizing the soldier's life. Their upbringing, their social relationships, their standard of living, and their standards of values all tended to incline them toward nonmilitary occupations and professions.

In view of this situation, it would seem that only by means denied the Germans by the Treaty — universal conscription and a broad reserve program — could those working-class and liberal middle-class elements which were hostile to or aloof from the Reichswehr have been brought into closer touch with it, so as to create an army more truly representative of the nation as a whole.

The same situation which resulted in greatly reduced representation of large social groups within the army had another even more damaging effect — hostility between the political parties representing these groups and the Reichswehr. The largest of these parties — and the largest party in the Republic — the Majority Socialist, represented many ideas which were anathema to almost all soldiers and followed policies which the army felt to be directly or indirectly aimed against itself or toward the disintegration and destruction of Germany as a nation.

The Majority Socialists, on the other hand, were, generally speaking, hostile to everything military and were especially suspicious of the Reichswehr because of the conservative complexion if its personnel and because of the family and economic ties which existed between many soldiers and members of the conservative parties. Despite the attempts of some leaders to take a more constructive stand toward military affairs, the party failed to adopt any positive military program. Its members more or less went their own way. In most cases this way led them to constant but ineffective attacks upon the military authorities and upon the army. After the acceptance of the Treaty of Versailles eliminated the possibility of a people's militia, these criticisms were almost uniformly negative and were seriously weakened by the ignorance of military activities and policy which characterized the party. . . .

Attempts were made, by groups on both sides, to heal the breach between party and army. These attempts were unsuccessful. Traditional hatreds, mutual distrust, and the actions of an irresponsible minority in both camps defeated every effort at reconciliation. The rift between the largest party in the Republic and the army was so wide and deep that only the utmost efforts of all concerned could have led to the development of cooperation and mutual respect. In the absence of such effort, the antagonism of these two powerful groups remained active and constituted one of the greatest potential dangers to the continued existence of the Republic.

The desire of the military to remain autonomous under the Republic, the general monarchist atmosphere within the Reichswehr, the scars left by war, defeat, and revolution, were all comparatively minor problems which could have been settled more or less amicably had the Reichswehr and the Majority Socialists achieved a *modus vivendi*. In the atmosphere of hatred, rivalry, and suspicion which resulted from their failure to attain this end, the significance of these problems became magnified and further inflamed an already unfortunate situation. Where the greater share of responsibility for the continuation of the pre-World War I feud lies and whether the most herculean efforts of all concerned could have altered the situation is a decision the reader must make for himself.

History tells us what has happened; it may also reveal unexploited possibilities, but it veils their potentialities in darkness. All that can be safely asserted is that the government of the Republic and the Reichswehr were able to cooperate. The largest party of the Republic and the Reichswehr were unable to cooperate. The resultant situation crippled the Republic vis-à-vis any third force which might arise to threaten it from within the nation, and played a part in making possible the eventual rise to power of Adolf Hitler and his evil cohorts.

45. THE OATH OF THE GERMAN SOLDIERS TO HITLER

The following oath, which does not differ much in form or substance from the oathes traditionally given by German soldiers to their sovereigns, was nevertheless to have fateful consequences. As long as they felt themselves bound by this oath, the great majority of the officer corps considered themselves powerless to stop Hitler, even when the more intelligent of them recognized that he had embarked upon a course which could only lead to disaster. In effect, by this oath, Hitler made the military his accomplices, be they willing or unwilling, in his whole policy of war.

I swear by God this sacred oath, that I will yield unconditional obedience to the Fuehrer of the German Reich and *Volk*, Adolf Hitler, the Supreme Commander of the Wehrmacht, and as a brave soldier, will be ready at any time to lay down my life for this oath.

Hans Rothfels

46. THE MILITARY RESISTANCE TO HITLER

It is generally acknowledged that most of the more traditionally Prussian elements within the German army were fundamentally antipathetic to the Nazis. They were the ones who were most active in the conspiracy of July 20, 1944. In the following selection taken from his book *The German Resistance*, Professor Hans Rothfels discusses the attitude of this group towards the Nazis, as well as the manner in which Hitler diminished or neutralized their influence within the army.

The relationship between army and party implies one of the major problems in the history of the Third Reich. It cannot be covered by any easy formula, neither by that of an allegedly "natural" clash of two "elites" — an older one, aristocratic and somewhat degenerate, versus a younger one, plebeian and biologically superior (the Goebbels explanation) — nor by the contrary assumption, likewise generalizing, of an allegedly "natural" alliance between "Prussian militarism and Nazism" (the official American thesis during the war). In reality the problem has run through several stages, and defies simplification. . . .

. . . As far as this military sector of the Third Reich is concerned, there can be no doubt that a certain cleavage existed from the beginning. Whatever the contribution of the Munich *Reichswehr* to the rise of the party, or that made by commanding officers in East Prussia (Von Blomberg and Von Reichenau) to Hitler's seizure of power, it was a support given with the same reservations which other upper-class groups maintained, inside as well as outside Germany. The hope was indulged of being able to use the "drummer," the "Bohemian corporal," the man with the funny mustache, as a tool, and then to throw him

away. This was a *proton pseudos* of large and fateful consequence. But besides the compromising attitude of military opportunists, there was that of uncompromising foes. The outstanding figure among these opponents is the Chief of Staff in the first year, Colonel General von Hammerstein-Equord — the "Red General," as he was often called — a passionate anti-Nazi and a man of deeply religious convictions. In January, 1933, he urged a military action against Hitler, but was prevented by Hindenburg, on the ground that politics were not the army's business.

The line of aloofness became then, in fact, the dominant one during the early years. It seemed to be in accordance with Prussian military traditions and with an aristocratic code, though the principle of keeping out of politics had had very different meanings before 1914, when meddling with public affairs seemed improper, and after 1919, when the *Reichswehr* was a sort of state within a state. With the conditions prevailing under the Nazi regime, however, this "hands-off" attitude was bound to gain a completely new meaning; it amounted practically to toleration of crime and murder on the part of those who had power to avert them; it thereby contra-

From Hans Rothfels, *The German Opposition to Hitler* (Hinsdale, Ill., 1948), pp. 63–75, abridged. Reprinted with the permission of Henry Regnery, Co.

dicted another, most honorable militarist and aristocratic tradition, that of *noblesse oblige* and of the protection of the weak. It is true many officers felt shame and indignation not only at the murder of Von Schleicher and the way it was hushed up, or at the incredible intrigues to which their own Commander in Chief, Von Fritsch, fell a victim; not only at the racial legislation which hit quite a number of their comrades or comrades' families, and destroyed the ties with, and the very existence of, so many Jewish veterans of the last war. They felt the same about the brutal things which took place outside their professional circle, about the scandals and outrages which they could not help seeing in the streets or hearing about. And the Protestant churches were never more crowded with officers in uniform — a rather unusual sight. There is no doubt that the army gave strong support to the Confessing Church and saw in the attack on Christianity a basic threat. A book published under the auspices of the War Ministry stressed this point. The whole climate of the regime, its boasting, its demagoguery, its appeal to the basest instincts, was certainly as anti-Prussian as possible. And yet no immediate reaction followed from the cleavage.

Of course, one can understand why Von Fritsch did not raise the standard of revolt for his own defense; but there were enough general issues of honor and morality which would have furnished a starting point, and the War Ministry was amply supplied with evidences of Nazi crimes. But none of these opportunities was seized upon, and discipline was too strict to allow spontaneous military actions against murder, plunder, and arson when they raged through German cities in November, 1938. It was only at the last minute, during the Polish campaign, that a genuine militarist tradition reasserted itself. Examples are known of regimental commanders, who, with armed interference, put a stop to the looting and the killing of civilians by the SS, and real battles were fought between soldiers and the black squadrons. But these instances of professional ethics and decency were not backed up or followed through, and another opportunity of saving the honor of the German army was missed.

While this sin of omission must be stated unmistakably, it is obvious that army aloofness was a sort of opposition in the same sense as the term has been applied to other "water-repellent" parts of the population. Even more effectively so. In fact, the army was the only social body within the state which was able and seemed determined to close all loopholes of infiltration. Party membership ceased under the colors, there were to be no politics, and the repeated "offers" of Dr. Ley to organize the soldier's leisure time ("strength through joy") were successfully warded off. Moreover, it was well known that Nazi functionaries, when called up, had a hard time in the army, and that top sergeants found an especial pleasure in deflating them. . . .

As a result, the army in the early years was to a large extent Nazi-proof. And this probably increased the illusory feeling that one could wait for some fruits of Hitler's revisionist and rearmament policies without incurring the danger of being carried away. The army actually appeared as a refuge for potential resisters. When Von Hammerstein was told about the growing number of high-school graduates who intended to choose a military career, he is said to have answered: "I know, this is simply another form of inner emigration."

In truth, however, the integrity of the army was gradually whittled down, partly through its own fault (especially the fault of Von Blomberg),[1] partly through an astute policy on the part of Hitler. . . . The first step was taken in August, 1934, a few hours after the death of Hindenburg, when the *Reichswehr* was tricked into an oath of unconditional obedience to the Führer's person. This constituted a moral bond, however immoral in content, and an obstacle which, in accordance with all traditional standards, could not easily be overcome.

[1]Minister of War between 1934 and 1938. [Editor's note]

The next step was the restoration of universal conscription in March, 1935. Beck, the successor and friend of Von Hammerstein, is on record as having opposed this measure, at least in its tempo and in its scope. He did so for technical as well as for political reasons. He foresaw not only a loss in quality and the dangerous trend toward bold adventures, but also the swamping effect as far as the anti-Nazi structure of the army was concerned.

In fact, the rapid increase opened the dike; it watered down army "separatism," which, however ambiguous in normal times, was an asset under circumstances as they then prevailed. It also opened splendid careers to young officers and unusual advancement to the higher ones. There is no doubt that Hitler's was a policy of deliberate bribery. While the very fact of the army's being the instrument of a criminal regime was in itself conducive of corruption, material temptation added greatly to the harmful effect. In many cases, "Prussianism" proved a hollow shell, just as the traditions of an austere past had vanished long ago among broad sections of the German people. In other words, officers were just as much infected by the poison of materialism which had spread since the late nineteenth century as were members of any other group. When generals had their *mésalliances* sanctioned, or their private debts settled, by the Führer—or, later on, were willing to receive large "personal" donations in money or estates from him—no link can be established between such an attitude and any militarist code or "categorical imperative" of an officer caste.

In addition, other factors worked against the resistance elements in the army. For one thing, Hitler's successes from the repudiation of the military sections of the Treaty of Versailles and the march into the Rhineland (March, 1936) through the annexation of Austria and the Sudetenland to the march into Prague (March, 1939), heightened his prestige. Having succeeded in one coup after another—and in all of them against the warnings of the army

—he could assume an "I-told-you-so" attitude which undermined the credit of his opponents. Moreover, shortly before the march into Vienna, Hitler dealt the army a severe blow. In the course of a knavish intrigue, the compromised War Minister von Blomberg as well as the unimpeachable Commander in Chief von Fritsch were dismissed. And on February 4, 1938, Hitler took unto himself the supreme command of the armed forces and established a new unified command *Oberkommando der Wehrmacht*, or OKW, under a typical yes-man (Keitel—or "Lackey-tel," as the resisters called him), who was made superior to the army Chief of Staff. At the same time a number of generals (ten to twelve commanders of corps and divisions), who had proved inaccessible—they were mostly bearers of old Prussian names—were also dismissed. It is less well known that this purge extended to about one hundred regimental commanders. Only one newspaper, in Silesia, dared to publish the list of the ousted men, and it was promptly suppressed as a result. The importance of this less conspicuous measure rests with the fact that regimental commanders decided on their own whether or not an officer candidate was to be accepted.

This was the situation when the war broke out. It explains something (though not all by far) of the defeat which the military part of the revolt suffered on July 20 at the hands of "loyal" officers; and it explains a good deal of the tantalizing story which unfolded through the years 1939–44. It was tantalizing from the viewpoint of those who urged military action, and it cannot fail to affect the historian, as an observer, with the same feeling.

A few remarks will suffice to characterize the "resistance against the resistance." Practically all witnesses, much as they differ in accent—Gisevius and Goerdeler, Hassell and Schlabrendorff—all agree in their complaints about hesitancy and evasiveness on the part of army and army group commanders. Some could eventually be won over, as were Field Marshals von

Kluge and Rommel; others had to be worked upon for months, only to slide back time and again. Whether this was due to conventional loyalty and misunderstood patriotism, or to faults of character, would have to be decided in each instance. The Captain of Reserves, Hermann Kaiser, who was attached to Colonel General Fromm, Commander of the Home Army, and who acted as an important liaison officer between Goerdeler and the military, noted in his diary on February 20, 1943: "the one is prepared to act upon order, the other to give orders when action has been taken." This is probably as objective an analysis of the average military attitude as can be given. Most of the high commanders were likely to follow the lead if a break occurred — or better still, if the formal bond of the oath were removed by Hitler's assassination; but, while they did not wish to commit themselves, they were equally unwilling to denounce those who tried to persuade them; not did they feel very sure about what the young officers would do. The conspirators looked with contempt upon such an attitude. "These cowards make out of me, an old soldier, an antimilitarist," Von Hammerstein is said to have exclaimed. Von Hassell spoke of the "hopeless sergeant majors." And in the diary quoted earlier, Kaiser remarked: "One need only to think of a Scharnhorst, or Clausewitz or Gneisenau to realize to what level the officer of today has descended." . . .

Against this background there stand out the names of those professional soldiers who were determined to "do something about it." Beck, though retired, remained the acknowledged leader of the military Resistance. He came from a middle-class family in the Rhineland, a man of liberal traditions and a scientific bent of mind. He has been described as "combining the universal culture and the European scope of the eighteenth century with the basic principles of the Prussian past." In fact, he recalls the forward looking generals and reformers of the years of 1807–1815, whose names were conjured up in Kaiser's diary. . . .

There were other men of an unusual type among the military conspirators, such as Colonel Count Claus Schenk von Stauffenberg. After having been severely wounded, he became Chief of Staff of the Home Army in 1943, and thus obtained a key position; it was he who placed the bomb on July 20. A Catholic from Bavaria, a member of the circle of disciples around the German poet Stefan George, he was undoubtedly as much concerned about the cultural and religious as about the social and political implications of the Nazi Regime and of totalitarianism in general. If looks mean anything, his picture will make one realize that this was no ordinary colonel and no man of narrow military ambitions, however brilliant a soldier he had been. . . .

The question may then be asked why, in spite of such an array of key officers, all military plans of action eventually fell short of the mark. For one thing, it is true that the officers were poorly trained for conspiratorial work, with the exception perhaps of those in the Intelligence Division. There was no revolutionary tradition extant in the Prusso-German army, such as exists in southern European countries or in Latin America. Another explanation suggests itself, and has been widely accepted: Nazi followers or vacillating non-Nazis foiled the attempts. There is truth in that, too. Much of the energy of the conspirators was consumed by the "labors of a Sisyphus," as has already been stated. . . . As long as the road to victory still seemed open, how could one convince the people and the army that Hitler was leading them to disaster? And conversely, with the threat of defeat imminent, how could one precipitate catastrophe by breaking up the front? We saw that Goerdeler spoke derisively of the policy of "waiting for the appropriate psychological moment." In fact, this policy was an excuse for all sorts of weaknesses and ambitions.

But within the merely military circle of thought, there was hardly a way out of the impasse. And without having been faced with the same problem, one had better withhold generalizing judgments. It required very strong convictions and a realization of a threat to the highest human values to break through the code of duty and patriotism to the point where one was prepared to revolt in the midst of an all-engulfing struggle, or eventually not only to wish and pray but also to work for the defeat of one's own country. . . .

47. GENERAL GUDERIAN ON THE JULY 20, 1944, PLOT

Although many German officers may have harbored serious reservations as to the methods and the ideals of the Nazis, their tradition of obedience to constituted authority prevented all but a few from taking any positive measures to restrain Hitler. In the following selection, General Heinz Guderian, one of the leading German exponents and practitioners of mechanized warfare, endeavors to justify this passive attitude. Of necessity he also condemns those who participated in the plot of July 20, 1944. The selection is taken from his book *Panzer Leader.*

From every point of view the results of the attempted assassination were frightful. For myself I refuse to accept murder in any form. Our Christian religion forbids it in the clearest possible terms. I cannot therefore approve of the plan of assassination. Apart from this religious reason, I must also say that neither the internal nor the external political situation was conducive to a successful *coup d'état.* The preparations made were utterly inadequate, the choice of personalities to fill the principal roles incomprehensible. The driving force had originally been Dr. Goerdeler, an idealist who believed that the *coup d'état* could be performed without the assassination. Both he and his fellow conspirators were undoubtedly convinced that what they were doing was in the higher interests of their nation. Dr. Goerdeler had also decided on the choice of the majority of the people destined by the conspirators to hold office in the new government. He had drawn up lists of names in this connection which, through his own carelessness, fell into the hands of the Gestapo. . . . By July 20th, 1944, the plan had been under discussion and debate for years on end. The number of people in the know increased constantly. It is hardly surprising that the Gestapo finally got wind of one or other of the groups of conspirators and that a wave of imprisonments threatened them all. This threat doubtless persuaded the impulsive Graf Stauffenberg to turn to assassination, a decision that the other conspirators were hardly likely to have reached on their own. The assassination was a failure. But the assassin was completely deceived as to the effect of his bomb and behaved with more than foolhardiness. . . .

Of course one question will always be asked: what would have happened had the assassination succeeded? Nobody can answer this. Only one fact seems beyond dispute: at that time the great proportion of the German people still believed in Adolf Hitler and would have been convinced that with his death the assassin had removed the only man who might still have been able to bring the war to a favourable conclusion. The odium thus created by his death would have been attached primarily to the corps of officers, the generals and the

From the book *Panzer Leader* by Heinz Guderian. Translated by Constantine Fitzgibbon. Published 1952 by E. P. Dutton & Co., Inc. and reprinted with their permission. Reprinted also with the permission of Michael Joseph Ltd.

general staff, and would have lasted not only during but also after the war. The people's hatred and contempt would have turned against the soldiers who, in the midst of a national struggle for existence, had broken their oath, murdered the head of the government and left the storm-wracked ship of state without a captain at the helm. It also seems unlikely that our enemies would have treated us any better in consequence than they actually did after the collapse.

The next question is: what should have happened? To this I can only reply: a very great deal has been spoken and written about resistance to the Hitler regime. But of those men who are still alive, the speakers and the writers, who had access to Hitler, which of them did, in fact, even once, offer any resistance to his will? Which of them dared, even once, to express opinions in Hitler's presence that were contrary to the dictator's and to argue with him to his face? That is what should have happened. During the months in which I attended Hitler's briefings and the countless conferences on military, technical and political subjects at which he was present, only very few men ever dared to contradict him, and of those few even fewer are still alive today. For I cannot call those men "resistance fighters" who only whispered their disapproval in corridors and only urged others on to act. This is a matter of profoundly differing attitudes. If a man disagreed with Hitler, then it was his duty to tell him so whenever he had an opportunity to do so. This was true particularly and primarily during the period when such expressed disagreement might have had an effect, that is to say in the period before the outbreak of war. Any man who was quite sure that Hitler's policy was bound to lead to war, that war must be prevented, and that a war would inevitably bring our nation to disaster, such a man was duty bound to seek and find occasions, before the war started, to say so without ambiguity both to Hitler and to the German people; if he could not do this from inside Germany, then he should have done so

from abroad. Did the responsible men at the time in fact do this? . . .

When National-Socialism, with its new, nationalistic slogans, appeared upon the scene the younger elements of the Officer Corps were soon inflamed by the patriotic theories propounded by Hitler and his followers. The completely inadequate state of the country's armaments had lain like a leaden weight on the Officer Corps for many long years. It is no wonder that the first steps towards rearmament inclined them to favour the man who promised to breathe fresh life into the armed forces after fifteen years' stagnation. The National-Socialist Party further increased its popularity in military circles since to begin with Hitler showed himself to be well disposed towards the Army and refrained from interfering in its private affairs. The previous gap in the Army's political life was now filled, and interest was aroused in political questions, though hardly in the manner that the democrats seem to have expected. Be that as it may, once the National-Socialists had seized power, the leaders of the armed forces could hardly remain aloof from National-Socialist politics, even had they wished to do so. The General Staff certainly played no leading role in this new development; if anything, the contrary was true. The prime example of the sceptical attitude of the General Staff was that of General Beck. He had a number of adherents at the centre, but no influence over the Army as a whole and even less in the other services. Beck and his successor, Halder, might try to put the brake on the swing towards National-Socialism at the hub of military authority; their effect on policy in general was nil and it simply followed its course without the support of, and in opposition to, the General Staff. Once again—as before the First World War—Germany found itself in a political situation from which there seemed to be no way out and which made the war look difficult, if not hopeless, before ever it began. Once again the soldiers, led by the generals and the General Staff Corps officers, had to find a way out of an impasse for which they were not responsible. ,

All the reproaches that have been levelled against the leaders of the armed forces by their countrymen and by the international courts have failed to take into consideration one very simple fact: that policy is not laid down by soldiers but by politicians. This has always been the case and is so today. When war starts the soldiers can only act according to the political and military situation as it then exists. Unfortunately it is not the habit of politicians to appear in conspicuous places when the bullets begin to fly. They prefer to remain in some safe retreat and to let the soldiers carry out "the continuation of policy by other means."

National policy conditions the theories of the soldiers in the preparations for war during the period of so-called "mental warfare." The international legal tribunals of the last few years have proved that up to 1938 the plans of the German General Staff were exclusively defensive in nature. The military and political condition of Germany permitted no other. Despite the rearmament that had been in progress since 1935, the specialists of the General Staff had no illusions concerning the long period of time that must elapse before the armed forces, and in particular the new weapons — the air force and the armoured force — would be fit for active service. It was only a direct order from Hitler, the political Head of the State, that forced another course of action on the unwilling soldiers.

Telford Taylor

48. THE GUILT OF THE GENERALS

The degree of responsibility that must be borne by the German officer corps, and especially the leading generals, for the coming to power of the Nazis and for the subsequent policy of the German state is an extremely subtle legal and moral question. In the following passage, from the conclusion to his book, *Sword and Swastika*, Telford Taylor, who was Chief American Counsel at the Nuremberg Trials, provides a balanced and perceptive statement as to the "guilt of the generals."

To understand is not necessarily to forgive, but understanding is the foundation of a just appraisal. Simple justice no less than charity requires that the officers' corps be judged for what it actually was, and not for what it is sometimes, but erroneously, imagined to have been. Despite the enormous prestige which the military profession enjoyed in Germany, the generals were not all-powerful and, partly as a result of their own blunders, their power decreased as Hitler's grew. The Reichswehr, small as it was, was far more dominant in the affairs of the Weimar Republic than was the Wehrmacht in those of the Third Reich. The idea that Hitler was a puppet who danced on strings pulled by the generals is utterly groundless; neither is the reverse the truth, although, in the later stages of the war, it approached the truth.

Neither is there the slightest warrant for picturing the generals as a coldly efficient

From Telford Taylor, *Sword and Swastika* (New York, 1952), pp. 367–373. Copyright 1952 by Telford Taylor. Reprinted by permission of Simon and Schuster, Inc.

coterie bent on world conquest. Cold they were, but their outlook was too archaic for efficiency, and their goal was not world conquest but the re-establishment of German military supremacy in Europe. With the exception of Seeckt they pursued this goal, not boldly and imaginatively, but with a narrow, cautious and often stodgy professionalism. It was precisely because Hitler brought boldness and imagination to the military leadership that the generals became his willing collaborators and, eventually, his followers.

Furthermore, it is futile to test the officers' corps by standards and values to which their leaders were almost totally oblivious. The generals were the product of imperial times and, almost to a man, they faithfully reflected the narrow, caste-conscious authoritarianism in which they had been trained. To "blame" such men, as individuals, for failing to risk their careers to preserve democracy in Germany is too much like blaming the crow for not singing sweetly. To expect German generals to "renounce war as an instrument of national policy" is to blind one's eyes to the hard facts of life.

But all this is merely a setting for the problem, not its solution. If nonconformity did not flourish under the Kaiser, neither did concentration camps. If the Jew was not highly regarded in imperial society, neither was he hounded and preyed upon, subjected to disgusting indignities, or officially labeled as subhuman. Neither the Kaiser nor the politicians of imperial times dealt with their opponents by massacre, as did Hitler in the Roehm purge. Least of all were generals and their wives murdered in their homes. All of these things and many more happened in the early years of the Third Reich, when the officers' corps was still powerful. It is one thing to understand that the generals were ill-equipped to become leaders in the movement for world order under the rule of law. It is quite another to forgive their becoming a pillar of the Reich.

But what duty did the officers' corps owe, and to whom? Even field marshals are

soldiers in the service of the state; is it for them to affect or check its course, even if depraved or suicidal? Were they not bound to follow Hitler, no less by their oath of allegiance than by the duty of obedience that every soldier owes? So many of them said during the years since the war, and even much earlier: "Brauchitsch hitches his collar a notch higher and says 'I am a soldier; it is my duty to obey,' " wrote von Hassell.

On this question much ink has been and will be spilled. A passage in one of General MacArthur's speeches, which attracted unfavorable editorial comment, touches the heart of the problem:

I find in existence a new and heretofore unknown and dangerous concept that the members of our armed forces owe primary allegiance or loyalty to those who temporarily exercise the authority of the Executive Branch of Government rather than to the country and its Constitution which they are sworn to defend. No proposition could be more dangerous.

This paragraph might easily have been written by Seeckt. Insofar as it speaks, literally, in terms of *allegiance*, which, of course, American officers owe to the Constitution (as Seeckt and his fellows owed it to the Weimar Republic), the sentiment is unexceptionable. But the setting of MacArthur's observation—a strongly worded attack on the policies of the administration—raised by clear implication the idea that an officer's duty of *obedience* to "those who temporarily exercise the authority of the Executive Branch" (by which he can only mean the President, who is the Constitutional Commander-in-Chief, just as were the German Presidents in Seeckt's time) is qualified by an overriding obligation to defend the Constitution.

Seeckt, too, conceived that he was under such a transcendent responsibility, though not to the Weimar Constitution. "Reichswehr will never shoot at Reichswehr," he had declared in 1920, as he flatly refused Noske's demand for military aid against the Kapp insurrection. "The Reichswehr . . . will stick to *me*," he coolly informed Ebert at the time of Hitler's "Beer-Hall

Putsch.'' This conception of the Army's unanswerability to the politicians of the moment was general throughout the officers' corps, and survived Seeckt. "We soldiers mistrusted all parties. . . . We all considered ourselves the trustees of the unity of Germany," declared Manstein at Nuremberg.

Seeckt and his colleagues have been much criticized for their unwillingness to give true fealty and full obedience to the political leaders of the Weimar Republic, and General MacArthur was relieved of his command on the ground that he, too, had refused fully to subordinate himself to the President. How, then, is there any basis for criticizing the German generals of the Third Reich? Did they not likewise owe full obedience to Adolf Hitler, who had been appointed Chancellor by Hindenburg, confirmed in office by popular election, and acclaimed in Hindenburg's political testament? Is it the duty of generals to obey to the letter the orders of a democratic government, but to confound, undermine and destroy an authoritarian regime?

The apparent dilemma is not superficial. It is a cardinal tenet of republicanism that the military are servants of the state, not an autonomous caste. Nor can we find any solution in the verbalism that generals may urge their views only on "purely military" matters. The adjective "military" has long since lost its purity, as Clausewitz cogently demonstrated. It is quite impossible for generals to analyze military problems without the analysis carrying a direct impact on political and diplomatic issues of the times.

Nevertheless, there is a profound and, I believe, sound public attitude that military leaders should enter these controversies as expert technical advisers, and not as advocates with a political stake in the decision. To this extent, Seeckt was on sure ground in excluding the Reichswehr from affinity with political parties. The spectacle of a military establishment in which generals take to the hustings, or covertly contrive to interject themselves (beyond their own ballot-box) in the political process, is not an appealing one to any believer in democratic government.

To this extent at least the military are under an obligation of political restraint to which the ordinary citizen is not subject. But the dilemma which we have posed arises only out of efforts to push this principle of political neutrality to much more distant limits. Are military men absolutely bound to follow the orders of *whatever* political regime holds sway, even though it be patently a bloody tyranny, bent on conquest? Are they mere janitors of the military machine, with no responsibility for the use to which it is put? Are they, in short, political eunuchs, deprived of the capacity of moral judgment on their own behalf?

If so, then surely history will acquit Brauchitsch and Rundstedt and even Keitel, and must condemn Beck and Witzleben and the other officers who attempted Hitler's murder and the overthrow of Nazism in 1944. Russian and Polish officers who oppose the designs of their Communist masters, whether by conspiracy or escape, must equally answer to the charge of unmilitary insubordination. What shall be their defense?

There come times in the affairs of nations when their very foundations are tested by a powerful challenge to basic tenets or governmental habits. These times we call "revolutionary," and the era of the Third Reich was truly revolutionary. The Third Reich was dedicated to the overthrow of many such tenets, among them those of government responsive to the popular will, justice under the rule of law, the equality of races, nationalities and sects before the law, and the dignity of the individual man.

These concepts touch the root of the governmental process and the social organism, and the issues they raise are commonly regarded as "revolutionary" in character by democrats and authoritarians of all hues. Is it either the privilege or the obligation of generals to stand aside from their solution, or to act by always putting their services at the disposal of the *de facto* regime, whatever its nature? In the answer to this question, I believe, lies the resolution of the dilemma we have posed.

In the case of the German generals, however, the question is not a naked abstraction, but is overlaid and colored by the established traditions of the officers' corps and the trust which the German people reposed in the generals. This trust was not only a fact—it was publicly proclaimed by the leaders of the officers' corps on all occasions. For Groener, the Army was "the rock upon which the state is built." In 1919, he had described it as "a center for the physical and moral education of German youth." As late as 1937, Beck wrote that the German people "place a confidence in the Wehrmacht which hardly knows limits. . . . To them the Wehrmacht is both people and state." In his testament, Hindenburg wrote of the Reichswehr as "the guardian of the state" and "the pattern of state conduct." And Stresemann, no soldier but a good nationalist, exalted "that old National Army on which we all depended. In this institution I have always seen the embodiment of the old Prussian idea of the state."

The trust was confidently extended and proudly acknowledged. It was not a trust to determine evanescent political issues, but to preserve the "old Prussian virtues" and safeguard the state. It was unpartisan, but nevertheless a political and social trust in the deepest sense. . . . The depth of the trust, even among intellectual and aristocratic civilians, was pathetically reflected in the hopes—at first confident, later agonized and despairing—that were reposed in the generals by von Hassell, Goerdeler, Gisevius, Schacht and other organizers of the clandestine anti-Hitler groups that spun their shadowy and futile plots during the later years of the Third Reich. "On the Reichswehr, . . . on its attitude, feeling, and inclination, depended primarily the fate of Germany and therewith of Europe, according to my opinion," writes the historian Meinecke.

Did the generals of the Hitler era live up to their own standards and discharge the trust? However one may assess the blame, the record of failure can hardly be gainsaid. By the end of 1938, there was precious little "Prussian cleanliness and simplicity" (Beck's phrase) left in the Third Reich. The scales of justice were sadly warped. The religion—Catholic or Protestant—which was a traditional ingredient of the military ethos was being deliberately and effectively discredited by the government. The battle for the mind of German youth was being lost. The honor of Schleicher and Fritsch was unredeemed. The power of the generals had declined immeasurably, and their control of strategic and even tactical military matters was gravely threatened. The emperors had always listened to them; now Hitler lectured them. The generals were convinced that Germany was not yet ready for war, but they no longer governed its timing. Their traditions were being flouted, and they were increasingly impotent to discharge their trust.

How had it all come about? Primarily, as we have seen, it was the wide area of agreement on objectives between Hitler and the generals that brought them together. Having become a pillar of the Third Reich, they were disinclined to bring the edifice crashing down about their own ears. In the struggle for mastery of the house, they were repeatedly outwitted, and the efforts of a few to reestablish their power were constantly set at naught by the individual ambitions of others.

The *esprit de corps* and unity inherited from the days of Moltke and Schlieffen had atrophied. And, as Hossbach put it, the officers' corps lacked any "Fuehrer-personality" to revitalize its leadership. Hammerstein, Blomberg, Fritsch, Beck, Rundstedt, Brauchitsch and their colleagues, individually and collectively, failed to manifest the capacity for aggressive and enlightened leadership that might have repulsed the onslaught of Nazism and safeguarded the integrity of the corps.

At bottom, the failure of the generals was due to the same political and social archaism that had characterized them during the First World War. The officers' corps was simply incapable of making the passage from century to century. They were in but not of modern times, and thus insensitive to many of the most important forces that played about their heads. Even today, this blindness is reflected in ways that would be amusing had not the consequences been so tragic. Manstein, proclaiming his dislike for the Nazis, explains through his apologist that "they were Bavarian, and Prussians do not think much of Bavarians. They were led by an Austrian corporal with, for all he knew, a bit of Czech or God knows what, about him." Men so provincial and caste-ridden were unlikely to grasp the dynamics of the twentieth-century western world, or hit upon ways and means of checking the versatile, terrible genius of Hitler, even had they so desired.

"History will indict the highest leaders of the Wehrmacht with blood-guilt if they do not act in accordance with expert and statesmanlike knowledge and assurance. Their duty of soldierly obedience finds its limit when their knowledge, conscience and responsibility forbid the execution of an order." So wrote Beck in July, 1938, as he reflected bitterly on the course events were taking, and on his inability to stir his brother generals to counteraction.

49. DE GAULLE ON THE ORIGINS OF THE FREE FRENCH MOVEMENT

The defeat of 1940 placed the French army before a moral crisis unparalleled in its long history. A small portion of the nation's armed forces, in whose name spoke a relatively unknown brigadier general, Charles de Gaulle, refused to accept the decision of the legally constituted government to call for an armistice. Claiming obedience to a France which they considered this government no longer to represent, de Gaulle and his followers found themselves obliged to institute in embryo a new political regime in exile. Given the French army's tradition of absolute obedience to the political regime of the moment, whatever its form, this was a profoundly revolutionary act. The victory of the Allied cause was to prove de Gaulle right, while those who had acted in accordance with the more traditional canons of military obedience were shown to have been mistaken. Nevertheless, in acting as he did, no matter how noble his motives, de Gaulle was establishing, as the history of the French army over the next two decades has amply demonstrated, a highly dangerous precedent. In the following selection, taken from the first volume of his *War Memoirs*, de Gaulle describes the reasons for his insurgency and its immediate consequences.

Go on with the war? Yes, certainly! But to what end and within what limits? Many, even among those who approved of the undertaking, wanted it to be no more than aid given by a handful of Frenchmen to the British Empire, still standing and in the fight. Not for a moment did I look at the enterprise in that way. For me, what had to be served and saved was the nation and the state.

I thought, in fact, that it would be the end of honour, unity, and independence if it were to be admitted that, in this world war, only France had capitulated and that she had let the matter rest there. For in that case, whatever might be the issue of the conflict—whether the country, after decisive defeat, would one day be rid of the invader by foreign arms, or would remain enslaved—its self-disgust and the disgust it would inspire in others would poison its soul and its life for many generations. As for the immediate future, in the name of what were some of its sons to be led out to a fight no longer its own? What was the good of supplying with auxiliaries the forces of another power? No! For the effort to be worth while, it was essential to bring back into the war not merely some Frenchmen, but France.

That was bound to involve the reappearance of our armies on the battlefields, the return of our territories to belligerence, participation by the country itself in the effort of its fighting men, and recognition by the foreign powers of the fact that France, as such, had gone on with the struggle—in short, to bring our sovereignty out from disaster and from the policy of wait-and-see, over to the side of war and, one day, of victory.

What I knew of men and things left me

From Charles de Gaulle, *The Call to Honor* (New York, 1955), pp. 81–85, 87–90, 93–94. Copyright © 1955 by Simon and Schuster, Inc. Reprinted by permission of the publishers Simon and Schuster, Inc., and Wiedenfeld & Nicolson Ltd.

with no illusions about the obstacles to be surmounted. There would be the power of the enemy, which could be broken only by a long process of wearing down and would have the help of the French official machine in opposing the belligerent recovery of France. There would be the moral and material difficulties which a long and all-out struggle would inevitably involve for those who would have to carry it on as pariahs and without means. There would be the mountain of objections, insinuations, and calumnies raised against the fighters by the sceptics and the timorous to cover their passivity. There would be the so-called "parallel" but in fact rival and opposing enterprises, to which the French passion for disputation would not fail to give rise, and of which the policy and services of the Allies would make use, in the customary way, in order to control them. There would be, on the part of those whose aim was subversion, the determination to side-track the national resistance in the direction of revolutionary chaos, to result in their dictatorship. There would be, finally, the tendency of the great powers to take advantage of our weakness in order to push their interests at the expense of France.

As for me, with a hill like that to climb, I was starting from scratch. Not the shadow of a force or of an organization at my side. In France, no following and no reputation. Abroad, neither credit nor standing. But this very destitution showed me my line of conduct. It was by adopting without compromise the cause of national recovery that I could acquire authority. It was by acting as the inflexible champion of the nation and of the state that it would be possible for me to gather the consent, even the enthusiasm, of the French and to win from foreigners respect and consideration. Those who, all through the drama, were offended by this intransigence were unwilling to see that for me, intent as I was on beating back innumerable conflicting pressures, the slightest wavering would have brought collapse. In short, limited and alone though I was, and precisely because I was so, I had

to climb to the heights and never then to come down.

The first thing to do was to hoist the colours. Broadcasting was to hand for that. Already in the afternoon of June 17 I outlined my intentions to Mr. Winston Churchill. Washed up from a vast shipwreck upon the shores of England, what could I have done without his help? He gave it me at once, and to begin with put the BBC at my disposal. We agreed that I should use it after the Pétain government had asked for the armistice. That very evening the news came that it had done so. Next day, at six p.m., I read out at the microphone the well-known text:

APPEAL BY GENERAL DE GAULLE TO THE FRENCH
June 18, 1940

The leaders who, for many years past, have been at the head of the French armed forces, have set up a government.

Alleging the defeat of our armies, this government has entered into negotiations with the enemy with a view to bringing about a cessation of hostilities. It is quite true that we were, and still are, overwhelmed by enemy mechanized forces, both on the ground and in the air. It was the tanks, the planes, and the tactics of the Germans, far more than the fact that we were outnumbered, that forced our armies to retreat. It was the German tanks, planes, and tactics that provided the element of surprise which brought our leaders to their present plight.

But has the last word been said? Must we abandon all hope? Is our defeat final and irremediable? To those questions I answer—No!

Speaking in full knowledge of the facts, I ask you to believe me when I say that the cause of France is not lost. The very factors that brought about our defeat may one day lead us to victory.

For, remember this, France does not stand alone. She is not isolated. Behind her is a vast Empire, and she can make common cause with the British Empire, which commands the seas and is continuing the struggle. Like England, she can draw unreservedly on the immense industrial resources of the United States.

This war is not limited to our unfortunate country. The outcome of the struggle has not been decided by the Battle of France. This is a world war. Mistakes have been made, there have been delays and untold suffering, but the fact remains that there still exists in the world everything we need to crush our enemies some day.

Today we are crushed by the sheer weight of mechanized force hurled against us, but we can still look to a future in which even greater mechanized force will bring us victory. The destiny of the world is at stake.

I, General de Gaulle, now in London, call on all French officers and men who are at present on British soil, or may be in the future, with or without their arms; I call on all engineers and skilled workmen from the armaments factories who are at present on British soil, or may be in the future, to get in touch with me.

Whatever happens, the flame of French resistance must not and shall not die.

As the irrevocable words flew out upon their way, I felt within myself a life coming to an end—the life I had lived within the framework of a solid France and an indivisible army. At the age of forty-nine I was entering upon adventure, like a man thrown by fate outside all terms of reference.

It was nonetheless my duty, while taking the first steps in this unprecedented career, to make sure that no authority better qualified than mine was willing to step forward to bring France and the Empire back into the struggle. As long as the armistice was not in force it was possible to imagine, though against all probability, that the Bordeaux government would at the last moment choose war. Even if there was only the feeblest chance, it must be encouraged. That is why, as soon as I reached London the afternoon of the 17th, I telegraphed to Bordeaux to offer my services in carrying on in the British capital the negotiations I had begun on the day before about the war matériel from the United States, the German prisoners, and the transport for North Africa.

The reply was a dispatch summoning me to return at once. On June 20 I wrote to Weygand, who had taken, in the midst of capitulation, the astonishing title of Minister of National Defence, to urge him to place himself at the head of the resistance and to assure him of my entire obedience if he did so. But this letter was to be returned to me by him, some weeks later, with a comment of which the least one can say is that it expressed his ill will. On June 30 the

so-called "French Embassy" notified me of the order to surrender myself prisoner at the Saint-Michel prison in Toulouse, there to be tried by the Conseil de Guerre. This condemned me, first, to a month's prison. Then—upon an appeal *a minima* demanded by the "Minister," Weygand—it condemned me to death. . . .

Thus, among the French as within the other nations, the immense convergence of fear, interest, and despair caused a universal surrender in regard to France. Though there were many feelings still loyal to her past and many interests eager to take advantage of the shreds yet left to her by the present, no responsible man anywhere acted as if he still believed in her independence, pride, and greatness. That she was bound henceforward to be enslaved, disgraced, and flouted was taken for granted by all who counted in the world. In face of the frightening void of the general renunciation, my mission seemed to me, all of a sudden, clear and terrible. At this moment, the worst in her history, it was for me to assume the burden of France.

But there is no France without a sword. To set up a fighting force was more important than anything. I began work on that at once. There were some military elements in England. First of all, there were the units of the Alpine Light Division, which, after some brilliant campaigning in Norway under General Béthouart, had been brought back to Brittany in the middle of June and reembarked there along with the last British troops. There were also some ships belonging to the Navy—nearly a hundred thousand tons in all—which had escaped from Cherbourg, Brest, and Lorient with many individuals and auxiliaries on board beside their crews, the whole totalling at least ten thousand sailors. There were, in addition, several thousand soldiers who had been wounded in Belgium and brought to hospital in Great Britain. The French military missions had organized the command and administration of all these elements with a view to keeping them under the orders of Vichy and preparing their general repatriation.

The mere act of making contact with these many dispersed fractions involved great difficulties for me. To begin with, I had only a very small number of officers, nearly all subalterns, full of immense good-will but powerless to storm the machinery of the hierarchy. What they could do—and did—was propaganda among those officers and men whom they managed to meet. The yield was bound to be small. A week after my appeal of June 18 the number of volunteers encamped in Olympia, which the British had lent us, amounted to only a few hundred.

It must be said that the British authorities did little to help our efforts. Certainly they had distributed a leaflet advising members of the French forces that they could choose between repatriation, joining General de Gaulle, and serving in His Majesty's forces. Certainly the instructions given by Churchill and the activities of Spears, whom the Prime Minister had made responsible for liaison between Free France and the British services, did sometimes succeed in vanquishing inertia or opposition. Certainly the press, the wireless, many associations, and countless individuals gave our enterprise a warm welcome. But the British High Command, which from one day to another expected the German offensive and perhaps invasion, was too much absorbed by its preparations to busy itself with a task which in its eyes was secondary. Besides, it was inclined by professional decorum and habit to respect the normal order of things—that is to say, Vichy and its missions. Finally, it looked with some mistrust upon these Allies of yesterday, humiliated by misfortune, dissatisfied with themselves and with others, and loaded with complaints. What would they do if the enemy gained a bridgehead? Wasn't the most sensible course to ship them away as quickly as possible? And what, after all, was the use of the few battalions without cadres and the crews without officers which General de Gaulle claimed he could rally?

On June 29 I went to Trentham Park, where the Light Mountain Division was encamped. The general commanding the division was himself anxious to return to France, though with the firm intention of getting back into the line one day—which indeed he was destined to do, effectively and with glory, later. But he had arranged for me to see the whole of each unit. This made it possible for me to rally a large part of the two battalions of the 13th Half-Brigade of the Foreign Legion with their leader, Lieutenant-Colonel Magrin-Verneret, known as Monclar, and his number two, Captain Koenig, two hundred Chasseurs Alpins, two-thirds of a tank company, some elements of gunners, engineers, and signals, and several staff and administrative officers, including Commandant de Conchard and Captains Dewavrin and Tissier. This in spite of the fact that, after I had left the camp, the British Colonels de Chair and Williams, sent by the War Office, had in turn had the troops paraded in order to tell them literally this: "You are perfectly free to serve under General de Gaulle. But it is our duty to point out to you, speaking as man to man, that if you do so decide you will be rebels against your government. . . ."

At the end of July the number of our effectives was barely seven thousand. That was all we would be able to recruit in Great Britain itself: those French troops who had not joined us had now been repatriated. With great difficulty we were recovering the arms and matériel they had left behind, seized often either by the English or by other allies. As for the ships, we were only able to man some of them, and it was heartbreaking to see the others sailing under a foreign flag. Little by little, in spite of everything, our first units took shape, equipped with an odd assortment of weapons, but formed of resolute men.

These were, in fact, of that strong type to which the fighting men of the French resistance, wherever they might be, were bound to belong. A taste for risk and adventure pushed to the pitch of art for art's sake, a contempt for the cowardly and the indifferent, a tendency to melancholy and so to quarreling during the periods without

197

danger, giving place to an ardent cohesion in action, a national pride sharpened to its extreme by their country's ill fortune and by contact with well-equipped allies, and, above all, a sovereign confidence in the strength and cunning of their own con- spiracy—such were the psychological characteristics of this elite, which started from nothing and was to grow, gradually, until it drew after it the whole nation and the whole of the Empire. . . .

Paul-Marie de La Gorce

50. THE COLLAPSE OF THE TRADITIONAL MILITARY ORDER

The armistice of June 1940 and de Gaulle's subsequent efforts to continue the war alone meant in effect that there were two separate governments, Vichy and Free France, each claiming to be the legitimate political regime of France, and each claiming the allegiance of the French military. The implications of this unprecedented situation are described in the following passage from *The French Army* by Paul-Marie de la Gorce.

The message broadcast by Marshal Pétain on June 17 that the fighting was to end marks the beginning of a new phase in the history of the Army, and in the history of public opinion. The few courageous engagements fought by small groups of isolated French soldiers, in the midst of the universal debacle, were a prefiguration of what, over the course of the years, would be the French return to the struggle. The hierarchies had collapsed, and from now on there could be no blind trust in the state, its institutions or its leaders. From now on, the duty of the citizen had to be decided by the individual conscience. But in this old-established country whose social framework was regarded as one of the oldest and most robust in existence anywhere, no one was prepared for such an unprecedented test.

Nothing was more revealing in this respect than the behavior of those who opposed the armistice before it was signed and who, until Paul Reynaud resigned, may even have included more than half his ministers. They were supported by the President of the Republic, the presiding officers of the Senate and the Chamber of Deputies. With them were the Governors General of the colonies, the High Commissioner in the Levant, the Residents General in Morocco and Tunisia and the main leaders of the military forces overseas. But a few days after the armistice, and especially after the affair of Mers-el-Kébir, those who were resolved to go on with the war had been reduced to a handful. The number of political figures who left to join de Gaulle was quite insignificant. Before 1942, not a single ambassador went over to Free France. De Gaulle's entire military entourage was made up of a few generals, almost all unknown, and of a single admiral. The spirit of resistance seemed to have abandoned almost all the Empire's top military and civilian officials. General Nogués, whose attitude had been decisive in determining that of the greater number of governors and residents general, bowed to the repeated vituperative orders of Pétain and

From Paul-Marie de la Gorce, *The French Army* (New York, 1963), pp. 308–313. Reprinted with the permission of George Braziller, Inc., and Weidenfeld & Nicolson Ltd.

Weygand. Addressing representatives of veterans' organizations, who begged him to carry on the struggle, he justified himself by explaining that nothing could be done without the aid of the fleet, which had decided to obey Vichy.

The acceptance of the armistice by so many officials of the Empire followed the irreversible decision taken at Bordeaux. It did not precede it. Their choice was no longer between those favoring and those hostile to a request for an armistice. It was a matter of obedience to the state, or open revolt. Almost every Frenchman would eventually have to face this alternative. Everything was thrown into turmoil for the Army which, by definition, was bound to practice collective obedience, following the orders of its leaders and subordinating itself to the state. After the shame of defeat, there began the tragedy of obedience.

Understood in this fashion, French military history may be said to have changed direction on June 18, 1940. As far back as one may go in the past, no trace can be found of the Army's openly opposing the state. Some generals may have lent their aid to some political maneuvers, but the military organization as a whole had never felt tempted to revolt, and had never succumbed. It had been the custom of Frenchmen to say that the Army—like the civil service—had served every regime with the same discipline and the same readiness. In the corps of officers, the reminder was voiced that the grandeur and servitude of military life directly implied the service of the state, whatever should occur. For France and the state were indistinguishable, as French history had exemplified on numberless occasions. The French state was one of the first in the world to exist as such.

In Italy and Germany, the officers for long had served rival or warring princes. Poles, Hungarians and Czechs had seen their countries disappear from the map for long stretches of time, and had found themselves serving the Czar, the Austrian Emperor or the King of Prussia. But in France the state was more deeply rooted than any-

where else. Its strength was increased by a homogeneous population and unbroken and relatively stable frontiers. In marked contrast with the succession of political regimes throughout the nineteenth century, the state had a permanence that guaranteed national stability. The Army was the symbol and instrument of this permanence. This was a dogma that nothing, it seemed, could ever shake. A province might be lost or an empire won, as the temporal authority of the day should decide; but the state remained. In this respect, there had been no fundamental change until the month of June, 1940.

The crisis that rent the Army little by little, after June 18, derived its gravity from its moral significance. Those who rebelled against established authority did so in the name of values transcending the traditional concepts of obedience and discipline. Later it would be pointed out that the state that established its headquarters in Vichy was entirely dependent on German good will and had, consequently, no real existence. That is true, but the fact can be established only by means of reasoning and argument. It was not any such analysis that motivated the overwhelming majority of the acts of resistance and rebellion that grew in number after the appeal broadcast on June 18 by General de Gaulle. They were an elemental revolt against capitulation, against the abandonment of the struggle while immense forces had not yet made any contribution. The feeling of honor was invoked to condemn obedience. Capitulation was judged to be dishonorable. Did not the teaching of the French Army forbid the laying down of arms before the soldier had exhausted "every means required by honor and the regulations"? No comparison can be sustained with the political revolutions that stud France's history. The issue was not the overthrow of a government that appeared detestable in order to replace it with another. Disobedience now did not merely challenge established authority; it overthrew the customary rules of the state.

For the defeat had left every hierarchy

intact. In the immense bewilderment that afflicted everyone, civilian and military alike, the instinctive reaction of the Army officers was to take refuge in obedience to the "great leaders," in a blind adherence to discipline. And blindness it indeed was, a deliberate blindness. Since no gleam of hope could be discovered, hope must be mysteriously secreted in some ulterior motive or double game whose nature the humble executant could not possibly divine. Blind trust was, in 1940, the temptation to which the Army cadres were most commonly exposed. The unshaken position of the hierarchies made it easy to go on with the usual obligations of the soldier's calling. Government, the law courts, the police and the civil service were where they always had been: however the armistice might be judged, the state seemed to have survived. To rebel against the government, in these circumstances, was to rebel against the apparatus of the state.

Yet from the very outset this semblance was challenged, this fiction was unveiled. Whatever immediate practical consequences it might have, the appeal broadcast by General de Gaulle on June 18 had a basic historical justification. By calling for war to the bitter end, in spite of the orders of leaders who had "yielded to panic and forgotten honor," de Gaulle confronted the French with an alternative. Each individual now knew that obedience was not the only possible course. At each instant the other side of the alternative remained available: dissidence and resistance. It is meaningful in itself that this momentous gesture should have been that of an officer. Emerging from an organ of the state which by its very nature had the obligation to execute unprotestingly the duties set by the hierarchy, this officer cast doubt on the hierarchy, discovered elsewhere the sources of duty, and spoke in the name of values that transcended discipline and respect for the leaders.

Accordingly, we may look on June 18 as the initiation of an adventure that would traverse the whole war and find no end in victory. This adventure is still going on and may, indeed, never entirely cease. Each man now had to ask himself what he should do, and on what date or in what circumstances he should take up arms once more. War had ceased to be a collective destiny that imposed its iron law on the totality of a nation, on an entire army and an entire people. It became a matter for the individual conscience. The Nation virtually ceased to recognize itself in the state. The state might continue in Vichy for a longer or shorter period and the civil service and the Army remain faithful to the government; dissidence might be limited to a few regions or spread on every hand; the resistance might be organized sooner or later. In any event, the continuation of the war in Europe, the struggle against the invader, the natural desire to free the country, the impossibility of remaining passive while two thirds of France was occupied, would all inevitably lead the French, at some point, to rise against their government and to deny the authority of the state.

For the Army, the traditional instrument of constituted power, this trial was all the more harrowing since it involved the upset of its own values. As to every other Frenchman, the choice appeared to the Army officers in the guise of a conflict of conscience. One man did not hesitate, being unable to accept the idea that France should capitulate while England, the French Empire and the French Navy were still intact and able to fight. Another would get ready to break away, but would be disturbed by the first clashes between the British and French fleets. If the former Ally had now turned against France, there could no longer be any question of fighting along with her. Yet another was revolted by the handshake exchanged at Montoire in October, 1940, between Hitler and Pétain. Many believed that underground resistance would be possible, with the Vichy state serving as cover, only to discover that the "double game" reduced their efforts to naught and that they must break with the government. But this decision was taken in secret and sometimes changed nothing in its author's external circumstances. Such was the strength of their habits of obedience that in 1942, although they were eager to get back into the war, most officers hesitated to play any part against Germany and Italy until some proof was offered them that they could still remain faithful to Pétain, Vichy, legality and hierarchy. General Juin succeeded in offering them this proof, relying on a telegram sent by Pétain to Darlan and which, in actual fact, was couched in the vaguest of terms.

"Between 1940 and 1945," wrote Vincent Monteil, a former officer with the Free French,

it was the officers who held in their hands the key of events, of the destiny of the fatherland, since everywhere they had taken charge of matters. Never to this extent had one seen so many things depend all at once on a few men—on their initiative, their faith, their imagination, their character, their sense of honor; or on their inertia, their doubts, their passivity, their spinelessness, their faithfulness to the externals of a deceitful discipline. To how many military leaders could one not at that time have applied the words of Saint Paul: ". . . troubled on every side, yet not distressed . . . perplexed, but not in despair; persecuted, but not forsaken, cast down, but not destroyed . . ."? These were the officers whose acts allowed a Free France to exist, to receive the support of various territories and to re-enter the combat. Others bowed to the relentless machinery of the hierarchy of rank and function, and to the fascination and ready compromises of obedience without any risk—if not without remorse.

Since military men were the most inclined by their outlook, traditions and social ambiance to opt for "order," and for obedience to the new regime, it is among them that the conflicting urges besetting all Frenchmen were the most agonizing. The choice facing the officers was never a theoretical one: in Syria, Dakar or Madagascar, they had to fight on one side or the other. War forced on them a total choice, for no Gaullist officer could be satisfied merely to stick up for his opinions in arguments with his fellows. He had to abandon everything: the uniform, regulations, discipline, the hierarchy. He could not take refuge in inactivity, bad temper or scoffing, for Vichy demanded discipline and nothing else. Dissidence and the Resistance demanded irrevocable decisions and total commitments.

Once flouted, the authorities and hierarchies turned against the recalcitrant officer. Sometimes they had recourse to almost unbearable moral pressures. Thus Captain Frenay, who called his movement "Combat," received letters from his mother pleading with him to return to "duty," and wondering whether she should not denounce her son. No longer did a straight and narrow path lie ahead for the Army. There was only the confused and passionate search for the path of honor and patriotism. And each man had to go it alone.

In the history of the military consciousness, we have reached the age of the individual. The position occupied in the hierarchy, and rank and training, weigh no more heavily than character, ideas, ambitions and desires. The remainder of the Second World War was to be an individual struggle in which each man took part, at the moment he himself chose and in the spirit that was intimately his own, not as the result of a collective decision imposed by the State. But the age of the individual would not rapidly expire when the war was ended. Later, other men were to invoke values that outranked obedience to the state, and would let themselves be drawn to other acts of dissidence.

For the French Army, the age of the individual began on June 18, 1940. A full twenty years later, it had not yet ended.

51. VICHY, DE GAULLE, AND THE FRENCH ARMY

The Vichy government, which lasted from the defeat of June 1940 until the Germans occupied all of France in November 1942, commanded the obedience of most of the French military, but the dissident Gaullist regime in London increasingly represented their real sentiments and aspirations. Unfortunately, the military forces of these two rival French governments on several occasions met in battle. The agony which such a situation created for the soldiers is depicted in the following passage from *Trois Siècles d'Obéissance Militaire* by Marshal Alphonse Juin. Juin, who was one of the leading generals under the Vichy government, later conducted a brilliant campaign at the head of the French detachment in the Allied armies in Italy.

After Dunquerque and the departure of the British and with the loss by the First French Army of most of its men and materiel, it was clear that the situation in the South was now irretrievable. The disparity between the strength of the two opposing armies no longer permitted any doubt in this matter. As the subsequent campaign was to show, there was no longer any solution worth considering but the conclusion of an armistice. . . .

In the despondency which struck France and the French people, there was no opposition to this decision, which, if it had been submitted to a referendum, would doubtless have been overwhelmingly approved. Our troops many of whom were prisoners did not raise any further objections either. Most of the military greeted with relief the clauses of the armistice which protected the existence of the army. In this matter, as well, the army gave proof of its perfect discipline vis-á-vis the civil authorities who assumed full responsibility.

But on June 18 from London, General de Gaulle in his appeal declared that if we had lost a battle, we had not for that reason lost the war. Certainly these were reassuring words for those who could listen to the broadcasts of the B.B.C. but they were words which entailed a break with the legal government. In any case he who had pronounced them was not a general like any other, since he had just before been made a member of the government. Thus in fact, it was a minister who rejected the principle of armistice, without as yet being able to be very precise as to what means he had at his disposal to annul it.

To make his way thus to England in order there to assert his resolution to continue the struggle under French colors, this was a decision which demonstrated great courage, even if he lacked a deliberately worked out plan. By resolutely cutting himself off from his country, which was almost unanimous in its attitude, de Gaulle had in mind only a rather vague idea of basing his endeavors on the mobilization of our empire, which appeared to be safe and intact. Such a gesture, however, involved him in a serious

From Marshal Alphonse Juin, *Trois Siècles d'Obéissance Militaire* (Paris, 1964), pp. 131–133, 139–141, 143–158, abridged. Reprinted with the permission of Librairie Plon. Translated by the editor.

question of conscience concerning his duty to obey, by which General de Gaulle, despite his title as a former minister, was naturally bound in so far as he was a member of the military hierarchy. . . .

The appeal of June 18 appeared to be an isolated instance, which only placed, by contrast, in sharper relief the attitude which the immense majority of French soldiers imposed upon themselves. Their almost unanimous reaction was to comply—not without some hesitation and serious consideration—with the instructions given by the political authorities. At a moment when everything was collapsing in France, except for the very idea of France, when institutions were giving way and the structure of the state itself was at issue and in doubt, the army, humiliated, broken, bleeding, continued to obey.

At the moment of the armistice, there were in England some thirty or thirty-five thousand French servicemen, most of them sailors. . . . The army was represented principally by units from the expeditionary force that had been sent to Norway, and which Béthouart had brought home from the victory at Narvik. . . . Of this number, except for the Thirteenth Demibrigade from the Foreign Legion, the attitude of which was not necessarily the same as that of a unit made up solely of Frenchmen, very few rallied to the banner of Free France. And it is to be noted that the first volunteers were above all young men and reservists for whom there were, after the armistice, no longer any military obligations. Among the sailors, to draw an example from what was the most numerous group of servicemen in England, by July 15 only about a dozen officers and some 500 men had joined Free France, while about 10,000 of them had been repatriated during the first weeks of the month, and 24,877 in all by the end of the year. . . .

The Germans had left us the direct administration of our overseas possessions, hoping in that way to keep them from becoming dissident. Further they had devised, in order to justify and to build up a bond between the colonies and the homeland, the maintenance in France of a free, sovereign zone, which in appearance enjoyed its full rights, as well as certain military forces. To put it another way, the Empire was linked to a government at Vichy, theoretically free and situated in an unoccupied zone, but a government which was only tolerated, it must be admitted, because of the Empire and to the degree that it would be able to guarantee its cohesion and its neutrality. The government and the unoccupied zone were thus no more than fictions, one might even say hostages, as was also Marshal Pétain during the four years that he spent at Vichy.

This would explain the efforts made by the members of his government in the course of the first two years following the armistice to manage things in such a way that the Empire was obedient to them or at least appeared to be obedient to them. It was their very existence and that of the unoccupied zone that was at stake in this game, since it was obvious to everyone that it would be the latter which would bear the costs of the slightest concerted attempt at secession. This would be the signal for the total occupation of France and for the deportation of large parts of its population. Here indeed was food for thought for the authorities stationed in North Africa. . . . The Germans had authorized the maintenance of our small transitional army only on condition that it bind itself to defend North Africa against an eventual aggression. Obviously, it was not to their own aggressive intentions that they were alluding here.

General Weygand, who had been named Commander-in-Chief in French Africa, translated this imperative by a simple order: "Defend North Africa against all comers." This was a formula which, while laying down the principle of neutrality for North Africa, also made it equally the duty of French troops to oppose, should the situation arise, any armed intervention by the Germans and the Italians.

It is to be supposed that the Axis powers

never paid much attention to the equivocal sense of this phrase "all comers." They doubtless counted on the Vichy government to avoid, if the moment should come, all possibility of hostility towards themselves. And yet, it was upon this formula which could be taken in two ways that the whole policy of the French high command in North Africa rested. In essence, the policy was one of obtaining from the Germans a reenforcement in our capacity to defend North Africa effectively against outsiders, but with the ulterior motive of using these arms against them in case they should make the first move or later seek to impose upon us an armed collaboration.

Thus, people were grateful to General Weygand for having through these simple measures lifted the morale of the little French army in North Africa and for having supplied it with a countersign which, at a time when the notion of duty was being subjected to a very severe trial, had for everyone a solid and stirring significance.

It was more than enough to give back to that army its soul.

We might note that all of this was done without there being any conflict between the civil and the military authorities and with full respect, apparent at least, for the instructions that had been given by the government. Once again, the basis for the conduct of the chiefs of the army was to be found in the concept of discipline. . . .

* * *

One may imagine the state of mind of General de Gaulle, arriving in London in the month of June 1940 practically as an outlaw, but with the stubborn determination to continue the struggle in the name of Free France. He found in England only a distrustful, if not a hostile climate. Many doors remained closed to him, for the British had other problems on their mind more urgent and more important than the offers of a French general who was in open rebellion against his own government. Moreover, this general was not an easy man to get along with. He would bristle as

soon as he thought that people were selling short the prestige of his country. . . .

Vichy had reacted against the Gaullist rebellion by having its chief sentenced in absentia at Clermont-Ferrand intending thereby to protect itself through intimidation against the attempts that might be made by other soldiers to join Free France. Those who rallied to this cause were in the beginning only isolated cases. Many in the African Army and in French West Africa consoled themselves in their sense of resignation after the defeat, with the idea that it was preferable to have two men to represent and defend the interests of our unfortunate country, one at home facing up to the occupying power, . . . and the other abroad, at London, able vis-à-vis the Allies to make the most of whatever possible help that France, reduced though she was, might eventually be able to offer them.

Certainly it was difficult to imagine how these two personages,[1] whose actions should have been complementary, would be able to harness their plans in unison, for one of them enjoyed a relative liberty of action over a vast area, and was able little by little to build up for himself the means by which he could act; while the other remained a hostage, whose sole concern was to protect those positions that were indispensable, if it should come about that the fighting was resumed. In such an allotment of duties, it was not the latter one who had chosen the more agreeable lot.

Thus, in the first days of his exile, General de Gaulle bent over his map as over an ordinary tactical exercise, looking for an opportunity that could be seized, in the degree that circumstances allowed . . . There was nothing to be attempted in the direction of French North Africa, which remained obedient to Vichy and which had at its disposal an army of 100,000 men. Besides, it was about to receive, as we have seen, Weygand as delegate general, a Weygand who would know how to lift its spirit and to whom General de Gaulle ten-

[1] De Gaulle and Pétain. [Editor's note]

dered an offer to rally to his cause, the terms of which were quite possibly calculated to prevent an unwanted adhesion.

There remained French West Africa and French Equatorial Africa, and especially Dakar, towards which de Gaulle's thoughts were immediately directed. Skilled emissaries brought about without too much difficulty, and above all without any bloodshed, the rallying of almost all of Equatorial Africa, which was isolated in the midst of British territories and practically cut off from the French homeland. With regard to Dakar, it was not the same. As a fortified base, it had the means to defend itself, but de Gaulle hoped that, if he appeared there with a strong force, the resistance would collapse of its own accord. This calculation proved to be wrong. The Governor General, Boisson, who represented the civil authorities, intended to defend the base which had been entrusted to him. The armed forces obeyed, in the air, at sea, and on land. After three days of fighting, the expedition had to withdraw. This time the blood had indeed flowed, and it would flow again, alas, six weeks later at Gabon.

Finally at Lake Chad, Leclerc was able to find the right path, and the victory at Koufra made all French hearts beat in unison, as they would be able to be inflamed in the month of April 1941 over the victory of the Montclar Brigade at Massowa at the time of the offensive which was to permit Wavell to liquidate the Italian Empire in East Africa.

Unfortunately, the next effort undertaken by Free France was directed towards Syria, where they acted with the aid of the British Middle East forces. Once again the defending units were placed before a frightful choice, but in Syria, as at Dakar, the army obeyed, whatever was to be the price of this obedience. In the same manner, they would obey again the following year, when on May 5, 1942 the British attacked Diego-Suarez. . . .

The landings of November 8, 1942 . . .

once again brought into dispute the loyalty of the army to the government of the French state. There has been much carping about the attitude of the men in command of the forces defending Algeria and Morocco at the moment of these landings. They have been blamed for having made a stand against the Allied forces which ultimately had no other aim than to drive the Axis out of North Africa, that is to say, to work for the common victory. But this is to frame the problem incorrectly. In reality, if there was one occasion when the psychological problem was relatively easy to resolve, it was at Algiers, Oran, and Casablanca, for the French soldiers had no choice. If the invader had appeared in broad daylight with all his forces deployed, the defending forces might well have asked themselves some questions. But everywhere the American forces came by night, arms in hand, under conditions which permitted not the slightest hesitation. What should . . . the sailors of Casablanca have done, when the American naval squadron, as a kind of calling card, dispatched shells and bombs? They answered with cannon shots, as had been provided for in their orders, without even having had the time to ask a single question, and without always knowing to whom they were replying. And not only did their attackers not for an instant bear them any ill will, because of this attitude, but they never lost an occasion to congratulate them for it. . . .

The ordeal was costly in dead, wounded, and missing. It was nevertheless one of which an army conscious of its traditions of loyalty and obedience might be proud. If there has been some dispute in France as to how much credit the soldiers deserved, for their attitude there has never been any question over the matter among the English or the Americans. Their losses were not negligible, but they were perfectly aware of the dangers to which they were exposing themselves by adopting a line of action which for various reasons seemed to have the most to recommend it.

If the defense of North Africa did not, in practice, create at the moment of the allied debarkments any problems for the soldiers and sailors stationed there, there were however problems of a different nature when Admiral Darlan decided to bring the Empire back into the war. It might well seem difficult to resume the fight alongside of people who had only recently opened fire on you and who had killed your comrades before your eyes. And above all, there was the oath of loyalty that had been sworn to Marshal Pétain, who officially repudiated the attitude of Admiral Darlan.

The crisis of conscience was resolved with great skill by Admiral Darlan who did not hesitate to assert that he was competent to speak in the name of the Marshal. In assuming this position, he was fortified by telegrams which Admiral Auphan had been able to get to him in clandestine fashion from Vichy, with the aim of better informing him of the intimate thoughts of the Chief of the State. These messages were to play a crucial role in determining the attitude of the military chiefs at Dakar, who chose a few days later to follow the same path as those in North Africa.

Just as they had not wanted to run the risk of warning the military chiefs in North Africa . . . the Allies had not informed General de Gaulle, . . . Whatever was the reason for this course of action, it was for de Gaulle a blow that hurt to note that under the circumstances the Allies had at Algiers approached two men, Admiral Darlan and General Giraud, who it was to be supposed in varying degrees owed allegiance to the government of Marshal Pétain.

The whole situation was overturned six weeks later as a consequence of the assassination of Admiral Darlan. This political crime was followed by "the quarrel of the Generals" at Algiers, an episode whose vicissitudes might have been fatal to the unity of the army. It was now however that everyone recovered themselves in the struggle against the common enemy. . . . Hindered at first by several attempts made by the Free French forces to win over supporters at the expense of the Army of Africa, . . . this unity, after having been reenforced on the battlefields of Tunisia, was fully realized in the summer of 1943, with the complete fusion of the former Free French Forces with those which had belonged to the army of the armistice. . . .

Reconstituted, reequipped, and modernized by the Americans, as a result of the Anfa accords, . . . these forces were henceforth prepared to participate with the Allies in the assault on the fortress of Europe.

52. GENERAL BOYER DE LA TOUR ON THE MARTYRDOM OF THE FRENCH ARMY

In May of 1958, the French army joined with the civilian population of Algeria in a revolt which brought about the downfall of the Fourth Republic. Behind this ultimate act of desperation there lay a decade and a half of frustration, as the army was assigned the thankless task of defending France's overseas empire against various native movements for independence. Rightly or wrongly, the military attributed their defeat in Indo-China to the unwillingness of the weak and vacillating governments of the Fourth Republic to furnish them adequate material or moral support. In Algeria they were certain that they were winning a military victory over the rebels, but they feared that it would be annulled by the persistence of the government in seeking a negotiated political solution. Rather than undergo yet another defeat, the army revolted against the government in Paris, thus paving the way for de Gaulle to come to power. Their realization that de Gaulle too wished to find a political solution to the rebellion in Algeria led the soldiers to connive at the civilian uprising of January 1960 and finally in May 1961 to stage another revolt, this time unsuccessfully, in an effort to impose their policy on the government. The state of mind of the French professional soldier in the years following World War II is depicted in the following selections from *Le Martyre de l'Armée Française,* by General Pierre Boyer de La Tour.

French decadence really began only at the end of the Second World War, for in 1940, even if France had been defeated in battle and had been occupied by the enemy, hope continued to exist. There were valiant men in the Resistance, in the Free French Forces, and after 1942, with the whole army of Africa, who embodied the will of the country not to die.

Since 1945, it has been otherwise. Our army has sustained a series of battles which have been shown to be in vain. It has lost the best of its sons by the tens of thousands. It has fought, suffered, and died while carrying out the orders of the various governments and regimes which have followed one upon another, but they have made light of its sufferings and have surrendered the territories for which they gave the order to fight.

During this same period, traitors at home have devoted their efforts to insulting our soldiers and to supporting our enemies, all with the tacit complicity of those in authority.

Thus, all the sacrifices which have been agreed upon have been shown to be useless and our sons have died for no apparent reason. The army has endured a martyrdom which still goes on and now those who hold power dimly perceive the end of the Algerian conflict only through a disguised capitulation although our troops in the field are victorious militarily.

Filled with anguish, sacrificed, martyred, and dishonored, the army is in the process

From General Pierre Boyer de La Tour, *Le Martyre de l'armée francaise* (Paris, n.d.), pp. 11–16, 290, 301–303, abridged. Reprinted with the permission of the author. Translated by the editor.

of searching out its conscience. Once the very model of confidence and discipline, it is close to losing its soul. . . .

Since the end of the Second World War we have been present at a hallucinating spectacle. The government of the Republic has given its army a mission in certain territories of what was once the Empire. Our soldiers have set about to fulfill it to the best of their ability. At the same time, without there being any reaction on the part of these in power, they have been slandered, outraged, insulted by a certain number of their compatriots who have taken the side of the enemy. Moreover, this government has, most of the time, deserted the cause that its soldiers have been defending, has disavowed them, unofficially at least, and has abandoned a portion of the national patrimony.

It is this that is new in our history, no regime ever having adopted a similar attitude, . . . No regime, be it a monarchy, empire, or republic, has ever ratified the abandonment of a parcel of national territory, unless it was constrained to do so in the wake of a defeat which left it in no condition to resist any further. . . .

The battles in Indo-China had taught the professional soldiers just what the nature of subversive war is. What is more, certain of them having been taken prisoner by the Viets, penetrated the meaning of this kind of conflict, understood it, and swore to themselves that, if a new battle were imposed upon them, they would win. . . .

In North Africa, the army understood its task, especially when those from the cadres who had fought and suffered in Indo-China were in command. The military conducted the struggle in resolute fashion and were on the point of winning, . . . Our army knew that in this kind of conflict it was by no means a matter of conquering terrain and destroying the enemy in pitched battles, but on the contrary, of winning over the people, in order with their help to proceed to the destruction of the rebel bands and to achieve pacification. All that really had to be done was to free

the people from the complex of terror into which they had been plunged, to give them reason to hope for a better future, and to give them certain assurance that they would never again fall under the yoke of the enemy. In subversive warfare, it has become evident that actions of a political nature are more important than military deeds. Our soldiers, through reading Mao Tse-tung, had completely assimilated this elementary truth. They realized, on one hand that they would have to embark on an arduous and harsh destruction of the hostile elements, but that on the other hand, they would also have to win over the sentiments of the people, and to provide them a sense of certainty in their future by asserting that France would never abandon them.

To win this struggle the army was obliged to commit itself politically. It was by no means a question of taking a stand against any of the political parties, but simply a matter of implementing a national policy, and with regard to Algeria, of maintaining the integrity of the nation's territory. For such a policy to succeed, it was necessary that the government agree to it. This agreement was never obtained, and that is why the war, having been won militarily, for the few rebel bands which had escaped were at the end of their rope, is going to be lost politically, for the Fifth Republic, just like its predecessor, has understood nothing about the problem which has been put to it.

For the great mass of the native population this problem is summed up in the following question: "Are you going to leave or stay?". . .

They are absolutely right and in Algeria one of the most tragic aspects of the drama lies with those who have sided with France.

The army swore to this people never to abandon them. Not being in the least bit racist, the men of the cadres being very fond of their Moslem compatriots, the army proclaimed: "We are brothers. France is the mother of us all. In Algeria, there are only

French citizens, whatever their race or religion." The military proclaimed the principle of fraternity. Greater and greater numbers of the native population were brought back to France. The army was on the point of triumphing, but political considerations were standing by. Although the army was victorious, it was disavowed. . . .

Everywhere we have abandoned to the persecutions of our enemies those who were loyal to us, in Indo-China, in Morocco, in Tunisia, . . . and even, under another form, in certain states of Black Africa. Who then can have confidence in France? She no longer keeps her word. What she affirms one day, she denies the next. Without being vanquished, she still capitulates. . . .

In Algeria, the military had the impression, after many disappointments, that the decision had been won, and militarily, this was true. Accepting and legalizing a revolt by the French population of Algeria who refused to die, the army in its ingenuousness believed that by calling upon him who symbolized the resistance in 1940, it could save Algeria.

The military were quickly made to understand that such was not the case, but even so they were ordered to continue to suffer and to die! . . .

Today the army is silent . . . and broken, with an atrocious sense of anguish in its heart. The military continue to die, although they know their struggle is futile. They suffer and they see that the authorities are driving them to despair. The army has made a promise and it will not be able to keep it. The French army is on the brink of death. If by some miracle, it escapes, decades will be needed for it to recover its soul!

Raoul Girardet

53. THE POLITICIZATION OF THE FRENCH ARMY UNDER THE FOURTH REPUBLIC

The basic principle of civil-military relations in France during the nineteenth and the first half of the twentieth centuries was that the army was politically neutral and played no role in the life of the state beyond its strictly military one. The history of the past twenty-five years would seem to represent a complete repudiation of this principle. The manner in which the French army, by the very nature of its military mission in the post-war years was led to take a political stand in opposition to the government is discussed in the following passage by Raoul Girardet, taken from his essay "Civil and Military Power in the Fourth Republic."

The elaboration of the doctrinal concepts of revolutionary war is a direct outgrowth of a study of tactical methods employed by the Viet Minh forces in Indochina. In effect, the army in Indochina was confronted by an unknown adversary which it could not defeat, in spite of recognized material superiority. The enemy had deliberately planned its strategy to thwart the French. The plan called for "war among the masses," in the words of Mao Tse-tung. Its main objective was the conquest of

From Raoul Girardet, "Civil and Military Power in the Fourth Republic," in *Changing Patterns of Military Politics*, ed. Samuel Huntington (New York, 1962). Reprinted with the permission of the *Revue francaise de science politique*.

people, not the taking of territory or the domination of a battlefield. The victor was the one who knew how to take hold of a population morally, then materially mobilize its strength. To achieve this end, the enemy in Indochina employed very specific techniques which were completely effective. They were constant propaganda, systematic terrorism, the deliberate dismemberment of existing social structures, and the establishment of "parallel hierarchies," which slowly replaced the hierarchies of legal order and enslaved the population in an increasingly tight web of steel. The French army was forced to admit that in such a struggle military action should be secondary to psychological action, propaganda, the collection and exploitation of political as well as operational information, police action, liaison with the people, and economic and social action. The French army discovered that its men not only had to be experts in the use of arms, but also, and perhaps above all, had to be political agitators, organizers, and leaders of partisans. In the end, the qualities and methods of the ideological crusader were more effective in obtaining final victory than the qualities and methods of the soldier. . . .

The war in Indochina marked the beginning of a grave period of tension between civil power and the military. The precepts of revolutionary war gradually tended to draw the military away from its traditional policy of political nonintervention. Algeria, however, was the decisive affair in which the army was to stand up to the government. This event cannot be fully understood unless an important fact, which seems to have escaped the majority of political observers, is considered. That fact is the progressive establishment, between 1954 and 1958, of a veritable "military province" in Algerian departments, the progressive assumption by the army of almost complete authority and administrative responsibility for this vast territory.

When the Algerian rebellion broke out at the end of 1954, the task assigned to the army was relatively simple: re-establish order—that is, suppress uprisings, and chase, destroy, or subdue the F.L.N. bands. However, since it was limited to a strictly military operation, the army's effort was doomed to almost irremediable failure. Deprived of information and cut off from any contact with the Moslem population, the "forces of law and order" wore themselves out thrusting at an elusive adversary. The experience of more than a century of colonial wars, the lessons of Galliéni and of Lyautey placed emphasis on the necessity of a policy of "pacification," closely coordinating military, psychological, and administrative action under one authority. The Indochinese precedent, constantly evoked by the doctrinaires of revolutionary war, was an indication of the dramatic conclusion that awaited combat unadapted to the methods of the adversary. The F.L.N., like the forces of Viet Minh, conducted a war "among the masses." Instead of hoping to achieve immediate military coups, the F.L.N. attempted to spread the network of its political and administrative structures over the entire Algerian population. Therefore, the French goal should have been, not the pursuit of its guerrillas, but the destruction of its political organization through the establishment of an opposition, through substitution of another political organization. The government could not help but recognize the validity of these observations. The police and traditional judiciary apparatus, accustomed to handling occurrences of an average criminal nature, were ridiculously impotent in the face of the systematic practice of terrorism carried on by the F.L.N. Algeria had only known inadequate administrative institutions, and in many places the all-too-weak existing structures began to crack at the beginning of the rebellion. There was an almost complete administrative void. At that time, only the army was in a position to fill it. Thus, gradually, from 1956 on, under the impetus of M. Lacoste, the resident Minister, increasingly greater responsibilities were confided in the military. The result was that, at least on a local level, the army had within its authority almost all repressive and administrative power. . . .

In fact, on the verge of the crisis of May 13, 1958, the army had not only supplanted civil administration in districts where the latter was incapable of handling its job, but the precepts of revolutionary war had also taken over from old colonial traditions, extending and developing them. With its newspapers, schools, teams of social workers, youth organizations, and women's clubs, the army tended to appear as an omnipotent party, even monopolizing public power in some regions of Algeria. The army had its own propaganda machine, and its own surveillance and repression system. At least on the local level, it controlled and animated the most dynamic elements of that part of the Moslem population that had escaped the claws of the rebellion. In short, the army had given Algeria many new institutions.

How can we avoid concluding that techniques of psychological action and of rehabilitation of the people are not, and cannot be, politically neutral? In reality, the mere fact that the army waged "a war among the masses," or, in more traditional terms, substituted "pacification" for "repression," inferred, even to the lowest echelons of the military hierarchy, the recognition of the development of a *particular Algerian policy.* Of course, the need for an all-inclusive policy attacking the entire Algerian problem was not immediately apparent to military circles. For a long while many officers refused to see beyond the narrow limits of the task assigned to them. For a long time as well the army in Algeria waited for the government to define and propose this sorely needed policy. . . .

It is quite evident that, because of the great division in political parties and public opinion, the government was powerless to promote the well-defined policy. . . . What was demanded was a plan of action for Algeria completely without ambiguity, containing a sufficiently broad outlook for the future. The government's indecision in this matter was not the only cause for discontent with civil power that existed in the military. The necessities of the struggle forced the army to determine this political program for itself. However, it does not seem, in spite of some assertions, that there was systematic agreement or a coordinated and deliberate quest on the part of its officers. The methods of pacification and their logical implications gradually led to the almost spontaneous elaboration of a coherent Algerian policy based on several essential assertions.

The first of these was the continuing presence of the French on Algerian soil. The essential task of pacification was, in effect, to win over, or to win back, the adherence of the Moslem population, which was basically insecure, hesitant, vacillating, and dominated by concern for the future. The reservations created by this situation were due more to fear of compromise than to open hostility. Any vagueness as to the future, any ambiguity as to France's will to maintain her sovereignty, ran the risk of irreparably paralyzing any action aimed at persuading and involving the country. Therefore, every French officer serving in Algeria, in order to properly fulfill his mission, of necessity had to declare that those remaining loyal would never be abandoned. Because of this, it can be understood why the army had to disagree with the policy of "cease fire, elections, negotiations" as defined in 1956 by the government of M. Guy Mollet. This formula was not aimed at securing the future; it allowed for the greatest diversity of solutions and left the way open to all possibilities. The "pacifying" officer, bound by the daily difficulties of his task, was led to believe, on the contrary, that future security was the first and most important condition for the effectiveness of his work. He had to proclaim that any retreat was unthinkable. Any break in the expression of his will or in the manifestation of his resolve would greatly compromise the pursuit of goals he had been ordered to achieve.

It was not, however, just a question of

obtaining the resigned or passive assent of the majority of the population. Even when secured, a guarantee of the continuance of French sovereignty was not enough to stand up to the mystique of the rebellion. Another faith and vision of the future had to be set in opposition to the faith and vision that sparked the adversary. This in turn led to a second, equally political, assertion: the need for the civic, economic, and social progress of the Moslems in Algeria. Since these Moslems were constantly dominated by a feeling of alienation from and frustration toward the population of European origin, the army thought that it would never win their deep faith or productively galvanize their energies and enthusiasm unless it offered them the concrete hope of a better and more dignified life. Thus, the army planned to concentrate on the most lowly, the outcasts. . . .

Finally, a revolution of the Kemalist type, overthrowing old institutions and aimed at the destruction of traditional inequalities was proposed to the Algerian masses. A new Algeria would grow out of the struggle, an Algeria where all citizens would have identical rights and similar opportunities. It was said that the Algerians of tomorrow would be "completely independent Frenchmen."

The army was soon to summarize its vast program in one simple phrase, "l'Algérie française," and in one word, "integration." However, it would be a mistake to think that the officers using this word accorded it an extremely precise institutional meaning. A great diversity of opinion existed in military circles about the nature of future administrative ties which ought to unite Algerian and metropolitan departments. Some were in favor of complete assimilation, while others were aware of an Algerian "personality" endowed with its own institutions. In fact, as it was used by the army until May 13, 1958, integration essentially corresponded to a synthesis of three major elements, the fundamental imperatives of military policy in Algeria: maintenance of French sovereignty, the

attainment by the Moslems of full civil equality, and economic and social progress.

. . . At this point, the military were quite far from their original task of re-establishing order. The army had set up a goal in the Algerian fight that, without expressly contradicting it, greatly transcended the goal sought by the government. On the basis of experience the army developed a complete, coherent Algerian policy closely linked to the imperatives and terms of the battle it had to fight. It was a fitting policy, defined by the army itself, which remained totally independent of the decisions of the government.

Above all, the pursuit of this Algerian policy was connected, within the ideological context of the French army, with a tenacious loyalty to certain strong and influential values. It must not be forgotten that the conquest of the French colonial empire, in the nineteenth century and at the beginning of the twentieth, was almost entirely the work of the army. It is not surprising that attachment to this empire occupied an important place in the moral patrimony of the French officer, that it was bound up with some of the most profound traditions inherited by the officer. Ties binding the army to the heritage of a colonial past were particularly numerous and strong in North Africa. How could this fund of memories, images, legends and collective pride be evoked? There were the legend of Lyautey and the great moments in the Moroccan epic, all living realities talked about at mess and taught at military academies. There was Algeria's role as a place of refuge from 1940 to 1943. The divisions that had fought in Italy and landed in France came to Algeria and found shelter. North African garrisons were a kind of sanctuary during the first years of the postwar period. The officers there enjoyed a higher standard of living and greater respect. Above all, there was great contact between the military and the Moslem population. Many officers had led North African units or fought at their side. Ties of friendship in battle, of respect and affection, developed and remained strong. The army was also proud of having assured perfect equality of treatment within its ranks for both North Africans and Frenchmen. Many such factors combined to grant North Africa a privileged place in the "sentimental geography" of the French army.

But there were graver considerations. The pursuit of the task of pacification ineluctably obliged the French officer to compromise a number of loyal Algerian Moslems with French authority, for which he felt directly responsible. To evacuate Algeria would amount to abandoning the loyal to the reprisals of the rebellion. To the officer who had granted his protection, this would mean forfeiting basic duties of loyalty and honor. Many men had already returned from Indochina with a feeling of guilt, bearing a heavy burden for having betrayed the commitments they had made to the Vietnamese partisans fighting by their side. . . .

. . . In the eyes of many officers the policy of pacification led to the establishment of a contract with the Moslem population, a personally binding contract that they had no right to break. Thus, it seemed impossible that the army should follow any policy other than the one to which the government had so deeply committed it. In consequence, the government lost the possibility of defining and imposing another policy. To the moral imperatives of obedience to legal government the army opposed other stronger imperatives, which grew out of the execution of the mission it had received.

It was a strange war, which, by its very form, led those who fought it to elaborate a policy committing them irrevocably to a particular path. It was an undertaking that conformed to the decision of legal government and was a legitimate outgrowth of national will; yet the struggle against the Algerian rebellion imperceptibly but irresistibly escaped the control of governmental authority. Under these conditions, it is hardly rash to assert that, by having developed all the logical consequences of the mission granted by civil power, the army finally arrived at opposing this power in decisive conflict. The army appears to have been borne along by the internal mechanism of the battle it was ordered to wage, a battle whose prime necessity and profound legitimacy seemed to be quite evident. Because the army suspected that a new government would try, in May, 1958, to force it to abandon a duty which had become part of its main existence, the army finally decided—against all its traditions and customs—to revolt, to stand up to the regime and impose its own law.

54. DE GAULLE ON THE 1960 AND 1961 UPRISINGS IN ALGERIA

The remarkable political career of General de Gaulle was founded on his courageous act of insubordination in 1940. Having become President of the Republic in 1958, following a military revolt, he himself then had to deal with the problems posed by an insubordinate army. The two passages below are drawn from radio addresses at the time of uprising of the European population of Algeria in January 1960 and the military revolt of April 1961.

ADDRESS OF JANUARY 29, 1960, AT THE
MOMENT OF THE INSURRECTION OF THE
EUROPEAN POPULATION OF ALGIERS

Frenchmen of Algeria, how can you listen to the liars and the conspirators who tell you that in granting a free choice to the Algerians, France and de Gaulle want to abandon you, to pull out of Algeria and hand it over to the rebellion? Is it abandoning you, is it wanting to lose Algeria, to send there and to maintain there an Army of 500,000 men equipped with tremendous amounts of matériel; to consent to the sacrifice there of a good many of our children; to pay out there, this very year, civil and military expenditures amounting to $2 billion, to undertake there a tremendous program of development; to draw from the Sahara, with great difficulty and at great expense, oil and gas in order to bring them to the sea?

How can you doubt that if, some day, the Moslems freely and formally decide that the Algeria of tomorrow must be closely united with France—how can you doubt that anything would bring greater joy to our country and to de Gaulle than to see them choose, between one solution or another, the one that would be the most French? How can you deny that all the work for the development of the Moslem populations, which was initiated eighteen months ago,

and is now still being pursued and which, after pacification, will have to be expanded yet more—how can you deny that this work tends precisely to create new and manifold ties between France and the Algerians? Above all else, how can you fail to see that, in rising up against the State and against the nation, you are surely heading toward ruin and at the same time you are running the risk of causing France to lose Algeria at the very moment when the decline of the rebellion is becoming evident? I solemnly appeal to you to return to law and order.

Next, I speak to the Army, which, thanks to its magnificent efforts, is in the process of winning the victory in Algeria; however, some of the elements of this Army might be tempted to think that this war is their war, not France's war, and that they have a right to a policy which would not be France's policy. To all our soldiers I say: in your mission there is no room for any equivocation or interpretation. You must liquidate the rebel force, which is seeking to drive France out of Algeria and to impose upon that land its dictatorship of want and sterility. At the same time that you are conducting the battle, you must contribute to the material and spiritual transformation of the Moslem populations so as to win their hearts and minds to France. When the time comes for the people to vote, it will be

From Charles de Gaulle, *Major Addresses, Statements, and Press Conferences of General Charles de Gaulle: May 19, 1958 — January 31, 1964* (New York: French Embassy — Press and Information Division, n.d.), pp. 73–74, 127–128.

your responsibility to guarantee the complete freedom and sincerity of this vote.

Yes, that is your mission, as France gives it to you, and it is France that you serve. What would the French Army become but an anarchic and absurd conglomeration of military feudalisms if it should happen that certain elements made their loyalty conditional? As you know, I have the supreme responsibility. It is I who bear the country's destiny. I must therefore be obeyed by every French soldier. I believe that I shall be obeyed, because I know you, because I have a high regard for you, because I feel affection for you, because I have confidence in General Challe whom I have placed at your head, soldiers of Algeria, and, finally, because I have need of you for France.

This having been said, listen to me carefully. In the presence of the insurrection in Algiers and in the midst of the agitation —bordering on a paroxism—the Delegate General, M. Paul Delouvrier, who is France in Algeria, and the Commander-in-Chief may, on their own responsibility, not have wanted to give the signal themselves for a pitched battle, but no soldier, under penalty of being guilty of a serious fault, may associate himself at any time, even passively, with the insurrection. In the last analysis, law and order must be re-established. The methods to be employed so that law and order will prevail may be of various sorts. But your duty is to bring this about. I have given, and am giving, this order.

Finally, I speak to France. Well, my dear country, my old country, here we are together, once again, facing a harsh test. By virtue of the mandate that the people have given me and of the national legitimacy that I have embodied for twenty years, I ask all men and women to support me, no matter what happens.

And while the guilty ones, who dream of being usurpers, take as a pretext, the decision that I have made concerning Algeria, let it be known everywhere, let it be clearly understood, that I do not intend to go back on that decision. To yield on this point and under these conditions would be to destroy the trump cards that we still hold in Algeria, but it would also be to make the State bow before the outrage that is being inflicted on it and the threat that is aimed at it. Thus France would become but a poor broken toy adrift on the sea of hazards.

Once again, I call upon all Frenchmen, wherever they may be, whoever they may be, to reunite themselves with France.

Vive la République! Vive la France!

ADDRESS BY PRESIDENT CHARLES DE GAULLE AFTER THE MILITARY INSURRECTION IN ALGERIA BROADCAST OVER FRENCH RADIO AND TELEVISION ON APRIL 23, 1961

An insurrectional power has set itself up in Algeria by a military pronunciamento. Those guilty of this usurpation have exploited the passion of officers of certain special units, the inflamed support of one part of the population of European origin, misguided by fears and myths, the impotence of authorities overwhelmed by the military conspiracy.

This power has an appearance: a quartet of retired generals. It has a reality: a group of partisan, ambitious and fanatical officers. This group and this quartet possess a limited and expeditious ability, but they see and know the nation and the world only as deformed by their fanaticism.

Their venture cannot but lead to a national disaster. For the immense effort of recovery in France—begun at the depths of the abyss on June 18, 1940; continued later despite everything until victory was gained, independence assured, the Republic restored; resumed three years ago in order to remake the State, maintain the national unity, rebuild our power, restore our position in the world, pursue our task overseas through a necessary decolonization—all this risks being made useless, on the very eve of success, by the odious and stupid adventure in Algeria.

Now the State is flouted, the nation defied, our power degraded, our international prestige lowered, our role and our place in Africa jeopardized. And by whom? Alas! Alas! By men whose duty, honor and reason for being was to serve and obey.

In the name of France, I order that all means—I say all means—be employed everywhere to bar the route to these men, until they are subjugated. I forbid any Frenchmen, and first of all any soldier, to execute any of their orders. The argument that it might be locally necessary to accept their command under the pretext of operational or administrative obligations can fool no one.

The civil and military leaders who have the right to assume responsibilities are those who have been legally named and precisely those the insurgents prevent from doing so.

The future of the usurpers should only be that provided for them by the rigor of the law.

In the face of the misfortune which looms over the country and the threat that hangs over the Republic, I have decided, having formally consulted the Constitutional Council, the Premier, the President of the Senate, the President of the National Assembly, to put into force Article 16 of our Constitution. As of today, I will take, if necessary directly, the measures that appear to me to be required by the circumstances.

In this way, I confirm myself in the French and republican legality which was conferred upon me by the nation and which I will maintain no matter what happens until the end of my term, or until I lack either force or life; and I will take measures to make sure that this legality remains after me.

Frenchwomen, Frenchmen, see where France risks going, compared with what she was again becoming.

Frenchwomen, Frenchmen, help me.

Suggestions for Reading

The place of the army in the evolution of the modern European state has not been much studied. There are thus relatively few books treating the question, particularly in English. The most readily available work is *Soldiers and Governments*, ed. Michael Howard (London, 1957), a collection of essays by British scholars on the subject of civil-military relations in some eight different countries. A general statement of the problem and an analysis of the German and Japanese experiences is given in the opening chapters of Samuel Huntington, *The Soldier and the State* (Cambridge, 1957). Hoffman Nickerson, *The Armed Horde* (New York, 1940), and Alfred Vagts, *A History of Militarism* (New York, 1959), both contain material of interest. In a more specific vein, Walter L. Dorn, *Competition for Empire* (New York, 1940), has an excellent and concise discussion of the standing army as a social and political institution, along with its effect on the society of eighteenth-century Europe. This is to be found in chapters I and III of Dorn's book.

With regard to the role of the army in the history of the particular countries studied in this volume, there is more on Germany than on the other states. The standard work here is the excellent Gordon A. Craig, *The Politics of the Prussian Army, 1640–1945* (Oxford, 1955). Also to be consulted are Herbert Rosinski, *The German Army* (London, 1939), and Walter Görlitz, *History of the German General Staff* (New York, 1953). For the effect of the Revolutionary and Napoleonic Wars on the military institutions of Prussia, see William O. Shanahan, *Prussian Military Reforms, 1786–1813* (New York, 1945). There are a number of good studies of the army in German political life after 1918, in particular John W. Wheeler-Bennett, *The Nemesis of Power: The German Army in Politics, 1918–1945* (London, 1953); also, Harold Gordon, *The Reichswehr and the German Republic* (Princeton, 1957), and Telford Taylor, *Sword and Swastika* (New York, 1952).

A good general history of the French army in English is lacking. Charles de Gaulle, *France and Her Army* (London, 1946), is little more than an adequate introduction to the subject. The effect of the French Revolution on the army is admirably treated in Robert R. Palmer, *Twelve Who Ruled* (Princeton, 1941). There is nothing in English on the French army in the first half of the nineteenth century, but for the period after 1870 Paul-Marie de la Gorce, *The French Army* (New York, 1963), is good, as is also Richard D. Challener, *The French Theory of the Nation in Arms, 1866–1939* (New York, 1955). Jere C. King, *Generals and Politicians* (Berkeley, 1951), deals with World War I, while George A. Kelly, *Lost Soldiers* (Cambridge, 1965), is on the subject of the political evolution of the French army after 1945.

The standard work on the British army is the massive John W. Fortescue, *A History of the British Army* (London, 13 vols., 1899–1930). For the place of the army in the evolution of the British constitutional system, one should consult J. S. Omond, *Parliament and the Army* (Cambridge, 1933). There are numerous books on the English Civil War and on the role of Cromwell and the New Model Army. Sir Charles Firth, *Cromwell's Army* (London, 1902), is a classic, while other studies include Leo F. Solt, *Saints in Arms* (Stanford, 1959), and Maurice P.

Ashley, *Cromwell's Generals* (London, 1954).

A great deal has been written on various aspects of the development of the Red Army. In addition to D. Fedotov White, *The Growth of the Red Army* (Princeton, 1944), and *The Soviet Army*, ed. Basil Liddell Hart (London, 1956), there is a good, concise account by Edward Mead Earle in *Makers of Modern Strategy*, ed. Edward Mead Earle (Princeton, 1943).

The literature on World War I is tremendous, and much pertaining to the problem of the army and the state may be found in the memoirs of the leading figures involved. Among those whose memoirs are readily available are David Lloyd George, Sir Douglas Haig, Sir William Robertson, Sir Winston Churchill, Raymond Poincaré, Marshal Foch, Marshal Joffre, Georges Clemenceau, General von Ludendorff, and General von Hindenburg, to mention a few. A suggestive study of the role of the civilian leader in an age of total war is presented in the essay by Harvey de Weerd in *Makers of Modern Strategy*.